Verse by Verse Commentary on

ISAIAH

Enduring Word Commentary Series

By David Guzik

The grass withers, the flower fades,
but the word of our God stands forever.
Isaiah 40:8

Commentary on Isaiah

Printed in the United States of America
or in the United Kingdom

Print Edition ISBN: 978-1-939466-64-8

Enduring Word

5662 Calle Real #184

Goleta, CA 93117

Electronic Mail: ewm@enduringword.com

Internet Home Page: www.enduringword.com

Contents

Isaiah 1 – Indictment and Invitation

A. God states His case and offers a cure.

1. (1) Introduction: **The vision of Isaiah, son of Amoz.**

The vision of Isaiah the son of Amoz, which he saw concerning Judah and Jerusalem in the days of Uzziah, Jotham, Ahaz, *and* Hezekiah, kings of Judah.

a. **The vision of Isaiah**: This book contains the prophecies of **Isaiah, the son of Amoz**, who ministered from about 740 to 680 B.C. For about 20 years, he spoke to both the northern kingdom of Israel and the southern kingdom of Judah. After Israel's fall to the Assyrians in 722 B.C., Isaiah continued to prophesy to Judah.

i. This period of Israel's history is told in 2 Kings 15 through 21 and 2 Chronicles 26 through 33. Isaiah was a contemporary of the prophets Hosea and Micah. By the time of Isaiah, the prophets Elijah, Elisha, Obadiah, Joel, Jonah, and Amos had already completed their ministry.

ii. By this time, Israel had been in the Promised Land for almost 700 years. For their first 400 years in Canaan, *judges* ruled Israel. These were spiritual, military, and political leaders whom God raised up as the occasion demanded. Then, for about 120 years, three kings reigned over all Israel: Saul, David, and Solomon. But in 917 B.C. Israel had a civil war and remained divided into two nations, Israel (to the north) and Judah (to the south) up until the time of Isaiah.

iii. Up until the time of Isaiah, the kingdom of Israel – the northern ten tribes – had some 18 kings, all of them bad and rebellious against the LORD. The kingdom of Judah – the two southern tribes – had some 11 kings before Isaiah's ministry, some good and some bad.

iv. In the time of Isaiah, Israel was a little nation often caught in the middle of the wars between three superpowers: Egypt, Assyria, and Babylon.

v. As Isaiah's ministry began, there was a national crisis in the northern kingdom of Israel. The superpower of Assyria was about to overwhelm the kingdom of Israel. During the span of Isaiah's ministry as a prophet, the southern kingdom of Judah was faced with repeated threats from the larger surrounding nations.

vi. Many modern scholars think that there was more than one author to the book of Isaiah. They use terms like "Deutero-Isaiah" and "Trito-Isaiah" or the "Isaianic School." Sometimes more than one author is supposed for the book of Isaiah because of changes of style and tone, and sometimes as a denial of Isaiah as predictive prophecy.

vii. However, the New Testament indicates that there was only one author of Isaiah. In John 12:37-41, John quotes from both the "first" part of Isaiah and the "second" part of Isaiah – the parts supposedly written by two or more different Isaiahs – and John specifically tells us it was the same Isaiah. The New Testament quotes Isaiah by name more than all the other prophetic authors combined.

viii. The book of Isaiah is filled with many wonderful prophecies of the Messiah, telling us about the person and work of Jesus Christ some seven hundred years before Jesus was born in Bethlehem. For this reason, sometimes Isaiah is called "The Fifth Gospel."

b. **Isaiah, son of Amoz**: The name **Isaiah** means *Salvation is of the Lord*. There are at least seven men by the name of **Isaiah** in the Bible, but only one is **Isaiah, the son of Amoz**.

i. Some have thought that **Amoz** and the prophet *Amos* were the same person, but this seems unlikely. Some ancient Jewish traditions say that **Amoz** was a brother of king Amaziah, but there is no biblical way to prove this.

ii. We know more about Isaiah than we do about many other of the prophets. Isaiah was married and was the father of at least two sons (Isaiah 7:3 and 8:3). He lived in Jerusalem (Isaiah 7:3, 22:1, 37:2, 38:5, and 39:3).

iii. There is "a strong Judeo-Christian tradition that holds that Isaiah also outlived Hezekiah and was sawn asunder by his successor Manasseh with a wooden saw after the prophet had hidden himself in a hollow tree from the angry king." (Bultema) Many think Hebrews 11:37 (*they were sawn in two*) is a reference to the martyrdom of Isaiah.

iv. Most of all, Isaiah was a great man of God. Isaiah "has the courage of a Daniel, the sensitivity of a Jeremiah, the pathos of a Hosea, and the raging anger of an Amos; and moreover he leaves all of them far behind in the unique art of holy mockery. His courage is of such a nature that he never, not even for a moment, shows himself to be weak or timid." (Bultema)

c. **In the days of**: The prophecy of this chapter probably took place in the time of Ahaz, king of Judah (2 Kings 16 and 2 Chronicles 28). Ahaz was an evil king, and in his reign Judah was invaded many times by surrounding nations.

2. (2-4) The complaint of the LORD against Judah.

Hear, O heavens, and give ear, O earth!
For the LORD has spoken:
"I have nourished and brought up children,
And they have rebelled against Me;
The ox knows its owner
And the donkey its master's crib;
***But* Israel does not know,**
My people do not consider."
Alas, sinful nation,
A people laden with iniquity,
A brood of evildoers,
Children who are corrupters!
They have forsaken the LORD,
They have provoked to anger
The Holy One of Israel,
They have turned away backward.

a. **Hear, O heavens, and give ear, O earth**: God called heaven and earth as witnesses against Judah. The leaders and people of Judah had resisted His will, and God now stated His case against them. We might think of heaven and earth as a "jury" that God presented the case before.

i. Romans 8:22 says, *For we know that the whole creation groans and labors with birth pangs together until now*. Creation is waiting for the deliverance that will come when the Messiah rules directly over all creation. When God's people disobey, we might say there is a sense in which they "delay" that resolution of all things. So, heaven and earth have an interest in our obedience.

b. **I have nourished and brought up children, and they have rebelled against Me**: The leaders and people of Judah were like rebellious children, who never appreciated all that their parents did for them.

i. As parents, we can appreciate how frustrating and galling it is for our children to disregard and disobey us. It fills us with righteous indignation, and we think, "After all I have done for them, they treat me like *this*?" But we have treated God even worse than any child has treated their parents.

c. **The ox knows its owner and the donkey its master's crib; but Israel does not know**: The leaders and people of Judah were not like dumb animals, such as the **ox** or the **donkey**. They were *dumber* than dumb animals. The **ox** at least **knows its owner**, but Judah didn't know who owned them. The **donkey** knows who takes care of him, but Judah didn't know who took care of them.

i. No animal has ever offended or resisted or rejected or disobeyed God the way every human being has. Any animal is a more faithful servant of God than the best human.

d. **Alas, sinful nation**: God clearly and strongly exposed their sin. They were **laden with iniquity, a brood of evildoers**, and they had **provoked** the LORD to **anger**.

3. (5-9) The desperate condition of Judah.

Why should you be stricken again?
You will revolt more and more.
The whole head is sick,
And the whole heart faints.
From the sole of the foot even to the head,
***There is* no soundness in it,**
***But* wounds and bruises and putrefying sores;**
They have not been closed or bound up,
Or soothed with ointment.
Your country *is* desolate,
Your cities *are* burned with fire;
Strangers devour your land in your presence;
And *it is* desolate, as overthrown by strangers.
So the daughter of Zion is left as a booth in a vineyard,
As a hut in a garden of cucumbers,
As a besieged city.
Unless the LORD of hosts
Had left to us a very small remnant,
We would have become like Sodom,
We would have been made like Gomorrah.

a. **Why should you be stricken again?** Despite their sin, God did not wish evil upon Judah. Instead, He longed for them to repent and to make it easy on themselves. God had chastised Judah, and they did not respond. They would continue to be **stricken** as long as they rebelled.

b. **Sick…the whole heart faints…. no soundness…wounds and bruises and putrefying sores**: Because of their rebellion against God, Judah was in a bad place. This is where their disobedience and lack of submission brought them.

c. **Your country is desolate, your cities burned with fire; strangers devour your land in your presence**: During the reign of Ahaz, the kingdom of Judah was attacked and pillaged by Israel, Syria, Edom, the Philistines, and Assyria (2 Chronicles 28). It was written of this period, *For the LORD brought Judah low because of Ahaz king of Israel, for he had encouraged moral decline in Judah and had been continually unfaithful to the LORD* (2 Chronicles 28:19).

i. For all this, Judah would not repent. Their sin brought them great trouble, but they still preferred their sin, with all of its trouble, than submitting to the LORD God. In fact, 2 Chronicles 28:22 says, *Now in the time of his distress King Ahaz became increasingly unfaithful to the LORD.*

d. **Unless the LORD of hosts had left to us a very small remnant, we would have become like Sodom, we would have been made like Gomorrah**: As bad as Judah's state was because of their sin, it could have been worse. It was only by the mercy of God that they survived at all. **Sodom** and **Gomorrah** were both totally destroyed, with not even a **very small remnant** to carry on. Even in the midst of judgment, God showed His mercy to Judah.

4. (10-15) God hates their empty religious ceremonies.

Hear the word of the LORD,
You rulers of Sodom;
Give ear to the law of our God,
You people of Gomorrah:
"To what purpose *is* the multitude of your sacrifices to Me?"
Says the LORD.
"I have had enough of burnt offerings of rams
And the fat of fed cattle.
I do not delight in the blood of bulls,
Or of lambs or goats.
When you come to appear before Me,
Who has required this from your hand,
To trample My courts?
Bring no more futile sacrifices;

Incense is an abomination to Me.
The New Moons, the Sabbaths, and the calling of assemblies—
I cannot endure iniquity and the sacred meeting.
Your New Moons and your appointed feasts
My soul hates;
They are a trouble to Me,
I am weary of bearing *them.*
When you spread out your hands,
I will hide My eyes from you;
Even though you make many prayers,
I will not hear.
Your hands are full of blood."

a. **You rulers of Sodom…you people of Gomorrah**: God was obviously trying to get the attention of the leaders and people of Judah. He did this by associating them with two cities synonymous with sin and judgment.

b. **To what purpose is the multitude of your sacrifices to Me?** Even in the midst of their rebellion, Judah continued its religious ceremony and ritual. They continued the **sacrifices**, they continued the **burnt offerings**, they continued offering the **fat of fed cattle**, they continued burning **incense**, they continued their **assemblies** and their **sacred meetings** – and God was sick of them all.

i. See how the LORD describes His reaction to these religious rituals: **I have had enough…. bring no more futile sacrifices…an abomination to Me…. I cannot endure…My soul hates…they are a trouble to Me…I am weary of bearing them.**

ii. This is a sobering thought. We can offer God all kinds of religious rituals and ceremonies, all kinds of religious service, *and He may hate it and consider it an abomination!* Perhaps, in the midst of all their calamity (described in Isaiah 1:5-9), Judah thought the answer was in religious ceremonies, in their ancient version of "church attendance" and a few dollars in the offering. But if their heart wasn't changed, and humbled, and surrendered to the LORD it made no difference. Without the right heart, God *hated* their religious ceremony and service.

iii. "When sinners are under the judgments of God they will more easily be brought to fly to their devotions than to forsake their sins and reform their lives." (Matthew Henry)

c. **When you spread out your hands**: This was the posture of prayer in that ancient culture. Instead of praying with heads bowed and hands folded, they would pray with the face turned towards heaven and the hands spread out to heaven. So, when they prayed, the LORD says, **"I will hide my eyes from you…I will not hear."**

i. We may be certain, that in the midst of all this religious ceremony, there were many fine prayers offered. Many eloquent, stirring, and emotional prayers were said. But they were empty, hollow, useless prayers, because God looked at Judah and said, **"Your hands are full of blood."**

5. (16-20) The LORD offers a cure.

"Wash yourselves, make yourselves clean;
Put away the evil of your doings from before My eyes.
Cease to do evil,
Learn to do good;
Seek justice,
Rebuke the oppressor;
Defend the fatherless,
Plead for the widow.
"Come now, and let us reason together,"
Says the LORD,
"Though your sins are like scarlet,
They shall be as white as snow;
Though they are red like crimson,
They shall be as wool.
If you are willing and obedient,
You shall eat the good of the land;
But if you refuse and rebel,
You shall be devoured by the sword";
For the mouth of the LORD has spoken.

a. **Wash yourselves, make yourselves clean…. Learn to do good, seek justice, rebuke the oppressor, defend the fatherless, plead for the widow**: The corruption of Judah's leaders and people was shown in their bad treatment of one another.

i. Many centuries later, the apostle John repeated the sense of Isaiah's message: *If someone says, "I love God," and hates his brother, he is a liar; for he who does not love his brother whom he has seen, how can he love God whom he has not seen?* (1 John 4:20) The leaders and people of Judah wanted to say they loved God by their religious ceremonies, but the LORD cared more about how they treated other people, especially the weak (**the fatherless…the widow**).

b. **"Come now, let us reason together," says the LORD**: The Lord GOD invites His people to come **reason** with Him. What He offers us isn't just offered because He is greater than us and has the right to dictate whatever terms please Him. God's direction for us is *reasonable.* It is *smart.* It is the *best way to live.*

i. It is *madness* to reject and resist a God of infinite wisdom, infinite love, infinite grace, and infinite power. True **reason** will drive any honest man to the humblest adoration and submission towards God.

ii. The angels surrounding the throne of God are covered with eyes, which speaks of their great ability to perceive and know (Revelation 4:6-8). These are perhaps the most intelligent, rational beings God ever created, and they spend every moment of their existence lost in total praise, total adoration, and total surrender to God. This is where the highest **reason** will drive us.

iii. It is just plain reasonable to follow God. Have you ever once heard of an old Christian, on their deathbed, gathering their children and friends around, and saying: "Now friends, watch out for that Christianity! I've followed Jesus my whole life and I'm so sorry I did! What a waste that was!" What nonsense! Quite the contrary, we find that Christians on their deathbed are trusting and loving God more than ever. It's just plain reasonable.

c. **Though your sins are like scarlet, they shall be as white as snow; though they are red like crimson, they shall be as wool**: The LORD offered a repentant, humbled Judah *true* and *complete* cleansing from sin. Their condition of sin could be transformed from deeply stained to become completely white.

i. In this passage, Isaiah says nothing about *how* this cleansing comes. But we know that it comes because Jesus took upon Himself our stain of sin, and God judged sin perfectly and completely in Jesus, so we can be accounted **white as snow** and as white as **wool**.

ii. There is tremendous hope in God's forgiveness! We really can be clean from the stain of sin. Our good works can't clean the stain. Our best intentions or promises can't clean the stain. Our suffering or pain can't clean the stain. Time can't clean the stain. Death can't clean the stain. Only the work of Jesus can make us **white as snow**! We really can have a break with the past, and a new beginning in Jesus Christ. The power of sin, the shame of sin, the guilt of sin, the domination of sin, the terror of sin, and the pain of sin can all be taken away in Jesus.

iii. "The Lord does not deny the truth of what the sinner has confessed, but he says to him, 'Though your sins be as scarlet, I meet you on that ground. You need not try to diminish the extent of your sin, or seek to make it appear to be less than it really is. No; whatever you say it is, it is all that, and probably far more. Your deepest sense of your sinfulness does not come up to the truth concerning your real condition; certainly, you do not exaggerate in the least. Your sins are scarlet, and crimson; it seems as though you have put on the imperial robe of sin, and made yourself a monarch of the realm of evil.' That is how a man's guilt appears before the searching eye of God." (Spurgeon)

iv. Spurgeon described people deeply stained by sin: "A wicked old wretch who has taken his degrees in Satan's college, has become a Master of Belial, a prince and chief of sinners – a Goliath amongst the Philistines – yet, to such a man, is this word sent today. Your hands are bloody with the souls of the young, you have kept a hellhouse; you have grit up public entertainments which have debauched and depraved the young; you have gold in your pocket to-day, which you have earned by the blood of souls; you have the fool's pence, and the drunkard's shillings, which have really come into your hands from the hearts of poor women, you have heard the cries of the starving children, and you have tempted their husbands to take the drink, and ruined their bodies and their souls. You have kept a place where the entertainment was so low, so grovelling, that you awoke the slumbering passions of evil in the minds of either young or old, and so you shall sink to hell with the blood of others on your head, as well as your own damnation, not with one millstone about your neck, but with many." All this may be true of you; yet God can forgive your sins and you can be made white as snow.

d. **Come now**: When we consider the greatness of God's cleansing and pardon, it is all the more reason for us to **come *now***. God wants the separation between you and He to be gone **now**. He doesn't want you to continue in your destructive path another moment. He wants the best for us **now**.

i. "Come now, no season can be better. If ye tardy till you're better, ye will never come at all. Come now; you may never have another warning; the heart may never be so tender as it is to-day. Come *now*; no other eyes may ever weep over you; no other heart may ever agonise for your salvation. Come *now, now, now,* for tomorrow you may never know in this world. Death may have sealed your fate, and the once filthy may remain filthy still. Come *now*; for to-morrow thy heart may become harder than stone, and God may give thee up. Come *now*; it is God's time; to-morrow is the devil's time. 'To-day if ye will hear his voice harden not your hearts, as in the provocation, when your fathers tempted me and proved me in the wilderness and saw my works.' Come now. Why delay to be happy? Would you put off your wedding-day? Will you postpone the hour when you are pardoned and delivered? Come *now*: the bowels of Jehovah yearn for you. The eye of your father sees you afar off, and he runs to meet you. Come *now*; the church is praying for you; these are revival times; ministers are more in earnest." (Spurgeon)

e. **If you are willing and obedient, you shall eat the good of the land; but if you refuse and rebel, you shall be devoured by the sword**: Here God offered Judah a choice. They could find hope in the midst of their chastisement, relief from empty religious ritual, and cleansing from their sin. But they had to surrender their heart before God, and not **refuse and rebel**. Instead, they had to be **willing and obedient**.

i. No one perfectly matches either phrase, but which phrase better describes your life? Is it **willing and obedient** or **refuse and rebel**? There is a consequence for either course: **eat of the good of the land** or **be devoured by the sword**. No wonder the LORD said, **"Come now, let us reason together!"**

B. A promise of redemption – with justice.

1. (21-23) The unjust leaders of Judah.

How the faithful city has become a harlot!
It was full of justice;
Righteousness lodged in it,
But now murderers.
Your silver has become dross,
Your wine mixed with water.
Your princes *are* rebellious,
And companions of thieves;
Everyone loves bribes,
And follows after rewards.
They do not defend the fatherless,
Nor does the cause of the widow come before them.

a. **The faithful city has become a harlot**: The **faithful city** was Jerusalem, the city once known for its faithfulness to the LORD. Now, Jerusalem **has become a harlot** – spiritually speaking, they have forsaken their "marriage" to the LORD and are committing spiritual adultery with their idolatry.

b. **It was full of justice**: The days of **justice** and **righteousness** were long past in Jerusalem. Now the city was filled with **murderers**, political corruption (**Your princes are rebellious**), **thieves**, fraud (**Your silver has**

become dross, your wine mixed with water), **bribes**, and favoritism against the weak (**They do not defend the fatherless, nor does the cause of the widow come before them**).

i. The LORD's accusation against Jerusalem shows, by contrast, what God values among political and civil leaders. God expects them to keep the peace (against **murderers**), have integrity (instead of being **rebellious** and the companion of **thieves**), and to defend the weak (the **fatherless** and **widows**).

ii. **Your wine mixed with water**: "The Lord Jesus made water into wine; sinners make wine into water." (Bultema)

iii. The spiritual adultery of Judah showed itself in this kind of sin. In a sense, the corruption among the leaders of Judah was a symptom of an even deeper spiritual problem.

2. (24-31) The LORD's plan of redemption with justice

Therefore the Lord says,
The LORD of hosts, the Mighty One of Israel,
"Ah, I will rid Myself of My adversaries,
And take vengeance on My enemies.
I will turn My hand against you,
And thoroughly purge away your dross,
And take away all your alloy.
I will restore your judges as at the first,
And your counselors as at the beginning.
Afterward you shall be called the city of righteousness, the faithful city."
Zion shall be redeemed with justice,
And her penitents with righteousness.
The destruction of transgressors and of sinners *shall be* together,
And those who forsake the LORD shall be consumed.
For they shall be ashamed of the terebinth trees which you have desired;
And you shall be embarrassed because of the gardens
Which you have chosen.
For you shall be as a terebinth whose leaf fades,
And as a garden that has no water.
The strong shall be as tinder,
And the work of it as a spark;
Both will burn together,
And no one shall quench *them*.

a. **The Lord of hosts, the Mighty One of Israel**: God now addresses Judah, introducing Himself with titles showing His power and majesty. He is the **Lord of hosts**, "**hosts**" referring to the armies of heaven. He is the **Mighty One of Israel**, whom it is futile to oppose. The title itself is a wake-up call.

i. Bultema on **the Lord of hosts**: "Describes Him as the Warrior who has all the angels as mighty soldiers at His disposal in the battle against the wicked. This is God's battle name and as a rule it signifies little good when He uses it in reference to His people, as is the case here. It usually implies that He considers and deals with His people as His enemies."

b. **I will rid Myself of My adversaries**: The problem with the leaders and people of Judah was that they had set themselves as **adversaries** of the Lord. They were acting like His **enemies**. They were putting themselves in the path of judgment. They would find the **hand** of the Lord **against** them, instead of for them.

c. **And thoroughly purge away your dross, and take away all your alloy**: **Dross** and **alloy** are impurities in metal. God promised to "turn up the heat" and refine Judah, taking away their impurities. His goal was not to destroy; instead He says, **"I will restore."** God will purify Jerusalem, to the point where **Afterward you shall be called the city of righteousness, the faithful city**.

d. **Zion shall be redeemed with justice**: God's redemption and restoration are always done with **justice** and **righteousness**. He never saves or redeems at the *expense* of His justice and righteousness.

e. **They shall be ashamed of the terebinth trees which you have desired**: These **terebinth trees** were sites of pagan worship which idol-loving Judah kept among them. When **Zion** is **redeemed with justice**, they would be **ashamed** of their former idolatries.

i. It is good to be **ashamed** and **embarrassed** over sin. There is something wrong with us when we are *shameless* or beyond embarrassment. God promised He would give Judah the gift of shame and embarrassment over sin again.

ii. "Sacred trees played an important part in the Canaanite fertility cult...for deciduous trees like the oak or terebinth may well have symbolized the death and rebirth of the god. The 'gardens' may be groves of these trees, or, alternatively, places of sacred springs or wells." (Grogan)

f. **As a terebinth tree whose leaf fades…as a garden that has no water…. The strong shall be as tinder…both will burn together**: The LORD spoke here of the spiritual *dryness* of Judah. Though they continued their religious ritual and ceremony, they were still spiritually dry. And as dry trees, dry gardens, and dry tinder are ready to burn, so was an unrepentant Judah ready to feel the fires of God's refining judgment.

Isaiah 2 – Hope and Fear

A. The hope of the Messiah's reign.

1. (1) A word concerning **Judah and Jerusalem.**

The word that Isaiah the son of Amoz saw concerning Judah and Jerusalem.

a. **The word that Isaiah the son of Amoz saw**: This was revealed to Isaiah in some kind of vision because this was a **word** that he **saw**.

b. **Concerning Judah and Jerusalem**: This prophecy (continuing on through Isaiah 4) is directed towards the southern kingdom **Judah** and its capital **Jerusalem**.

i. Isaiah 2:1-3 is repeated in Micah 4:1-3. Since Isaiah and Micah were contemporary prophets, it isn't surprising that the same Spirit of the LORD could give these two prophets the same vision, to establish and emphasize His word.

2. (2-3) The exaltation of Judah and Jerusalem

Now it shall come to pass in the latter days
***That* the mountain of the LORD's house**
Shall be established on the top of the mountains,
And shall be exalted above the hills;
And all nations shall flow to it.
Many people shall come and say,
"Come, and let us go up to the mountain of the LORD,
To the house of the God of Jacob;
He will teach us His ways,
And we shall walk in His paths."
For out of Zion shall go forth the law,
And the word of the LORD from Jerusalem.

a. **In the latter days**: In context, the term **latter days** refers to the "time of the Messiah," when the Anointed of the LORD reigns over the earth. Broadly, this speaks of the time many refer to as the *millennium*, the thousand-year reign of Jesus on this earth (Psalm 72, Isaiah 11:4-9, Jeremiah 23:5-6, Luke 1:32-33 and 19:12-27, Matthew 5:18).

b. **The mountain of the LORD's house shall be established on the top of the mountains, and shall be exalted above the hills; and all nations shall flow to it**: During the millennium, Israel will be the "superpower" of the world. It will be the leading nation in all the earth, and the center of Israel will be **the mountain of the LORD's house** – the temple mount, which will be the "capital" of the government of the Messiah. **All nations shall flow** to the "capital" of the government of Jesus.

c. **Come, let us go to the mountain of the LORD…He will teach us His ways, and we shall walk in His paths**: During the millennium, the citizens of earth will acknowledge and submit to the Lordship of Jesus. It will be a time of perfectly administrated enforced righteousness on this earth.

3. (4) The peaceful nature of the Messiah's reign

He shall judge between the nations,
And rebuke many people;
They shall beat their swords into plowshares,
And their spears into pruning hooks;
Nation shall not lift up sword against nation,
Neither shall they learn war anymore.

a. **They shall beat their swords into plowshares, and their spears into pruning hooks**: During the reign of the Messiah, there will be no more war. There will still be conflicts between nations and individuals, but they will be justly and decisively resolved by the Messiah and those who reign with Him (**He shall judge between the nations, and shall rebuke many people**).

i. It isn't the reign of the Messiah itself that will change the heart of man. Citizens of the earth will still need to trust in Jesus, and His work on their behalf, for their personal salvation during the millennium. But war and armed conflict will not be tolerated.

b. **Nation shall not lift up sword against nation, neither shall they learn war anymore**: It is important to see that this is not the peace of surrender. This is the peace of enforced righteousness. There would be no more war, and no more need for **swords** and **spears**, so it made sense to make them into **plowshares** and **pruning hooks**. But there will be no more war because there will be a new ruler on earth, Jesus Christ. Psalm 2:9 tells us what the Messiah will do to the disobedient in that day: *You shall break them with a rod of iron; You shall dash them to pieces like a potter's vessel.*

i. We long for the day when there is no more need for a military budget, when the money that goes for weapons and armies can go to schools and parks. But we are only safe doing that when the Messiah reigns among us.

ii. "Men yearn for peace, but they will not acknowledge the hopelessness of their own efforts to achieve it. It is only when the word of the Lord goes forth from Jerusalem, when He Himself is reigning over the nations, that lasting peace will come." (Martin)

B. The threat of coming judgment.

1. (5) A plea to **walk in the light of the Lord**.

O house of Jacob, come and let us walk
In the light of the Lord.

a. **Oh house of Jacob**: After painting the picture of the glory of the Messiah's reign, Isaiah then challenges Judah (**house of Jacob**) to live in the Messiah's reign right now.

b. **Walk in the light of the Lord**: This means to order your life after God's truth and God's ways. The ultimate reign of the Messiah may be many years away, but Jesus can reign in our lives, in our minds, and in our hearts right now. We don't have to wait for the *enforced* righteousness of the millennium to have the blessing of Jesus' righteousness in our lives right now.

c. **Walk in the light of the Lord**: This means you enjoy the *blessings* of the Messiah's reign right now. You don't have to live a dark, depressing, discouraging Christian life. You can **walk in the light of the Lord**.

i. What is it that gets you down, that brings darkness into your life? How can it compare to the **light of the Lord**? Is the *darkness* of spiritual attack, of unfaithful friends, of bad circumstances, of shame, of guilt, of anything greater than the **light of the Lord**? It cannot be so.

ii. "You know that, if you were to go to Australia in a good sound ship, you would get there even if you were always to lie down in the hold among the luggage and the rats; but I should like to go in a first-class cabin, and I do not see why you and I, if we are going to heaven, should not go first-class." (Spurgeon)

2. (6-9) The sins that prevent Judah from walking in the light of the Lord.

For You have forsaken Your people, the house of Jacob,
Because they are filled with eastern ways;
They *are* soothsayers like the Philistines,
And they are pleased with the children of foreigners.
Their land is also full of silver and gold,
And there is no end to their treasures;
Their land is also full of horses,
And there is no end to their chariots.
Their land is also full of idols;
They worship the work of their own hands,
That which their own fingers have made.
People bow down,
And each man humbles himself;
Therefore do not forgive them.

a. **They are filled with eastern ways…they are soothsayers like the Philistines…they are pleased with the children of foreigners**: Judah had allowed the false gods of foreigners to capture their attention.

i. This was not an anti-immigrant statement. God is not against the cultures and customs of other peoples, except where those customs and cultures honor and worship false gods. Perhaps in the name of "diversity," the leaders and people of Judah were allowing the worship of false gods.

b. **Their land is also full of silver and gold**: Judah had allowed the false gods of wealth and materialism to captivate their attention. Because Judah was in a time of economic prosperity (**full of silver and gold…no end to their treasures…full of horses…no end to their chariots**), they were far more prone to economic idolatry.

i. This was not an anti-wealth statement. God is not against wealth and riches and may choose to bless some with significant resources. This is a rebuke to those who *love* riches and *trust* in wealth.

c. **Their land is also full of idols**: Judah had allowed idols to captivate their attention. Because everyone has an innate tendency to worship themselves (**the work of their own hands, that which their own fingers have made**), we are tempted to worship what we have made and accomplished instead of worshipping the One who made us.

i. This was not an anti-work statement. God wants us to work hard, and be pleased with the **work** of our **own hands**, and to see the accomplishments that our **own fingers have made**. This is a rebuke against those who *worship* what they have made and what they have done.

d. **People bow down, and each man humbles himself**: There was plenty of worship (**bow down**) in Judah, and plenty of people humbling themselves. They were simply worshipping the wrong things and humbling themselves before the wrong things!

i. We know how to **bow down**, we know how to humble ourselves; we just don't find it easy to direct it properly towards the LORD. We are more than happy to **bow down** and humble ourselves for something of our choosing but often find it difficult to do it for the LORD.

ii. The application is sobering: **Therefore do not forgive them**. Their worship of foreign gods, of riches, and of idols was sincere. It may have been ennobling or helpful to society. But it was a rejection of the LORD God and was therefore unforgivable.

3. (10-22) A description of the Day of Judgment.

Enter into the rock, and hide in the dust,
From the terror of the LORD
And the glory of His majesty.
The lofty looks of man shall be humbled,
The haughtiness of men shall be bowed down,
And the LORD alone shall be exalted in that day.
For the day of the LORD of hosts
***Shall come* upon everything proud and lofty,**
Upon everything lifted up—
And it shall be brought low—
Upon all the cedars of Lebanon *that are* high and lifted up,
And upon all the oaks of Bashan;
Upon all the high mountains,
And upon all the hills *that are* lifted up;
Upon every high tower,
And upon every fortified wall;
Upon all the ships of Tarshish,
And upon all the beautiful sloops.
The loftiness of man shall be bowed down,
And the haughtiness of men shall be brought low;
The LORD alone will be exalted in that day,
But the idols He shall utterly abolish.
They shall go into the holes of the rocks,
And into the caves of the earth,
From the terror of the LORD
And the glory of His majesty,
When He arises to shake the earth mightily.

In that day a man will cast away his idols of silver
And his idols of gold,
Which they made, *each* for himself to worship,
To the moles and bats,
To go into the clefts of the rocks,
And into the crags of the rugged rocks,
From the terror of the LORD
And the glory of His majesty,
When He arises to shake the earth mightily.
Sever yourselves from such a man,
Whose breath *is* in his nostrils;
For of what account is he?

a. **From the terror of the LORD and the glory of His majesty**: The beginning of the chapter described the glory of the Messiah's reign (Isaiah 2:1-4). The second part of the chapter described the current corruption of Judah (Isaiah 2:6-9). How will the earth be transformed from its current corruption to the glory of the Messiah's reign? It will happen by the victory of the Messiah in **the day of the LORD of hosts**.

i. The term **day of the LORD** (used more than 25 times in the Bible) does not necessarily refer to one specific day. It speaks of "God's time." The idea is that now is the *day of man*, but the day of man will not last forever. One day, the Messiah will end the day of man and bring forth the **day of the LORD**.

b. **The day of the LORD of hosts shall come**: In the **day of the LORD**, men will be terrified. God tells them to **enter into the rock, and hide in the dust, from the terror of the LORD and the glory of His majesty**. In the **day of the LORD**, men will be humbled: **The lofty looks of man shall be humbled, the haughtiness of men shall be bowed down, and the LORD alone shall be exalted in that day**. In that day, there will be no more idolatry; **the LORD alone shall be exalted**. In that day, God will be glorified, and all will see **the terror of the LORD and the glory of His majesty**.

i. The **high tower**, the **fortified wall**, the **ships of Tarshish** and the **beautiful sloops** – these are all expressions of the **loftiness of man** and the **haughtiness of men**. In the *day of the LORD*, every proud, arrogant achievement of man will be brought to nothing, and **the LORD alone will be exalted in that day**.

ii. "Man in all matters of religion, and in all his dealings with God, is proud. It is wonderful how apparently humble men will be when they worship false gods. They will cut themselves with knives, and roll themselves in the mire. We have known some votaries to kneel before the representation of the Virgin Mary and lick the very pavement with their tongues by way of penance, and perform the most degrading rites in honor of their false gods. Man seems to be humble enough in his dealings with a false deity, but as soon as ever he comes to deal with the true God, the first things that have to be got out of him are his pride, his high looks, his haughtiness." (Spurgeon)

c. **Sever yourselves from such a man**: Because the days of idols and human pride are coming to an end, it is not wise to associate with those who cling to what will certainly be defeated. We should see that such men are of no **account**, and *walk in the light of the LORD* instead.

i. What strange sin in us, to make us give more account to men who can only hold as much breath as their nostrils will contain – who depend on every breath for life – than to the LORD God who will **shake the earth mightily**! It simply makes sense for us to honor and obey God rather to follow men into sin.

d. **For of what account is he?** If men are only men, why do we give so much attention to the opinions of men? Why rise so high on the praise of men, and get so low at their disapproval? We have something – Someone – better to live for.

i. "'*But they say.*' What do they say? Let them say. It will not hurt you if you can only gird up the loins of your mind, and cease from man. 'Oh, but they have accused me of this and that.' Is it true? 'No, sir, it is not true, and that is why it grieves me.' That is why it should not grieve you. If it were true it ought to trouble you; but if it is not true let it alone. If an enemy has said anything against your character it will not always be worth while to answer him. Silence has both dignity and argument in it." (Spurgeon)

ii. "Brethren in Christ, let us think more of God and less of man. Come, let the Lord our God fill the whole horizon of our thoughts. Let our love go forth to him; Iet us delight ourselves in him. Let us trust in him that liveth for ever, in him whose promise never faileth, in him who will be with us in life, and in death, and through eternity. Oh that we lived more in the society of Jesus, more in the sight of God! Let man go behind our back, and Satan too. We cannot spend our lives in seeking the smiles of men, for pleasing God is the one object we pursue. Our hands, and our heads, and our hearts, and all that we have and are, find full occupation for the Lord, and therefore we must 'Cease from man.'" (Spurgeon)

Isaiah 3 – The Sins of Judah

A. Profile of a society under judgment.

1. (1-7) Shortages of food, water, and competent leaders.

For behold, the Lord, the LORD of hosts,
Takes away from Jerusalem and from Judah
The stock and the store,
The whole supply of bread and the whole supply of water;
The mighty man and the man of war,
The judge and the prophet,
And the diviner and the elder;
The captain of fifty and the honorable man,
The counselor and the skillful artisan,
And the expert enchanter.
"I will give children *to be* their princes,
And babes shall rule over them.
The people will be oppressed,
Every one by another and every one by his neighbor;
The child will be insolent toward the elder,
And the base toward the honorable."
When a man takes hold of his brother
In the house of his father, *saying,*
"You have clothing; you be our ruler,
And *let* these ruins *be* under your power,"
In that day he will protest, saying,
"I cannot cure *your* ills,
For in my house *is* neither food nor clothing;
Do not make me a ruler of the people."

a. **For behold, the Lord, the LORD of hosts, takes away from Jerusalem and from Judah the stock and the store**: God's judgment on Judah, at this point, includes taking away their food (**stock and the store**) and **water**.

i. Isaiah 3:1 is a good example of the way two Hebrew words may be used, each translated **Lord**. In this verse, the first time **Lord** is used, it translates the Hebrew word *adonai*, which means "master, owner, sovereign." It is a broad word that can be applied to a human master as well as the Lord GOD, the ultimate Master. The second time **LORD** is used, and is printed in small capitals, it translates the Hebrew word *Yahweh*, which is the sacred name of the Triune God. So, it may be that the Hebrew Bible could use the phrase *adonai Yahweh*, which could be translated into English as *Lord LORD*, but actually means "Master Yahweh." That phrase appears more than 300 times in the Old Testament. Most of the time, the phrase is translated *Lord GOD* in the New King James Version.

ii. The specific phrase here – **the Lord, the LORD of hosts** – is used more than 15 times in the Old Testament, and often by Isaiah (Isaiah 1:24, 3:1, 3:15, 10:23-24, 10:33, 19:4, 22:5, 22:12, 22:14-15, and 28:22). It emphasizes the majesty and power of God because the idea behind **LORD of hosts** is that God is "Commander in Chief" of heaven's armies.

iii. So when it is "The Master of All, Yahweh of Heaven's Armies" (**the Lord, the LORD of hosts**) who has taken food and water from **Jerusalem and from Judah**, they would be wise to repent and get right with Him. "This is also the reason why he calls God *the Lord* and *Jehovah of hosts*, that the majesty of God may terrify their drowsy and sluggish minds; for God has no need of titles, but our ignorance and stupidity must be aroused by perceiving his glory." (Calvin)

b. **The mighty man and the man of war, the judge and the prophet**: The judgment is worse than just taking away food and water. God also brought judgment on **Jerusalem** and **Judah** by depriving them of godly, competent leaders on every level: **the mighty man and the man of war, the judge and the prophet, and the diviner and the elder; the captain of fifty and the honorable man, the counselor and the skillful artisan, and the expert enchanter**. Instead of wise, competent leaders, God **will give children to be their princes, and babes shall rule over them**.

i. The eventual fulfillment of this prophecy is found in 2 Kings 24:14: *Also he carried into captivity all Jerusalem: all the captains and all the mighty men of valor, ten thousand captives, and all the craftsmen and smiths. None remained except the poorest people of the land.*

ii. But this *principle* of God's judgment endures to this day. One way God may bring judgment on a nation is to curse them with incompetent, ungodly leaders. Often, this is the simplest avenue of judgment: giving people what their wicked hearts desire. This crisis of leadership can happen even in economically prosperous times (Isaiah 2:7 is part of this same prophecy). The terrible effect of this judgment of God, the granting of incompetent and ungodly leaders, may not be immediately seen, but it will be certainly seen, apart from the repentance of a nation and the mercy of God.

c. **The people will be oppressed**: This comes from the ungodly, incompetent leadership, and there will be a breakdown of order in society (**The child will be insolent toward the elder, and the base toward the honorable**).

i. "For there is hardly any conduct more offensive, or more fitted to disturb our minds, than when the worst examples of every sort are publicly exhibited by magistrates, while no man utters a syllable against them, but almost all give their approbation." (Calvin)

d. **You have clothing, you be our ruler, and let these ruins be under your power**: Things will become so bad, that in the minds of the people, the smallest achievements will qualify a man for leadership. Yet even such a man will not want to lead: **In that day, he will protest, saying, "I cannot cure your ills...do not make me a ruler of the people."**

i. "It is astonishing how realistically the prophet is here able to describe the consequences of a total collapse of the state. Anyone who remembers the months that followed May 1945 in Germany will have the sensation in reading this passage of being carried right back to these days." (Kaiser, cited in Grogan)

2. (8-12) Why Judah is ripe for judgment.

For Jerusalem stumbled,
And Judah is fallen,
Because their tongue and their doings
***Are* against the LORD,**
To provoke the eyes of His glory.
The look on their countenance witnesses against them,
And they declare their sin as Sodom;
They do not hide *it.*
Woe to their soul!
For they have brought evil upon themselves.
"Say to the righteous that *it shall be* well *with them,*
For they shall eat the fruit of their doings.
Woe to the wicked! *It shall be* ill *with him,*
For the reward of his hands shall be given him.
***As for* My people, children *are* their oppressors,**
And women rule over them.

O My people! Those who lead you cause *you* to err,
And destroy the way of your paths."

a. **Their tongues and their doings are against the Lord**: Jerusalem and Judah have sinned in what they *say* and in what they *do*. In fact, what they *say* and what they *do* **provoke the eyes of His glory**.

i. It is much easier to think that what we *do* is offensive to God than to think that what we *say* can **provoke the eyes of His glory**. But we are commanded to glorify God by what we *say* just as much as by what we *do*. Jesus said, *for every idle word men may speak, they will give account of it in the day of judgment. For by your words you will be justified, and by your words you will be condemned.* (Matthew 12:36-37)

b. **The look on their countenance witnesses against them**: The very look on their faces is evidence of their guilt. Either they have the smirk of the reprobate or the downcast gaze of those under conviction.

i. "Impure propensities are particularly legible in the eyes: whoever has beheld the face of a *debauchee* or a *prostitute* knows this; of these it may be said, they wish to appear what they really are. They glory in their iniquity. This is the highest pitch of ungodliness." (Clarke)

c. **And they declare their sin as Sodom; they do not hide it**: Their sin is openly displayed, and they have no sense of shame. The cultural dynamic in Isaiah's day was probably much the same as in our time. In the name of "frankness" and "honesty" and "let's not be hypocrites," all kinds of sin are approved, and no one is "allowed" to proclaim a standard unless they live up to it perfectly.

i. Outward decency *is* important. It is important not to talk about many sins, even though they exist, and sometimes touch the church. It is through these means that God's people *declare a standard*, even though they or the world do not perfectly measure up to a standard. Ephesians 5:12 matters here: *For it is shameful even to speak of those things which are done by them in secret.*

ii. One of the most destructive lies of our time is that it is wrong or hypocritical to have a standard that we don't live up to. No one has *always* told the truth, yet it is right and good to teach our children, "Don't lie." It would be wrong, and destructive, for someone to answer, "You can't tell your child not to lie. You have lied in the past. You are a hypocrite." This attitude in our society translates into a certain result: *a wholesale lowering of standards*. Also, the charge of *hypocrisy* is false. It is not hypocritical to promote a standard you don't perfectly meet.

Hypocrisy is when you *pretend* to keep the standard but do not or when you do not *keep the standard* but think that others *should*.

iii. "The maintenance of external decency is at least some evidence of a conscience not altogether seared." (Jennings)

d. **Woe to their soul! For they have brought evil upon themselves**: God did not have to do anything unique or special to bring this judgment on Jerusalem and Judah. All He had to do was leave them alone and allow them to **have brought evil upon themselves**.

i. When the LORD gives a nation the leadership they desire and deserve, it can be either a blessing or a curse. In Judah's case in the time of Isaiah, it was a curse.

e. **Say to the righteous that it shall be well with them, for they shall eat the fruit of their doings**: Even in the midst of judgment, God knows how to bless and protect His people. Sometimes this is only seen in the perspective of eternity, but God assures us that the righteous will never share the same fate as the wicked. Abraham knew this principle well when he said to the LORD, *"Far be it from You to do such a thing as this, to slay the righteous with the wicked, so that the righteous should be as the wicked; far be it from You! Shall not the Judge of all the earth do right?"* (Genesis 18:25)

f. **They shall eat the fruit of their doings.... for the reward of his hands shall be given him**: God will give both the righteous and the wicked the reward they deserve. For the righteous, this is a comfort, for the wicked, it is a curse.

i. Spurgeon on **Woe to the wicked! It shall be ill with him**: "It shall be ill with the wicked, and let no present appearance lead you to doubt it.... The eyes that never weep for sin here will weep in awful anguish for ever.... It will be a profitable thing for thee to feel the wrath of God heavy on thy spirit now, for if not, it will crush thee, crush thee down and down without hope, world without end. It shall be ill with you."

g. **As for My people, children are their oppressors, and women rule over them**: Again, the LORD both declares and bemoans His judgment on Judah, that they have been given incompetent and ungodly leadership. **Those who lead you cause you err, and destroy the way of your paths**.

i. **Women rule over them**: this was seen as a curse, not a blessing. Certainly, God may raise up particular women at particular times to be leaders in different spheres. Deborah (Judges 4-5) and Esther are examples of this. But this is entirely different from a society where, in general, **women rule over them**. Such a society is cursed, not blessed.

B. God's case against Judah.

1. (13-15) Their ill treatment of the poor.

The Lord stands up to plead,
And stands to judge the people.
The Lord will enter into judgment
With the elders of His people
And His princes:
"For you have eaten up the vineyard;
The plunder of the poor *is* in your houses.
What do you mean by crushing My people
And grinding the faces of the poor?"
Says the Lord God of hosts.

a. **The Lord stands up to plead, and stands to judge the people**: Here, the Lord is both a *prosecutor* (**stands up to plead**) and a **judge** against Judah. When you are in court, and the prosecutor and the judge are the same person, you know you are going to be found guilty.

b. **The plunder of the poor is in your houses. What do you mean by crushing My people, and grinding the faces of the poor?** God's charge against the **elders** and the **princes** of Israel is not that they have *failed to help the poor*. That would be bad in itself. But far worse than that, they have *robbed* the poor, and taken advantage of their poverty to enrich themselves.

2. (16-23) The sinful women of Judah, and the judgment of the Lord against them.

Moreover the Lord says:
"Because the daughters of Zion are haughty,
And walk with outstretched necks
And wanton eyes,
Walking and mincing *as* they go,
Making a jingling with their feet,
Therefore the Lord will strike with a scab
The crown of the head of the daughters of Zion,
And the Lord will uncover their secret parts."
In that day the Lord will take away the finery:
The jingling anklets, the scarves, and the crescents;
The pendants, the bracelets, and the veils;
The headdresses, the leg ornaments, and the headbands;
The perfume boxes, the charms, and the rings;
The nose jewels, the festal apparel, and the mantles;
The outer garments, the purses, and the mirrors;
The fine linen, the turbans, and the robes.

a. **The daughters of Zion are haughty, and walk with outstretched necks**: The women of Judah were *proud.* They were taken with themselves and loved to consider themselves better than others (**are haughty**).

i. This proud heart was the basis for the rest of the sin among the **daughters of Zion**. "To meet their unfounded accusations, he lays open the inward disease, which is manifested in the whole of their outward dress." (Calvin)

ii. In contrast, women of God are called to *in lowliness of mind let each esteem others better than* [themselves] (Philippians 2:3).

b. **Wanton eyes**: The women of Judah were sexually seductive and promiscuous. They wanted to leer at men and draw them into sexual immorality with their flirtations.

i. "What he adds about *wandering eyes* denotes shameless lust, which for the most part is expressed by the *eyes*; for unchaste *eyes* are the heralds of an unchaste heart; but the *eyes* of chaste women are sedate, and not wandering or unsteady." (Calvin)

ii. In contrast, women of God are called *to be discreet* and *chaste* (Titus 2:5).

c. **Walking and mincing as they go, making a jingling with their feet**: The women of Judah were obsessed with **finery**, luxury, and "accessories." They devoted far too much of their lives to their appearance and image.

i. For emphasis, the prophet declared a list of the "accessories" and luxury items the women of Judah longed for and devoted too much of their lives to: **The jingling anklets, the scarves, and the crescents; the pendants, the bracelets, and the veils; the headdresses, the leg ornaments, and the headbands; the perfume boxes, the charms, and the rings; the nose jewels, the festal apparel, and the mantles; the outer garments, the purses, and the mirrors; the fine linen, the turbans, and the robes**. Apparently, there was good shopping in Jerusalem.

ii. This love of finery, luxury, and the obtaining of it all is not unique to women. Many men have a problem with it also. But it is definitely a problem among many women. A 1992 story in the *Los Angeles Times* told about Michelle, a successful writer and editor, who feared the day her husband might discover her secret stash of credit cards, her secret post office box or the other tricks she used to hide how much money she spent shopping for herself. "I make as much money as my husband.... If I want a $500 suit from Ann Taylor, I deserve it and don't want to be hassled about it. So the easiest thing to do is lie," she explained. Last year, when her husband forced her to destroy one of her credit cards, Michelle went out and got a new one without telling him. "I do live in fear. If he discovers this new VISA, he'll kill me."

iii. In the same article, a school teacher explained more: "Men just don't understand that shopping is our drug of choice," she joked, even while admitting that some months her salary goes exclusively to paying the minimum balance on her credit cards. "Walking through the door of South Coast Plaza is like walking through the gates of heaven. God made car trunks for women to hide shopping bags in." A young professional named Mary explained: "Shopping is my recreation. It's my way of pampering myself. When you walk into [a mall] and you see all the stores, it's like something takes over and you get caught up in it."

iv. "It is worthy of notice that the Prophet had good reason for reproving, with so great earnestness and vehemence, the luxury of women; for while they are chargeable with many vices, they are most of all inflamed with mad eagerness to have fine clothes. Covetous as they naturally are, still they spare no expense for dressing in a showy manner, and even use spare diet, and deprive themselves of what nature requires, that their clothes may be more costly and elegant. So grievously are they corrupted by this vice, that it goes beyond every other." (Calvin)

v. "Nothing can exceed the curiosity which dwells in woman. Indeed there is no end to those contrivances; and it was not without reason that the ancients called the collection of a woman's ornaments *a world*; for if they were collected into one heap, they would be almost as numerous as the parts of the world." (Calvin)

vi. In contrast, women of God are commanded: *Do not let your adornment be merely outward; arranging the hair, wearing gold, or putting on fine apparel; rather let it be the hidden person of the heart, with the incorruptible beauty of a gentle and quiet spirit, which is very precious in the sight of God.* (1 Peter 3:3-4)

d. **Therefore the Lord will strike with a scab the crown of the head of the daughters of Zion, and the LORD will uncover their secret parts**: Their obsession with their appearance, their love of luxury, and their promiscuity made the **daughters of Zion** ripe for judgment. Their "crown" will be **a scab**, and instead of being beautifully adorned, they will be exposed and humiliated. Also, **the Lord will take away the finery**.

i. In Isaiah's time, these judgments were connected with the coming invasions. Because of scarcity and disease, the haughty **daughters of**

Zion would be sick and diseased. They would be raped and humiliated. And all their wonderful "accessories" would be taken away.

ii. Because of their role in the nurture of children, it is important that women of God live and think like women of God. When the women of a culture become degenerate, then the hope for the next generation is gone. But when the women of a culture turn to the LORD and His ways, there is great hope for the future.

iii. "In short, both men and women are instructed to make a sober use of the gifts of God, both in food and in clothing, and in the whole conduct of life. For the Lord cannot endure extravagance, and absolutely must inflict severe punishment on account of it; for it cannot be restrained by a lighter chastisement." (Calvin)

3. (24-26) More of the judgment of the LORD on the sinful daughters of Zion.

And so it shall be:
Instead of a sweet smell there will be a stench;
Instead of a sash, a rope;
Instead of well-set hair, baldness;
Instead of a rich robe, a girding of sackcloth;
And branding instead of beauty.
Your men shall fall by the sword,
And your mighty in the war.
Her gates shall lament and mourn,
And she *being* desolate shall sit on the ground.

a. **Instead of…Instead of…Instead of…Instead of…instead of**: The LORD will replace their finery with the marks of captivity and humiliation. They will live the **stench**, the **baldness**, the **branding** and the general deprivation of captivity.

i. Do we realize how quickly God can take it all away? How much more reason to honor God with what we have, instead of indulging ourselves.

ii. "Now there cannot befall us anything worse than that we should be hardened against chastisements, and not perceive that God chastiseth us. When we labour under such stupidity, our case is almost hopeless." (Calvin)

b. **Your men shall fall by the sword, and your mighty in the war**: without doubt, one reason the daughters of Zion loved all the luxury and finery was because it made them more attractive to men. They felt they could "get" men that way. But their ungodly love of luxury and finery resulted in the loss of their men.

c. **She being desolate shall sit on the ground**: A Roman medal, struck after Jerusalem's fall, shows a Jewish woman **being desolate**, sitting under a palm tree next to a Roman soldier.

Isaiah 4 – The Messiah's Community

A. Judgment on the daughters of Zion and a glorious hope.

1. (1) The desperate condition of the daughters of Zion.

And in that day seven women shall take hold of one man, saying,

**"We will eat our own food and wear our own apparel;
Only let us be called by your name,
To take away our reproach."**

a. **And in that day**: As a result of the judgments of the LORD detailed in Isaiah 3:16-26, the daughters of Zion will have few men to choose from as husbands.

b. **Seven women shall take hold of one man**: So many men *shall fall by the sword* (Isaiah 3:25), that **seven women** would chase after **one man**. They would be so desperate for marriage that would not expect their husbands to provide for them at all (**We will eat our own food and wear our own apparel**).

c. **Only let us be called by your name**: Instead, it would be enough to simply take the name of a husband so that it would **take away** the **reproach** of being unmarried and childless.

i. In a broader sense, this shows that it is *not good* for women to be too desperate for marriage. They may marry unwisely, and for the wrong reasons. It is also bad when women do not expect their husbands to provide for the household.

2. (2) The glorious hope of **the Branch of the LORD**.

**In that day the Branch of the LORD shall be beautiful and glorious;
And the fruit of the earth *shall be* excellent and appealing
For those of Israel who have escaped.**

a. **In that day the Branch of the LORD shall be beautiful and glorious**: The **Branch of the LORD** is a Messianic title, speaking of Jesus Christ.

i. This image is repeated in Isaiah 11:1: *There shall come forth a Rod from the stem of Jesse, and a Branch shall grow out of his roots.* It is repeated in Jeremiah 23:5: *"Behold, the days are coming," says the LORD, "That I will raise to David a Branch of righteousness; a King shall reign and prosper, and execute judgment and righteousness in the earth."* It is repeated in Jeremiah 33:15: *In those days and at that time I will cause to grow up to David a Branch of righteousness; He shall execute judgment and righteousness in the earth.* It is repeated in Zechariah 3:8: *For behold, I am bringing forth My Servant the BRANCH.*

ii. The ideas behind the title **Branch of the LORD** are those of fruitfulness and life. Jesus used the same image when He said *I am the vine, you are the branches* (John 15:5).

b. **In that day**: This does not mean that the Messiah would appear when these judgments were taking place on the daughters of Zion. It means that the *promise* of the Messiah would be all the more **beautiful and glorious** to them in the midst of their suffering.

c. **And the fruit of the earth shall be excellent and appealing for those of Israel who have escaped**: For the remnant preserved through judgment, the promise of the Messiah would be all the more beautiful, dear, and life-giving. **Fruit** would sprout and grow from the **Branch of the LORD**, even as they simply trusted in the promise of the Messiah before He came.

B. Zion under the government of *the Branch of the LORD*.

1. (3) Holiness marks the society where *the Branch of the LORD* reigns.

And it shall come to pass that *he who is* left in Zion and remains in Jerusalem will be called holy—everyone who is recorded among the living in Jerusalem.

a. **Will be called holy**: In the days of the sinful daughters of Zion, they were called beautiful, they were called delicate, they were called attractive, they were called fashionable, and they were called sexy. But they were *not* **called holy**.

i. "Christ's holiness shall be both imputed and imparted unto them: he shall both expiate their sins and heal their natures, pay their debts, and give them a stock of grace and holiness, so that men shall call them a 'holy people.'" (Trapp)

b. **Everyone who is recorded**: In the days when the *Branch of the LORD* reigns, the distinguishing mark of all, including the daughters of Zion, will be that they **will be called holy**.

i. **Holy** does not mean "super-spiritual." It does not mean sinless perfection. It does not mean spiritually superior and obnoxious. It means a life, a heart, a mind, and a body that is genuinely separated to the LORD. It is a life lived *apart* from the thinking and heart of this world, this flesh, and the devil, and lived *apart* to the LORD.

2. (4-6) More characteristics of the society where *the Branch of the LORD* reigns.

When the Lord has washed away the filth of the daughters of Zion, and purged the blood of Jerusalem from her midst, by the spirit of judgment and by the spirit of burning, then the LORD will create above every dwelling place of Mount Zion, and above her assemblies, a cloud and smoke by day and the shining of a flaming fire by night. For over all the glory there *will be* a covering. And there will be a tabernacle for shade in the daytime from the heat, for a place of refuge, and for a shelter from storm and rain.

a. **The Lord has washed away the filth of the daughters of Zion**: When *the Branch of the LORD* reigns, there will be cleansing. The cleansing will not come easily; it will come **by the spirit of judgment and the spirit of burning**. But it will be worth it.

i. "Sin is the excrement of the soul, the superfluity or garbage of naughtiness, the devil's vomit. From this abominable filth Christ hath 'loved and washed his with his own blood, that he may make them kings and priests unto God and his Father.'" (Trapp)

ii. "He not only washeth his people from their sins, but taketh away their swinish natures, whereby they would else return to their former wallowing in the mire." (Trapp)

b. **A cloud and smoke by day and the shining of a flaming fire by night**: When *the Branch of the LORD* reigns, there will be the tangible presence of the LORD. Just as in the days of the Exodus, God will be as real as a pillar of cloud by day and a pillar of fire by night (Exodus 13:21-22).

c. **And there will be a tabernacle for shade...a place of refuge, and for a shelter from storm and rain**: When *the Branch of the LORD* reigns, there will be protection that comes from the LORD. The LORD's people will be safe and secure, washed, and in the abiding presence of the LORD.

i. "Nothing is more necessary than that we follow our calling, and perform our duty faithfully. It belongs equally to the condition of the good and of the bad that they suffer many inconveniences; but bad men have no refuge, no place of concealment in which they may hide themselves, and they must be utterly overwhelmed. But blessed is the condition of the godly; for although they endure heat and cold, still they have a safe refuge in God." (Calvin)

ii. If we are really born again, we *want* to be washed, have the presence of the LORD, and enjoy His protection. Many people only want the LORD's constant presence and protection. But He doesn't grant those apart from His cleansing.

Isaiah 5 – The Vineyard of the LORD

A. The parable of the vineyard.

"For exquisite beauty of language and consummate skill in effective communication, this parable is virtually peerless. One difficulty of a literary masterpiece is that a would-be translator who is not the literary equal of the author faces an impossible task.... It is in fact an outstanding example of the way the inspiring Spirit employed human language to convey the divine message." (G.W. Grogan)

1. (1-2) The unproductive vineyard

Now let me sing to my Well-beloved
A song of my Beloved regarding His vineyard:
My Well-beloved has a vineyard
On a very fruitful hill.
He dug it up and cleared out its stones,
And planted it with the choicest vine.
He built a tower in its midst,
And also made a winepress in it;
So He expected *it* to bring forth *good* grapes,
But it brought forth wild grapes.

a. **Now let me sing**: The story is about a vineyard that had many advantages. It belonged to a loving person (**my Well-beloved**). It was planted on **a very fruitful hill**. The ground was carefully prepared (**dug it up and cleared out its stones**). It was planted with good stock (**planted it with the choicest vine**). It was protected (**a tower in its midst**). Provision was made for the fruit to be processed (**made a winepress in it**).

i. "No possession is dearer to a man than *a vineyard*, and there is none that demands more constant and persevering toil. Not only, therefore, does the Lord declare that we are his beloved inheritance, but at the same time points out his care and anxiety about us." (Calvin)

ii. "I have been thinking of the advantages of my own position towards the Lord, and lamenting with great shamefacedness that I am not bringing forth such fruit to him as my position demands. Considering our privileges, advantages, and opportunities, I fear that many of us have need to feel great searchings of the heart." (Spurgeon)

b. **He expected it to bring forth good grapes**: This is not surprising, considering all the advantages the vineyard had. What else would be expected? But instead **it brought forth wild grapes**.

i. **Wild grapes**: "We are dealing here with something worse than unfruitfulness. The New Testament also speaks of a faith that brings forth fruit, but the fruit is *dead works*, which pollute the air like a cadaver. The wolfsbane, or wild vine (2 Kings 4:39), does bear beautiful berries, but they are bitter, foul-smelling and poisonous in nature. This is a precise description of the self-willed and false religion of the unfaithful covenant people." (Bultema)

ii. Clarke on **wild grapes**: "Poisonous berries...not merely useless, unprofitable grapes, such as wild grapes; but grapes offensive to the smell, noxious, poisonous."

iii. **Wild grapes** means that the vineyard produced just what you would expect it to produce if *nothing had been done to it*. All the love, care, time, work, and investment had no result.

2. (3-4) God asks Jerusalem and Judah to consider the story of the vineyard.

"And now, O inhabitants of Jerusalem and men of Judah,
Judge, please, between Me and My vineyard.
What more could have been done to My vineyard
That I have not done in it?
Why then, when I expected *it* to bring forth *good* grapes,
Did it bring forth wild grapes?"

a. **Judge, please, between Me and My vineyard**: The question is simple. Who is to blame for the harvest of only *wild grapes*? Is it the fault of the owner of the vineyard, or is it the fault of the vineyard itself?

i. We know, and they knew, that farming is a matter of cause and effect. Literally, one could never "blame" a vineyard for lack of production. But in the LORD's vineyard, the will of man is a factor.

b. **What more could have been done to My vineyard**: In the story, there was nothing left undone by the owner of the vineyard. He did all he could do. In the same way, God cannot be blamed at all for the **wild grapes** Israel brought forth. God did all He could do, apart from making men robots, acting apart from or against their wills.

i. The fault lies with man, not God. "It will be seen then...that every soul of man had the chance of becoming a fruitful vineyard; and if it became the reverse, it was due to no failure in either the wisdom or grace of God." (Meyer)

ii. "O you that profess to be his people, what more could Christ have done for you? What more could the Holy Spirit have done? What richer promises, what wiser precepts, what kinder providences, what more gracious patience?" (Spurgeon)

c. **Why then, when I expected it to bring forth *good* grapes, did it bring forth wild grapes?** It is possible for God to do a work in His people, but for His people to receive that work *in vain*. Paul warned, *we then, as workers together with Him also plead with you not to receive the grace of God in vain.* (2 Corinthians 6:1)

i. Of course, a literal vineyard doesn't "do" anything. But we, as God's vineyard, are called to work with the grace of God, so that grace is not received in vain. Grace isn't given because of any works, past, present or promised; yet it is given to *encourage* work, not to say work is unnecessary. God doesn't want us to receive His grace and become passive. Paul knew that God gives His grace, we work hard, and the work of God is done.

ii. Jesus used this same image in His parable of the wicked tenants and the vineyard (Matthew 21:33-46).

iii. "Has it been so with us? Have we rewarded the Wellbeloved thus ungratefully for all his pains? Have we given him hardness of heart, instead of repentance; unbelief, instead of faith; indifference, instead of love; idleness, instead of holy industry; impurity, instead of holiness?" (Spurgeon)

3. (5-7) God's judgment on the unproductive vineyard.

"And now, please let Me tell you what I will do to My vineyard:
I will take away its hedge, and it shall be burned;
And break down its wall, and it shall be trampled down.
I will lay it waste;
It shall not be pruned or dug,
But there shall come up briers and thorns.
I will also command the clouds
That they rain no rain on it."
For the vineyard of the LORD of hosts *is* the house of Israel,
And the men of Judah are His pleasant plant.

He looked for justice, but behold, oppression;
For righteousness, but behold, a cry *for help.*

a. **I will take away its hedge**: All the owner of the vineyard must do is *stop providing special protection* to the vineyard, and it **shall be burned…it shall be trampled down**.

i. In a limited sense, God has given the responsibility of "taking away hedges" to the church. When a Christian is stubbornly unrepentant, it may be the job of the church to "turn them over" to Satan, so they will feel the pain of their sin and repent (1 Timothy 1:20; 1 Corinthians 5:4-5). The church does this by putting such ones outside the spiritual protection found among God's people.

b. **I will lay it waste; it shall not be pruned or dug**: The vineyard will receive *nothing* from the LORD. The vineyard resisted and protested the "pruning" and "digging" and "watering" the owner did. So now, the owner says, "Fine. No more pruning or digging or watering. You will see for yourself if that is better."

i. Many discouraged children of God wish the LORD would stop pruning, stop digging, stop watering. Those things may be hard, but it is *even worse* when the LORD stops doing them.

c. **He looked for justice, but behold oppression; for righteousness, but behold, a cry for help**: The prophet plays on words here. In the Hebrew, he wrote "**He looked for** *mishpat*, **but behold** *mispat*; **for** *tsedaqua*, **but behold** *tseaqua*."

B. Woe to the nation ripe for judgment.

1. (8-10) Woe to the land barons.

Woe to those who join house to house;
They add field to field,
Till *there is* no place
Where they may dwell alone in the midst of the land!
In my hearing the LORD of hosts *said*,
"Truly, many houses shall be desolate,
Great and beautiful ones, without inhabitant.
For ten acres of vineyard shall yield one bath,
And a homer of seed shall yield one ephah."

a. **Woe to those who join house to house**: The picture is of greedy real estate buying and development.

i. "For it cannot be condemned as a thing in itself wrong, if a man *add field to field and house to house*; but he looked at the disposition of mind, which cannot at all be satisfied, when it is once inflamed by the desire of gain. Accordingly, he describes the feelings of those who never have enough, and whom no wealth can satisfy." (Calvin)

ii. "Covetous persons are of the dragon's temper, who, they say, is so thirsty, that no water can quench his thirst. Covetousness is a dry drunkenness, saith one, an insatiable dropsy, and like hell itself." (Trapp)

b. **Many houses shall be desolate, great and beautiful ones, without inhabitant**: In judgment, their real estate deals will not be successful, and they will have many vacant and unsold houses.

i. "When men are covetous after the things of this world, God has a way of making them to be filled with disappointment and with bitterness." (Spurgeon)

2. (11-17) Woe to those who party endlessly and celebrate everything but God.

Woe to those who rise early in the morning,
***That* they may follow intoxicating drink;**
Who continue until night, *till* wine inflames them!
The harp and the strings,
The tambourine and flute,
And wine are in their feasts;
But they do not regard the work of the LORD,
Nor consider the operation of His hands.
Therefore my people have gone into captivity,
Because *they have* no knowledge;
Their honorable men *are* famished,
And their multitude dried up with thirst.
Therefore Sheol has enlarged itself
And opened its mouth beyond measure;
Their glory and their multitude and their pomp,
And he who is jubilant, shall descend into it.
People shall be brought down,
Each man shall be humbled,
And the eyes of the lofty shall be humbled.
But the LORD of hosts shall be exalted in judgment,
And God who is holy shall be hallowed in righteousness.
Then the lambs shall feed in their pasture,
And in the waste places of the fat ones strangers shall eat.

a. **Woe to those who rise early in the morning, that they may follow intoxicating drink**: The picture is of those who "work hard" to party and endlessly celebrate. Their lives are filled with substance abuse and music – **but they do not regard the work of the Lord, nor consider the operation of His hands.**

i. What is wrong with the party life and the addiction to entertainment? Simply put, God is forgotten. Though men may claim to remember Him in some way, they do not **regard the work of the Lord, nor consider the operation of His hands**. Anyone who really does **regard the work of the Lord**, and really does **consider the operation of His hands**, will live as if God is real and as if there is much more to life than partying and entertainment.

b. **Therefore My people have gone into captivity**: Those who forget about God because of their partying and entertainment will be judged by a captivity that will end the laughs (**he who is jubilant, shall descend into it**), exalt the Lord (**the Lord of hosts shall be exalted in judgment**), and reward the meek (**the lambs shall feed in their pasture**).

3. (18-21) Woe to those who confuse moral issues, who think that they know better than God does.

Woe to those who draw iniquity with cords of vanity,
And sin as if with a cart rope;
That say, "Let Him make speed *and* hasten His work,
That we may see *it;*
And let the counsel of the Holy One of Israel draw near and come,
That we may know *it.*"
Woe to those who call evil good, and good evil;
Who put darkness for light, and light for darkness;
Who put bitter for sweet, and sweet for bitter!
Woe to *those who are* wise in their own eyes,
And prudent in their own sight!

a. **Woe to those who draw iniquity with cords of vanity**: They pull their sin to themselves with ropes of emptiness!

i. "They flatter themselves by imagining that what is sin is not sin, or by some excuse or idle pretence they lessen its enormity. These, then, are *cords*, wicked *ropes*, by which they *draw iniquity*." (Calvin)

ii. "That are not only drawn to sin by the allurements of the world, or by the persuasions of wicked men, being surprised and overtaken by sin, as sometimes good men are...but are active and industrious in drawing sin to themselves, or themselves to sin; that greedily and steadily pursue sin, and the occasions of it, and are not at rest until they have overtaken it; that sin wilfully, and resolvedly, and industriously." (Poole)

iii. "With vain and deceitful arguments and pretences, whereby sinners generally draw themselves to sin." (Poole)

b. **Let the counsel of the Holy One of Israel draw near and come, that we may know it**: In saying these empty words, they showed their arrogant contempt of the LORD. It is as if they said, "Go ahead, God. We are ready for your judgment."

i. "He either cannot or will not do us any harm: we do not fear him, let him do his worst; let him begin as soon as he pleaseth. Not that any of the Israelites were so impudent as to use these expressions; but this was the plain language of their actions; they lived as if they were of this opinion; their presumption and security showing their desperate contempt of God, and of all his judgments." (Poole)

c. **Woe to those who call evil good, and good evil**: Using clever and deceptive words, they blur moral issues and excuse their sin. They look at their own **evil** and call it **good**, and they look at the **good** of others and call it **evil**. Isaiah is describing a deep state of moral confusion.

i. "They were the Nietzschians of that day with their *Unwertung aller Werten*, the devaluation of all values, the overturning of all values and basic concepts." (Bultema)

d. **Woe to those who are wise in their own eyes**: They were full of pride and rejected the wisdom and standards of God. "The Bible? It's so judgmental. Judge not lest you be judged. It's all how you interpret it. You have your interpretation and I have mine." All this thinking exalts the wisdom of man over the word of God.

4. (22-23) Woe to the corrupt, who place greater value on drinking than on fairness and justice.

Woe to men mighty at drinking wine,
Woe to men valiant for mixing intoxicating drink,
Who justify the wicked for a bribe,
And take away justice from the righteous man!

a. **Woe to the men mighty at drinking**: These were men of accomplishment, of high achievement – in sin.

i. "The prophet inveigheth against this vice a second time, because it was grown so common. Drunkards also are a sottish kind of creatures, and had therefore more than need to be double dealt with.... Many of these sots take it for a great glory that they are mighty to drink wine." (Trapp)

ii. "When one was commended to King Alphonsus for a great drinker, and able to bear it, he answered that that was a good praise in a sponge, but not in a prince." (Trapp)

iii. "Nothing is more base or disgraceful than for a man to make trial of his strength in swallowing food or in guzzling wine, and this struggling with himself so as to cram down as much as his belly can hold. Such men keep no rule of life, and do not know why God gives them nourishment; for we eat and drink to support the body, and not to destroy it." (Calvin)

b. **Who justify the wicked for a bribe, and take away justice from the righteous man**: These are men who care only for their own pleasure and entertainment, and care nothing for others.

5. (24-30) The Lord promises a sure and complete judgment.

Therefore, as the fire devours the stubble,
And the flame consumes the chaff,
***So* their root will be as rottenness,**
And their blossom will ascend like dust;
Because they have rejected the law of the Lord of hosts,
And despised the word of the Holy One of Israel.
Therefore the anger of the Lord is aroused against His people;
He has stretched out His hand against them
And stricken them,
And the hills trembled.
Their carcasses *were* as refuse in the midst of the streets.
For all this His anger is not turned away,
But His hand *is* stretched out still.
He will lift up a banner to the nations from afar,
And will whistle to them from the end of the earth;
Surely they shall come with speed, swiftly.
No one will be weary or stumble among them,
No one will slumber or sleep;
Nor will the belt on their loins be loosed,
Nor the strap of their sandals be broken;
Whose arrows *are* sharp,
And all their bows bent;
Their horses' hooves will seem like flint,
And their wheels like a whirlwind.
Their roaring *will be* like a lion,
They will roar like young lions;
Yes, they will roar

And lay hold of the prey;
They will carry *it* away safely,
And no one will deliver.
In that day they will roar against them
Like the roaring of the sea.
And if *one* looks to the land,
Behold, darkness *and* sorrow;
And the light is darkened by the clouds.

a. **As the fire devours the stubble, and the flame consumes the chaff**: **Stubble** and **chaff** are both very flammable. God is warning of sudden, complete, and severe judgment.

b. **Because they have rejected the law of the LORD of hosts, and despised the word of the Holy One of Israel**: Every one of Judah's sins could be traced back to a time of rejecting and despising what God says. Man's opinion was far more important to them than God's word.

c. **He will lift up a banner to the nations from afar, and will whistle to them from the end of the earth**: God will call foreign nations to come and invade Judah, making them instruments of His judgment upon them.

d. **They shall come with speed, swiftly.... No one will be weary or stumble among them...Nor will the belt on their loins be loosed... Whose arrows are sharp, and all their bows bent**: The armies God would call against Judah would all business. They would be totally focused, prepared, and readied – while the strong men of Judah would use their strength for drinking contests! This would be a great mismatch, and a soft, drunk, and flabby Judah would certainly fall against such dedicated enemies.

i. If we will not be strong for our own sakes, or even for the sake of the LORD, should we not at least be strong for the sake of our enemies? If they are strong and focused against us, should we not be strong in the LORD, and focused on the LORD, to overcome such strong enemies?

e. **Behold, darkness and sorrow; and the light is darkened by the clouds**: This is a distressing place. Why would the LORD put Judah in such a place? Because He loves them. These words were harsh but merciful; yet these words were a slap in the face to prevent total and eternal destruction. The only question is, "Will we *listen* to God's warning?"

i. "God's woes are better than the devil's welcomes." (Spurgeon)

Isaiah 6 – Isaiah's Conviction, Cleansing and Call

A. The conviction of the prophet.

1. (1-2) What Isaiah saw.

In the year that King Uzziah died, I saw the Lord sitting on a throne, high and lifted up, and the train of His *robe* filled the temple. Above it stood seraphim; each one had six wings: with two he covered his face, with two he covered his feet, and with two he flew.

a. **In the year that King Uzziah died**: King Uzziah of Judah had a long and distinguished reign, described in 2 Chronicles 26 and in 2 Kings 15:1-7 (**Uzziah** is called *Azariah* in 2 Kings 15).

i. Uzziah began his reign when he was only 16 years old, and he reigned 52 years. Overall, he was a good king, and 2 Kings 15:3 says, *he did what was right in the sight of the LORD, according to all that his father Amaziah had done.* 2 Chronicles 26:5 says, *He sought God in the days of Zechariah, who had understanding in the visions of God; and as long as he sought the LORD, God made him prosper.*

ii. Uzziah also led Israel in military victories over the Philistines and other neighboring nations, and he was a strong king. Uzziah was an energetic builder, planner, and general. 2 Chronicles 26:8 says of Uzziah, *His fame spread as far as the entrance of Egypt, for he became exceedingly strong.*

iii. But Uzziah's life ended tragically. 2 Chronicles 26:16 says, *but when he was strong his heart was lifted up, to his destruction, for he transgressed against the LORD his God by entering the temple of the LORD to burn incense on the altar of incense.* In response, God struck Uzziah with leprosy, and he was an isolated leper until his death.

iv. So, to say **in the year King Uzziah died** is to say a lot. It is to say, "In the year a great and wise king died." But it is also to say, "In the year a great and wise king who had a tragic end died." Isaiah had great reason to be discouraged and disillusioned at the death of King Uzziah, because a great king had passed away, and because his life ended tragically. Where was the LORD in all this?

b. **I saw the LORD sitting on a throne**: Where was the LORD in all this? The LORD was **sitting on a throne**! God was still enthroned in heaven and was still in charge of all creation.

i. There is a throne in heaven, and the LORD God sits upon it as the sovereign ruler of the universe! This is the central fact of heaven; that there is *an occupied throne* in heaven. God does not sit on a *chair* in heaven. Anyone might sit on a *chair*. But *sovereign kings* sit on thrones. *Judges* sit on thrones. Those with proper *authority and sovereignty* sit on thrones.

ii. Isaiah was not alone in seeing God's throne. Almost everyone in the Bible who had a vision of heaven, was taken to heaven, or wrote about heaven spoke of God's throne.

- The prophet Michaiah saw God's throne (1 Kings 22:19).
- Job saw God's throne (Job 26:9).
- David saw God's throne (Psalm 9:4 and 9:7, 11:4)
- The Sons of Korah saw God's throne (Psalm 45:6, 47:8).
- Ethan the Ezrahite saw God's throne (Psalm 89:14).
- Jeremiah saw God's throne (Lamentations 5:19)
- Ezekiel saw God's throne (Ezekiel 1:26, 10:1).
- Daniel saw God's throne (Daniel 7:9).
- The Apostle John saw God's throne (Revelation 4:1-11). In fact, the book of Revelation may as well be called "the book of God's throne," because God's throne is specifically mentioned more than 35 times in that book.

iii. The core belief of atheism or materialism is that there *is no throne*; there is no seat of authority or power all the universe must answer to. The core belief of humanism is that there is a throne – but *man* sits upon it. But the Bible makes it clear that there *is a throne* in heaven, and *no fallen man* sits on the throne, but the *Lord GOD is enthroned in heaven.*

iv. Isaiah may have been depressed or discouraged because a great leader of Judah was no longer on the throne. God in heaven now shows Isaiah, "Don't worry about it, Isaiah. Uzziah may not be on his throne, but I am on My throne."

c. **High and lifted up**: The throne was exalted and majestic. The throne set its Occupant in a superior position.

d. **The train of His robe filled the temple**: Kings of that time would wear robes with long trains because they were difficult to maneuver and work in. Wearing a long train meant, "I am important enough that I don't have to work. I am a person of honor and dignity. Others must serve me and wait upon me." Essentially, the same is said when a bride wears a dress with a long train today.

i. God is so honored, so important, so dignified, that **the train of His robe filled the temple**. That's a long train.

e. **Above it stood seraphim**: Surrounding the throne of God are angels known here as **seraphim**. In many other passages, these angels are known as *cherubim* (Psalm 80:1; Isaiah 37:16; Ezekiel 10:3) or as the *living creatures* of Revelation 4:6-11. This is the only chapter in the Bible where these creatures are named **seraphim**.

i. Some deny that *cherubim* and **seraphim** refer to the same beings. But the name **seraphim** means, "burning ones." Ezekiel 1:13 describes cherubim (see also Ezekiel 10:15) this way: *their appearance was like burning coals of fire, like the appearance of torches going back and forth among the living creatures. The fire was bright, and out of the fire went lightning.* That certainly seems to describe *burning ones.*

f. **Each one had six wings**: In Revelation 4:8, the Apostle John also mentions their **six wings**. They need the six wings, so each can cover **his face** (to show they are too lowly to look upon the LORD), so each can cover **his feet** (to hide this "humble" area of the body, so nothing even possibly deficient is seen in the LORD's presence), and so each can fly.

i. The LORD said to Moses, "*You cannot see My face; for no man shall see Me, and live*" (Exodus 33:20). Apparently, the same is true even for angels, so the **seraphim** cover their faces.

ii. "The *two wings* with which the angels *fly* mean nothing else than their ready and cheerful performance of the commandments of God.... The *two wings* with which they *cover their face* show plainly enough that even angels cannot endure God's brightness, and that they are dazzled by it in the same manner as when we attempt to gaze upon the radiance of the sun." (Calvin)

iii. "For the seraph remembers that even though sinless he is yet a creature, and therefore he conceals himself in token of his nothingness and unworthiness in the presence of the thrice Holy One." (Spurgeon)

g. **Each one had six wings: with two he covered his face, with two he covered his feet, and with two he flew**: The **seraphim** used four of their wings to express their humility and used two of their wings to express their willingness and ability to serve God. This is the proper balance.

i. "Thus they have four wings for adoration and two for active energy; four to conceal themselves, and two with which to occupy themselves in service; and we may learn from them that we shall serve God best when we are most deeply reverend and humbled in his presence. Veneration must be in larger proportion than vigor, adoration must exceed activity. As Mary at Jesus' feet was preferred to Martha and her much serving, so must sacred reverence take the first place, and energetic service follow in due course." (Spurgeon)

2. (3-4) What Isaiah heard.

And one cried to another and said:

"Holy, holy, holy *is* the LORD of hosts;
The whole earth *is* full of His glory!"

And the posts of the door were shaken by the voice of him who cried out, and the house was filled with smoke.

a. **One cried to another and said**: The *seraphim* are not even directly addressing the LORD God here. They are proclaiming His glorious nature and character to one another, in the presence of the LORD.

b. **Holy, holy, holy is the LORD of hosts**: Why do they repeat "**holy**" three times? Wasn't it enough to simply say that the LORD was "**holy**" once? It wasn't enough. They say it three times because there are Three Persons in the One God.

i. Calvin didn't think that this was the best verse to prove the Trinity, but he still saw the truth of the Trinity here. "The ancients quoted this passage when they wished to prove that there are three persons in one essence of the Godhead…. I have no doubt that the angels here describe One God in Three Persons."

c. **Holy, holy, holy is the LORD of hosts**: Why do they repeat "**holy**" three times? Wasn't it enough to simply say that the LORD was "**holy**" once? It wasn't enough. In the Hebrew language, intensity is communicated by *repetition*. To say the LORD is **holy** says something. To say the LORD is **holy, holy**, says far more. To say, **holy, holy, holy is the LORD** is to declare His holiness in the highest possible degree.

i. What does it mean that God is **holy**, and **holy** in the highest possible sense? **Holiness**, at its root, has the idea of *apartness*. It describes someone, or something, which is *set apart* from other people or things. An object can be holy if it is set apart for sacred service. A person is holy if they are set apart for God's will and purpose.

ii. What is the Lord set apart from? He is set apart from *creation*, in that the Lord God is not a creature, and He exists outside of all creation. If all creation were to dissolve, the Lord God would remain. He is set apart from *humanity*, in that His "nature" or "essence" is *Divine*, not *human*. God is not a *super-man* or the *ultimate man*. God is not merely *smarter* than any man, *stronger* than any man, *older* than any man, or *better* than any man. You can't measure God on man's chart at all. He is *Divine*, and we are *human*.

iii. Yet, because we are made in the image of God (Genesis 1:26-27), humanity is *compatible* with Divinity. They are different, but they do not automatically *oppose* each other. This is how Jesus, the Second Person of the Trinity, could *add humanity to His deity* when He became a man. Unfallen humanity is not deity, but it is compatible with it.

iv. God's holiness is a part of everything He is and does. God's power is a *holy power*. God's love is a *holy love*. God's wisdom is a *holy wisdom*. Holiness is not an aspect of God's personality; it is one characteristic of His entire Being.

d. **The whole earth is full of His glory**: The *seraphim* surrounding the throne of God could see this probably more clearly than Isaiah could. We are often blind to the obvious glory of God all around us.

e. **The posts of the door were shaken by the voice of him who cried out**: The *seraphim* are majestic beings, and their voice carries *weight*. When they speak, the doorposts of God's throne room shake! The idea may be that Isaiah was watching from the doorway, and when the *seraphim* cried out, he could feel the doorposts shake.

i. Yet these high, majestic beings – perhaps the highest beings in all of God's creation – have *one occupation*. Their existence is given over to the praise and worship and honor of the Lord God who is enthroned in heaven. What could we possibly do that is a higher calling than that?

ii. They sang so powerfully the doorposts were shaken! Shouldn't we sing with the same passion, the same heart, the same intensity? Do those angels have more to thank and praise God for than we do?

f. **The house was filled with smoke**: This **smoke** reminds us of the pillar of cloud that represented the presence of God (Exodus 13:21-22), the smoke on Mount Sinai (Exodus 19:18), and the cloud of God's Shekinah glory that filled the temple (1 Kings 8:10-12). A cloud of glory often marks the presence of the LORD.

3. (5) What Isaiah felt.

So I said:
"Woe *is* me, for I am undone!
Because I *am* a man of unclean lips,
And I dwell in the midst of a people of unclean lips;
For my eyes have seen the King,
The LORD of hosts."

a. **Woe is me, for I am undone**: What made Isaiah feel like he was coming apart? Two things. First, the sight and sound of the *seraphim*. Second, the vision of the Lord GOD.

i. When Isaiah saw the angels, in all their holy humility, obedience, and praise to God, he realized not only that he was unlike the Lord GOD, he was also unlike the angels. They could cry out *Holy, holy, holy* and praise God so beautifully, but he could not because he was **a man of unclean lips**. "I am a man of unclean lips; I cannot say, Holy, holy, holy! which the seraphs exclaim. They are holy; I am not so: they see God and live; I have seen him, and must die, because I am unholy." (Clarke)

ii. When Isaiah saw the LORD, he knew what kind of man *he* was. As poorly as he compared to the *seraphim,* that was nothing in relation to how he compared to the LORD. This vision (or actual experience) of the throne of God did not immediately make Isaiah feel *good.* The more clearly he saw the LORD, the more clearly he saw how bad his state was.

iii. Isaiah's deep sense of depravity is consistent with the experience of other godly men in the presence of the LORD. Job (Job 42:5-6), Daniel (Daniel 10:15-17), Peter (Luke 5:8) and John (Revelation 1:17) each had similar experiences.

iv. **I am undone** is not a bad place to be. "God will never do anything with us till he has first of all undone us." (Spurgeon)

b. **Because I am a man of unclean lips, and I dwell in the midst of a people of unclean lips**: Isaiah saw his sinfulness, and the sinfulness of his people, mainly in terms of *sinful speech.*

i. By nature, our lips are full of flattery and false intent: *With flattering lips and a double heart they speak* (Psalm 12:2). By nature, our lips lie and are proud: *Let the lying lips be put to silence, which speak insolent things proudly and contemptuously against the righteous* (Psalm 31:18).

By nature, our lips deceive: *Keep your tongue from evil, and your lips from speaking deceit* (Psalm 34:13). By nature, our lips are violent: *Swords are in their lips* (Psalm 59:7). By nature, our lips bring death to others: *The poison of asps is under their lips* (Psalm 140:3).

ii. Isaiah did not think for a moment that this was his *only* sin, but he saw that this was an example of the *great and incurable disease of sin* in him and his people.

c. **For my eyes have seen the King, the Lord of hosts**: Isaiah was a righteous, godly man by all outward appearance. Yet when he saw the enthroned **King**, the **Lord of hosts**, he saw how sinful he was in comparison.

i. Isaiah's life may have been as brilliant as a diamond. But when you lay a diamond against a perfectly black background and have the right light upon it, you can see every flaw and imperfection – flaws that were invisible before. Even so, when Isaiah's righteous life lay against the background of God's perfection, it looked different.

B. The cleansing of the prophet.

1. (6) A seraphim brings a coal from the altar.

Then one of the seraphim flew to me, having in his hand a live coal *which* he had taken with the tongs from the altar.

a. **One of the seraphim flew to me**: These angelic beings, surrounding the throne of God, ministered to Isaiah. One flew to Isaiah with **a live coal** – which means the **coal** was still hot and burning. It was so hot that even an angel had to use **the tongs from the altar**.

b. **The altar**: This must be heaven's version of the altar of incense that was set before the holy of holies in the tabernacle of God (Exodus 30:1-10). We know that the earthly tabernacle God instructed Moses to build was made after the pattern of a heavenly reality (Exodus 25:9).

i. The *throne* is for God; that is where He rules and reigns. **The altar** is for us; that is where we find cleansing and purging from sin. We should never confuse the two.

ii. "The fire was *taken from the altar*, to intimate that it was divine or heavenly; for the law forbade any *strange fire* to be brought to it, because in sacred things every human mixture is absolute profanation. By this figure, therefore, Isaiah was taught that all purity flows from God alone." (Calvin)

2. (7) A coal from the altar cleanses Isaiah's lips.

And he touched my mouth *with it*, and said:

"Behold, this has touched your lips;
Your iniquity is taken away,
And your sin purged."

a. **And he touched my mouth with it**: This must have been painful; a burning hot coal applied to the lips, one of the more sensitive areas of the body. Yet, nothing is written that Isaiah reacted in pain. Either there was no pain, because of a special blessing by God, or the pain did not matter because of the majesty of the surroundings and the goodness of the cleansing.

i. Isaiah knew he did not serve the LORD like these *seraphim*, the *burning ones*. So God said, "I will light a fire in you, also!" That is why a burning coal was used to purify Isaiah. "Jehovah, who is a consuming fire, can only fitly be served by those who are on fire, whether they be angels or men." (Spurgeon)

ii. Isaiah cried out, *Woe is me, for I am undone!* (Isaiah 6:5) We might think that a burning coal to the lips would be more painful than a vision of the holy God. But for Isaiah, it was more disturbing to see the holiness of God, and to see his lack of holiness, than it was to have a burning coal applied to his lips.

b. **Your iniquity is taken away, and your sin purged**: Isaiah's sin had to be *burned* away; the fire of judgment was applied to his place of sin.

i. This was obviously a *spiritual* transaction. If one has a sinful mouth, it will do nothing to place a burning hot coal on their lips. That will not take away or purge their sin.

ii. Yet, the same principle works on our behalf in regard to Jesus' work on Calvary. Our sin was placed upon Him, and He was burned with the fire of God's judgment. Yet because He was holy and righteous Himself, the fire of God's judgment did not harm Him; it only burned away the sin, our sin.

iii. Once Isaiah had *met* with the LORD, been *convicted* of his sin, and *cleansed* from its guilt, then he was ready to serve God. "The effect of that live coal will be to fire the lip with heavenly flame. 'Oh,' says one man, 'a flaming coal will burn the lip so that the man cannot speak at all.' That is just how God works with us; it is by consuming the fleshly power that he inspires the heavenly might. Oh let the lip be burnt, let the fleshly power of eloquence be destroyed, but oh for that live coal to make the tongue eloquent with heaven's flame; the true divine power which urged the Apostles forward, and made them conquerors of the whole world." (Spurgeon)

C. The commission of the prophet.

1. (8) God calls and Isaiah responds.

Also I heard the voice of the Lord, saying:

"Whom shall I send,
And who will go for Us?"
Then I said, "Here *am* I! Send me."

a. **Whom shall I send, and who will go for Us?** God looked for someone to **send**. He wanted someone to **go**.

i. How strange it is for God to ask a question at all! What does God wonder about? What questions would He have? What does God not know? But God was asking for a *person* because God wants to reach the world, and He wants to reach it through willing people. It isn't that God doesn't know who these people are. It is that God is waiting for ready hearts to reveal themselves.

ii. How strange it is that this God of majesty, sovereignty, and power *asks for volunteers*! He could easily *create* robots to do His work or *command angels* to carry out His will. But God wants willing, surrendered servants. Have you been waiting for God to *force* you to serve Him? He looks for *volunteers.*

b. **Whom shall I send**: This means that the missionary, the Christian worker, the witness of Jesus Christ, is *sent.* This is a divine commission. **Who will go for Us** means that the missionary, the Christian worker, the witness of Jesus Christ, *has decided to go*. God's divine will to send and the human will to go are in perfect cooperation

i. Here we see another subtle reference to the Trinity. Who is sending? **I** or **Us**? It seems to be the same Person speaking in both the singular and the plural. It is the same Person! "The change of the number, *I* and *us*, is very remarkable; and both being meant of one and the same Lord, do sufficiently intimate a plurality of the persons in the Godhead." (Poole)

c. **Here am I! Send me**: Isaiah *emphatically* answered God's call. He did not hesitate. *Isaiah wanted to be the answer to God's question.*

i. What created this kind of heart in Isaiah? First, he had a heart that had been in the presence of God. He had a heart that knew its own sinfulness. He had a heart that knew the need among the people, the need for God's word. He had a heart that had been touched by God's cleansing fire. And he had a heart that *heard* God's heart to reach the nations.

d. **Send me**: This meant Isaiah was submitted to the LORD in all his service. He didn't even say, "Here I am, I will go." Isaiah would not go at all unless he knew he was *sent* by the LORD. Many are quick to say, "Here I am, I will go" but never wait for the LORD to **send** them.

2. (9-10) His mission described.

And He said, "Go, and tell this people:
'Keep on hearing, but do not understand;
Keep on seeing, but do not perceive.'
Make the heart of this people dull,
And their ears heavy,
And shut their eyes;
Lest they see with their eyes,
And hear with their ears,
And understand with their heart,
And return and be healed."

a. **And He said, "Go"**: When we say, "*Here am I! Send me*" to the LORD, we should expect that He will say **"Go."** He may say, "**Go** and serve Me here" or "**Go** and serve me there" or "**Go** and be prepared for future service," but God always has a "**Go**" for us.

b. **Go and tell these people, "Keep on hearing, but do not understand; keep on seeing but do not perceive"**: God told Isaiah to go and preach to a people who wouldn't respond so that their guilt would be certain. As Trapp wrote, Isaiah would "Preach them to hell."

c. **Make the heart of this people dull, and their ears heavy, and shut their eyes**: This is an unsatisfying audience and ministry for any preacher. Isaiah might not be satisfied with this ministry. The people might not be satisfied with it. But God would be satisfied with it.

d. **And understand with their heart, and return and be healed**: This shows what the word of God *can* accomplish when it is received with open eyes, open ears, and an open heart. It brings *understanding* to our hearts, it makes us *return*, and it brings *healing* to our lives. If you are under the word of God and these things *aren't* happening to you, ask God to work with your eyes, ears, and heart.

3. (11-13) Isaiah is told how long he must prophesy this way.

Then I said, "Lord, how long?"
And He answered:
"Until the cities are laid waste and without inhabitant,
The houses are without a man,
The land is utterly desolate,

The LORD has removed men far away,
And the forsaken places *are* many in the midst of the land.
But yet a tenth *will be* in it,
And will return and be for consuming,
As a terebinth tree or as an oak,
Whose stump *remains* when it is cut down.
So the holy seed *shall be* its stump."

a. **Lord, how long?** This is a logical question from anyone who is given such a difficult commission. "Do I have to preach to those who won't hear, and their rejection of my message will ultimately seal their doom? How long will I have to serve in that kind of ministry?"

b. **Until the cities are laid waste and without inhabitant**: This answered the question of how long Isaiah was to preach. He should preach until destruction comes. He should preach in hope of the restoration of a remnant (**yet a tenth will be in it, and will return**). Even though Isaiah's ministry was difficult, it was not without hope.

c. **And be for consuming**: The remnant will indeed return, but even the remnant will eventually be judged. Israel was not done being disobedient when they returned from the Babylonian captivity, and God was not done bringing His judgment on a disobedient Israel.

i. "The devastation, great as it was to be, would not be total; but even its survivors would have to submit to further judgment. The illustration from nature, however, introduces an element of hope." (Grogan)

ii. We would expect this dramatic call of Isaiah to open the book. But the Bible clearly states that the *message* is more important than the *messenger*. Isaiah's *message* was more important than Isaiah the *messenger*.

iii. When Isaiah *saw the LORD*, who did he see? He saw God in the Second Person of the Trinity, he saw Jesus before He added humanity to His deity. We know this because the Apostle John quotes Isaiah 6:10, and under the inspiration of the Holy Spirit, adds: *These things Isaiah said when he saw His glory and spoke of Him* (John 12:41).

Isaiah 7 – Shear-Jashub and Immanuel

A. The sign of Shear-Jashub.

1. (1-2) The northern nation of Israel and Syria combine to attack Judah.

Now it came to pass in the days of Ahaz the son of Jotham, the son of Uzziah, king of Judah, *that* Rezin king of Syria and Pekah the son of Remaliah, king of Israel, went up to Jerusalem to *make* war against it, but could not prevail against it. And it was told to the house of David, saying, "Syria's forces are deployed in Ephraim." So his heart and the heart of his people were moved as the trees of the woods are moved with the wind.

a. **In the days of Ahaz the son of Jotham**: **Ahaz** was a wicked king of Judah, worshipping other gods and even sacrificing his son to Molech (2 Kings 16:1-4). The only good thing Ahaz seemed to do was to father Hezekiah, who became a good king of Judah.

i. "He was a cowardly, superstitious and hypocritical ruler, one of the worst kings Judah ever had." (Bultema)

b. **Rezin king of Syria and Pekah...king of Israel**: The alliance between these two nations and their unsuccessful attack on Jerusalem is described in 2 Kings 16.

i. The attack on Jerusalem was ultimately unsuccessful, but the war against Judah greatly weakened the kingdom southern tribes. 2 Chronicles 28:6 documents the damage: *For Pekah the son of Remaliah killed one hundred and twenty thousand in Judah in one day, all valiant men, because they had forsaken the LORD God of their fathers*. 2 Chronicles 28:5 says that the Syrian army *carried away a great multitude of them as captives*. The king of Israel also captured 200,000 men, women and children, but sent them back to Judah at the command of the prophet Oded (2 Chronicles 28:8-15).

ii. All in all, when the events of this chapter unfold, the nation of Judah had faced terrible calamity and was devastated. As the combined armies of Israel and Syria approached Jerusalem, it looked like *everything* would be lost. Ahaz was challenged to trust God when things were bad, and it looked like soon, all would be lost.

c. **Went up to Jerusalem to make war against it, but could not prevail against it**: How was Ahaz saved from this attack? Because he entered into an ungodly alliance with *Tiglath-Pileser king of Assyria,* and even gave Tiglath-Pileser *silver and gold that was found in the house of the LORD* as a present to win his favor and protection (2 Kings 16:7-9).

i. When Ahaz went to meet Tiglath-Pileser, his new master, in Damascus, he saw the pagan altars and places of sacrifice. He copied these designs and remodeled the temple of the LORD in Jerusalem after the pattern of the pagan temple and altars in Damascus. Ahaz is a powerful, extreme example of someone who enters into an ungodly alliance for "good" reasons yet becomes thoroughly corrupted and compromised (2 Kings 16:10-18).

ii. It is important to understand that the events of this chapter happened *before* Ahaz made his final decision to put his trust in Tiglath-Pileser, king of Assyria. Though we are told the end result of the attack in Isaiah 7:1-2 (**could not prevail against it**), Isaiah is telling us the end result *before* he describes his prophecy to Ahaz. This disregard for chronological order may be frustrating to us but is completely natural to the ancient Hebrew mind.

d. **Syria's forces are deployed in Ephraim**: *Ephraim* is another title for the northern nation of Israel. King Ahaz heard that Syria and Israel had joined together to make war against Judah.

e. **So his heart and the heart of his people were moved as the trees of the woods are moved with the wind**: King Ahaz and his people react with *fear* instead of with *trust in God.* They are *shaken* and *unstable* in their hearts.

i. In this, the people of Judah really are the people of *Ahaz* (**his people**), not the people of the LORD. God was not shaken or unsettled by this threat. If the king of Judah and the people of Judah had put their trust in the LORD, they would have had the peace of God in this conflict.

2. (3-9) The word of the LORD to Ahaz through Isaiah.

Then the LORD said to Isaiah, "Go out now to meet Ahaz, you and Shear-Jashub your son, at the end of the aqueduct from the upper pool, on the highway to the Fuller's Field, and say to him: 'Take heed, and be quiet; do not fear or be fainthearted for these two stubs of smoking firebrands,

for the fierce anger of Rezin and Syria, and the son of Remaliah. Because Syria, Ephraim, and the son of Remaliah have plotted evil against you, saying, "Let us go up against Judah and trouble it, and let us make a gap in its wall for ourselves, and set a king over them, the son of Tabel"—thus says the Lord GOD:

"It shall not stand,
Nor shall it come to pass.
For the head of Syria *is* Damascus,
And the head of Damascus *is* Rezin.
Within sixty-five years Ephraim will be broken,
***So that it will* not *be* a people.**
The head of Ephraim *is* Samaria,
And the head of Samaria *is* Remaliah's son.
If you will not believe, surely you shall not be established."'"

a. **You and Shear-Jashub your son**: Isaiah was told to take his son, named **Shear-Jashub**, and bring a word from the LORD to Ahaz. He brought his son as a walking object lesson because the name **Shear-Jashub** means, "*A Remnant Shall Return*."

b. **At the end of the aqueduct from the upper pool, on the highway to the Fuller's Field**: These seemingly irrelevant details make an important point. All this happened to real people at a real time and in real places. This isn't make-believe or fairy tales. This is real.

c. **Take heed, and be quiet**: Seemingly, Ahaz needed to pay attention (**take heed**) and stop his talking about the problem (**be quiet**). He needed to trust God and take courage in the LORD (**do not fear or be fainthearted**).

i. Perhaps also, the calamity and devastation that had wracked Judah so far had made Ahaz stop trusting in God. "If God loves me, why am I in this mess at all? Trust Him now, after all He has allowed to happen? Are you crazy?"

d. **Do not fear or be fainthearted**: It was hard for Ahaz to do this because he didn't see the situation the way the LORD did. Ahaz looked at Israel and Syria and saw a terrible threat. God looked at Israel and Syria and saw **two stubs of smoking firebrands**. To the LORD, they were all smoke and no fire.

i. "One would think that they are endued with so great power that they could burn and destroy the whole world. To put down the excess of terror, the Lord declares that what we imagined to be a burning, and a perpetual burning, is but a slight smoke and of short duration." (Calvin)

ii. "Calleth them in contempt a couple of firebrands, such as would do mischief but cannot, because smoking and not burning, and but the tails of smoking firebrands neither, such as are smoking their last, and shall shortly be utterly extinct. In a word, they have more pride than power, being a mere flash." (Trapp)

e. **It shall not stand, nor shall it come to pass**: Certainly, the king of Israel and the king of Syria had their plans – they **plotted evil against** Judah. They wanted to attack Jerusalem, defeat the capital of Judah (**make a gap in its wall**), then depose Ahaz and set up their own king. But God was not worried about their plans. They looked like a big, flaming threat to Ahaz, but God looked and saw **two stubs of smoking firebrands**, and simply said, "**It shall not stand, nor shall it come to pass.**"

i. Their plans will not succeed because the nations are led by ungodly men (**Rezin** and **Remaliah's son**), and not by the LORD. This is God's promise, and Isaiah calls Ahaz to trust in the LORD and in His promise.

f. **If you will not believe, surely you shall not be established**: Here is the challenge to Ahaz. God has promised, now the king of Judah must believe. If he **will not believe**, it will not affect the outcome of the attack against Jerusalem. God has already decreed that their attack would not succeed. But it would affect the course of Ahaz's life and reign as king (**surely you shall not be established**).

i. As it happened, Ahaz did not **believe**. He did not put his trust in the LORD. He put his trust in carnal methods and the king of Assyria. Jerusalem was spared, and Ahaz no doubt believed he was successful, and his plan had worked. But if he would have just trusted in the LORD, Jerusalem would have been spared, and Ahaz would have been blessed.

ii. Isaiah brought his son **Shear-Jashub** (Isaiah 7:3) because his name meant *A Remnant Shall Return*, and God wanted Ahaz to know that because of the kind of ungodly trust he put in the king of Assyria, Judah would eventually be taken into captivity, and only a remnant would return.

B. The sign of Immanuel.

1. (10-12) Ahaz will not ask for a sign.

Moreover the LORD spoke again to Ahaz, saying, "Ask a sign for yourself from the LORD your God; ask it either in the depth or in the height above." But Ahaz said, "I will not ask, nor will I test the LORD!"

a. **Ask a sign for yourself**: Through the prophet Isaiah, God invites Ahaz to ask for a sign. God has just challenged Ahaz to believe and be blessed, and now God offers to give Ahaz a basis for belief – **a sign for yourself**.

b. **But Ahaz said, "I will not ask, nor will I test the LORD"**: This *sounds* very spiritual from Ahaz. He almost seems to say what Jesus said in Matthew 4:7: "*You shall not tempt the LORD your God.*" Though the words are similar, the hearts are far apart. Ahaz refused to ask for a sign, because when God fulfilled the sign, he would be "obligated" to believe.

i. This was not tempting or testing God in a wrong way. It is never testing God to do as He says, and if the LORD invites us to test Him, we should. For example, in Malachi 3:10, the LORD invited Israel to give as He commanded, and thereby to *try Me now in this.*

ii. Again, perhaps Ahaz was bitter against the LORD, because of all the disaster Judah had already been through at the hands of Israel and Syria. Perhaps his mind is, "I want nothing to do with the God who allowed it to get this bad."

iii. Haven't we, in some way, to some degree, been in the same state of mind as Ahaz? Haven't we rejected the gracious, free gifts of God for silly and strange reasons? "Here let us each descend and dive into his own conscience, to see whether we also have not matched Ahaz in his madness, or at leastwise coasted too near upon his unkind usage of the Lord, by rejecting his sweet offers of grace and motions of mercy, by slighting his holy sacraments, those signs and seals of the righteousness that is by faith." (Trapp)

2. (13-16) The LORD's sign to Ahaz: the sign of *Immanuel.*

Then he said, "Hear now, O house of David! *Is it* a small thing for you to weary men, but will you weary my God also? Therefore the Lord Himself will give you a sign: Behold, the virgin shall conceive and bear a Son, and shall call His name Immanuel. Curds and honey He shall eat, that He may know to refuse the evil and choose the good. For before the Child shall know to refuse the evil and choose the good, the land that you dread will be forsaken by both her kings."

a. **Is it a small thing for you to weary men, but will you weary my God also?** The rulers of Judah treated other people poorly, but they treated the LORD even more poorly. If many of us expressed the same distrust we have towards the LORD towards other people, we might get a punch in the nose.

i. "How heartily angry is the prophet, how blessedly blown up in this case to so great dishonour done to God! We should be so too." (Trapp)

ii. Spurgeon spoke well to this point: "Did I not hear some one say, 'Ah, sir, I have been *trying to believe* for years.' Terrible words! They make the case still worse. Imagine that after I had made a statement, a man should declare that he did not believe me, in fact, he could not believe me though he would like to do so. I should feel aggrieved certainly; but it would make matters worse if he added, 'In fact I have been for years trying to believe you, and I cannot do it.' What does he mean by that? What can he mean but that I am so incorrigibly false, and such a confirmed liar, that though he would like to give me some credit, he really cannot do it? With all the effort he can make in my favour, he finds it quite beyond his power to believe me? Now, a man who says, 'I have been trying to believe in God,' in reality says just that with regard to the Most High."

b. **Therefore the Lord Himself will give you a sign: Behold, the virgin shall conceive and bear a Son, and shall call His name Immanuel**. This is one of the most famous prophecies regarding the birth of Jesus the Messiah in the Bible. It also illustrates a principle of prophecy, that prophecy may have both a *near fulfillment* and a *far fulfillment*.

i. Spurgeon said of this passage, that it is said to be "One of the most difficult in all the Word of God. It may be so; I certainly did not think it was until I saw what the commentators had to say about it, and I rose up from reading them perfectly confused."

ii. "It is characteristic of predictive prophecy that it often mingles different times together in one composite picture" (Martin)

c. **For before the Child shall know to refuse the evil and choose the good, the land that you dread will be forsaken by both her kings**: The *near fulfillment* of this prophecy centered around Ahaz, Jerusalem, and the attack from Israel and Syria. For Ahaz, the sign centered on this time span. Simply put, God would give Ahaz a sign that within a few years, both Israel and Syria would be crushed. This was a sign of deliverance to Ahaz.

i. Many commentators think that this was immediately fulfilled when a young woman in the royal household shortly married, conceived a son, and unknowingly naming him "*Immanuel.*" Before this boy came to eat solid food, Israel and Syria would be defeated. It is also possible that God is just referring in a figurative way to a year or two period of time.

ii. "The name 'Immanuel' was a rebuke to Ahaz. If 'God is with us,' then why should he have feared the enemy?" (Wolf)

iii. "The 'sign' of the child, therefore, constitutes an indication that the all-sovereign and all-knowing God has the situation completely in hand, and it rebukes the king's lack of faith in him." (Grogan)

d. **Behold, the virgin shall conceive and bear a Son**: The *far* or *ultimate fulfillment* of this prophecy goes far beyond Ahaz, to announce the miraculous virgin birth of Jesus Christ.

i. We know this passage speaks of Jesus because the Holy Spirit says so through Matthew: *"Behold, the virgin shall be with child, and bear a Son, and they shall call His name Immanuel," which is translated, "God with us."* (Matthew 1:23)

ii. We know this passage speaks of Jesus because the prophecy is addressed not only to Ahaz, but also to David's entire house (**O house of David!**).

iii. We know this passage speaks of Jesus because it says **the virgin shall conceive**, and that conception would be **a sign** to David's entire house. Those who deny the virgin birth of Jesus like to point out that the Hebrew word translated **virgin** (*almah*) can also be translated as "young woman." The idea is that Isaiah was simply saying that a "young woman" would give birth, not a virgin. While the *near fulfillment* may have reference to a young woman giving birth, the *far* or *ultimate fulfillment* clearly points to a woman miraculously conceiving and giving birth. This is especially clear because the Old Testament never uses the word in a context other than **virgin** and because the Septuagint translates it categorically **virgin** (*parthenos*).

iv. We know this passage speaks of Jesus because it says He will be known as **Immanuel**, meaning "God with Us." This was true of Jesus *in fact*, not only as a title. **Immanuel** speaks both of the deity of Jesus (*God* with us) and His identification and nearness to man (God *with us*).

e. **Call His name Immanuel**: Jesus is truly **Immanuel**, *God with us*. "Christ, indeed, was not called by this name Immanuel that we anywhere read of... but the import of this name is most truly affirmed and acknowledged to be fully made good in him." (Trapp)

i. "He is, therefore, called *God with us*, or *united to us*; which cannot apply to a man who is not God...it denotes not only the power of God, such as he usually displays by his servant, but a union of person, by which Christ became God-man." (Calvin)

ii. "In what sense then, is Christ GOD WITH US? Jesus is called Immanuel, or *God with us*, in his *incarnation*; *God with us*, by the influences of his *Holy Spirit*, in the *holy sacrament*, in the *preaching* of his *word*, in *private prayer*. And *God with us*, through every *action* of our life, that we begin, continue, and end in his name. He is *God with us*, to *comfort*, *enlighten*, *protect*, and *defend* us, in every time of *temptation* and *trial*, in the hour of *death*, in the day of *judgment*; and *God with us* and *in us*, and we *with* and *in* him, to all eternity." (Clarke)

3. (17-25) Assyria, the nation Ahaz trusted, will also bring ruin to Judah.

"The Lord will bring the king of Assyria upon you and your people and your father's house—days that have not come since the day that Ephraim departed from Judah."

And it shall come to pass in that day
***That* the Lord will whistle for the fly**
That *is* in the farthest part of the rivers of Egypt,
And for the bee that *is* in the land of Assyria.
They will come, and all of them will rest
In the desolate valleys and in the clefts of the rocks,
And on all thorns and in all pastures.
In the same day the Lord will shave with a hired razor,
With those from beyond the River, with the king of Assyria,
The head and the hair of the legs,
And will also remove the beard.
It shall be in that day
***That* a man will keep alive a young cow and two sheep;**
So it shall be, from the abundance of milk they give,
That he will eat curds;
For curds and honey everyone will eat who is left in the land.
It shall happen in that day,
***That* wherever there could be a thousand vines**
***Worth* a thousand *shekels* of silver,**
It will be for briers and thorns.
With arrows and bows men will come there,
Because all the land will become briers and thorns.
And to any hill which could be dug with the hoe,
You will not go there for fear of briers and thorns;
But it will become a range for oxen
And a place for sheep to roam.

a. **The Lord will bring the king of Assyria upon you**: This was bad news to Ahaz, who had been foolishly trusting in Assyria instead of the Lord. It is as if the Lord is saying, "It will seem to you like trusting in Assyria is a clever move, because the armies of Syria and Israel will be defeated. But the Assyrians will end up defeating you also."

i. "Thou mightest have remained at home and at ease, and mightest have received the assistance of God; but thou choosest rather to call in the Assyrians. Thou shalt find them to be worse than thine own enemies." (Calvin)

ii. If Ahaz understood and believed what the LORD said, it would have terrified him. The Assyrians were well known for their sheer cruelty, especially over the nations they conquered. They delighted in torture and humiliation (**shave with a hired razor...the head and the hair of the legs**).

iii. "To shave off the beard of an Oriental was an unbearable shame to him and was a sign of great sadness and mourning as well as despicable slavery." (Bultema) We see this principle illustrated by the actions of David in 2 Samuel 10:4-5.

b. **The LORD will whistle for the fly that is the farthest part of the rivers of Egypt, and for the bee that is in the land of Assyria. They will come**: Judah would not only be attacked by the Assyrians, they would also be invaded by the Egyptians. God would pinch Judah between these mighty nations to the north and south.

i. These invasions would bring Judah low, so that they could not farm as normally, and thus **curds and honey everyone will eat who is left in the land**. Normal agriculture would be devastated (**wherever there could be a thousand vines...it will be for briars and thorns**). Former farms will be suitable only for grazing (**it will become a range for oxen and a place for sheep to roam**).

Isaiah 8 – The Sign of Maher-Shalal-Hash-Baz

A. The coming Assyrian invasion against Syria and Israel.

1. (1-4) The invasion is announced by the naming of Isaiah's son.

Moreover the LORD said to me, "Take a large scroll, and write on it with a man's pen concerning Maher-Shalal-Hash-Baz. And I will take for Myself faithful witnesses to record, Uriah the priest and Zechariah the son of Jeberechiah." Then I went to the prophetess, and she conceived and bore a son. Then the LORD said to me, "Call his name Maher-Shalal-Hash-Baz; for before the child shall have knowledge to cry 'My father' and 'My mother,' the riches of Damascus and the spoil of Samaria will be taken away before the king of Assyria."

a. **Moreover the LORD said to me**: This prophecy continues from Isaiah 7, where God assured Ahaz, king of Judah, that he would not be overthrown by the combined forces of Syria and Israel. God announced judgment against Syria and Israel, saying of their attack against Judah: *It shall not stand, nor shall it come to pass.... Within sixty-five years Ephraim will be broken, so that it will not be a people.* Here, God gives Isaiah a sign to explain more about *how soon* the defeat of Syria and Israel will come.

b. **Take a large scroll**: It isn't often that the prophets are commanded to write, but here is one instance. Isaiah will write **concerning Maher-Shalal-Hash-Baz**, which means *speed to the spoil, hurry to the plunder.*

c. **Write on it with a man's pen**: Isaiah's message was meant to be public, and at a level any man could read and understand.

i. Calvin on **with a man's pen**: It "denotes any man of ordinary rank; and the meaning is, that not even the most ignorant and uneducated persons may be unable to read the writing."

d. **I will take for Myself faithful witnesses to record**: The LORD appointed two **witnesses**, so the validity of this word would be established. *By the* *mouth of two or three witnesses the matter shall be established.* (Deuteronomy 19:15)

e. **Then I went to the prophetess**: This refers to Isaiah's wife. She is called a **prophetess**, though it could be in the sense of simply being the wife of the prophet. However, she clearly brought forth prophecy on at least one occasion. The birth and naming of her son **Maher-Shalal-Hash-Baz** was a word from God, so she certainly "brought forth" that prophecy.

i. There are many examples of prophetesses in the Bible: Miriam (Exodus 15:20), Deborah (Judges 4:4), Huldah (2 Kings 22:14), Noadiah (Nehemiah 6:14), Anna (Luke 2:36), and Philip's four daughters (Acts 21:8-9). So, it may be that the wife of Isaiah had a prophetic ministry in her own right. But it may also be that she was simply the wife of the prophet, and her "prophecy" was giving birth to **Maher-Shalal-Hash-Baz.**

f. **For before the child shall have knowledge to cry "My father" and "My mother"**: Through the birth and naming of **Maher-Shalal-Hash-Baz**, the LORD gives a time frame for the invasion of Assyria that will punish Syria and Israel.

i. This is essentially the same as the *near meaning* of the Immanuel sign of Isaiah 7:10-17, but this sign was more public and plainer.

2. (5-10) Judah will be afflicted also.

The LORD also spoke to me again, saying:

"Inasmuch as these people refused
The waters of Shiloah that flow softly,
And rejoice in Rezin and in Remaliah's son;
Now therefore, behold, the Lord brings up over them
The waters of the River, strong and mighty—
The king of Assyria and all his glory;
He will go up over all his channels
And go over all his banks.
He will pass through Judah,
He will overflow and pass over,
He will reach up to the neck;
And the stretching out of his wings
Will fill the breadth of Your land, O Immanuel.
"Be shattered, O you peoples, and be broken in pieces!
Give ear, all you from far countries.
Gird yourselves, but be broken in pieces;
Gird yourselves, but be broken in pieces.

Take counsel together, but it will come to nothing;
Speak the word, but it will not stand,
For God *is* with us."

a. **These people refused the waters of Shiloah that flow softly**: The people of the northern kingdom of Israel did not appreciate their humble streams (**the waters of Shiloah**). Instead, they rejoiced in wicked leaders (**in Rezin and Remaliah's son**). So, God will give them a different kind of river – **the waters of the River, strong and mighty**.

i. "The little stream of Shiloah sprung from Mount Zion on the southwesterly side of Jerusalem. It flowed as softly as oil without any murmur. Jerusalem's existence and continuation depended on it." (Bultema)

ii. The capital of the Assyrian Empire was Nineveh, and the city of Nineveh was founded on a great river: the Tigris. The Assyrian Empire was also centered across another mighty river: the Euphrates. The whole land of Israel simply did not have a river like the Euphrates or the Tigris. God is using the difference between the small, humble, yet adequate waters of Israel and the mighty, yet uncontrolled rivers of Assyria to make a point. It is as if God is saying, "You don't like what I have given you? You persist in rejecting what I give you? Then I will give you something different, but you won't like it either."

iii. "The small and gentle waters should be more highly valued by us than the large and rapid rivers of all the nations, and we ought not to envy the great power of the ungodly." (Calvin)

b. **He will go up over all his channels and go over all his banks**: Like a large river in a flood, the Assyrian army will not stay confined to its "banks." Instead, they will "flow over" their attack on Israel and Syria, and "flood" Judah with violence and destruction (**He will pass through Judah**).

c. **He will reach up to the neck**: Assyria would completely conquer the northern nation of Israel. The ten northern tribes would cease to be a nation after the Assyrians conquered them. But the Assyrians would not conquer the southern nation of Judah. They would "flood" them (**fill the breadth of Your land**), and **reach up to the neck**, but not over their heads. Judah would survive the Assyrian invasion but suffer much destruction from the Assyrians.

i. Indeed, 2 Kings 18:13 describes the extent of the Assyrian invasion against Judah: *And in the fourteenth year of King Hezekiah, Sennacherib king of Assyria came up against all the fortified cities of Judah and took them*. Yet, Hezekiah was able to keep the king of Assyria away from Jerusalem, and barely able to survive, by buying his favor with riches from the temple – even stripping gold from the temple doors to appease the pagan king.

ii. "The sacred history assures us that these things were fulfilled...for the Assyrians, whom the Jews called to their assistance, destroyed them. This was the just punishment of their distrust; and we see in it a striking instance of the wicked greediness of men, who cannot be satisfied with the promise and assistance of God." (Calvin)

d. **Your land, O Immanuel**: This refers back to the "Immanuel" prophecy of Isaiah 7:14. The land the Assyrians will invade doesn't really belong to Judah or to King Ahaz. It belongs to the LORD God, to the coming Messiah, to **Immanuel**.

e. **Gird yourselves, but be broken in pieces.... speak the word, but it will not stand, for God is with us**: The victims of this Assyrian invasion (Syria, Israel, and Judah) could prepare for the invasion all they wanted (**gird yourselves**). But all their preparation would not protect them (**but be broken in pieces**). They could **take counsel together, but it will come to nothing**. All their plans and words and ideas **will not stand, for God is with us**. God's will was going to be done, despite all the plans and preparations Syria, Israel, and Judah might make against it.

i. Who is the **us** of **God is with us**? In one sense the **us** is the Assyrian army because they were the instruments of God's judgment against Syria, Israel, and Judah. Nothing could stop the Assyrian army, because even if they did not know it, or even if their own hearts were wrong in the matter, God was using them. But the **us** is also the prophet himself. As a messenger of God, his word would come to pass no matter what the three nations did to prepare against it.

ii. **God is with us** also alludes to the **Immanuel** prophecy, because **Immanuel** means "God is with us."

B. How Judah can prepare for this invasion.

1. (11-15) Prepare by fearing God, not Assyria.

For the LORD spoke thus to me with a strong hand, and instructed me that I should not walk in the way of this people, saying:

"Do not say, 'A conspiracy,'
Concerning all that this people call a conspiracy,
Nor be afraid of their threats, nor be troubled.
The LORD of hosts, Him you shall hallow;

***Let* Him *be* your fear,**
And *let* Him *be* your dread.
He will be as a sanctuary,
But a stone of stumbling and a rock of offense
To both the houses of Israel,
As a trap and a snare to the inhabitants of Jerusalem.
And many among them shall stumble;
They shall fall and be broken, be snared and taken."

a. **Do not say, "A conspiracy"…nor be afraid of their threats**: Isaiah, and all the people of Judah, were tempted to give in to fear and panic, knowing the dangerous place they were in. At the time of this prophecy, the combined armies of Israel and Syria had destroyed much of Judah. Their armies either encircled Jerusalem or were on the way. They planned to depose King Ahaz of Judah and set their own man on the throne (Isaiah 7:6). Now, Isaiah's prophecy declared the armies of Syria and Israel would not succeed in conquering Judah, but the Assyrians (who they trusted to help them) would attack them and do much damage. In the midst of all this, it would be easy to let your heart or mind settle on conspiracies and threats. But God tells them not to.

b. **The Lord of hosts, Him you shall hallow; let Him be your fear**: Instead of fearing conspiracies and threats, fear God. Don't see yourself at the mercy of opposing armies; you are in God's hands. Worry about your place with the Lord instead of your enemies.

c. **He will be as a sanctuary**: The Lord will be our *sacred place* and our *place of protection*. He will keep us safe from our enemies.

d. **But a stone of stumbling and a rock of offense**: For those who trust Him, the Lord **will be as a sanctuary**. But for those who don't, He will be **a stone of stumbling and a rock of offense**. Instead of finding protection from the Lord, they will "trip" over Him, falling to destruction. Indeed, **many among them shall stumble; they shall fall and be broken**.

i. We love to sing the song, "What A Friend We Have in Jesus," and every line of the song is true. But for those who reject the Lord, they could sing, "What an Enemy I Have in God." Instead of being **as a sanctuary**, He will be **a trap and a snare**. Instead of being protected, they **shall fall and be broken**. No wonder Psalm 2:12 says, *Kiss the Son, lest He be angry, and you perish in the way, when His wrath is kindled but a little. Blessed are all those who put their trust in Him.*

ii. We know that Jesus is this **stone of stumbling and a rock of offense** (1 Peter 2:6-8). This is a strong statement of the deity of Jesus, because clearly in Isaiah 8:13-14, the LORD of hosts is the stone, and clearly in 1 Peter 2:6-8, Jesus Christ is the stone.

iii. This same idea is behind the statement of Simeon when he held the child Jesus, as recorded in Luke 2:34: *Behold, this Child is destined for the fall and rising of many in Israel, and for a sign which will be spoken against.*

2. (16-18) Prepare by waiting on the LORD.

Bind up the testimony,
Seal the law among my disciples.
And I will wait on the LORD,
Who hides His face from the house of Jacob;
And I will hope in Him.
Here am I and the children whom the LORD has given me!
We are **for signs and wonders in Israel**
From the LORD of hosts,
Who dwells in Mount Zion.

a. **And I will wait on the LORD**: Waiting on the LORD is not passive inactivity. It means to **wait on the LORD** as a waiter would *wait on* a table. It means to be totally attentive to the LORD, focused on His every move, and responsive to His every desire. At times it means inactivity, but even that is an "active inactivity," where we stand before the LORD, totally focused on Him, waiting for what He wants next.

i. At the time Isaiah spoke, the leaders and the people of Judah were waiting on the armies of Israel and Syria, because they were under attack. As they heard of the danger from the Assyrians, they would be tempted to put their focus on them. But their focus was on these armies, not on the LORD. Isaiah says, "Battle against Syria and Israel by setting your focus on the LORD. Prepare for the coming attack from Assyria by waiting on the LORD instead of your enemies."

b. **Bind up the testimony, seal the law among my disciples**: Waiting on the LORD is connected with His word. We can wait on the LORD by waiting on His word.

c. **Here am I and the children whom the LORD has given me! We are for signs and wonders in Israel**: Isaiah had been called to prophesy, and to use his children in his prophetic messages (Isaiah 7:3, 8:3). So, he declared, **Here am I and the children whom the LORD has given me!** It is as if he is said, "Look at us! We are the message!"

i. The name *Maher-Shalal-Hash-Baz* means, "Speed to the spoil, hurry to the plunder." This spoke of the coming attack on Syria, Israel, and

Judah by Assyria. The name *Shear-Jashub* means, "A Remnant Shall Return." This spoke of the restoration God would eventually bring. The name *Isaiah* means, "Salvation is of the LORD." This spoke of the attitude and hope Judah needed to have.

ii. We are also the children of God, and we are *His* message. Hebrews 2:11-13 quotes this passage to communicate this truth: *For both He who sanctifies and those who are being sanctified are all of one, for which reason He is not ashamed to call them brethren, saying.... "Here am I and the children whom God has given Me."* Just as much as Isaiah's children were living witnesses of the truth of God's word, so are we as God's children.

3. (19-22) Prepare by seeking His light and word, not the darkness of the occult.

And when they say to you, "Seek those who are mediums and wizards, who whisper and mutter," should not a people seek their God? *Should they seek* the dead on behalf of the living? To the law and to the testimony! If they do not speak according to this word, *it is* because *there is* no light in them. They will pass through it hard pressed and hungry; and it shall happen, when they are hungry, that they will be enraged and curse their king and their God, and look upward. Then they will look to the earth, and see trouble and darkness, gloom of anguish; and *they will be* driven into darkness.

a. **Seek those who are mediums and wizards**: In the present danger from Syria and Israel, and in the coming danger from Assyria, Judah will be tempted to seek guidance and comfort from **those who are mediums and wizards**. Isaiah exposes the foolishness of this, when he says, "**Should not a people seek their God? Should they seek the dead on behalf of the living?**"

i. When you are in trouble, shouldn't you seek your God? If you can't rely on your God when you are in trouble, then what good is your God?

ii. What sense does it make to **seek the dead on behalf of the living?** The dead are the dead, the living are the living. The living God speaks through His living Word and His living people to guide us. There is no reason to **seek the dead**.

iii. This passage also exposes the foolishness of praying to the saints. The exact same question should be asked: **Should they seek the dead on behalf of the living?**

b. **To the law and to the testimony**: Forget about **mediums** and **wizards** and the **dead**. Instead of all that deception and foolishness, **To the law and to the testimony!** Go to God's word.

i. **Law** and **testimony** each refer to God's word. We might say that **law** refers to God's holy commands, and **testimony** refers to His dealings with His people as recorded in His Word. But that may be slicing it too thin, because often similar terms for God's word are repeated, not for the sake of distinction, but for the sake of emphasis.

ii. How it needs to be proclaimed *to* our preachers today: **To the law and to the testimony!** Enough with the over-use of anecdotes and jokes. Enough with the emphasis on entertainment and sappy stories. Enough with the catering to itching ears. Enough with the hobbyhorses and pet peeves. **To the law and to the testimony!**

iii. "Let us remember, as ministers of the Gospel, what M'Cheyne beautifully said; 'Depend upon it,' said he, 'it is God's Word not man's comment upon God's Word, that saves souls;' and I have marked, that if ever we have a conversion at any time, in ninety-nine cases out of a hundred, the conversion is rather traceable to the text, or to some Scripture quoted in the sermon, than to any trite or original saying by the preacher. It is God's Word that breaks the fetters and sets the prisoner free, it is God's Word instrumentally that saves souls, and therefore let us bring everything to the touchstone." (Spurgeon)

c. **If they do not speak according to this word, it is because there is no light in them**: If there is a disagreement between God's word and the word of the messenger, it isn't hard to figure out who is wrong. The messenger is wrong. The word judges the messenger; the messenger doesn't judge the word.

d. **They will be driven into darkness**: When they forsake God's word and trust in **mediums** and **wizards** and the **dead**, they are courting darkness, not light.

Isaiah 9 – Unto Us A Child Is Born

A. Hope for Israel.

1. (1-2) A day of light for the northern tribes.

Nevertheless the gloom *will* not *be* upon her who *is* distressed,
As when at first He lightly esteemed
The land of Zebulun and the land of Naphtali,
And afterward more heavily oppressed *her*,
***By* the way of the sea, beyond the Jordan,**
In Galilee of the Gentiles.
The people who walked in darkness
Have seen a great light;
Those who dwelt in the land of the shadow of death,
Upon them a light has shined.

a. **Nevertheless the gloom**: The **gloom** carries over from Isaiah 8, where Isaiah warned Judah about the coming invasion from Assyria. Isaiah 8:22 said, *then they will look to the earth, and see trouble and darkness, gloom of anguish; and they will be driven into darkness.* The invasion of the Assyrians would be terrible for the Jewish people, especially for the northern regions of the Promised Land, **the land of Zebulun and the land of Naphtali**.

b. **The gloom will not be upon her who is distressed**: In this context, the promise of Isaiah 9:1 is all the more precious. The northern regions of the Promised Land – around the Sea of Galilee (**Galilee of the Gentiles**) – were most severely ravaged when the Assyrians invaded from the north. The promise is that this land, once seemingly **lightly esteemed** by the LORD, will one day have a special blessing.

c. **The people who walked in darkness have seen a great light...upon them a light has shined**: The northern tribes were the first to suffer from the Assyrian invasions, so in God's mercy, they will be the first to see the light of the Messiah.

i. Matthew 4:13-16 quotes this passage as clearly fulfilled in the Galilean ministry of Jesus. Since the majority of Jesus' ministry took place in this northern area of Israel, around the Sea of Galilee, God certainly did have a special blessing for this once **lightly esteemed** land.

2. (3-5) Joy in the Messiah's deliverance and victory.

You have multiplied the nation
***And* increased its joy;**
They rejoice before You
According to the joy of harvest,
As *men* rejoice when they divide the spoil.
For You have broken the yoke of his burden
And the staff of his shoulder,
The rod of his oppressor,
As in the day of Midian.
For every warrior's sandal from the noisy battle,
And garments rolled in blood,
Will be used for burning *and* fuel of fire.

a. **You have multiplied the nation and increased its joy**: The ministry of the Messiah would bring joy and gladness to Israel. Jesus said His ministry was like having a wedding party (Matthew 9:14-15). They will rejoice **according to the joy of harvest**, the time when the hard work has paid off and the bounty comes off. They will rejoice **as men rejoice when they divide the spoil**, with a celebration of victory, as in the locker room of a championship team.

b. **As in the day of Midian**: This refers to Gideon's great victory over Midian in Judges 7. As wonderfully complete, joyous, and victorious as Gideon's victory over Midian was, this is the same kind of victory the Messiah will enjoy and give.

i. And the victory is *complete*. The reference to **every warrior's sandal... garments rolled in blood, will be used for burning and fuel of fire** means that the battle is *over*. This is what you did when the battle was finished, and you had won.

c. **You have broken the yoke of his burden**: Each of these promises – the reference to great *joy*, the breaking of **the yoke of his burden** and the **rod of his oppressor**, and the complete victory over all enemies has spiritual application to Jesus' work in our lives. These things are ours in Jesus.

i. When is Jesus sad or worried or afraid? When does Jesus groan under **the yoke of his burden**? When does Jesus feel the sting of the **rod of**

his oppressor? When is Jesus' victory incomplete? The risen, glorified, ascended Jesus experiences none of these things, and He has *raised us up together, and made us sit together in the heavenly places in Christ Jesus* (Ephesians 2:6). As we are in Jesus Christ, we share in His victory: *We are more than conquerors through Him who loved us* (Romans 8:37).

3. (6) The glory of the Messiah who will reign.

For unto us a Child is born,
Unto us a Son is given;
And the government will be upon His shoulder.
And His name will be called
Wonderful, Counselor, Mighty God,
Everlasting Father, Prince of Peace.

a. **For unto us a Child is born, unto us a Son is given**: Most straightforwardly, Isaiah used the Hebrew literary tool of *repetition* to emphasize the point. The **Child is born**, the **Son is given**. At the same time, we recognize the hand of the Holy Spirit in the specific wording.

b. **For unto us a Child is born**: This glorious prophecy of the birth of Messiah reminds Israel that the victory-bringing Messiah would be a *man*. Theoretically, the Messiah could have been an angel. Or, the Messiah could have been God without humanity. But in reality, neither of those options would have qualified the Messiah to be our Savior and High Priest as Jesus is. The **Child** had to be **born**.

i. What amazing mystery! There is nothing weaker, more helpless, more dependent than a *child*. Theoretically, the Messiah could have come as a fully-grown man, created as an adult even as Adam was created. But for Jesus to fully identify with humanity, and to display in His life the servant nature that is in God, He *made Himself of no reputation, taking the form of a bondservant, and coming in the likeness of men* (Philippians 2:7).

c. **Unto us a Son is given**: This **Child** would be a man, but more than a man. He is also the eternal **Son** of God, the Second Person of the Godhead. Theoretically, the Messiah didn't have to be God. He might have been a sinless angel, or merely a perfect man like Adam. But in reality, neither of those options would have qualified the Messiah to be our Savior and High Priest as Jesus is. The **Son** had to be **given**.

i. What glorious truth! We needed a perfect, infinite Being to offer a perfect, infinite atonement for our sins. We needed *Immanuel, God is with us* (Isaiah 7:14).

ii. The **Child** could be **born** because the *humanity* of Jesus had a starting point. There was a time when humanity *was not* added to His deity. The **Son** had to be given, because the Second Person of the Trinity is eternal, and existed forever as the Son, even before adding humanity to His deity.

iii. While Isaiah may have intended the repetition merely for the sake of emphasis, we rejoice in the Holy Spirit's guidance in every word! Jesus, the Messiah, is *fully God and fully man*. There was a time when the eternal Son of God, the Second Person of the Holy Trinity, added humanity to His deity. He never became less God, but He added a human nature to His divine nature, and so became one person with two distinct natures, functioning together in perfect harmony.

iv. That Jesus is both God and man tells us that man really is made in the image of God (Genesis 1:26) and that perfect humanity is more compatible with deity than we imagine. It says that our problem is not our humanity, but our fallenness. To say "I'm only human" is wrong because Jesus was fully human yet perfect. It is more accurate to say, "I'm only fallen." But remember that the humanity that Jesus added to His Divine nature was not the sinful humanity we commonly know, but the perfect humanity of Adam and Eve before the fall.

v. Jesus remains a man eternally (Acts 7:55-56, 1 Timothy 2:5). He did not relinquish His humanity on His ascension; but He is now a man in a resurrection body, as we will one day have.

vi. If Jesus were not fully man, He could not stand in the place of sinful man and be a substitute for the punishment man deserves. If He were not fully God, His sacrifice would be insufficient. If Jesus is not fully God and fully man, we are lost in sin.

d. **And the government will be upon His shoulder**: Ultimately, this will be fulfilled in the Millennium, when Jesus Christ will rule the earth as King of Kings and Lord of Lords (Revelation 20:4-6, Psalm 72, Isaiah 2:1-4, Isaiah 11, Isaiah 65:17-25, Zechariah 14:6-21).

i. This ultimate fulfillment of this promise is still waiting. But we can still see **the government...upon His shoulder** in many ways. Gayle Erwin writes about **the government** God promises, both ultimately and right now:

What might such a government look like? First of all, it would look like its king. Politicians of this day look for what they can get from you. Jesus looks for what He can do for you.

Leaders of this day surround themselves with servants. Jesus surrounds us with His servanthood.

Leaders of this day use their power to build their empire. Jesus uses his power to wash our feet and make us clean and comfortable.

Leaders of this day trade their influence for money. God so loved that he gave…

Generals of this day need regular wars to keep their weapons and skills up to date and insure their own advancement. Jesus brings peace and rest to hearts.

The higher the plane of importance one reaches in this world, the more inaccessible he becomes. Jesus was Emanuel, "God with us."

Leaders of this day are desperate to be seen and heard. Jesus sought anonymity so He could be useful.

Obviously, Jesus is not in charge of the halls of Washington, London, Moscow, Baghdad, Paris or Bonn. So, how can we ever believe the "government will be upon His shoulders"?

Actually, His government shows its workings in wonderful ways. Whenever I see someone who miraculously leaves a life of drugs or alcohol and is restored to his family and work, I can see that he is now governed by God.

Whenever I see loving Christians gently caring for orphans and those rejected by family, I know I am watching people governed by God.

Whenever I see people eagerly learning the Bible and joyously praising, I know who the governor is.

Whenever I see people give up lucrative careers simply to go and share the Good News of Jesus, I know they are governed by God.

When I see pastors carefully teach and lead the flock God has given them, I know they are getting signals from the great King.

When I see people leave family to live and teach in distant lands because they love the people who have not heard, I know they are governed by God.

So, indeed, the government is alive and working. Often silently, mostly unseen. We can be and are, by choice, governed by God. Hope and joy and peace and rest cover its subjects. Justice, mercy and grace, amazingly coexist. I like this Kingdom. The borders are open. Come on in.

e. **His name will be called**: The idea isn't that these will be the literal names of the Messiah. Instead, these are aspects of His character, they describe who He is and what He has come to do.

i. "In Semitic thought, a name does not just identify or distinguish a person, it expresses the very nature of his being." (Longenecker)

ii. Calvin, on the greatness of these titles: "This ought to be the more carefully considered, because the greater part of men are satisfied with his mere name, and do not observe his power and energy, though that ought to be chiefly regarded."

f. The Messiah is **Wonderful**: The glory of who He is and what He has done for us should fill us with *wonder*. You can never really look at Jesus, really know Him, and be bored. He is **Wonderful** and will fill your heart and mind with *amazement*.

i. As well, this is a reference to the deity of Jesus. "The word 'wonderful' has overtones of deity" (Grogan). This is also seen in Judges 13:18.

g. The Messiah is our **Counselor**: Jesus is the One fit to guide our lives and should be the Christian's immediate resource as a counselor. *Jesus can help you with your problems.* He may use the presence and the words of another Christian to do it, but Jesus is our **Counselor**.

i. How we need Jesus as our **Counselor**! "It was by a Counsellor that this world was ruined. Did not Satan mask himself in the serpent, and counsel the woman with exceeding craftiness, that she should take unto herself of the fruit of the tree of knowledge of good and evil, in the hope that thereby she should be as God? Was it not that evil counsel which provoked our mother to rebel against her Maker, and did it not as the effect of sin, bring death into this world with all its train of woe? Ah! beloved, it was meet that the world should have a Counsellor to restore it, if it had a Counsellor to destroy it." (Spurgeon)

ii. Jesus is our **Counselor** in the sense that as God the Son, He takes counsel with the Father and the Holy Spirit for our good. The High Council of the Godhead brought forth our salvation. "Hence you read in the book of Zechariah, if you turn to the sixth chapter and the thirteenth verse, this passage – 'The council of peace shall be between them both.' The Son of God with his Father and the Spirit, ordained the council of peace. Thus was it arranged. The Son must suffer, he must be the substitute, must bear his people's sins and be punished in their stead; the Father must accept the Son's substitution and allow his people to go free, because Christ had paid their debts. The Spirit of the living God must then cleanse the people whom the blood had pardoned, and so they must be accepted before the presence of God, even the Father. That was the result of the great council." (Spurgeon)

iii. The Great Counselor guides our lives. "Remember, there is nothing that happens in your daily life, but what was first of all devised in eternity, and counselled by Jesus Christ for your good and in your behalf, that all things might work together for your lasting benefit and profit…. Oh, how strange providence seems to you and to me! Does it not look like a zig-zag line, this way and that way, backward and forward, like the journeyings of the children of Israel in the wilderness? Ah! my brethren, but to God it is a straight line. Directly, God always goes to his object. And yet to us, he often seems to go round about…. Let us learn to leave providence in the hand of the Counsellor." (Spurgeon)

iv. Jesus' counsel is *necessary* counsel. Jesus' counsel is *faithful* counsel, without any self-interest. Jesus' counsel is *hearty* counsel. It isn't detached and unemotional. Jesus' counsel is *sweet* counsel. "Christian, do you know what sweet counsel is? You have gone to your Master in the day of trouble, and in the secret of your chamber you have poured out your heart before him. You have laid your case before him, with all its difficulties, as Hezekiah did Rabshakeh's letter, and you have felt, that though Christ was not there in flesh and blood, yet he was there in spirit, and he counselled you. You felt that his was counsel that came from the very heart. But he was something better than that. There was such a sweetness coming with his counsel, such a radiance of love, such a fullness of fellowship, that you said, 'Oh that I were in trouble every day, if I might have such sweet counsel as this!' Christ is the Counsellor whom I desire to consult every hour, and I would that I could sit in his secret chamber all day and all night long, because to counsel with him is to have sweet counsel, hearty counsel, and wise counsel, all at the same time." (Spurgeon)

v. "Why, you may have a friend that talks very sweetly with you, and you will say, 'Well, he is a kind, good soul, but I really cannot trust his judgment.' You have another friend, who has a good deal of judgment, and yet you say of him, 'Certainly, he is a man of prudence above a great many, but I cannot find out his sympathy; I never get at his heart, if he were ever so rough and untutored, I would sooner have his heart without his prudence, than his prudence without his heart,' But we go to Christ, and we get wisdom; we get love, we get sympathy, we get everything that can possibly be wanted in a Counsellor." (Spurgeon)

h. The Messiah is **Mighty God**: He is the God of all creation and glory, the LORD who reigns in heaven, the One worthy of our worship and praise.

i. It is difficult to think of a more straightforward declaration of the deity of the Messiah. Yet some groups (such as Jehovah's Witnesses) try to make a distinction between **Mighty God** and *Almighty God.* Scripturally, there is no distinction, because both titles are used of Jesus *and* Yahweh specifically (*Almighty* is applied to Jesus in Revelation 1:8).

ii. In Isaiah 10:21, the prophet uses the exact same phrase to refer to Yahweh: *The remnant will return, the remnant of Jacob, to the Mighty God.* Therefore, this is a clear statement of absolute deity

iii. "And indeed, if Christ had not been *God*, it would have been unlawful to glory in him; for it is written, *Cursed be he that trusteth in man*. (Jeremiah 17:5)" (Calvin)

iv. "We extend the right hand of fellowship to all those who love the Lord Jesus Christ in sincerity and truth; but we cannot exchange our Christian greetings with those who deny him to be 'very God of very God.' And the reason is sometimes asked; for say our opponents, 'We are ready to give the right hand of fellowship to you, why don't you do so to us?' Our reply shall be given thus briefly: 'You have no right to complain of us, seeing that in this matter we stand on the defensive. When you declare yourselves to believe that Christ is not the Son of God, you may not be conscious of it, but you have charged us with one of the blackest sins in the entire catalogue of crime.' The Unitarians must, to be existent, charge the whole of us, who worship Christ, with being idolaters. Now idolatry is a sin of the most heinous character; it is not an offense against men it is true, but it is an intolerable offense against the majesty of God." (Spurgeon)

v. "If Christ were not the Son of God, his death, so far from being a satisfaction for sin, was a death most richly and righteously deserved. The Sanhedrin before which He was tried was the recognised and authorised legislature of the country. He was brought before that Sanhedrin, charged with blasphemy, and it was upon that charge that they condemned him to die, because he made himself the Son of God." (Spurgeon)

i. The Messiah is the **Everlasting Father**: The idea in these Hebrew words is that Jesus is the source or author of all eternity, that He is the Creator Himself. It *does not* mean that Jesus Himself is the Person of the *Father* in the Trinity.

j. The Messiah is the **Prince of Peace**: He is the One who makes peace, especially between God and man.

i. "Whenever, in short, it appears to us that everything is in a ruinous condition, let us recall to our remembrance that Christ is called *Wonderful*, because he has inconceivable methods of assisting us, and because his power is far beyond what we are able to conceive. When we need counsel, let us remember that he is the *Counselor*. When we need strength, let us remember that he is *Mighty* and *Strong*. When new terrors spring up suddenly every instant, and when many deaths threaten us from various quarters, let us rely on that *eternity* of which he is with good reason called the Father, and by the same comfort let us learn to soothe all temporal distresses. When we are inwardly tossed by various tempests, and when Satan attempts to disturb our consciences, let us remember that Christ is *The Prince of Peace*, and that it is easy for him quickly to allay all our uneasy feelings. Thus will these titles confirm us more and more in the faith of Christ, and fortify us against Satan and against hell itself." (Calvin)

4. (7) The glory of the Messiah's reign.

Of the increase of *His* government and peace
***There will be* no end,**
Upon the throne of David and over His kingdom,
To order it and establish it with judgment and justice
From that time forward, even forever.
The zeal of the LORD of hosts will perform this.

a. **Of the increase of His government and peace there will be no end... even forever**: The reign of the Messiah will not last merely 1,000 years, though the millennium is a special aspect of His reign. **There will be no end** to the reign of the Messiah, and He will rule for all eternity.

i. Handel had it right in the Hallelujah chorus of *Messiah*: "And He shall reign forever and ever."

b. **Upon the throne of David**: Jesus will rule on David's throne and over **his kingdom** (that is, David's kingdom – Israel). This is a fulfillment of God's great covenant with David in 2 Samuel 7.

c. **The zeal of the LORD of hosts will perform this**: All this may sound too good to be true, but it will be done. God – the LORD of all heavenly armies – has promised to accomplish this word, and part of it has been accomplished already.

i. Jesus can be *Wonderful, Counselor, Mighty God, Everlasting Father, Prince of Peace* for everyone now. One day, these offices will be imposed upon the world. For now, they are real for those who receive Jesus and submit to Him.

B. Coming judgment on the Northern Kingdom of Israel.

This section (Isaiah 9:8-10:4) is in four parts, each part concluding with "For all this His anger is not turned away, but His hand (of judgment) is stretched out still." Some have called this section, "The Speech of the Outstretched Hand."

1. (8-12) Because of their unholy pride, Israel will be defeated by her enemies.

The LORD sent a word against Jacob,
And it has fallen on Israel.
All the people will know—
Ephraim and the inhabitant of Samaria—
Who say in pride and arrogance of heart:
"The bricks have fallen down,
But we will rebuild with hewn stones;
The sycamores are cut down,
But we will replace *them* with cedars."
Therefore the LORD shall set up
The adversaries of Rezin against him,
And spur his enemies on,
The Syrians before and the Philistines behind;
And they shall devour Israel with an open mouth.
For all this His anger is not turned away,
But His hand *is* stretched out still.

a. **The LORD sent a word against Jacob, and it has fallen on Israel**: The idea is that the LORD brought a word against all His people (**against Jacob**) and the word has scored a "direct hit" against the Northern Kingdom of **Israel**.

b. **Ephraim and the inhabitant of Samaria**: The tribe of **Ephraim** was the largest and most influential tribe in the Northern Kingdom of Israel. So, often the LORD refers to the Kingdom of Israel by the name **Ephraim**. **Samaria** was the capital of the Northern Kingdom of Israel. There isn't any doubt whom this prophecy is directed to.

c. **Who say in pride and arrogance of heart: "The bricks have fallen down, but we will rebuild with hewn stones; the sycamores are cut down, but we will replace them with cedars"**: In their pride, the leaders and the people of the Northern Kingdom of Israel said, "Who cares if God judges us? Whatever is torn down, **we will rebuild with** something better. We have nothing to fear from what God can bring against us."

i. "Instead of humbling themselves before the face of God on account of the many calamities that had already descended on them, they still entertained a lighthearted optimism regarding the future. This optimism manifested itself in the slogans that were current in that day and apparently on everybody's lips." (Bultema)

ii. "What a brief but deeply psychological picture this is of an unfaithful generation that keeps dreaming of better times to come and lightheartedly ignores the severe judgments of God." (Bultema)

d. **Therefore the LORD shall set up the adversaries**: Because they believed they would be able to weather the storm of attack and then rebuild, God would send successive waves of enemies against Israel (**The Syrians before and the Philistines behind**). The destruction of Israel would be complete, and their proud promise to rebuild would be unfulfilled.

e. **For all this, His anger is not turned away, but His hand is stretched out still**: For the first time, the chorus is said. The judgment against Israel's pride was not enough. There was still sin to judge, and God wasn't ready to stop His work of judgment.

i. Calvin could say of his day, more than 300 years ago: "How many are the distresses with which Europe has been afflicted for thirty or forty years? How many are the chastisements by which she has been called to repentance? And yet it does not appear that those numerous chastisements have done any good. On the contrary, luxury increases every day, lawless passions are inflamed, and men go on in crimes and profligacy more shamelessly than ever. In short, those very calamities appear to have been so many excitements to luxury and splendour. What then should we expect but to be bruised with heavier blows?"

2. (13-17) Because they refuse to repent, there will be an overthrow of leadership.

For the people do not turn to Him who strikes them,
Nor do they seek the LORD of hosts.
Therefore the LORD will cut off head and tail from Israel,
Palm branch and bulrush in one day.
The elder and honorable, he *is* the head;
The prophet who teaches lies, he *is* the tail.
For the leaders of this people cause *them* to err,
And *those who are* led by them are destroyed.
Therefore the LORD will have no joy in their young men,
Nor have mercy on their fatherless and widows;
For everyone *is* a hypocrite and an evildoer,
And every mouth speaks folly.

For all this His anger is not turned away,
But His hand *is* stretched out still.

a. **For the people do not turn to Him who strikes them**: Each episode of judgment was followed by Israel's refusal to **turn to** the LORD. They were like dumb animals that resist even more when they are beaten.

b. **Therefore the LORD will cut off head and tail from Israel**: Those who lead in Israel (**the elder and honorable...the prophet who teaches lies... the leaders of this people**) will be **cut off**, which often means to be killed.

i. "The expression *branch and rush* indicates the same thing as *head and tail.* A branch grows upward and hence refers to the high and important people of the population; the rush grows in muddy marshes and refers to the lowest element of the population, the scum." (Bultema)

c. **For all this, His anger is not turned away, but His hand is stretched out still**: This chorus is repeated. The judgment against Israel's impenitence was not enough. There was still sin to judge, and God wasn't ready to stop His work of judgment.

3. (18-21) Because of prevailing wickedness they will attack their own brothers.

For wickedness burns as the fire;
It shall devour the briers and thorns,
And kindle in the thickets of the forest;
They shall mount up *like* rising smoke.
Through the wrath of the LORD of hosts
The land is burned up,
And the people shall be as fuel for the fire;
No man shall spare his brother.
And he shall snatch on the right hand
And be hungry;
He shall devour on the left hand
And not be satisfied;
Every man shall eat the flesh of his own arm.
Manasseh *shall devour* Ephraim, and Ephraim Manasseh;
Together they *shall be* against Judah.
For all this His anger is not turned away,
But His hand *is* stretched out still.

a. **For wickedness burns as the fire**: The prophet sees the wickedness of Israel as a raging wildfire: unstoppable, swift, uncontrolled, and devouring everything it touches.

b. **And the people shall be as fuel for the fire**: This wildfire of God's judgment is fueled by **the people**, in two senses. First, their wickedness *supplies fuel* to the fire of God's judgment. If the wickedness was taken away, the fire would have no more fuel. Second, they are *burnt up and destroyed* by the fire.

c. **No man shall spare his brother**: In gruesome detail, the prophet speaks of the carnage that one Israelite will inflict on another. The wildfire of God's judgment burns, but God merely lets the evil, hateful passions of men burn wild among themselves. God did not need to start the fire or fan the flames; He simply took away the "fire retardant" that had held the evil, hate-filled passions of men in check.

d. **For all this, His anger is not turned away, but His hand is stretched out still**: A third time the chorus is presented. The judgment against Israel's wickedness was not enough. There was still sin to judge, and God wasn't ready to stop His work of judgment.

4. (10:1-4) Because of social injustice, they will be exiled and slain.

"Woe to those who decree unrighteous decrees,
Who write misfortune,
***Which* they have prescribed**
To rob the needy of justice,
And to take what is right from the poor of My people,
That widows may be their prey,
And *that* they may rob the fatherless.
What will you do in the day of punishment,
And in the desolation *which* will come from afar?
To whom will you flee for help?
And where will you leave your glory?
Without Me they shall bow down among the prisoners,
And they shall fall among the slain."
For all this His anger is not turned away,
But His hand *is* stretched out still.

a. **Woe to those who decree unrighteous decrees…rob the needy of justice…take what is right from the poor of My people, that widows may be their prey**: The leaders and people of Israel were simply *unfair* to others and preyed on the weak.

b. **What will you do in the day of punishment…. To whom will you flee for help?** The idea is, "When you have forsaken others in their time of need, who will you go to for help when you are in need?"

c. **Without Me they shall bow down among the prisoners, and they shall fall among the slain**: All God needs to do to bring extreme judgment on Israel is to *withdraw His protection*. The LORD declared that "**Without Me** you have no hope before your enemies."

i. "As the people had hitherto lived *without God* in worship and obedience; so they should now be *without* his help, and should perish in their transgressions." (Clarke)

d. **Without Me they shall bow down**: When the Assyrians conquered other nations, it wasn't enough for them to just win a military victory. They had a perverse pleasure in humiliating and subjugating their conquered foes. They would do everything they could to bring them low. Here, God said, "You have rejected Me, so **without Me** you **shall bow down** in humiliation and degradation before your enemies."

i. One of the Hebrew words commonly translated *worship* in the Old Testament is *shachah*. It means to bow down, to reverently bow or stoop, to pay homage. But this is another word for **bow down**, the Hebrew word *kara*. It isn't a good word; it means to sink, to drop, to bring low, or to subdue. We might say that we will either *bow down* to the LORD in worship, or it will be said of us, **without Me they shall bow down** in suffering and humiliation. Which will it be?

e. **For all this, His anger is not turned away, but His hand is stretched out still**: Once again, this chorus is heard. The judgment against Israel's injustice was not enough. There was still sin to judge, and God wasn't ready to stop His work of judgment.

i. The repetition of the phrase reminds us that God's judgment is *persistent*. It moves from phase to phase until it finds repentance. This means that it makes sense for us to repent *now*, because God's judgment is persistent for all eternity. "If even physical death does not satisfy the fierce anger of this holy God, what dread and punishment lies beyond the grave?" (Grogan)

ii. It makes perfect sense for this message of coming judgment to follow the announcement of the Messiah. His coming was announced, but the people were not ready for Him, and the predicted judgment would come before they were ready.

Isaiah 10 – Assyria Judged

Since Isaiah 10:1-4 connects with Isaiah 9, it is examined in the previous chapter.

A. God's judgment on arrogant Assyria.

1. (5-7) Assyria, the unintentional instrument in the hand of the Lord.

"Woe to Assyria, the rod of My anger
And the staff in whose hand is My indignation.
I will send him against an ungodly nation,
And against the people of My wrath
I will give him charge,
To seize the spoil, to take the prey,
And to tread them down like the mire of the streets.
Yet he does not mean so,
Nor does his heart think so;
But *it is* in his heart to destroy,
And cut off not a few nations.

a. **Woe to Assyria, the rod of My anger**: In the previous section (Isaiah 7:1 through 10:4), the Lord revealed that He would use Assyria as an instrument of judgment against Syria, Israel, and Judah. But what about Assyria? Weren't they even more wicked than Syria, Israel, or Judah? Yes, the Assyrians were wicked; yet the Lord could use them as **the rod of My anger**. At the same time, none of this excused Assyria, so the Lord says, "**woe to Assyria**."

i. "A similar shift in the object of divine judgment occurred in the case of the Babylonians. God raised up the Babylonian armies between 605 and 686 B.C. to punish Judah (Habakkuk 1:6-11), and then He announced judgment on Babylon (Habakkuk 2:6-17; Isaiah 14:5)." (Wolf)

b. **The rod of My anger…the staff in whose hand is My indignation**: The **rod** and the **staff** were sticks used by shepherds to guide and correct their sheep. God is saying that Assyria was like a stick in His hand, used to correct Syria, Israel, and Judah.

c. **I will send him against an ungodly nation, and against the people of My wrath**: In this sense, Assyria was on a mission from God. They were doing the LORD's will, running His errands when they came against Syria, Israel, and Judah. God gave them permission (**I will give them charge**) to **seize the spoil, to take the prey, and to tread them down like the mire of the streets.**

d. **Yet he does not mean so, nor does his heart think so**: Since Assyria was an instrument in God's hand, since they were doing the will of the LORD, does this excuse their attack on Syria, Israel, and Judah? *Not at all!* Though they were instruments in God's hand, they did **not mean so, nor does his heart think so**. They *didn't care at all* about God's will or glory in the matter. Instead, **it is in his heart to destroy, and cut off not a few nations**. Assyria didn't care about the will or glory of God; they wanted to **destroy** and **cut off** many nations.

i. Psalm 76:10 says *Surely the wrath of man shall praise You*. God can use the wickedness and carnality of man to further His will, *without ever approving of the wickedness or carnality*. In fact, God is totally justified in *judging* the very wickedness and carnality that He used.

ii. The pattern is repeated over and over through the Scriptures. Joseph's brothers sinned against Joseph, but God used it for His purpose, and disciplined Joseph's brothers. Saul sinned against David, but God used it for His purpose, and judged Saul. Judas sinned against Jesus, but God used it for His purpose, and judged Judas.

iii. This should help with questions that trouble many people. The first question is "How can God bring any good through an evil thing that was done to me?" We can't often know in advance exactly *how* God will bring the good, but we can trust that He will as we continue to yield to Him and seek Him. The second question is "Doesn't God care about what they did to me?" He does care, and God will bring His correction or judgment according to His perfect will and timing.

2. (8-14) The arrogance of Assyria.

"For he says,
'*Are* not my princes altogether kings?
***Is* not Calno like Carchemish?**
***Is* not Hamath like Arpad?**
***Is* not Samaria like Damascus?**
As my hand has found the kingdoms of the idols,

Whose carved images excelled those of Jerusalem and Samaria,
As I have done to Samaria and her idols,
Shall I not do also to Jerusalem and her idols?'"

Therefore it shall come to pass, when the LORD has performed all His work on Mount Zion and on Jerusalem, *that He will say,* "I will punish the fruit of the arrogant heart of the king of Assyria, and the glory of his haughty looks."

For he says:
"By the strength of my hand I have done *it,*
And by my wisdom, for I am prudent;
Also I have removed the boundaries of the people,
And have robbed their treasuries;
So I have put down the inhabitants like a valiant *man.*
My hand has found like a nest the riches of the people,
And as one gathers eggs *that are* left,
I have gathered all the earth;
And there was no one who moved *his* wing,
Nor opened *his* mouth with even a peep."

a. **Are not my princes altogether kings**: Assyria had such an inflated view of themselves that they regarded their **princes** to be on the level of the **kings** of other nations.

b. **As I have done to Samaria and her idols, shall I not do also to Jerusalem and her idols?** Here, the LORD described the proud, arrogant heart of the Assyrians. **Samaria** was the capital of the northern kingdom of Israel, which was given over to gross idolatry. **Jerusalem** was the capital of the southern kingdom of Judah, which still maintained *some* worship of the Lord GOD. In their pride, the Assyrians thought the Lord GOD nothing more than one of the idols that they had conquered in Samaria or in many other cities. The Assyrians were in for a rude wake-up call.

i. "The cities mentioned in verses 9 and 10 came under Assyrian control between 740 and 721 B.C., and none of the gods of these areas had provided the slightest help. It was assumed that the 'idols' (v.10) of Jerusalem were equally impotent." (Wolf)

c. **I will punish the fruit of the arrogant heart of the king of Assyria, and the glory of his haughty looks**: The pride of Assyria and her king was found in his **arrogant heart** and exposed by **his haughty looks**. How much pride can be revealed by a *haughty look*.

i. The Bible describes God's opinion of **haughty looks**: *A haughty look, a proud heart, and the plowing of the wicked are sin.* (Proverbs 21:4)

The one who has a haughty look and a proud heart, him I will not endure (Psalm 101:5). *For You will save the humble people, but will bring down haughty looks* (Psalm 18:27).

d. **By the strength of my hand I have done it**: Again, the LORD revealed the heart of Assyria. They gloried in their own **strength** and wisdom (**by my wisdom, for I am prudent**). They exaggerated their power (**I have gathered all the earth**).

i. Julius Caesar had this heart of pride when he said of his military conquests: *Veni, vidi, vici* ("I came, I saw, I conquered"). Charles V had a better heart when he said of his military conquests, *Veni, vidi, sed Christus vicit* ("I came, I saw, but Christ conquered").

3. (15-19) God assesses the arrogance of Assyria.

Shall the ax boast itself against him who chops with it?
***Or* shall the saw exalt itself against him who saws with it?**
As if a rod could wield *itself* against those who lift it up,
***Or* as if a staff could lift up, *as if it were* not wood!**
Therefore the Lord, the Lord of hosts,
Will send leanness among his fat ones;
And under his glory
He will kindle a burning
Like the burning of a fire.
So the Light of Israel will be for a fire,
And his Holy One for a flame;
It will burn and devour
His thorns and his briers in one day.
And it will consume the glory of his forest and of his fruitful field,
Both soul and body;
And they will be as when a sick man wastes away.
Then the rest of the trees of his forest
Will be so few in number
That a child may write them.

a. **Shall the ax boast itself against him who chops with it?** The LORD uses the pictures of an **ax**, a **saw**, a **rod**, and a **staff** to make the point that the *instrument* should never take credit for what the *worker* does with the instrument. The scalpel can't take credit for what the surgeon does; the strength and the skill are in the user, not in the instrument.

i. If it is easy for an unknowing instrument of God to become proud, it is also easy for a willing instrument of God to become proud. Jesus said we should have a different attitude: *So likewise you, when you have done all those things which you are commanded, say, "We are unprofitable servants. We have done what was our duty to do."* (Luke 17:10) As wonderful as it is to be an instrument in the hand of God, the instrument deserves no special glory.

b. **Therefore the Lord...will send leanness among his fat ones**: Assyria sat "fat and sassy" at the time, but God would **send leanness** to them. His judgment will be **like the burning of a fire** among them, **and it will consume the glory of his forest and of his fruitful field**. The Lord will leave Assyria just a shadow of its former self.

i. Bultema on **both soul and body**: "Calvin warned against inferring from this that the soul is not immortal. What is meant, according to this keen expositor, is that the soul of this tyrant will have to pay for his wicked deeds on earth after the destruction of His body."

B. Despite the coming attack of the Assyrians, God will preserve a remnant of Israel.

1. (20-27) God tells His people: **Do not be afraid of the Assyrian.**

And it shall come to pass in that day
***That* the remnant of Israel,**
And such as have escaped of the house of Jacob,
Will never again depend on him who defeated them,
But will depend on the LORD, the Holy One of Israel, in truth.
The remnant will return, the remnant of Jacob,
To the Mighty God.
For though your people, O Israel, be as the sand of the sea,
A remnant of them will return;
The destruction decreed shall overflow with righteousness.
For the Lord GOD of hosts
Will make a determined end
In the midst of all the land.

Therefore thus says the Lord GOD of hosts: "O My people, who dwell in Zion, do not be afraid of the Assyrian. He shall strike you with a rod and lift up his staff against you, in the manner of Egypt. For yet a very little while and the indignation will cease, as will My anger in their destruction." And the LORD of hosts will stir up a scourge for him like the slaughter of Midian at the rock of Oreb; *as* His rod was on the sea, so will He lift it up in the manner of Egypt.

It shall come to pass in that day
***That* his burden will be taken away from your shoulder,**
And his yoke from your neck,
And the yoke will be destroyed because of the anointing oil.

a. **It shall come to pass in that day**: The LORD told Judah to not trust in Assyria as their deliverer when the threat from Syria and Israel came (Isaiah 7). The LORD promised that He would deliver them from Syria and Israel and that they did not have to trust in Assyria. But Ahaz, king of Judah, did not take God's counsel and trusted in Assyria. The LORD would then use Assyria to defeat Syria and Israel as He had promised, but He would also use Assyria to judge Judah. Now, the LORD wants to prepare Judah for the attack from Assyria, reminding them that He is still in charge and they can still trust Him.

i. This shows the remarkable grace and longsuffering of God. We would not criticize the LORD if He said, "You want to trust in the Assyrians and not in Me? Fine. You are now on your own. Good luck." But even in the midst of the judgment they *deserved*, brought through the Assyrians, God wants to comfort His people and bring them hope.

b. **The remnant of Israel...will never again depend on him who defeated them, but will depend on the LORD**. The LORD promises His people, "You are going through this now because you will not trust Me. But I am going to change you so that you trust Me again, and you will once again **depend on the LORD**."

c. **A remnant of them will return**: The suffering of God's people at the hands of the Assyrians and others would make them feel as if they would certainly be destroyed. God assures them that this is not the case. He will always preserve His **remnant**.

d. **The destruction decreed shall overflow with righteousness**: When God allows destruction – whether in outright judgment or loving correction – it is always *righteous*, and never unfair. In fact, His judgment *overflows with righteousness.*

e. **For the Lord GOD of hosts will make a determined end**: An end of what? An end of Judah's trust in nations like Assyria. They will **never again depend on him who defeated him**.

f. **Therefore...do not be afraid of the Assyrian**: The LORD is telling His people, "Judgment and correction are coming, and it will hurt. But I have a plan, so don't be afraid." This is a hard word to believe because judgment and correction, by their very nature, *hurt!* Yet we can *decide* to **not be afraid** and trust in the LORD, even when it hurts.

i. **He shall strike you with a rod**, yet do not be afraid. He will **lift up his staff against you**, but do not be afraid. Why shouldn't they fear? Because the Assyrians are not in charge, the LORD is. In **a very little while...the indignation will cease, as will My anger**. We can always be comforted by the fact that God will never leave His people to the mercy of their enemies. Even when He uses the Assyrians to bring judgment and correction, He is still in charge.

g. **And the LORD of hosts will stir up a scourge for him like the slaughter of Midian**: Judah should trust the LORD because He will indeed take care of the Assyrians. He will take care of them like He took care of **Midian at the rock of Oreb**. The LORD will strike Assyria **as His rod was upon the sea.**

i. Judges 7:25 describes Gideon's victory over the Midianites **at the rock of Oreb**. As miraculous and complete as Gideon's victory was, that is how miraculous and complete God's judgment on Assyria would be. As it happened, this was exactly the case. 2 Kings 19:35 describes how God simply sent the angel of the LORD and killed 185,000 Assyrians in one night. When the people woke up, there were 185,000 dead Assyrian soldiers.

ii. Exodus 14:16 describes how the LORD used the rod of Moses to divide the Red Sea. In the same way, He would do something totally miraculous against Assyria.

iii. The LORD even took care of the king of the Assyrians according to His justice. 2 Kings 19:36-37 describes that when the king of the Assyrians returned home after attacking Judah, he was murdered by his own sons as he worshipped in the temple of Nisroch his god.

h. **It shall come to pass in that day that his burden will be taken from your shoulder, and his yoke from your neck**: Assyria would indeed trouble and oppress Judah, but not forever. Instead, **the yoke will be destroyed because of the anointing oil**. Because of the presence and power of the Holy Spirit among Judah (represented by **the anointing oil**), the yoke of bondage would be **destroyed.**

i. Bultema thinks that **because of the anointing oil** should really be seen as *because of the Anointed One*, the Messiah, Jesus Christ. He is the source of our victory and freedom from the yoke of bondage.

2. (28-32) A prophetic description of the arrival of the army of the Assyrians.

He has come to Aiath,
He has passed Migron;
At Michmash he has attended to his equipment.
They have gone along the ridge,
They have taken up lodging at Geba.
Ramah is afraid,
Gibeah of Saul has fled.

Lift up your voice,
O daughter of Gallim!
Cause it to be heard as far as Laish—
O poor Anathoth!
Madmenah has fled,
The inhabitants of Gebim seek refuge.
As yet he will remain at Nob that day;
He will shake his fist at the mount of the daughter of Zion,
The hill of Jerusalem.

a. **He has come to Aiath**: Because of the word of comfort and encouragement in the previous section, Judah might think that God wouldn't send judgment among them at all. This section, with the specific mention of many cities of Judah, is meant to show that God will indeed allow the invasion of the Assyrians, even though He will restore after the attack.

b. **Aiath…Migron…Michmash…. Geba…. Nob**: The listing of cities flows from the north to the south, describing the course of the Assyrian invasion. **Nob** is right on the outskirts of Jerusalem. This is as far as the army of the Assyrians came against Judah. They were stopped here when the Lord killed 185,000 Assyrian soldiers in one night.

i. "With a deft poetic touch, Isaiah told how the enemy moved through twelve different locations, coming ever closer to the capital." (Wolf)

3. (33-34) The Lord humbles the proud among the people of Judah.

Behold, the Lord,
The Lord of hosts,
Will lop off the bough with terror;
Those of high stature *will be* hewn down,
And the haughty will be humbled.
He will cut down the thickets of the forest with iron,
And Lebanon will fall by the Mighty One.

a. **Those of high stature will be hewn down**: The Lord promises that His judgment will extend even against **those of high stature**. A mighty forest seems invincible and seems as if it will stand forever, but the Lord can cut it down. Even so, the Lord will cut down the proud and **those of high stature** among Judah. All that will be left in a once-mighty forest will be stumps.

b. **And Lebanon will fall by the Mighty One**: The forests of **Lebanon** were known for their large, mighty cedar trees. God will judge the proud among Judah – and all the nations for that matter – and leave a once mighty forest of **those of high stature** as if they were just stumps. The bigger they are, the harder they fall down.

Isaiah 11 – The Branch and Root of Jesse

A. The character of the King.

1. (1) A stem sprouts forth from the stump of Jesse.

There shall come forth a Rod from the stem of Jesse,
And a Branch shall grow out of his roots.

a. **There shall come forth a Rod from the stem of Jesse**: Isaiah 10:33-34 left with the idea of the LORD chopping down the proud as if they were mighty trees. Now, the picture is of the LORD looking over these stumps, and causing **a Branch** to grow out of one of them, the root of the family of **Jesse**, King David's father.

i. Indeed, Jesus did come from the *stump* of Jesse. The royal authority of the house of David was dormant for 600 years when Jesus came as King and Messiah. When Jesus came forth, it was like a new green **Branch** coming from an apparently dead stump.

ii. The LORD wanted Judah to know that even though the Assyrians and others would come and bring judgment, God would still use them and bring forth life from them. Even if they looked like a long-dead stump, God could bring forth life. Glorious restoration under the Messiah was promised.

iii. "We see a bare, withered tree stump, robbed of its trunk and top, and it looks as though the stump will never bear any fruit any more. But, a small shoot sprouts from the root of this dry stump which is the Davidic dynasty. Because of its unsightliness and misery, it is not named after David but after his father. When Christ was born, there was nothing royal about that dynasty. But a new shoot sprang from this old stem." (Bultema)

b. **A Rod from the stem of Jesse**: In using this title, the LORD emphasized the humble nature of the Messiah. **Jesse** was the much less famous father of King David. It is far humbler to say, "from Jesse" than to say, "from King David."

2. (2) The spiritual empowerment of the Messiah.

The Spirit of the Lord shall rest upon Him,
The Spirit of wisdom and understanding,
The Spirit of counsel and might,
The Spirit of knowledge and of the fear of the Lord.

a. **The Spirit of the Lord shall rest upon Him**: The *Branch* that comes from the apparently dead stump isn't just barely alive. It is full of life, and full of the **Spirit of the Lord**. We see here that the Messiah has seven – the number of fullness and completion – aspects of the **Spirit of the Lord**.

i. **The Spirit of the Lord** is upon the Messiah. Jesus did not have a false spirit or a deceiving spirit, or even the spirit of a man. The **Spirit of the Lord** God of Israel rests upon the Messiah. On one occasion Jesus rebuked the disciples saying, *You do not know what manner of spirit you are of* (Luke 9:55). Jesus was of the **Spirit of the Lord**, and He knew it.

ii. The **Spirit of wisdom** is upon the Messiah. Jesus is perfectly wise in all things. He showed this during his earthly ministry, and He shows it now in His continuing ministry in heaven for His people. 1 Corinthians 1:30 says that Jesus *became for us wisdom from God*. It isn't just that Jesus *has* wisdom; He *is* wisdom.

iii. The **Spirit of...understanding** is upon the Messiah. Jesus understands all things, and He understands us perfectly. He is perfectly suited to be our sympathetic High Priest in heaven (Hebrews 4:15-16). **Understanding** in Hebrew has the idea of a sharp sense of smell. John Trapp said this word describes Jesus' "Sharpness of judgment in smelling out a hypocrite...His sharp nose easily discerneth and is offended with the stinking breath of the hypocrite's rotten lungs, though his words be never so scented and perfumed with shows of holiness."

iv. The **Spirit of counsel** is upon the Messiah. Jesus has perfect **counsel** to give us at all times. He has both the **wisdom** and the **understanding** to be a perfect counselor.

v. The **Spirit of...might** is upon the Messiah. Jesus has the power to do what He desires to do. Many people would help us if they could but are powerless to help. Others may have the power to help us, but they don't care about us. Jesus has both the love and the **might** to help us.

vi. The **Spirit of knowledge** is upon the Messiah. Jesus knows everything. He knows our hearts and He knows all the facts. Many times we have made decisions that seemed strange or wrong to others because they didn't have the **knowledge** that we have. Jesus has **knowledge** that we don't have, so it shouldn't surprise us that sometimes His decisions seem strange or wrong to us or to others.

vii. The **Spirit of...the fear of the Lord** is upon the Messiah. Jesus willingly kept Himself in a place of submission, respect, and honor to God the Father.

b. **The Spirit of the Lord...of wisdom and understanding...of counsel and might...of knowledge and of the fear of the Lord**: These seven aspects of the Spirit of God are not the only characteristics of the Holy Spirit. But they are grouped together in a "seven" to show the fullness and perfection of the Holy Spirit.

i. This passage is behind the term *the sevenfold Spirit of God* used in Revelation 1:4, 3:1, 4:5, and 5:6. It isn't that there are seven different spirits of God, rather the Spirit of the Lord has these characteristics, and He has them all in fullness and perfection.

ii. The seven-branched lampstand that held the oil lamps for the tabernacle was also an illustration of the seven aspects of the Holy Spirit. "This candlestick had one stem in the center from which protruded three branches to the right and three to the left. Similarly, in this text, three pairs of the names of the Spirit are grouped around the central stem." (Bultema)

c. **Shall rest upon Him**: Jesus the Messiah lived and ministered as a man filled with the Spirit of God. The **wisdom**, **understanding**, **counsel**, **might**, **knowledge**, and **fear of the Lord** Jesus displayed in His ministry flowed not from His "own" divine resources, but from His reliance on the Spirit of the Lord who filled Him.

i. As truly God, Jesus has all these attributes from eternity. But when Jesus emptied Himself at the incarnation, He allowed the Holy Spirit to fill Him as a man, being an eternal example *to* us and a sympathizer *with* us. When Jesus added humanity to His deity, in no way did He stop being God. But as Philippians 2:5-8 tells us, there is some sense in which Jesus choose to "empty Himself" of some of the privileges or prerogatives of deity. Instead, Jesus chose to rely on the **Spirit of the Lord**.

ii. Jesus displayed the fruit of the Spirit to the uttermost because He was a perfect vessel. Jesus received the Spirit without measure (John 3:34).

iii. There seem to have been times when Jesus did operate beyond what a Spirit-filled man could do, such as when He was transfigured (Matthew 17:1-9) or when Jesus performed some of His miracles over nature. But certainly, Jesus fought all His battles as a man filled with the Holy Spirit.

d. **The Spirit of the Lord**: These seven characteristics describe the nature of the **Spirit of the Lord**. They also describe the nature of Jesus. There is no difference between the nature of Jesus and the nature of the Holy Spirit. When we see Jesus, we see God the Father (John 14:9). When we see the Spirit of the Lord at work, it should look like the ministry and the nature of Jesus.

3. (3-5) The perfect character of the Messiah.

His delight *is* in the fear of the Lord,
And He shall not judge by the sight of His eyes,
Nor decide by the hearing of His ears;
But with righteousness He shall judge the poor,
And decide with equity for the meek of the earth;
He shall strike the earth with the rod of His mouth,
And with the breath of His lips He shall slay the wicked.
Righteousness shall be the belt of His loins,
And faithfulness the belt of His waist.

a. **His delight is in the fear of the Lord**: Nothing pleased Jesus more than doing the will of His Father. *My food is to do the will of Him who sent Me, and to finish His work.* (John 4:34)

b. **With righteousness He shall judge**: Jesus did not rely on outward appearance, or on the mere words that someone said. He judged with **righteousness**. He didn't cheat the poor of justice, and if the poor and the weak are given justice, then everyone will be.

c. **He shall strike the earth with the rod of His mouth**: The mere words of Jesus have the power to judge the wicked. He only has to announce a judgment and it is done.

i. Bultema quotes Dr. V. Hepp on **with the breath of His lips He shall slay the wicked**: "From of old, the Rabbis have adhered to the first interpretation and seen in this wicked (one)...the Jewish Antichrist...this prediction of the wicked (one) may be unhesitatingly applied to the Antichrist." Dr. V. Hepp made this remark in light of

2 Thessalonians 2:8: *And then the lawless one will be revealed, whom the Lord will consume with the breath of His mouth and destroy with the brightness of His coming.*

d. **Righteousness shall be the belt of His loins**: The qualities of **righteousness** and **faithfulness** are so close to Jesus they are like belts around His waist. Everything Jesus does is touched by His **righteousness** and **faithfulness**.

B. The glorious reign of the King.

1. (6-9) The new ecology of the reign of the Messiah.

"The wolf also shall dwell with the lamb,
The leopard shall lie down with the young goat,
The calf and the young lion and the fatling together;
And a little child shall lead them.
The cow and the bear shall graze;
Their young ones shall lie down together;
And the lion shall eat straw like the ox.
The nursing child shall play by the cobra's hole,
And the weaned child shall put his hand in the viper's den.
They shall not hurt nor destroy in all My holy mountain,
For the earth shall be full of the knowledge of the LORD
As the waters cover the sea.

a. **The wolf also shall dwell with the lamb**: When the Messiah reigns, nature will be transformed. No longer will there be predators among the animals, and it seems that all animals will be herbivores (plant-eaters) only (**the cow and the bear shall graze...the lion shall eat straw like the ox**).

i. Romans 8:19-22 tells us more about this transformation of creation: *The earnest expectation of the creation eagerly waits for the revealing of the sons of God. For the creation was subjected to futility, not willingly, but because of Him who subjected it in hope; because the creation itself also will be delivered from the bondage of corruption into the glorious liberty of the children of God. For we know that the whole creation groans and labors with birth pangs together until now.* Nature is waiting for the transformation that will come when the Messiah reigns and believers are glorified.

b. **And a little child shall lead them**: When the Messiah reigns, not only will the way animals relate to each other be changed, but the way they relate to humans will be changed. **A little child** will be safe and able to lead a **wolf** or a **leopard** or a **young lion** or a **bear**. Even the danger of predators like cobras and vipers will be gone.

i. In Genesis 9:2-3, the LORD gave Noah, and all mankind after him, the permission to eat meat. At the same time, the LORD put the *dread* of man in animals, so they would not be effortless prey for humans. Now, in the reign of the Messiah, that is reversed. For this reason, many think that in the reign of the Messiah, the Millennium, humans will return to being vegetarians, as it seems they were before Genesis 9:2-3.

c. **For the earth shall be full of the knowledge of the LORD as the waters cover the sea**: When the Messiah reigns, the **knowledge of the LORD** – in a relational sense, not merely an intellectual sense – will cover the entire earth. The Millennial reign of the Messiah will be glorious.

2. (10-12) The new Exodus of the Millennial reign of the Messiah

"And in that day there shall be a Root of Jesse,
Who shall stand as a banner to the people;
For the Gentiles shall seek Him,
And His resting place shall be glorious."
It shall come to pass in that day
***That* the LORD shall set His hand again the second time**
To recover the remnant of His people who are left,
From Assyria and Egypt,
From Pathros and Cush,
From Elam and Shinar,
From Hamath and the islands of the sea.
He will set up a banner for the nations,
And will assemble the outcasts of Israel,
And gather together the dispersed of Judah
From the four corners of the earth.

a. **For the Gentiles will seek Him**: The glory of the reign of the Messiah will be not only for the Jewish people but also for the Gentiles. He **shall stand as a banner to the people**, lifted high to draw all peoples to Him.

i. In Isaiah 5:26 the banner was used to call the nations to judgment against Israel. Now the **banner** calls the nations to the blessings of the Messiah.

b. **The second time to recover the remnant of His people who are left**: In the reign of the Messiah, there will be another Exodus of the Jewish people, delivering them not only from Egypt but from all nations where they have been **dispersed**.

3. (13-16) The peace of the reign of the Messiah.

Also the envy of Ephraim shall depart,
And the adversaries of Judah shall be cut off;
Ephraim shall not envy Judah,
And Judah shall not harass Ephraim.
But they shall fly down upon the shoulder of the Philistines toward the west;
Together they shall plunder the people of the East;
They shall lay their hand on Edom and Moab;
And the people of Ammon shall obey them.
The LORD will utterly destroy the tongue of the Sea of Egypt;
With His mighty wind He will shake His fist over the River,
And strike it in the seven streams,
And make *men* cross over dryshod.
There will be a highway for the remnant of His people
Who will be left from Assyria,
As it was for Israel
In the day that he came up from the land of Egypt.

a. **Ephraim shall not envy Judah…Judah shall not harass Ephraim**: In the reign of the Messiah, the nations will not go to war anymore. Conflicts will be justly and swiftly settled by the Messiah and His government. Disobedient nations (here, described as **the Philistines and Edom and Moab** and **the people of Ammon**, traditional enemies of Israel) will be punished.

b. **There will be a highway for the remnant of His people**: Any obstacle to the gathering of those dispersed among the nations will be taken away. Nothing can oppose the government of the Messiah.

Isaiah 12 – Words from a Worshipper

A. The worshipper speaks to the Lord.

1. (1) Praise to the Lord after His anger has passed

And in that day you will say:
"O Lord, I will praise You;
Though You were angry with me,
Your anger is turned away, and You comfort me.

a. **And in that day you will say**: Isaiah chapter 11 spoke powerfully of the reign of the Messiah as king over all the earth. This brief chapter of praise comes from the heart of the one that has surrendered to the Messiah as king and enjoys the benefits of His reign.

b. **O Lord, I will praise You; though You were angry with me**: The worshipper *decides* to praise the Lord, even though he has felt the Lord's anger against him.

i. Under the New Covenant, does God get **angry** with us? There is a sense in which all the anger and wrath of God against us was poured out upon the Son of God on the cross. In this sense, there is no more anger from God towards us because His anger has been "exhausted." But there is also a sense in which we receive *chastening* or *discipline* from the Lord, which certainly *feels* like His anger. This chastening feels unpleasant (Hebrews 12:11), but it really shows the *fatherly love* of God instead of His hatred.

c. **Your anger is turned away**: It is wonderful when the **anger** of God is **turned away**. In the larger sense, His **anger is turned away** because of what Jesus did on the cross. Jesus put Himself in between us and the anger of the Lord and receiving that anger in Himself, He **turned away** God's anger.

i. In the sense of God's chastening or discipline in our lives, how wonderful it is when His **anger is turned away**, and "spanking" stops.

d. **And You comfort me**: When God disciplines us, He does so as a perfect parent, knowing perfectly how to comfort us after we have been chastened. Sometimes, like rebellious children, we refuse the comfort of God after discipline, but that is always our fault, not His.

i. "Satan also tempts us by all methods, and employs every expedient to compel us to despair. We ought, therefore, to be fortified by this doctrine, that, though we feel the anger of the Lord, we may know that it is of short duration, and that we shall be comforted as soon as he has chastened us." (Calvin)

2. (2) A declaration of thanks and confidence in the LORD.

Behold, God *is* my salvation,
I will trust and not be afraid;
'For YAH, the LORD, *is* my strength and song;
He also has become my salvation.'"

a. **Behold**: The worshipper wants others to *see* what he says is true. He is excited about what God has done in his life and invites all to **behold** the work of the LORD.

b. **God is my salvation**: This *is* salvation. To say **God is my salvation** is also to say, "I am not my salvation. My good works, my good intentions, my good thoughts do not save me. **God is my salvation**."

i. Many don't ever feel the *need* for **salvation**. Instead, they think their lives are fine, and come to God for a little help when they feel they need it. But they never see themselves as drowning men in need of rescue or see themselves as hell-destined sinners in need of **salvation**.

ii. The worshipper is so immersed in this idea that he repeats it in the same verse: **God is my salvation…He also has become my salvation**.

c. **I will trust and not be afraid**: This peace and security comes from knowing that **God is my salvation**. When we are our own salvation, it is hard to **trust and not be afraid** in ourselves. But when God is our salvation, we can **trust and not be afraid**.

i. Paul repeated the same idea in Romans 5:1: *Therefore, having been justified by faith, we have peace with God through our Lord Jesus Christ.* The place of peace and trust and "no fear" comes only from seeing our salvation in God, and not in ourselves.

d. **I will trust and not be afraid**: This is a confident statement reflecting the **will** of the worshipper. He is *deciding* to **trust and not be afraid**. There are *feelings* of trust, but that is different than the *decision* to trust. We can say to our **will**, "**I will trust and not be afraid**."

i. "Hearken, O unbeliever, you have said, 'I cannot believe,' but it would be more honest if you had said, 'I *will* not believe.' The mischief lies there. Your unbelief is your fault, not your misfortune. It is a disease, but it is also a crime: it is a terrible source of misery to you, but it is justly so, for it is an atrocious offense against the God of truth. (Spurgeon)

ii. "The talk about trying to believe is a mere pretence. But whether pretence or no, let me remind you that there is no text in the Bible which says, 'Try and believe,' but it says 'Believe in the Lord Jesus Christ.' He is the Son of God, he has proved it by his miracles, he died to save sinners, therefore trust him; he deserves implicit trust and child-like confidence. Will you refuse him these? Then you have maligned his character and given him the lie." (Spurgeon)

e. **For Yah, the Lord, is my strength and song**: The Lord is not only the worshipper's salvation, He is also his **strength and song**. Some find it easier to consider the Lord their salvation in a distant "bye-and-bye" sense than to take Him today as their **strength** and **song**.

i. When the Lord is our **strength**, it means that He is our resource, He is our refuge. We look to Him for our needs and are never unsatisfied. "Nor is he here called a part or an aid of our strength, but our complete *strength*; for we are strong, so far as he supplies us with strength." (Calvin)

ii. When the Lord is our **song**, it means that He is our joy, He is our happiness. We find our purpose and life in Him, and He never disappoints.

iii. "The word *Yah* read here is probably a mistake; and arose originally from the custom of the Jewish scribes, who, when they found a line too short for the word, wrote as many letters as filled it, and then began the next line with the whole word." (Clarke)

3. (3) The result of the salvation of the Lord.

Therefore with joy you will draw water
From the wells of salvation.

a. **You will draw water from the wells of salvation**: Jesus promised us *whoever drinks of the water that I shall give him will never thirst. But the water that I shall give him will become in him a fountain of water springing up into everlasting life.* (John 4:14) We can come to Jesus and **draw water from the wells of salvation**.

i. When we remember the semi-arid climate of Israel, we see what a beautiful picture **the wells of salvation** paint. When water is rare, a well is life. A reliable source of something that is absolutely necessary (like **water**) is a precious gift. God's gift of **salvation** is just that precious.

ii. The LORD's resource is not limited. There is not one *well of salvation*. There are many **wells of salvation**. This doesn't mean that there are many ways to be saved. All of the wells draw from the same reservoir of salvation, Jesus Christ. But many wells can bring water from the same water table.

b. **You will draw water**: This means there is something for us to *do*. God doesn't meet our needs as we sit in passive inactivity. We must reach out and **draw** what He has provided. At the same time, it is His *water*, His *well*, His *rope*, and His *bucket* that we draw with.

c. **Therefore with joy**: Because it is all of the LORD, we draw from the wells of salvation **with joy**. There should be no somber faces at the LORD's well of salvation. We draw water **with joy**.

i. "Joy is the just man's portion, and Christ is the never-failing fountain whence by a lively faith he may infallibly fetch it." (Trapp)

ii. "Be of good courage, you very, very timid ones, and alter your tone. Try to put a 'Selah' into your life, as David often did in his Psalms. Frequently, he put in a 'Selah,' and then he changed the key directly. In like manner, change the key of your singing; you are a great deal too low. Let the harp-strings be screwed up a bit, and let us have no more of these flat, mournful notes. Give us some other key, please, and begin to say, with the prophet Isaiah, 'O Lord, I will praise thee: though thou wast angry with me, thine anger is turned away, and thou comfortedst me. Behold, God is my salvation, I will trust, and not be afraid.'" (Spurgeon)

B. The worshipper declares the greatness of God to everyone.

1. (4) Exalting God among the peoples.

And in that day you will say:
"Praise the LORD, call upon His name;
Declare His deeds among the peoples,
Make mention that His name is exalted."

a. **Praise the LORD, call upon His name**: This is an exhortation to praise, and an encouragement to worship the LORD and trust in Him. The worshipper has received from the *wells of salvation*, and now that living water is flowing out of him, encouraging others to worship and trust in the LORD.

i. It is as if the job of praising God is too big for this worshipper, and he needs to call in others to help him. "The saints are unsatisfiable in praising God for the great work of their redemption, and do therefore call in help, all that may be." (Trapp)

b. **Declare His deeds...Make mention that His name is exalted**: The worshipper can't stop talking about God's greatness and the great things He has done.

2. (5-6) Singing praise to the LORD.

"Sing to the LORD,
For He has done excellent things;
This *is* known in all the earth.
Cry out and shout, O inhabitant of Zion,
For great *is* the Holy One of Israel in your midst!"

a. **Sing to the LORD**: First, the LORD was the song of the worshipper (Isaiah 12:2). Now, he sings this song of the LORD to whoever will listen! If the LORD has become your song, then *sing it*.

b. **Cry out and shout**: This is *excited* praise. It is wrong to manipulate or push God's people into an artificial sense of enthusiasm in their worship. Yet there may often be a sincere and appropriate joy and energy as we worship God. If our worship will *never* **cry out and shout**, there is something missing in it.

i. "We ought not to worship God in a half-hearted sort of way; as if it were now our duty to bless God, but we felt it to be a weary business, and we would get it through as quickly as we could, and have done with it; and the sooner the better. No, no; 'All that is within me, bless his holy name.' Come, my heart, wake up, and summon all the powers which wait upon thee! Mechanical worship is easy, but worthless. Come rouse yourself, my brother! Rouse thyself, O my own soul!" (Spurgeon)

c. **For great is the Holy One of Israel in your midst**: This gives two reasons for great praise. First, because of *who* God is – **the Holy One of Israel**. Second, because of *where* God is – **in your midst**. Each of these gives everyone reason to praise God.

Isaiah 13 – The Burden against Babylon

Isaiah 13 begins a section ending at Isaiah 23:18 where he prophesies against the nations. It is fitting for judgment to begin at the house of God, so the LORD has first spoken to Israel and Judah. But now, the LORD speaks against the nations, beginning with Babylon.

A. Judgment upon Babylon.

1. (1) The burden against Babylon.

The burden against Babylon which Isaiah the son of Amoz saw.

a. **Burden**: In the prophets, a **burden** is a "heavy" message of weighty importance, heavy in the sense that it produces sorrow or grief.

i. "*Massa* comes from the verb 'to lift up' (*nasa*), and so it can mean 'to carry' or 'to lift up the voice.' From the first meaning comes the translation 'burden,' or 'load'; and from the second meaning we get the translation 'oracle,' or 'utterance.'" (Wolf)

ii. Grammatically, we may be able to translate the idea as "an oracle." But since these are *heavy* oracles, we are justified in calling them *burdens*.

b. **Against Babylon**: Isaiah finished his prophetic career in 685 B.C., almost 100 years before Judah finally fell before the Babylonian Empire (586 B.C.). At the time of this prophecy, Babylon was a significant nation, but they were definitely behind the Assyrian Empire in status. Yet the LORD who knows the end of all things can speak of the judgment on the pride of Babylon hundreds of years before the judgment comes.

i. This **burden against Babylon** will last until the end of Isaiah 14. Adam Clarke says of this passage, "The former part of this prophecy is one of the most beautiful examples that can be given of elegance of composition, variety of imagery, and sublimity of sentiment and diction, in the prophetic style; and the latter part consists of an ode of supreme and singular excellence."

ii. Why did God speak to **Babylon**? This prophecy was probably never published in Babylon, so it wasn't really given as a warning to them. Instead, the reason was for the help of the people of God. First, by showing them that God was indeed just, and would judge the wicked nations around them. Israel and Judah were feeling the sting of God's discipline, and in such times we wonder if God is unfairly singling us out. This is assurance to them that He isn't. Second, Babylon (and other nations in this section) were nations that had come against Israel and Judah, and God showed His love to His people by announcing His vengeance against their enemies.

2. (2-8) An army comes against Babylon.

"Lift up a banner on the high mountain,
Raise your voice to them;
Wave your hand, that they may enter the gates of the nobles.
I have commanded My sanctified ones;
I have also called My mighty ones for My anger—
Those who rejoice in My exaltation."
The noise of a multitude in the mountains,
Like that of many people!
A tumultuous noise of the kingdoms of nations gathered together!
The LORD of hosts musters
The army for battle.
They come from a far country,
From the end of heaven—
The LORD and His weapons of indignation,
To destroy the whole land.
Wail, for the day of the LORD *is* at hand!
It will come as destruction from the Almighty.
Therefore all hands will be limp,
Every man's heart will melt,
And they will be afraid.
Pangs and sorrows will take hold of *them*;
They will be in pain as a woman in childbirth;
They will be amazed at one another;
Their faces *will be like* flames.

a. **The LORD of hosts musters the army for battle**: This is an army of judgment against the Babylonian Empire, prophesied decades before they were even a superpower. This powerful army is described vividly, with sights and sounds of battle presented.

b. **They will be amazed at one another**: When Babylon fell suddenly by a clever, surprise attack by Cyrus, the citizens of the city were completely shocked (Daniel 5).

3. (9-16) The terrors of judgment upon Babylon.

Behold, the day of the LORD comes,
Cruel, with both wrath and fierce anger,
To lay the land desolate;
And He will destroy its sinners from it.
For the stars of heaven and their constellations
Will not give their light;
The sun will be darkened in its going forth,
And the moon will not cause its light to shine.
"I will punish the world for *its* evil,
And the wicked for their iniquity;
I will halt the arrogance of the proud,
And will lay low the haughtiness of the terrible.
I will make a mortal more rare than fine gold,
A man more than the golden wedge of Ophir.
Therefore I will shake the heavens,
And the earth will move out of her place,
In the wrath of the LORD of hosts
And in the day of His fierce anger.
It shall be as the hunted gazelle,
And as a sheep that no man takes up;
Every man will turn to his own people,
And everyone will flee to his own land.
Everyone who is found will be thrust through,
And everyone who is captured will fall by the sword.
Their children also will be dashed to pieces before their eyes;
Their houses will be plundered
And their wives ravished."

a. **The day of the LORD comes**: Isaiah now speaks in the "prophetic tense," having in mind both a *near* fulfillment (the day of judgment against the Babylonian Empire), and an *ultimate* fulfillment (the final day of judgment at the return of Jesus).

i. **The day of the LORD** is an important phrase, used some 26 times in the Bible. It speaks not of a single day of judgment, but of the season of judgment when the LORD sets things right. It is as if today is man's day, but the LORD's day is coming.

b. **The stars of heaven and their constellations will not give their light; the sun will be darkened**: Several prophetic passages describe the cosmic disturbances that will precede and surround the return of Jesus (Joel 2:10, Revelation 6:12-14, Isaiah 34:4). In fact, Jesus was probably quoting or paraphrasing this passage from Isaiah in Matthew 24:29: *Immediately after the tribulation of those days the sun will be darkened, and the moon will not give its light; the stars will fall from heaven, and the powers of the heavens will be shaken.*

i. In the near fulfillment of the judgment of Babylon, they *felt* like the whole world was coming apart. In the ultimate fulfillment connected with the return of Jesus, the whole world *will* be falling apart.

c. **I will punish the world for its evil**: This prophetic identification of Babylon with the world, ripe for ultimate judgment, is consistent through the Scriptures. We aren't surprised that Isaiah has prophetically combined the vision of Babylon's judgment with the judgment of the whole **world for its evil**.

i. Babylon is mentioned 287 times in the Scriptures, more than any other city except Jerusalem.

ii. Babylon was a literal city on the Euphrates river. Genesis 11:1-10 tells us that it was at Babylon where, soon after the flood, mankind formally organized in the rebellion against God. In this sense, Babylon "Was the seat of the civilization that expressed organized hostility to God." (Tenney, *Interpreting Revelation*).

iii. Later, Babylon was also the Capital of the empire that cruelly conquered Judah. "Babylon, to them (the Jews), was the essence of all evil, the embodiment of cruelty, the foe of God's people, and the lasting type of sin, carnality, lust and greed." (Tenney)

iv. To those familiar with the Old Testament, the name Babylon is associated with organized idolatry, blasphemy and the persecution of God's people. In the New Testament, the world's system of the last days is characterized both religiously and commercially as Babylon (Revelation 17 and 18). Therefore, Babylon is a "Suitable representation...of the idolatrous, pagan world-system in opposition to God." (Martin)

d. **Therefore I will shake the heavens, and the earth will move out of her place**: Haggai 2:6 and Hebrews 12:25-28 echo this same thought. Since God can shake the heavens and move the earth, and since God Himself is unshakable, it makes a lot more sense to trust in God than even the ground we stand on and the air we breathe.

e. **It shall be as the hunted gazelle**: The idea is that God's judgment, upon both Babylon and the world in general, is *unrelenting*. It is like a nature film where the **hunted gazelle** is overtaken by the lion, and is utterly consumed. There is no escape from God's unrelenting judgment.

i. If you take comfort in Jesus, remember that this is the same *unrelenting* judgment that was poured out upon Him on the cross. In this picture from Isaiah, *Jesus was the* **hunted gazelle**, and *willingly* made Himself so.

B. Desolate Babylon.

1. (17-22) Babylon is laid waste.

"Behold, I will stir up the Medes against them,
Who will not regard silver;
And *as for* gold, they will not delight in it.
Also *their* bows will dash the young men to pieces,
And they will have no pity on the fruit of the womb;
Their eye will not spare children.
And Babylon, the glory of kingdoms,
The beauty of the Chaldeans' pride,
Will be as when God overthrew Sodom and Gomorrah.
It will never be inhabited,
Nor will it be settled from generation to generation;
Nor will the Arabian pitch tents there,
Nor will the shepherds make their sheepfolds there.
But wild beasts of the desert will lie there,
And their houses will be full of owls;
Ostriches will dwell there,
And wild goats will caper there.
The hyenas will howl in their citadels,
And jackals in their pleasant palaces.
Her time *is* near to come,
And her days will not be prolonged."

a. **I will stir up the Medes against them**: If this prophecy was made decades before the Babylonian Empire defeated the Assyrian Empire and became a superpower, it was even longer before the time when **the Medes** came **against** the Babylonians, conquering them as instruments of God's judgments.

i. It is specifically worded passages like this that drive skeptics of the Bible crazy, pushing them to regard Isaiah as written *after* the events prophesied. But doesn't God know the future, and know it specifically?

ii. **Will be as when God overthrew Sodom and Gomorrah**: "The phrase 'Sodom and Gomorrah' suggests not only complete destruction but also its moral cause." (Grogan)

b. **It will never be inhabited**: The ancient city of Babylon, once conquered, **will never be inhabited** again.

i. "When Cyrus conquered Babylon, he did not devastate the city. The walls were left standing until 518 B.C., and general desolation did not set in until the third century B.C. Babylon gradually fell into decay, and the prophecy of Isaiah was fulfilled. Babylon became completely depopulated by the time of the Muslim conquest in the seventh century A.D., and to this day it lies deserted." (Wolf)

ii. This is also true in its ultimate fulfillment. When Jesus returns in glory and conquers the world system, He will rule the earth for 1,000 years. As He does, there will be no more "world system" in opposition to God as we know it. In this sense, the world system in opposition to God **will never be inhabited** again.

c. **Owls…ostriches…wild goats…hyenas**: The animals mentioned here are impossible to identify precisely. The picture is of the darkness and confusion surrounding the fall of Babylon.

i. "The 'wild goats' (v. 21) are sometimes associated with demons in goat form that are called 'satyrs' (Leviticus 17:7; 2 Chronicles 11:15)." (Wolf)

ii. John Calvin applied the truth of Isaiah 13 in this manner: "Whenever therefore we behold the destruction of cities, the calamities of nations, and the overturning of kingdoms, let us call those predictions to remembrance, that we may be humbled under God's chastisements, may learn to gather wisdom from the affliction of others, and may pray for an alleviation of our own grief."

Isaiah 14 – Babylon and Lucifer

A. The fall of the King of Babylon.

1. (1-2) Judgment on Babylon means mercy on Israel.

For the Lord will have mercy on Jacob, and will still choose Israel, and settle them in their own land. The strangers will be joined with them, and they will cling to the house of Jacob. Then people will take them and bring them to their place, and the house of Israel will possess them for servants and maids in the land of the Lord; they will take them captive whose captives they were, and rule over their oppressors.

a. **For the Lord will have mercy on Jacob**: Isaiah 13 ended with the desolation and gloom that would come upon Babylon. Since Babylon was Judah's great enemy, any judgment on Babylon was an expression of mercy to Israel. So, Isaiah followed the pronouncement of judgment on Babylon with **the Lord will have mercy on Jacob, and will still choose Israel**.

i. **Will still choose Israel**: Sometimes we feel that God chose us, but if He had to choose again, God would change His choice! We almost feel that God is "stuck" with us now and would choose differently if He could. Here, the Lord reminds His children that He does **still choose** us and would choose us all over again.

b. **And settle them in their own land**: The promise of restoration to their own land was also important. The Babylonians had forcibly exiled most of the population of Judah, so the promise of return to **their own land** was precious.

i. "This promise had a measure of fulfillment when Israel was brought back from Babylon; and still is it true that, when God's people come to their worst, there is always something better before them. On the other hand, it is equally sure that, when sinners come to their best, there is always something terrible awaiting them." (Spurgeon)

c. **The strangers will be joined with them**: The invitation to Gentiles was precious. The regathered and restored Israel would invite Gentiles to receive the goodness of God with them.

d. **They will take them captive whose captives they were, and rule over their oppressors**: In inviting **the strangers** to come and be **joined with them**, Israel would eliminate their enemies. The ultimate way to conquer an enemy is to make them your friend.

2. (3-8) The joy of the earth at the fall of the king of Babylon.

It shall come to pass in the day the LORD gives you rest from your sorrow, and from your fear and the hard bondage in which you were made to serve, that you will take up this proverb against the king of Babylon, and say:

"How the oppressor has ceased,
The golden city ceased!
The LORD has broken the staff of the wicked,
The scepter of the rulers;
He who struck the people in wrath with a continual stroke,
He who ruled the nations in anger,
Is persecuted *and* no one hinders.
The whole earth is at rest *and* quiet;
They break forth into singing.
Indeed the cypress trees rejoice over you,
***And* the cedars of Lebanon,**
***Saying,* 'Since you were cut down,**
No woodsman has come up against us.'

a. **In the day the LORD gives you rest from your sorrow, and from your fear and the hard bondage in which you were made to serve**: The LORD announces a day when He will give real **rest** to believing Israel. They will have **rest** from **sorrow**, from **fear**, and from their **hard bondage**.

i. This **rest** is the birthright of every believer in Jesus Christ. Jesus said, *"Come to Me, all you who labor and are heavy laden, and I will give you rest."* (Matthew 11:28). Do you have **rest** from **sorrow**? Do you have **rest** from **fear**? Do you have **rest** from **hard bondage**?

b. **That you will take up this proverb against the king of Babylon**: In the day of restoration, the defeat and weakness of the **king of Babylon** will be exposed, and Israel will rejoice.

i. As this prophecy continues from the context of Isaiah 13, it is important that we remember that Isaiah has two aspects of prophetic fulfillment in mind. First, there is the immediate and partial fulfillment regarding the empire of Babylon and its king. Second, there is the distant and ultimate fulfillment regarding the spiritual empire of Babylon – the world system – and its king, Satan.

ii. Some strongly disagree and see this passage as *only* referring to the king of literal Babylon and having *no reference* to Satan at all.

iii. John Calvin is an example of those who do not see any reference to Satan: "The exposition of this passage, which some have given, as if it referred to Satan, has arisen from ignorance; for the context plainly shows that these statements must be understood in reference to the king of the Babylonians. But when passages of Scripture are taken up at random, and no attention is paid to the context, we need to wonder that mistakes of this kind frequently arise... But as these inventions have no probability whatever, let us pass by them as useless fables."

iv. Adam Clarke also did not see any reference to Satan here: "But the truth is, the text speaks nothing at all concerning *Satan* nor his *fall*, nor the *occasion* of that fall, which many divines have with great confidence deduced from this text... This chapter speaks not of the ambition and fall of Satan, but of the pride, arrogance, and fall of Nebuchadnezzar." (Clarke)

v. Nevertheless, there is good reason to see this as *both* a reference to the ancient king of Babylon and the spiritual power behind that king. Biblical prophecy often has both a near and a distant fulfillment.

vi. So, **this proverb against the king of Babylon** was, in a partial sense, in the mouth of the returning exiles when Babylon was finally conquered, and the people of Judah could return to the Promised Land. But in an ultimate sense, **this proverb against the king of Babylon** will be in the mouth of God's people when the world system and her king, Satan, are each conquered and destroyed.

vii. Why does God tell His people – either in an immediate or an ultimate sense – the destiny of Babylon and her king? So that we can think and live *now*, knowing the ultimate fate of the world system and Satan. We often have said, "If I only knew then what I know now" once we see how things turn out. Here, God is allowing us the opportunity to know *now* what we will see *then*, and to allow it to affect our thinking and our actions.

viii. The literary form of this passage is important. "Its form is really that of the funeral dirge, with the characteristic limping rhythm of a Hebrew lament, so plaintive and yet ominous to the sensitive ear.... There is a considerable element of irony, so that the whole song becomes a taunt in the guise of a lament." (Grogan) This is a funeral song that mocks and taunts the dead, who in fact receives no burial.

c. **How the oppressor has ceased**: God wants us to know *now* that He has numbered the days of the king of spiritual Babylon – Satan. There will come a day when his oppression **has ceased**, and when the **Lord** will break **the staff of the wicked**, and **the scepter of the rulers**.

i. Sometimes we get so weary and discouraged from Satan's attack, it is almost as if we think his day will last forever. If we remember that one reason Satan works so hard is because even he knows his time is short, this is an encouragement to us. We can remain steadfast; we can outlast him.

d. **He who struck the people in wrath…who ruled the nations in anger**: Both the king of literal Babylon and the king of spiritual Babylon were mighty, oppressive rulers over the **people** and the **nations**. But now, the one who once persecuted is himself **persecuted and no one hinders**, and as a result, the **whole earth is at rest and quiet**, and they even **break forth into singing**.

i. "The whole Near East rejoiced over Babylon's fall because her rule was harsh and oppressive." (Wolf)

ii. Even the **trees rejoice** over the fall of the king of Babylon. This is true of the king of literal Babylon because the attacking kings cut down thousands of trees for both fuel and lumber, leaving Israel and Lebanon deforested. "Since the twelfth century B.C. the kings of Mesopotamia had imported lumber from Lebanon. Nebuchadnezzar used large supplies of such choice timbers in his extensive building efforts in Babylon after 605 B.C." (Wolf)

iii. The trees also rejoice at the fall of the king of spiritual Babylon, because *the creation itself also will be delivered from the bondage of corruption into the glorious liberty of the children of God.* (Romans 8:21)

3. (9-11) Hell receives the fallen king of Babylon.

"Hell from beneath is excited about you,
To meet *you* at your coming;
It stirs up the dead for you,
All the chief ones of the earth;
It has raised up from their thrones
All the kings of the nations.
They all shall speak and say to you:
'Have you also become as weak as we?
Have you become like us?

Your pomp is brought down to Sheol,
***And* the sound of your stringed instruments;**
The maggot is spread under you,
And worms cover you.'"

a. **Hell from beneath is excited about you**: Hell itself is excited to meet the king of Babylon because it can't wait to be the place where the one who tortured so many is tortured himself. This was true both for the king of literal Babylon, and the king of spiritual Babylon.

i. God wants us to know *now* that Satan is destined for hell. He isn't a winner, he is a loser, and he certainly *isn't* the boss or lord of hell. Satan will go to hell as a victim, as the ultimate prisoner in the dungeon of darkness, and hell will be *happy* to receive him this way.

b. **Have you also become as weak as we? Have you become like us?** When he went to hell, the king of literal Babylon was exposed as a mere man, though he thought of himself as greater than that. As well, when the king of spiritual Babylon goes to hell, all will be amazed to see that he was *only a creature.*

i. We often – to his great delight – exaggerate Satan's status and importance. We think of him as the *opposite* of God; as if God were light and Satan were darkness, as if God were hot and Satan were cold. Satan *wishes* he was the opposite of God, but God wants us to know *now* what everyone will know *someday* – that Satan is a mere creature and is in *no way* the opposite of God. If Satan has an opposite, it is not God the Father or God the Son, it would be a high-ranking angelic being such as Michael.

c. **Your pomp is brought down…the maggot is spread under you, and worms cover you**: In the end, it just won't be a *defeat* for the king of Babylon. Both for the literal and spiritual kings of Babylon, their defeat in hell will be *disgusting* and *degrading.*

i. Knowing this now – how *disgusting* and *degrading* the end of Satan will be – why would any of us serve him or work for his cause, even for a minute? Who wants to end up with the maggots and the worms?

d. **And the sound of your stringed instruments**: Before his fall, Satan was associated with music in heaven. Ezekiel 28:13 says of Satan before his fall, *the workmanship of your timbrels and pipes was prepared for you on the day you were created.* Apparently, the musical career of Satan did not end with his fall, because the **sound of** his **stringed instruments** is only brought down when he is imprisoned in hell.

4. (12-15) The fall of Lucifer.

"How you are fallen from heaven,
O Lucifer, son of the morning!
***How* you are cut down to the ground,**
You who weakened the nations!
For you have said in your heart:
'I will ascend into heaven,
I will exalt my throne above the stars of God;
I will also sit on the mount of the congregation
On the farthest sides of the north;
I will ascend above the heights of the clouds,
I will be like the Most High.'
Yet you shall be brought down to Sheol,
To the lowest depths of the Pit."

a. **How you are fallen from heaven, O Lucifer, son of the morning**: Here, the prophet identified the king of Babylon as **Lucifer, son of the morning**. Some debate if **Lucifer** is a *name* or a *title*; the word means *morning star* or *day star*, referring to a brightly shining object in the heavens. Whether it is a title or a name makes little difference; this once brightly shining king of Babylon is now **fallen from heaven**.

i. In the prophetic habit of speaking to both a near and a distant fulfillment, the prophet will sometimes speak *more* to the near or *more* to the distant. Here is a good example of Isaiah speaking *more* to the distant, ultimate fulfillment. It is true that the king of literal Babylon shined brightly among the men of his day and fell as hard and as completely as if a man were to fall from heaven. But there was a far more brightly shining being who inhabited heaven and fell even more dramatically – the king of spiritual Babylon, Satan.

b. **Fallen from heaven**: In fact, there are four falls of Satan, and this passage refers to his final, fourth fall.

i. Satan fell from glorified to profane (Ezekiel 28:14-16). This is what Jesus spoke of in Luke 10:18 when He says He *saw Satan fall like lightning from heaven*. This is the only fall of Satan that has already happened.

ii. Satan will fall from having access to heaven (Job 1:12, 1 Kings 22:21, Zechariah 3:1) to restriction on the earth (Revelation 12:9).

iii. Satan will fall from his place on the earth to bondage in the bottomless pit for 1,000 years (Revelation 20:1-3).

iv. Finally, as mentioned here in Isaiah 14:12, Satan will fall from the bottomless pit to the lake of fire, which we commonly know as *hell* (Revelation 20:10).

c. **Son of the morning**: This is a title of glory, beauty, and honor, which fit Lucifer well before his fall. The morning is glorious, and in Hebrew thinking, the **son of** "x" is characterized by "x." So, before his fall, Lucifer was characterized by the glory **of the morning**.

i. Jesus Himself is called the *Bright and Morning Star* (Revelation 22:16). Satan, though a created being, had some of these glorious qualities in himself. No wonder that *Satan himself transforms himself into an angel of light* (2 Corinthians 11:14), deceiving many with his apparent glory, beauty, and goodness.

d. **How you are cut down to the ground**: What a contrast! This being, once so high, once so shining, once so bright, is now **cut down to the ground**.

e. **For you have said in your heart**: Here, God tells us the reason behind the fall of both the literal and spiritual king of Babylon. The fall was prompted by something he **said**, even though he may have never said it with his lips – it was enough that he **said** it in his **heart**.

f. **I will**: The pride, the grasping selfish ambition, the self-will of the king of Babylon is powerfully expressed in five **I will** statements. This is the essence of the self-focused and self-obsessed life.

- **I will ascend into heaven**: It was as if Satan said, "Heaven will be my home and my place of honor."
- **I will exalt my throne above the stars of God**: "I will be enthroned and will be exalted above all other angelic beings."
- **I will also sit on the mount of the congregation**: "I will sit in the place of glory and honor and attention."
- **I will ascend above the heights**: "I will continue to rise, even in heaven, until all see me in my bright shining glory."
- **I will be like the Most High**: "I will be glorious, and be set equal to God, far above all other created beings."

i. We see in these statements not so much a desire to exalt one's self above God, but the desire to exalt one's self above one's *peers*. From this passage, it seems that Satan's desire was not so much to be above God, but to be honored and regarded as the highest *angel*, **above the** [other] **stars of God**, receiving the glory and attention one would receive being next to God, equal with God, **like the Most High**. We don't have to want to be exalted higher than God to be like Satan. It is enough to want to be exalted above other people.

ii. Lucifer was certainly a glorious angel (*day star*, **son of the morning**, and also called *the seal of perfection, full of wisdom and perfect in beauty…the anointed cherub who covers* in Ezekiel 28:12 and 14). Yet, there came a time when despite all his beauty and glory, he departed from the heart of God by wanting to exalt himself above his peers. Instead, the heart of Jesus says, "The status of equality with God is not something to hang on to. I will let it go. I will give up My reputation, be a servant, live humbly among men, and even die an excruciating and humiliating death." (Philippians 2:5-8) When Lucifer departed from this heart, he fell from glory.

iii. "It is a strange paradox that nothing makes a being less like God than the urge to be his equal, for he who was God stepped down from the throne of his glory to display to the wondering eyes of men the humility of God." (Grogan)

g. **I will be like the Most High**: What *prompted* Satan's desire to exalt himself above all other creatures? What *prompted* these five **I will** statements?

i. Why did Lucifer rebel? Perhaps because he rejected God's plan to create an order of beings made in His image (Genesis 1:26), who would be beneath the angels in dignity (Hebrews 2:6-7a; 2 Peter 2:11) yet would be served by angels in the present (Hebrews 1:14; 2:7-8; Psalm 91:11-12) and would one day be lifted in honor and status above the angels (1 Corinthians 6:3; 1 John 3:2). Satan wanted to be the highest among all creatures, equal to God in glory and honor, and the plan to create man would eventually put men above angels. He was apparently able to persuade one-third of the angelic beings to join him in his rebellion (Revelation 12:3-4, 7, and 9).

ii. If this is the case, it explains well Satan's present strategy against man: to obscure the image of God in man through encouraging sin and rebellion, to cause man to serve him, and to prevent the ultimate glorification of man.

h. **Yet you shall be brought down**: Despite Satan's desire to exalt himself, he will not be exalted at all. Certainly, there is a sense in which he is exalted right now, but this is but an eye-blink in the scope of eternity. Satan, like all those who desire to exalt themselves, **shall be brought down**.

i. 1 Peter 5:6 expresses the true path to being exalted: *Therefore humble yourselves under the mighty hand of God, that He may exalt you in due time*. In Mark 9:35, Jesus said If anyone desires to be first, he shall be last of all and servant of all.

5. (16-17) The nations are amazed at the fall of the king of Babylon.

"Those who see you will gaze at you,
And* consider you, *saying:
'*Is* this the man who made the earth tremble,
Who shook kingdoms,
Who made the world as a wilderness
And destroyed its cities,
***Who* did not open the house of his prisoners?'**

a. **Those who see you will gaze at you…"Is this the man who made the earth tremble…Who did not open the house of his prisoners?"** When the king of literal Babylon fell, his weakness was exposed, and others were amazed that at one time he had so much power, and so many feared him. The same will happen when the king of spiritual Babylon falls. People will see him for what he really is and be amazed at how much power he actually had.

6. (18-23) The amazing and bloody destruction of Babylon.

"All the kings of the nations,
All of them, sleep in glory,
Everyone in his own house;
But you are cast out of your grave
Like an abominable branch,
***Like* the garment of those who are slain,**
Thrust through with a sword,
Who go down to the stones of the pit,
Like a corpse trodden underfoot.
You will not be joined with them in burial,
Because you have destroyed your land
***And* slain your people.**
The brood of evildoers shall never be named.
Prepare slaughter for his children
Because of the iniquity of their fathers,
Lest they rise up and possess the land,
And fill the face of the world with cities."
"For I will rise up against them," says the LORD of hosts,
"And cut off from Babylon the name and remnant,
And offspring and posterity," says the LORD.
"I will also make it a possession for the porcupine,

And marshes of muddy water;
I will sweep it with the broom of destruction," says the LORD of hosts.

a. **All the kings of the nations**: In this brief section, Isaiah brings his focus back more upon the king of literal Babylon. He notes the comfort and ease the other kings of the earth enjoy, but not the fallen king of Babylon, who is instead **cast out of your grave like an abominable branch**.

i. "But now a terrible thing has happened; he was not given the honorable burial deemed so important for monarchs. Even the common man regarded proper burial as essential." (Wolf) Instead of a proper burial, the king of Babylon gets a bed of maggots and a blanket of worms! (Isaiah 14:11).

ii. "The corpse of the king of Babylon would be thrown out like a rejected branch (*neser*). What a contrast to the Branch from the stump of Jesse that would bear abundant fruit! (Isaiah 11:1)" (Wolf)

b. **I will sweep it with the broom of destruction**: The destruction of Babylon – both literal and spiritual – will be complete. The LORD will **cut off from Babylon the name and remnant**. There will not even be a **remnant** of Babylon left.

i. "Rubbish fit only for the broom of judgment – this was God's verdict on mighty Babylon!" (Grogan)

ii. "If God's enemies have a bright day or two, it shall soon be showery weather with them. They may for the moment exult over God's people, but he knows that their day of reckoning is coming." (Spurgeon)

B. Judgment to come on Assyria and the Philistines.

1. (24-27) The coming judgment on Assyria.

The LORD of hosts has sworn, saying,
"Surely, as I have thought, so it shall come to pass,
And as I have purposed, *so* it shall stand:
That I will break the Assyrian in My land,
And on My mountains tread him underfoot.
Then his yoke shall be removed from them,
And his burden removed from their shoulders.
This *is* the purpose that is purposed against the whole earth,
And this *is* the hand that is stretched out over all the nations.
For the LORD of hosts has purposed,
And who will annul *it*?
His hand *is* stretched out,
And who will turn it back?"

a. **Surely, as I have thought, so it shall come to pass**: God's thoughts are as good as actions. All God has to do is think a thought, and worlds can be created. What a comfort to know that God thinks good thoughts towards His people: *I know the thoughts that I think toward you, says the* Lord, *thoughts of peace and not of evil, to give you a future and a hope.* (Jeremiah 29:11)

b. **I will break the Assyrian in My land**: God did this powerfully when the Assyrians invaded Judah. 2 Kings 19:35 describes how God simply sent the angel of the Lord and killed 185,000 Assyrians in one night. When the people woke up, there were 185,000 dead Assyrian soldiers.

c. **For the Lord of hosts has purposed, and who will annul it?** God always accomplishes His purpose! His plan is never frustrated! Even when we have no trust at all in our own plan, we can fully trust God's purpose.

2. (28-31) The coming judgment on the Philistines.

This is the burden which came in the year that King Ahaz died.
"Do not rejoice, all you of Philistia,
Because the rod that struck you is broken;
For out of the serpent's roots will come forth a viper,
And its offspring *will be* a fiery flying serpent.
The firstborn of the poor will feed,
And the needy will lie down in safety;
I will kill your roots with famine,
And it will slay your remnant.
Wail, O gate! Cry, O city!
All you of Philistia *are* dissolved;
For smoke will come from the north,
And no one *will be* alone in his appointed times."

a. **Do not rejoice, all you of Philistia, because the rod that struck you is broken**: There was constant warfare between Israel and the Philistines, and so on many occasions, Israel was **the rod that struck** the Philistines. Now, when Israel and Judah would be humbled, God did not want the Philistines to glory in it.

b. **All you of Philistia are dissolved**: God's judgment would come against the Philistines also. They should not think that just because God was judging the Israelites, that they had somehow escaped.

3. (32) A word for the **messengers of the nation**.

What will they answer the messengers of the nation?
That the Lord has founded Zion,
And the poor of His people shall take refuge in it.

a. **What will one then answer the messengers of the nation?** In the midst of the judgment of the nations, what does God have to say to His people and to all the nations, when nations are being judged?

i. "No doubt the 'envoys' were Philistine diplomats sent to Jerusalem to encourage solidarity against the common Assyrian foe. As elsewhere, Isaiah's message encouraged trust in God, not in alliances." (Grogan)

b. **The Lord has founded Zion**: This was God's simple answer. When judgment comes, what is **founded** on the Lord is made evident. The storm comes and beats against the house and tests its foundation. When **the Lord has founded** something, it is evident to everyone in the midst of judgment.

c. **The poor of His people shall take refuge in it**: This was the second part of God's answer. God's place of security is not for the rich and self-sufficient. It is for the **poor of His people**. It is the poor in spirit who find refuge in God's city.

Isaiah 15 – The Burden Against Moab

A. A night invasion of Moab.

1. (1a) **The burden against Moab.**

The burden against Moab.

a. **Moab**: The founder of the people of Moab was the son born of the incestuous relationship between Lot and one of his daughters, when his daughters made Lot drunk, after the destruction of Sodom and Gomorrah (Genesis 19:30-38). The Moabites settled in the plains to the south-east of Israel, in what is modern-day Jordan.

b. **Moab**: At times, the Moabites were great enemies of Israel.

- It was Balak, king of Moab, who hired Balaam the prophet, hoping that he could curse Israel (Numbers 22-25).
- It was Eglon, king of Moab, who oppressed Israel in the days of the Judges (Judges 3:12-30).

i. During the time of Saul and David, Israel established a firm control over Moab, but later kings of Israel were not always able to keep them under Israeli dominance.

c. **Moab**: At the same time, there was a Moabite connection with Israel.

- First, they were related to Israel because Lot was Abraham's nephew. Because of this, God told Israel in Deuteronomy 2:9 that they were not to destroy Moab and take their land.
- As well, David, Israel's greatest king, was one-quarter Moabite. His paternal grandmother Ruth was from Moab, and David entrusted his father and mother to the protection of the king of Moab when he was a fugitive from Saul (1 Samuel 22:3-4).

i. For these reasons, there is a great deal of sadness and empathy on Isaiah's part as he describes the coming judgment on Moab.

2. (1b-4) The cities and soldiers of Moab fall under a night attack.

Because in the night Ar of Moab is laid waste
***And* destroyed,**
Because in the night Kir of Moab is laid waste
***And* destroyed,**
He has gone up to the temple and Dibon,
To the high places to weep.
Moab will wail over Nebo and over Medeba;
On all their heads *will be* baldness,
***And* every beard cut off.**
In their streets they will clothe themselves with sackcloth;
On the tops of their houses
And in their streets
Everyone will wail, weeping bitterly.
Heshbon and Elealeh will cry out,
Their voice shall be heard as far as Jahaz;
Therefore the armed soldiers of Moab will cry out;
His life will be burdensome to him.

a. **Because in the night Ar of Moab is laid waste and destroyed…Kir of Moab…Heshbon and Elealeh**: God announced coming judgment on Moab, against these cities.

i. "Most of these sites were originally part of Israel's territory when Moses and Joshua defeated Sihon, King of the Amorites. All the cities north of the Arnon River...once belonged to the tribe of Reuben. Throughout the years, however, the Moabites had persistently pushed the Israelites out of these regions." (Wolf)

b. **He has gone up to the temple**: The picture is of a Moabite man fleeing the destruction of his city, running to his temple and his pagan gods for protection and mourning (**To the high places to weep**).

c. **They will clothe themselves with sackcloth…everyone will wail, weeping bitterly**: At this invasion, and as a result of it, there will be great distress and mourning in Moab.

i. Jeremiah 48 also prophesies the judgment of Moab, and also gives the reason why. *"Moab has been at ease from his youth; he has settled on his dregs, and has not been emptied from vessel to vessel, nor has he gone into captivity. Therefore his taste remained in him, and his scent has not changed. Therefore behold, the days are coming," says the* Lord, *"That I shall send him wine-workers who will tip him over and empty his vessels and break the bottles."* (Jeremiah 48:11-12) When we are at ease and are never "poured" from vessel to vessel, we "settle on the dregs" and are never refined. God uses the "pouring" process to refine us.

B. Refugees flee Moab.

1. (5-7) The flight of the refugees from Moab.

"My heart will cry out for Moab;
His fugitives *shall flee* to Zoar,
***Like* a three-year-old heifer.**
For by the Ascent of Luhith
They will go up with weeping;
For in the way of Horonaim
They will raise up a cry of destruction,
For the waters of Nimrim will be desolate,
For the green grass has withered away;
The grass fails, there is nothing green.
Therefore the abundance they have gained,
And what they have laid up,
They will carry away to the Brook of the Willows."

a. **His fugitives shall flee to Zoar**: The connection is interesting because **Zoar** was the city Lot and his daughters escaped from, hiding in the mountains, before Lot's daughters committed incest with their father, and gave birth to the child *Moab*, the father of the Moabites.

i. Bultema on **Zoar**: "This town is called *a heifer of three years old*, apparently to indicate that it had never been under the yoke of strangers."

b. **The green grass has withered away**: The beautiful plains of Moab were wonderful grazing land. But now, under the hand of God's judgment, **the green grass has withered away**.

c. **Therefore the abundance they have gained…they will carry away to the Brook of the Willows**: The picture is of fleeing refugees, carrying all their possessions with them.

2. (8-9) The cry of the refugees from Moab.

"For the cry has gone all around the borders of Moab,
Its wailing to Eglaim
And its wailing to Beer Elim.
For the waters of Dimon will be full of blood;
Because I will bring more upon Dimon,
Lions upon him who escapes from Moab,
And on the remnant of the land."

a. **The cry has gone all around the borders of Moab**: Their pain in the midst of judgment would be evident to all. Everyone **around the borders of Moab** would see God's judgment against them.

b. **Lions upon him who escapes from Moab**: If the judgment of the night attack did not complete the work of judgment, God would send **lions upon him who escapes**. God will finish His work of judgment.

Isaiah 16 – The Burden Against Moab (continued)

A. Counsel to Moab.

1. (1-2) **Send the lamb...**

Send the lamb to the ruler of the land,
From Sela to the wilderness,
To the mount of the daughter of Zion.
For it shall be as a wandering bird thrown out of the nest;
***So* shall be the daughters of Moab at the fords of the Arnon.**

a. **Send the lamb to the ruler of the land**: The idea behind this is that Moab should resume their bringing of tribute to Jerusalem, thereby submitting themselves to God again. This kind of tribute is described in 2 Kings 3:4-5, where Mesha, King of Moab, who once paid tribute to Israel, stopped doing so when King Ahab of Israel died. Here, Isaiah counsels Moab to resume this payment of tribute.

b. **As a wandering bird thrown out of the nest**: Isaiah paints a powerful picture of the helpless, confused state of Moab under the hand of God's judgment. They are like a **wandering bird thrown out of the nest**, confused, weak, and vulnerable. Their only recourse is to submit themselves to Jerusalem and its King again.

2. (3) Isaiah's word to Judah as she observes Moab under judgment.

"Take counsel, execute judgment;
Make your shadow like the night in the middle of the day;
Hide the outcasts,
Do not betray him who escapes.

a. **Hide the outcasts**: Here, in the compassion of his prophecy, Isaiah pleads with the rulers of Judah to **hide the outcasts** of Moab. Again, his great sympathies are probably due to the connection between Moab and the royal house of David.

b. **Do not betray him who escapes**: Isaiah wanted Judah to be a place of refuge and protection for Moab under judgment. This is exactly what the church should when people receive the judgment that fits their rebellion against God. If they humbly flee for refuge among God's people, the church should be a place that will **hide the outcasts** and receive **him who escapes**, never to **betray** them.

3. (4-5) A plea for refuge among Moab in the day of the righteous King.

"Let My outcasts dwell with you, O Moab;
Be a shelter to them from the face of the spoiler.
For the extortioner is at an end,
Devastation ceases,
The oppressors are consumed out of the land.
In mercy the throne will be established;
And One will sit on it in truth, in the tabernacle of David,
Judging and seeking justice and hastening righteousness."

a. **Let My outcasts dwell with you, O Moab**: This is a sudden and curious change of focus. In Isaiah 16:3, Judah was counseled to receive the outcasts of Moab. Now, Moab is asked to receive the outcasts of Judah. Bultema thinks that Isaiah 16:4-5 is an end-times prophecy of how Moab will be a place of refuge for Jews escaping the fury of the Antichrist after the abomination of desolation.

i. In a coming day, Israel, will flee from the fury of the Antichrist and will find refuge in places like Moab (Revelation 12:6, 12:13-14). They will be protected **from the face of the spoiler** until **devastation ceases** and **the oppressors are consumed out of the land**.

b. **In mercy the throne will be established**: In those end times, the **throne** of the Messiah **will be established**, and the Messiah Himself will sit on the throne: **One will sit on it in truth, in the tabernacle of David**. His reign will be wonderful, **judging and seeking justice and hastening righteousness**.

B. The pain of the prophet.

1. (6-8) The pain in Moab at the judgment of God.

We have heard of the pride of Moab—
***He is* very proud—**
Of his haughtiness and his pride and his wrath;
***But* his lies *shall* not *be* so.**
Therefore Moab shall wail for Moab;
Everyone shall wail.

For the foundations of Kir Hareseth you shall mourn;
Surely *they are* stricken.
For the fields of Heshbon languish,
***And* the vine of Sibmah;**
The lords of the nations have broken down its choice plants,
Which have reached to Jazer
And wandered through the wilderness.
Her branches are stretched out,
They are gone over the sea.

a. **We have heard of the pride of Moab**: Here is the only place where the sin of Moab is detailed. It is significant that Moab's sin was **pride** because they were a fairly small and insignificant nation. We can easily understand how the great empires of Babylon or Assyria might fall through pride. The seemingly small can be just as consumed with pride as the great.

i. "Like Assyria and Babylon, Moab was extremely proud. Isaiah piled term upon term to show that the nation's relative insignificance did not make it immune to pride." (Wolf)

ii. This applies to our lives. We are often slow to see pride in what we think of as small things. It is not only the great and famous of this world who are in danger of pride.

b. **The pride of Moab**: This **pride** is also referred to in the prophecy of judgment found in Jeremiah 48:1-13. God would judge the proud nation, so that **Moab shall wail for Moab**. The Moabites took great pride in their vineyards, but God used the **lords of the nations** to break them down and to destroy everything Moab took pride in.

i. "Even though Moab had been advised to seek help from Zion's King, the seer foresaw at the same time the futility of this advice on account of Moab's pride. Whenever pride is not broken by humility, it will have to be broken by justice." (Bultema)

2. (9-12) Isaiah's sorrow of heart for Moab.

Therefore I will bewail the vine of Sibmah,
With the weeping of Jazer;
I will drench you with my tears,
O Heshbon and Elealeh;
For battle cries have fallen
Over your summer fruits and your harvest.
Gladness is taken away,
And joy from the plentiful field;
In the vineyards there will be no singing,

Nor will there be shouting;
No treaders will tread out wine in the presses;
I have made their shouting cease.
Therefore my heart shall resound like a harp for Moab,
And my inner being for Kir Heres.
And it shall come to pass,
When it is seen that Moab is weary on the high place,
That he will come to his sanctuary to pray;
But he will not prevail.

a. **I will bewail the vine of Sibmah…I will drench you with my tears**: As Isaiah prophesied of the judgment coming upon Moab, he wasn't happy. He was not pleased that judgment was coming upon a rival nation. As far as he was concerned, **Gladness is taken away, and joy from the plentiful field**. In fact, Isaiah would not even let others be happy at a time like this: **I have made their shouting cease**. He hurts so badly for Moab that he says, **"my heart shall resound like a harp for Moab."**

b. **When it is seen that Moab is weary on the high place, that he will come to his sanctuary and pray; but he will not prevail**: At the same time, Isaiah knew that Moab looked in the wrong places for answers. The prophet knew the pain of seeing calamity come and watching people turn to the *wrong* places in the midst of the destruction.

i. This was the same attitude Jesus had when He wept for Jerusalem: *O Jerusalem, Jerusalem, the one who kills the prophets and stones those who are sent to her! How often I wanted to gather your children together, as a hen gathers her chicks under her wings, but you were not willing! See! Your house is left to you desolate; for I say to you, you shall see Me no more till you say, "Blessed is He who comes in the name of the Lord!"* (Matthew 23:37-39) When Jesus saw the desolation to come upon the city that rejected Him, He did not rejoice. Jesus also knew that in the midst of their calamity, they would turn to themselves instead of the Lord.

3. (13-14) Three years until judgment comes on Moab.

This *is* the word which the Lord has spoken concerning Moab since that time. But now the Lord has spoken, saying, "Within three years, as the years of a hired man, the glory of Moab will be despised with all that great multitude, and the remnant *will be* very small *and* feeble."

a. **Within three years**: Isaiah, speaking for the Lord, announced that judgment would come upon Moab in this time period. The judgment will humble Moab: **The glory of Moab will be despised**.

b. **Within three years**: Since we don't know the exact date of Isaiah's prophecy, it is impossible to independently verify the accuracy of the **within three years** prediction. But in the phrasing **this is the word which the LORD has spoken concerning Moab since that time**, we gather that most of Isaiah 15-16 was given at an earlier time, and the **within three years** aspect was added at the right time, at a later date.

i. "Apparently King Sargon of Assyria conducted a major operation against the Arabians in 715 B.C., and he may have devastated Moab en route to encountering those tribes." (Wolf)

ii. We see this applies in at least three ways.

- In this prophecy, God announced the time frame for His judgment to be a *warning* to Moab and an invitation for their humble repentance (it wasn't unthinkable that this prophecy would get to the Moabites somehow).
- This prophecy was a *lesson* for God's people on how the LORD judges the proud.
- This prophecy *assured* God's people that the LORD would deal with other more wicked nations as He also dealt with Israel.

Isaiah 17 – The Burden Against Syria and Israel

A. A prophecy of doom upon Syria and Israel.

1. (1-6) The LORD speaks to Damascus and Ephraim.

The burden against Damascus.
"Behold, Damascus will cease from *being* a city,
And it will be a ruinous heap.
The cities of Aroer *are* forsaken;
They will be for flocks
Which lie down, and no one will make *them* afraid.
The fortress also will cease from Ephraim,
The kingdom from Damascus,
And the remnant of Syria;
They will be as the glory of the children of Israel,"
Says the LORD of hosts.
"In that day it shall come to pass
***That* the glory of Jacob will wane,**
And the fatness of his flesh grow lean.
It shall be as when the harvester gathers the grain,
And reaps the heads with his arm;
It shall be as he who gathers heads of grain
In the Valley of Rephaim.
Yet gleaning grapes will be left in it,
Like the shaking of an olive tree,
Two *or* three olives at the top of the uppermost bough,
Four *or* five in its most fruitful branches,"
Says the LORD God of Israel.

a. **Damascus**: This was one of the great cities of the ancient world and the capital of the ancient nation of Syria. Syria is positioned to the immediate north-east of Israel, and the northern tribes, around the Sea of Galilee, had constant contact and interaction with Syria.

b. **Behold, Damascus will cease from being a city, and it will be a ruinous heap**: Damascus was one of the most beautiful cities of the ancient world, but the coming Assyrian judgment would reduce it to a heap of ruins.

c. **The fortress will also cease from Ephraim**: As is often the case, the northern kingdom of Israel is referred to by its dominant tribe, **Ephraim**. At this time, Israel and Syria were closely aligned against Judah. Since they were such close friends, God announced His judgment against **Ephraim**, against Israel, at the same time He spoke to Syria. 2 Kings 15:29 and 16:9 describe the fulfillment of this prophecy.

i. Israel's modern interaction with Syria is interesting, and a potential hotspot for future conflict. When Syria occupied the Golan Heights, a strategically crucial high plateau above the whole region of Galilee, Israel was under constant threat of invasion and shelling from Syrian placements on the Golan. But when Syria eventually made a full-on invasion of Israel from the Golan, Israel miraculously beat them back and captured the Golan Heights. Since then, Syria has often insisted that this strategically crucial region is theirs and must be given back. The Israelis are adamant that they will never give back land that belongs to them and is necessary for their security. In the meantime, Syria has often fought Israel through terrorism and their support of militia groups in Lebanon. The dream of a "Greater Syria," encompassing Syria, Lebanon, and parts of northern Israel is a powerful influence in the Syrian leadership.

2. (7-9) The humble response to the judgment of the Lord.

In that day a man will look to his Maker,
And his eyes will have respect for the Holy One of Israel.
He will not look to the altars,
The work of his hands;
He will not respect what his fingers have made,
Nor the wooden images nor the incense altars.
In that day his strong cities will be as a forsaken bough
And an uppermost branch,
Which they left because of the children of Israel;
And there will be desolation.

a. **In that day a man will look to his Maker, and his eyes will have respect for the Holy One of Israel**: In the midst of such severe judgment, some will respond as they should, with humble **respect** for God.

b. **He will not look to the altars, the work of his hands**: One of God's purposes in judgment is to turn our focus away from our idols and the things we have trusted in instead of Him. This speaks of this purpose being fulfilled.

c. **His strong cities will be as a forsaken bough**: In judgment, God would strip away from Israel every wrong thing they might have trusted in – pagan **altars**, **wooden images**, **incense altars**, and even their **strong cities** would give no protection. Their only hope was in the LORD.

i. "When the Israelites came into the land of Canaan many years before, the strong cities of the land were abandoned to them.... However, the situation has changed, and the same cities will be abandoned by the Israelites themselves as they are under the judging hand of God." (Grogan)

3. (10-11) God's judgment will bring man's work to nothing.

Because you have forgotten the God of your salvation,
And have not been mindful of the Rock of your stronghold,
Therefore you will plant pleasant plants
And set out foreign seedlings;
In the day you will make your plant to grow,
And in the morning you will make your seed to flourish;
***But* the harvest *will be* a heap of ruins**
In the day of grief and desperate sorrow.

a. **You will plant pleasant plants…you will make your seed to flourish; but the harvest will be a heap of ruins**. One aspect of the LORD's judgment against Israel will be to bring their hard work to nothing. They will work hard to plant and grow crops (both literally and figuratively), but **the harvest will be a heap of ruins.**

i. This can be one of the most devastating aspects of the LORD's judgment. Haggai 1:6 speaks of this work of the LORD: *You have sown much, and bring in little; you eat, but do not have enough; you drink, but you are not filled with drink; you clothe yourselves, but no one is warm; and he who earns wages, earns wages to put into a bag with holes.* How much better it is to be listening to Jesus and to have our service directed and blessed by Him (Luke 5:1-10).

b. **Because you have forgotten the God of your salvation**: This was why the LORD brought this judgment on Israel. In one way, this does not seem like a "great" sin. After all, why does God need us to remember Him? Why can't we just leave Him alone, and He leave us alone? It is a sin to forget **the God of your salvation** because He created you, and because He is **the God of your salvation**. If you forget Him, you can forget about your salvation.

i. Satan does not need to make us bank robbers or murderers to destroy us. It is quite enough to simply make us *forget*. We can forget because of sleepiness, we can forget because of a lack of attention, we can forget because we are distracted. Satan doesn't care much about how he does it, but he does want us to forget the God of our salvation.

ii. "We are thus reminded that we ought not to be so impatient in enduring chastisements, which cure us of the fearfully dangerous disease of apostasy." (Calvin)

B. God will destroy the nation that brings doom upon Syria and Israel.

1. (12-13a) The rush of the nations against Syria and Israel.

Woe to the multitude of many people
***Who* make a noise like the roar of the seas,**
And to the rushing of nations
***That* make a rushing like the rushing of mighty waters!**
The nations will rush like the rushing of many waters.

a. **The nations will rush like the rushing of many waters**: God will use other nations to bring judgment against Syria and Israel. They will come against them like a flash flood that can't be stopped.

2. (13b-14) God's judgment against the nations that rush against Israel.

But *God* will rebuke them and they will flee far away,
And be chased like the chaff of the mountains before the wind,
Like a rolling thing before the whirlwind.
Then behold, at eventide, trouble!
***And* before the morning, he *is* no more.**
This *is* the portion of those who plunder us,
And the lot of those who rob us.

a. **God will rebuke them**: When God brings the rush of nations against Israel, it doesn't mean that the nations He uses to judge will be walking right with Him and exempt from judgment. Instead, **God will rebuke them and they will flee far away**. God can use one sinner to judge another, and then judge the sinner He just used.

b. **This is the portion of those who plunder us**: This is a comforting principle: Even in the midst of judgment, God shows mercy. As bad as it was going to be for Israel, it could have been worse. Instead, God would allow it for a time, then He would **rebuke** those attacking Israel. Israel was not at the mercy of circumstances or their enemies; they were at the mercy of God.

Isaiah 18 – Concerning Ethiopia

"To us, this brief chapter is the most difficult one of all the sixty-six chapters of Isaiah" (Bultema). "Although the prophecy is a short one, it probably ranks as the most obscure chapter in this entire section" (Wolf). "This is one of the most obscure prophecies in the whole Book of Isaiah" (Clarke).

A. No need to make an alliance with Ethiopia.

1. (1-2) A word directed to Ethiopia.

Woe to the land shadowed with buzzing wings,
Which *is* beyond the rivers of Ethiopia,
Which sends ambassadors by sea,
Even in vessels of reed on the waters, *saying,*
"Go, swift messengers, to a nation tall and smooth *of skin,*
To a people terrible from their beginning onward,
A nation powerful and treading down,
Whose land the rivers divide."

a. **Which is beyond the rivers of Ethiopia**: In the days of Isaiah, Ethiopia was a major world power, ruling Egypt and a chief rival to Assyria. Since Judah was caught in the middle of this conflict, it might make sense for Judah to align herself with Ethiopia against Assyria.

i. "In 715 B.C. an Ethiopian named Shabako gained control of Egypt as founder of the twenty-fifth dynasty. Ethiopian domination continued until 633 B.C. when a native Egyptian regained the throne." (Wolf)

ii. "The term designates a much larger area than present-day Ethiopia – an area including the Sudan and Somalia." (Grogan)

b. **Shadowed with buzzing wings**: The Nile Valley is famous for its many whirring insects.

c. **Which sends ambassadors by sea**: The scene pictures Ethiopian ambassadors who come to make an alliance with Judah and the other nations of the region against Assyria.

d. **Go, swift messengers, to a nation tall and smooth of skin**: As the Ethiopian ambassadors invite Judah to rebel against the Assyrians, they ask Judah to send **swift messengers** back to Ethiopia (**to a nation tall and smooth of skin…a nation powerful**), and the Ethiopians would hope to hear that Judah has rebelled against Assyria and aligned itself with Ethiopia and Egypt.

2. (3-6) The Lord rejects the offer of help from the Ethiopians.

All inhabitants of the world and dwellers on the earth:
When he lifts up a banner on the mountains, you see *it*;
And when he blows a trumpet, you hear *it*.
For so the Lord said to me,
"I will take My rest,
And I will look from My dwelling place
Like clear heat in sunshine,
Like a cloud of dew in the heat of harvest."
For before the harvest, when the bud is perfect
And the sour grape is ripening in the flower,
He will both cut off the sprigs with pruning hooks
And take away *and* cut down the branches.
They will be left together for the mountain birds of prey
And for the beasts of the earth;
The birds of prey will summer on them,
And all the beasts of the earth will winter on them.

a. **The Lord said to me, "I will take My rest"**: The Lord God rejected the alliance with Ethiopia because He was more than able to deal with the Assyrians Himself. He could *take His rest* without the help of the Ethiopians. If God had wanted to muster an army against Assyria, He would have raised a banner or sounded a trumpet. God was fully able to do it and would do it when the time was right.

i. Significantly, there is no rebuke or judgment against Ethiopia announced in this chapter. It wasn't as if God was going to judge Ethiopia for their offer of an alliance. Perhaps the idea is that it is a well-intentioned but unnecessary offer. Instead, Judah was to trust in the Lord.

b. **He will both cut off the sprigs with pruning hooks and take away and cut down the branches**: God can "prune" Assyria all by Himself. He will destroy the Assyrian army so completely that **they will be left together for the mountain birds of prey**.

B. Ethiopians come and worship God.

1. (7) The Ethiopians come to Mount Zion.

In that time a present will be brought to the LORD of hosts
From a people tall and smooth *of skin*,
And from a people terrible from their beginning onward,
A nation powerful and treading down,
Whose land the rivers divide—
To the place of the name of the LORD of hosts,
To Mount Zion.

a. **A present will be brought to the LORD of hosts**: Isaiah announces a day when Ethiopians will come and worship the LORD and bring gifts to Him **to the place of the name of the LORD of hosts, to Mount Zion**.

b. **To the place of the name of the LORD**: Instead of Israelite messengers bringing news to Ethiopia of an alliance against the Assyrians, the day will come when Ethiopians will come and worship at **Mount Zion**.

i. This may have been fulfilled in some way close to Isaiah's time. But we know it was fulfilled in Acts 8:26-40, when an Ethiopian came to worship the LORD at Jerusalem, and then trusted in Jesus at the preaching of Philip. It was also fulfilled in the strong Ethiopian church of the first few centuries, and the enduring Ethiopian church today.

Isaiah 19 – The Burden Against Egypt

A. God strikes Egypt.

1. (1-4) The LORD strikes Egypt by giving them over to civil war and submission to a cruel master.

The burden against Egypt.
Behold, the LORD rides on a swift cloud,
And will come into Egypt;
The idols of Egypt will totter at His presence,
And the heart of Egypt will melt in its midst.
"I will set Egyptians against Egyptians;
Everyone will fight against his brother,
And everyone against his neighbor,
City against city, kingdom against kingdom.
The spirit of Egypt will fail in its midst;
I will destroy their counsel,
And they will consult the idols and the charmers,
The mediums and the sorcerers.
And the Egyptians I will give
Into the hand of a cruel master,
And a fierce king will rule over them,"
Says the Lord, the LORD of hosts.

a. **The LORD rides on a swift cloud, and will come into Egypt**: Egypt was one of the great powers of the ancient world, and being situated immediately to the south of Israel, it was an empire that Israel constantly had to reckon with. Many times, Egypt had been the enemy of Israel, at times Egypt had been a refuge for Israel, and sometimes Egypt offered a tempting but ungodly alliance to Israel. In this chapter, the LORD presents both a prophecy *against* and *for* Egypt.

b. **The idols of Egypt will totter at His presence**: Egypt was known for its worship of many, many different gods. Through His hand of judgment, the LORD will "knock over" these many different gods.

i. "In Isaiah's day there was no other nation on earth that was so much in the grip of superstition and filthy idolatry as Egypt. Apes, cats, frogs, crocodiles, lizards – everything was venerated by them." (Bultema)

ii. At the time of the Exodus, when the Pharaoh of Egypt would not release the children of Israel from their captivity, the LORD also made **the idols of Egypt** to **totter at His presence**. He directed each of the plagues against a particular idol of Egypt.

- The LORD knocked down the god *Khnum*, the guardian of the Nile, the god *Hapi*, the spirit of the Nile, and the god *Osiris* (who had the Nile as his bloodstream) when the waters were turned to blood.
- The LORD knocked down the goddess *Heqt*, the frog-goddess of fertility, with the plague of frogs.
- The LORD knocked down the goddess *Hathor*, a cow-like mother goddess, with the plague on livestock.
- The LORD knocked down the god *Imhotep*, the god of medicine, with the plague of boils.
- The LORD knocked down the god *Nut*, the sky goddess, with the plague of hail.
- The LORD knocked down the whole system of Egyptian worship of their gods with loathsome lice and swarms of insects.
- The LORD knocked down the god *Seth*, thought to be the protector of crops, with the plague of locusts.
- The LORD knocked down the god *Ra*, thought to be the sun god, with the plague of darkness.
- The LORD knocked down *Osiris*, the Egyptian god thought to be the giver of life, and the supposed deity of Pharaoh himself, with the plague against the firstborn.

iii. In the days of the Exodus, God made all **the idols of Egypt** to **totter at His presence**. Here, Isaiah tells us the LORD will do it again.

c. **I will set Egyptians against Egyptians**: Isaiah prophesies a coming civil war in Egypt, which was indirectly the hand of God's judgment against them.

i. "Not many years after this time it was divided into twelve several kingdoms, between whom there were many and cruel wars, as is related by the historians of those times." (Poole)

d. **I will destroy their counsel, and they will consult the idols and the charmers**: When a nation is under the judgment of God, He often seems to "remove" sound **counsel** and wisdom from their leaders, and they turn to vain, pagan things for wisdom instead (**idols and the charmers**).

i. "Egypt was renowned for her class of wise men (1 Kings 4:30), but they would not be able to cope with this judgment from the Lord." (Wolf)

e. **The Egyptians I will give into the hand of a cruel master, and a fierce king will rule over them**: God may judge a nation through their leadership in two ways. First, by removing competent leadership (**I will destroy their counsel**). Second, by giving them **cruel** and oppressive rulers. This is a curse and a judgment to any people.

2. (5-10) The Lord strikes Egypt by drying up the Nile, thus wrecking their economy.

The waters will fail from the sea,
And the river will be wasted and dried up.
The rivers will turn foul;
The brooks of defense will be emptied and dried up;
The reeds and rushes will wither.
The papyrus reeds by the River, by the mouth of the River,
And everything sown by the River,
Will wither, be driven away, and be no more.
The fishermen also will mourn;
All those will lament who cast hooks into the River,
And they will languish who spread nets on the waters.
Moreover those who work in fine flax
And those who weave fine fabric will be ashamed;
And its foundations will be broken.
All who make wages *will be* troubled of soul.

a. **The river will be wasted and dried up**: The Nile River was the key to Egypt's agriculture and economy. For it to suffer a severe drought or lowering would have a devastating effect on the lives of Egyptians. God promises this will happen as a judgment against Egypt.

b. **The rivers will turn foul**: Because of this ecological disaster, the workers of Egypt would cry out. **The fishermen also will mourn…they will**

languish who spread nets on the waters.... those who weave fine fabric will be ashamed.... all who make wages will be troubled of soul.

3. (11-15) The LORD strikes Egypt by sending them with foolish counsel.

Surely the princes of Zoan *are* fools;
Pharaoh's wise counselors give foolish counsel.
How do you say to Pharaoh, "I *am* the son of the wise,
The son of ancient kings?"
Where *are* they?
Where are your wise men?
Let them tell you now,
And let them know what the LORD of hosts has purposed against Egypt.
The princes of Zoan have become fools;
The princes of Noph are deceived;
They have also deluded Egypt,
***Those who are* the mainstay of its tribes.**
The LORD has mingled a perverse spirit in her midst;
And they have caused Egypt to err in all her work,
As a drunken man staggers in his vomit.
Neither will there be *any* work for Egypt,
Which the head or tail,
Palm branch or bulrush, may do.

a. **Surely the princes of Zoan are fools; Pharaoh's wise counselors give foolish counsel**: As the LORD strikes Egypt, not only does He give them cruel rulers, but He also gives those cruel rulers **foolish counsel**.

b. **Where are your wise men? Let them tell you now, and let them know what the LORD of hosts has purposed against Egypt**: Here, the LORD reminds us of what true wisdom is. It is knowing **what the LORD of hosts has purposed**. True wisdom isn't knowing all kinds of facts and plans and strategies. *The fear of the LORD is the beginning of wisdom, and the knowledge of the Holy One is understanding.* (Proverbs 9:10).

4. (16-17) When God strikes Egypt, there will be terror among the people.

In that day Egypt will be like women, and will be afraid and fear because of the waving of the hand of the LORD of hosts, which He waves over it. And the land of Judah will be a terror to Egypt; everyone who makes mention of it will be afraid in himself, because of the counsel of the LORD of hosts which He has determined against it.

a. **Because of the waving of the hand of the LORD of hosts**: All the LORD will need to do is to wave His hand, and the people of Egypt will respond in terror, they will **be afraid and fear**.

b. **The land of Judah will be a terror to Egypt**: This is a dramatic change. For thousands of years, the **land of Judah** lay submissively in the shadow of the great Egyptian Empire. The LORD prophesies a day when Judah will be mightier than Egypt, and **the land of Judah will be a terror to Egypt**.

B. God saves Egypt

1. (18-22) Egypt turns to the LORD.

In that day five cities in the land of Egypt will speak the language of Canaan and swear by the LORD of hosts; one will be called the City of Destruction. In that day there will be an altar to the LORD in the midst of the land of Egypt, and a pillar to the LORD at its border. And it will be for a sign and for a witness to the LORD of hosts in the land of Egypt; for they will cry to the LORD because of the oppressors, and He will send them a Savior and a Mighty One, and He will deliver them. Then the LORD will be known to Egypt, and the Egyptians will know the LORD in that day, and will make sacrifice and offering; yes, they will make a vow to the LORD and perform *it*. And the LORD will strike Egypt, He will strike and heal *it;* they will return to the LORD, and He will be entreated by them and heal them.

a. **Five cities in the land of Egypt** will become more identified with the LORD than with Egypt. A better translation of the phrase **City of Destruction** may be, *City of the Sun*, which was a well-known Egyptian city known as *Heliopolis*.

b. **Egypt will speak the language of Canaan**: This prophecy announces a day when Egypt will worship the LORD, with **an altar to the LORD**, and will memorialize God's great works with **a pillar to the LORD**. When Egypt is brought under this oppression, they will **cry to the LORD because of the oppressors**, and then **He will send them a Savior and a Mighty One, and He will deliver them**.

i. "In the time of the Maccabees, the high priest Onias IV was forced to flee to Egypt, and there he built a temple that was similar to the one in Jerusalem. Some commentators relate the 'altar' of verse 19 to this structure." (Wolf) This may relate to the *City of the Sun* prophecy because the temple Onias IV built was in the province of Heliopolis.

ii. **He will send them a Savior and a Mighty One**: "The text says the Saviour is a great one. Oh! I wanted a great Saviour. A little

Saviour would not have answered my turn, for great sin wanted a great atonement, and my hard heart wanted great grace to soften it down." (Spurgeon)

c. **The Egyptians will know the LORD in that day**: There did come to be a widespread knowledge of the LORD in Egypt. In the days of Jesus, more than a million Jews lived in Egypt. In the early days of Christianity, there was a strong, vital church in Egypt for more than 600 years.

i. This prophecy may have additional fulfillment during the Millennium, but it certainly has been fulfilled in history. In the fourth century, the great theologian Athanasius, wrote this from Egypt: "The thing is happening before our very eyes, here in Egypt; and thereby another prophecy is fulfilled, for at no other time have the Egyptians ceased from their false worship save when the Lord of all, riding as on a cloud, came down here in the body and brought the error of idols to nothing and won over everybody to Himself and through Himself to the Father." (From *On the Incarnation*, cited by Grogan)

ii. The altar and sacrifice described most likely are fulfilled during the Millennium, when sacrifice will be allowed as a memorial of Jesus' great work, but never as atonement. "For just as restored Israel will bring blood sacrifices unto the Lord to keep in remembrance of the all-sufficient blood sacrifice of Christ, so this may also take place in Egypt on that memorable day." (Bultema)

d. **He will strike and heal it**: Whatever judgment God allowed, His desire was that people would repent and return to Him so they could be healed.

2. (23-25) An amazing peace between three formerly hostile enemies.

In that day there will be a highway from Egypt to Assyria, and the Assyrian will come into Egypt and the Egyptian into Assyria, and the Egyptians will serve with the Assyrians. In that day Israel will be one of three with Egypt and Assyria—a blessing in the midst of the land, whom the LORD of hosts shall bless, saying, "Blessed *is* Egypt My people, and Assyria the work of My hands, and Israel My inheritance."

a. **Israel will be one of three with Egypt and Assyria**: God promises the day will come when there will be peace between Israel, Egypt, and Assyria. There will be trade and travel between the three nations (**a highway from Egypt to Assyria**). In that day, the LORD will bless all three nations.

b. **Blessed is Egypt My people, and Assyria, the work of My hands, and Israel is My inheritance**: What an amazing work of redemption! This shows that God's salvation will extend to the nations, and He will call forth His own even from **Egypt** and **Assyria**, not only from **Israel**.

i. It was powerful to say this of Egypt; it was almost unbelievable to say it about Assyria, the nation Jonah hated so much. "In Isaiah's day, Assyria was the one power feared by every little nation in the Fertile Crescent. The calculated brutality of the Assyrians probably made them more of an object of general hatred than any other nation of antiquity. The Egyptians, Babylonians, and Persians were all capable of inhuman acts, but the Assyrian record for callous cruelty is difficult to parallel." (Grogan)

ii. "Who, standing amid the terrors of the plagues, could ever have supposed that Egypt would be addressed as 'my people'? Who could have thought that Assyria, the tyrant persecutor, would ever be called 'the work of my hands'? Yet these are the trophies and triumphs of divine grace." (Meyer)

iii. "But Israel is always his inheritance. There he finds rest and home, for the Lord's portion is his people. Oh to know the riches of the glory of his inheritance in the saints!" (Meyer) We are also the Lord's inheritance; in Ephesians 1:18, Paul prayed *that you may know what is the hope of His calling, what are the riches of the glory of His inheritance in the saints*. God's people are *His* riches and inheritance and glory.

c. **Blessed is Egypt My people**: From this passage regarding the conversion of Egypt, Spurgeon drew the following points (from his sermon, *The Fruits of Grace*).

- God's grace often comes to the very worst of men.
- God's grace sends a Savior.
- Grace changes men's language.
- God's grace sets men on holy service.
- God's grace teaches men to pray.
- God's grace instructs men.
- Grace makes even trouble a blessing to a man.
- God's grace changes the relations of men to each other.
- God's grace makes men to be blessed, and to be a blessing to others.

Isaiah 20 – Don't Trust in Egypt

A. Isaiah acts out a sign.

1. (1) The political setting for the sign.

In the year that Tartan came to Ashdod, when Sargon the king of Assyria sent him, and he fought against Ashdod and took it,

a. **In the year that Tartan came to Ashdod**: This describes the time when the army of Assyria conquered the Philistine city of **Ashdod**. Isaiah's sign was a response to this victory of Assyria.

i. This invasion has a concrete marking point in secular history: 711 B.C.

b. **He fought against Ashdod and took it**: The Philistines were both neighbors and thorns to Israel, and the fall of **Ashdod** would certainly make Judah think, "We're next. We need protection."

2. (2) The LORD gives Isaiah a sign to act out.

At the same time the LORD spoke by Isaiah the son of Amoz, saying, "Go, and remove the sackcloth from your body, and take your sandals off your feet." And he did so, walking naked and barefoot.

a. **Remove the sackcloth from your body, and take your sandals off your feet**: Before this, Isaiah wore an outer garment of **sackcloth** – clothes of mourning. Now, God tells him to remove his outer garment of **sackcloth** and to take his **sandals off**.

i. "God would sometimes have his prophets to add to their word a visible sign, to awaken people's minds to a more serious consideration of the matters proposed to them." (Poole)

b. **And he did so, walking naked and barefoot**: We shouldn't think that Isaiah was nude, completely without clothing. Instead, he only wore the inner garment customary in that day – sort of like wearing only your underwear or a nightshirt. The message wasn't *nudity*, it was complete *poverty* and *humiliation.* Isaiah dressed as the poorest and most destitute would dress.

i. "One need not imagine that Isaiah walked around stripped for the entire three years or that Ezekiel lay on his side for 390 days without getting up (Ezekiel 4:9). Perhaps part of each day was used for those designated purposes." (Wolf)

ii. "Not stark naked, but stripped as a prisoner, his mantle or upper garment cast off." (Trapp)

iii. "Other prophets were asked to go through equally difficult experiences as signs to Israel. Hosea endured a trying marriage, and Ezekiel's wife died as an illustration for the nation (Ezekiel 24:16-24)." (Wolf)

B. The meaning of the sign.

1. (3-4) The sign announces the judgment and humiliation of Egypt.

Then the LORD said, "Just as My servant Isaiah has walked naked and barefoot three years *for* a sign and a wonder against Egypt and Ethiopia, so shall the king of Assyria lead away the Egyptians as prisoners and the Ethiopians as captives, young and old, naked and barefoot, with their buttocks uncovered, to the shame of Egypt."

a. **My servant Isaiah has walked naked and barefoot three years for a sign and wonder against Egypt**: Under the command of the LORD, Isaiah dressed in this poor and humble way for three years. It was a message **against Egypt** because **the king of Assyria** would **lead away the Egyptians as prisoners**.

b. **To the shame of Egypt**: As the Assyrians took the Egyptians captive, they would humiliate them by stripping them and leading them away as prisoners. This would all be **to the shame of Egypt**.

i. "So dealeth the devil with all his wretched captives, whom he driveth away hellward, naked and barefoot with their buttocks uncovered, the shame of their nakedness exposed to public view for want of the white raiment of Christ's righteousness that they might be clothed." (Trapp)

2. (5-6) The sign's message to Judah.

"Then they shall be afraid and ashamed of Ethiopia their expectation and Egypt their glory. And the inhabitant of this territory will say in that day, 'Surely such *is* our expectation, wherever we flee for help to be delivered from the king of Assyria; and how shall we escape?'"

a. **They shall be afraid and ashamed of Ethiopia their expectation and Egypt their glory**: When God judges Ethiopia and Egypt, it will be evident how foolish it was for Judah to look to them for protection against Assyria.

i. Whenever our **expectation** is in something wrong, or our **glory** is in something wrong, the LORD will find a way to make those things disappoint us. Judah set their **expectation** on Ethiopia, and looked to Egypt for **glory**, but now they are left **afraid and ashamed**.

ii. "There is no place of security for the people of God, other than that to be found in the rule of God. All expectation not centred in God, is doomed to disappointment and discomfiture." (Morgan)

b. **How shall we escape?** The LORD allowed Judah to be backed into a corner, caught between two mighty Empires (Egypt and Assyria), without being able to trust either one. There was no **escape** – except in the LORD.

i. Because of the glorious promise of revival and restoration among Egypt in Isaiah 19, Judah might have been even more tempted to say, "Well, we can trust in Egypt. They are all going to come to the LORD someday anyway!" But with the dramatic three-year sign, Isaiah shows Judah how vain it was to make Egypt their **expectation** or **glory**.

Isaiah 21 – Burdens Against Babylon, Edom and Arabia

A. The burden against Babylon.

1. (1-2) An army from Persia marches on Babylon.

The burden against the Wilderness of the Sea.
As whirlwinds in the South pass through,
***So* it comes from the desert, from a terrible land.**
A distressing vision is declared to me;
The treacherous dealer deals treacherously,
And the plunderer plunders.
Go up, O Elam!
Besiege, O Media!
All its sighing I have made to cease.

a. **The burden against the Wilderness of the Sea**: Babylon is called the **Wilderness of the Sea** because the great plain of Babylon was divided with lakes and marshes, so it was referred to as a "sea."

i. "And the title of *the sea* might well be given to the waters of Babylon, because of the great plenty and multitude of them...the name of *sea* being given by the Hebrews to every great collection of waters." (Poole)

b. **Go up, O Elam! Besiege, O Media**: **Elam** and **Media** are the ancient names for the peoples of Persia, modern day Iran. The Persian Empire conquered the Babylonian Empire, and Isaiah here prophetically sees their armies marching on Babylon.

i. "God oft maketh use of one tyrant to punish another; as here he stirreth up the Persians to plunder and waste the Babylonians. So the Persians were afterwards in like sort punished by the Macedonians, the Macedonians by the Romans, those Romans by the Huns, Vandals,

Lombards, Saracens, Turks; all whom Christ shall destroy at his last coming." (Trapp)

2. (3-10) The fall of Babylon.

Therefore my loins are filled with pain;
Pangs have taken hold of me, like the pangs of a woman in labor.
I was distressed when *I* heard *it*;
I was dismayed when *I* saw *it*.
My heart wavered, fearfulness frightened me;
The night for which I longed He turned into fear for me.
Prepare the table,
Set a watchman in the tower,
Eat and drink.
Arise, you princes,
Anoint the shield!
For thus has the Lord said to me:
"Go, set a watchman,
Let him declare what he sees."
And he saw a chariot *with* a pair of horsemen,
A chariot of donkeys, *and* a chariot of camels,
And he listened earnestly with great care.
Then he cried, "A lion, my Lord!
I stand continually on the watchtower in the daytime;
I have sat at my post every night.
And look, here comes a chariot of men with a pair of horsemen!"
Then he answered and said,
"Babylon is fallen, is fallen!
And all the carved images of her gods
He has broken to the ground."
Oh, my threshing and the grain of my floor!
That which I have heard from the LORD of hosts,
The God of Israel,
I have declared to you.

a. **Pangs have taken hold of me, like the pangs of a woman in labor**: As the people collapse from fear and pain, the nation prepares for war (**Arise, you princes, anoint the shield!**).

i. "Nothing is more hopeless and crestfallen than a wicked man in distress: for why? his life and hopes end together." (Trapp)

b. **Babylon is fallen, is fallen**: This report came to the watchman. This dramatic scene was fulfilled when the Medo-Persian Empire conquered Babylon, but it also has a prophetic application. Revelation 18:2 describes the cry of an angel when God judges the world system, both *commercial* Babylon and *spiritual* Babylon: *And he cried mightily with a loud voice, saying, "Babylon the great is fallen, is fallen, and has become a dwelling place of demons, a prison for every foul spirit, and a cage for every unclean and hated bird!"* The repetition of the phrase **is fallen, is fallen** connects the two passages.

i. The same panic and terror the people of Babylon felt when that great city was conquered by the Medes and Persians will be seen again. When the LORD strikes the world system, both *spiritual Babylon* and *commercial Babylon*, the world will be terrified and mourn the same way (Revelation 18:9-19). But God's people rejoice over the fall of Babylon (Revelation 18:20).

B. Burdens against Edom and Arabia.

1. (11-12) The burden against Edom (**Dumah**).

The burden against Dumah.
He calls to me out of Seir,
"Watchman, what of the night?
Watchman, what of the night?"
The watchman said,
"The morning comes, and also the night.
If you will inquire, inquire;
Return! Come back!"

a. **The burden against Dumah**: This was another ancient name for the kingdom of *Edom,* in the mountainous region of **Seir**. The Edomites descended from Esau, the brother of Jacob (Israel). They settled in the land to the south-east of Israel and were the sometimes enemies of Israel.

b. **He calls to me out of Seir**: This is a vague, mysterious **burden against Dumah**. It may speak to the confusion and darkness striking Edom at the time of their judgment. Bultema wrote of these verses, "This brief burden has always been a great burden to expositors!"

c. **Watchman, what of the night?** Using a powerful dramatic scene of a cry to a watchman in the night, Isaiah paints the picture of the judgment and terror that will come upon Edom.

i. On the burden against Edom: "What he may be saying is that the long night of Assyrian oppression is almost over, and the night of Babylonian rule would follow a brief 'morning' of respite." (Wolf)

2. (13-17) The burden against Arabia.

The burden against Arabia.
In the forest in Arabia you will lodge,
O you traveling companies of Dedanites.
O inhabitants of the land of Tema,
Bring water to him who is thirsty;
With their bread they met him who fled.
For they fled from the swords, from the drawn sword,
From the bent bow, and from the distress of war.

For thus the LORD has said to me: "Within a year, according to the year of a hired man, all the glory of Kedar will fail; and the remainder of the number of archers, the mighty men of the people of Kedar, will be diminished; for the LORD God of Israel has spoken *it*."

a. **The burden against Arabia**: Isaiah pictured the refugees from an attack on Arabia. They are **traveling companies of Dedanites**; they are **thirsty**, and they need **bread**, because they **fled from the swords** and from the **bent bow, and from the distress of war**.

b. **Within a year...the glory of Kedar will fail**: Reckoning from Isaiah's time, the attack upon Arabia would come soon, **within a year**.

i. Poole on **according to the year of a hired man**: "An exact year; for hirelings diligently observe and wait for the end of the year, when they are to receive their wages."

Isaiah 22 – Judgment on Jerusalem

A. Isaiah denounces the city of Jerusalem.

1. (1-4) Isaiah is grieved over a joyous city.

The burden against the Valley of Vision.
What ails you now, that you have all gone up to the housetops,
You who are full of noise,
A tumultuous city, a joyous city?
Your slain *men are* not slain with the sword,
Nor dead in battle.
All your rulers have fled together;
They are captured by the archers.
All who are found in you are bound together;
They have fled from afar.
Therefore I said, "Look away from me,
I will weep bitterly;
Do not labor to comfort me
Because of the plundering of the daughter of my people."

a. **The burden against the Valley of Vision**: This is Jerusalem, a city on a hill but surrounded by a still higher hill, and in the midst of three valleys. Since Jerusalem was a center for the worship of God and some of the prophets of God (including Isaiah), it is called **the Valley of Vision**.

i. "It is strange to find a prophecy against Judah and Jerusalem in a section that deals with the nations. But since Judah had chosen to behave like her neighbors and to desert the Lord, she deserved to be judged." (Wolf)

b. **What ails you now, that you have all gone up to the housetops**: The idea is that people have come out of their houses and up to their **housetops** to see the coming calamity.

i. "As they used to do in times of great confusion and consternation, that they might mourn, and look, and cry to Heaven for help." (Poole)

c. **A tumultuous city, a joyous city**: In his prophecy, Isaiah saw the commotion all around Jerusalem, and asked, "Is it the result of an evil tumult, or is it an expression of joy?"

d. **Your slain men are not slain with the sword**: When Jerusalem was conquered by the Babylonians, many of the men of Judah did not bravely die in battle. They died either being starved to death in the siege of the city or as they fled in cowardly retreat.

i. "Either by famine or pestilence in the siege, as many died, Jeremiah 14:18; 38:2, or in their flight, as others were; both which were inglorious kinds of death." (Poole)

e. **I will weep bitterly, do not labor to comfort me**: We usually think of Jeremiah as the "weeping prophet." But Isaiah also said "**I will weep bitterly**" when he saw God's judgment coming against God's people.

2. (5-7) Isaiah sees a coming army, and the LORD brings no deliverance.

For *it is* a day of trouble and treading down and perplexity
By the Lord GOD of hosts
In the Valley of Vision—
Breaking down the walls
And of crying to the mountain.
Elam bore the quiver
With chariots of men *and* horsemen,
And Kir uncovered the shield.
It shall come to pass *that* your choicest valleys
Shall be full of chariots,
And the horsemen shall set themselves in array at the gate.

a. **For it is a day of trouble**: Isaiah saw an army full of arrows and chariots coming against Jerusalem. He prophesied the attack and overthrow of Jerusalem by the Babylonians.

i. **Elam bore the quiver**: "Because Elam, Babylon's neighbor to the east, had strongly supported the Babylonians and the Chaldeans in the struggle against Assyria, the Elamites were probably allies of the Babylonians." (Wolf)

b. **Your choicest valleys shall be full of chariots, and the horsemen shall set themselves in array at the gate**: Attacking armies will once again surround Jerusalem, and in that day the LORD will not deliver them.

3. (8-14) Jerusalem makes all the wrong preparations for a coming battle.

He removed the protection of Judah.
You looked in that day to the armor of the House of the Forest;
You also saw the damage to the city of David,
That it was great;
And you gathered together the waters of the lower pool.
You numbered the houses of Jerusalem,
And the houses you broke down
To fortify the wall.
You also made a reservoir between the two walls
For the water of the old pool.
But you did not look to its Maker,
Nor did you have respect for Him who fashioned it long ago.
And in that day the Lord GOD of hosts
Called for weeping and for mourning,
For baldness and for girding with sackcloth.
But instead, joy and gladness,
Slaying oxen and killing sheep,
Eating meat and drinking wine:
"Let us eat and drink, for tomorrow we die!"
Then it was revealed in my hearing by the LORD of hosts,
"Surely for this iniquity there will be no atonement for you,
Even to your death," says the Lord GOD of hosts.

a. **You gathered together the waters of the lower pool.... to fortify the wall**: When Jerusalem was faced with this subsequent attack, they prepared the city for battle and for siege, strengthening the wall of the city and making sure there was adequate water for a siege.

b. **He removed the protection of Judah**: All their care in defending the city would not matter because God had **removed the protection of Judah**. Instead of their building projects, the best thing Jerusalem could do for her protection was to turn her heart toward the LORD, **but you did not look to its Maker, nor did you have respect for Him who fashioned it long ago**.

c. **In that day the Lord GOD of hosts called for weeping and mourning**: Instead of preparing Jerusalem for an attack, they should have turned their hearts in humble repentance to the LORD. Instead of humbly seeking the LORD, the people of Jerusalem had both confidence in their own preparation (**joy and gladness**), and a fatalistic outlook toward the future (**"Let us eat and drink, for tomorrow we die!"**).

d. **For this iniquity there will be no atonement for you**: What is this sin that can't be forgiven, that has **no atonement**? It is the sin of ignoring God, of refusing to humble yourself before the LORD and repent. Jerusalem was doing everything except the *essential* thing they had to do to prepare for the attack, and because they rejected the LORD, there would be **no atonement for** them.

i. "Our hearts are top-full of harlotry, ready to shift and shark in every by-corner for comfort; to hang their hopes on every hedge, rather than to roll themselves upon God, 'the hope of Israel.'" (Trapp)

B. Isaiah denounces Shebna, the king's chief steward.

1. (15-19) Shebna had a high and honorable office, yet he used it to glorify himself.

Thus says the Lord GOD of hosts:
"Go, proceed to this steward,
To Shebna, who *is* over the house, *and say*:
'What have you here, and whom have you here,
That you have hewn a sepulcher here,
***As* he who hews himself a sepulcher on high,**
Who carves a tomb for himself in a rock?
Indeed, the LORD will throw you away violently,
O mighty man,
And will surely seize you.
He will surely turn violently and toss you like a ball
Into a large country;
There you shall die, and there your glorious chariots
***Shall be* the shame of your master's house.**
So I will drive you out of your office,
And from your position he will pull you down.

a. **Shebna, who is over the house**: Shebna was a servant of King Hezekiah, both a **steward...over the house** and a scribe (2 Kings 18:18, Isaiah 37:2). These were both positions of honor and responsibility. Shebna was one of King Hezekiah's chief assistants.

i. "The king of Judah at this time was Hezekiah – a good king – so the condemnatory judgment fell on the next person in line. Shebna and the populace in general did not share the godly principles of King Hezekiah." (Wolf)

b. **What have you here, and whom have you here**: The LORD spoke to Shebna, that proud man, and essentially said, "Who do you think you are? What do you think you have? You really are nothing and you have nothing."

c. **As he who hews himself a sepulcher on high**: This shows what Shebna did with his position of honor and authority. He made himself a fancy and prestigious tomb. In that day, this was a display of significant power and wealth. In this, Shebna represented all of Jerusalem with his obsessive self-interest.

i. Isaiah had prophesied that the people of Judah and Jerusalem would be carried away into exile, but Shebna didn't believe it. He built this elaborate tomb to himself in Jerusalem, as if to say, "I will never be carried away in exile. I am so certain that I will die here that I will build my tomb here."

d. **He will surely turn violently and toss you like a ball into a large country; there you shall die.... so I will drive you out of your office**: Shebna sought honor and glory but would never find it. Instead, the LORD would make certain that he was never even buried in his prestigious, expensive tomb, but would die in exile instead.

i. Shebna is the same kind of man Jesus spoke about in Luke 12:16-21, in the parable of the rich fool. That man spent his time planning and his money building great things, but in the end, he died without God and it all meant nothing. Now, all of Shebna's accomplishments – the beautiful tomb, the **glorious chariots** – meant worse than nothing; they were a *shame* to him instead.

2. (20-24) The LORD lifts up Eliakim instead of Shebna.

'Then it shall be in that day,
That I will call My servant Eliakim the son of Hilkiah;
I will clothe him with your robe
And strengthen him with your belt;
I will commit your responsibility into his hand.
He shall be a father to the inhabitants of Jerusalem
And to the house of Judah.
The key of the house of David
I will lay on his shoulder;
So he shall open, and no one shall shut;
And he shall shut, and no one shall open.
I will fasten him *as* a peg in a secure place,
And he will become a glorious throne to his father's house.

They will hang on him all the glory of his father's house, the offspring and the posterity, all vessels of small quantity, from the cups to all the pitchers."

a. **Eliakim the son of Hilkiah**: This man is mentioned in passages like 2 Kings 18:18 and Isaiah 36:3 as another assistant to King Hezekiah. He should be distinguished from Eliakim the son of Josiah, who was a puppet king established by Pharaoh (2 Kings 23:34).

b. **My servant**: What a glorious title for Eliakim! Both Shebna and Eliakim were servants of Hezekiah, but Shebna's heart was directed towards selfish ambition and glory, and Eliakim's heart was turned towards the LORD.

c. **Eliakim the son of Hilkiah**: The place of **Eliakim** before Hezekiah is somewhat obscure in the Scriptures; he is only mentioned in six passages, and the only description of him is that he *was over the household* (2 Kings 18:18, 37 and Isaiah 36:3, 22). But Eliakim was famous in heaven! **He shall be a father to the inhabitants of Jerusalem and to the house of Judah**.

d. **I will clothe him with your robe and strengthen him with your belt; I will commit your responsibility into his hand**: The LORD would take the office and authority of the unfaithful Shebna and give it to Eliakim instead. God will get His work done! If a Shebna is unfaithful, the LORD will remove him from his office, strip him of his authority, and give it to another.

e. **The key of the house of David I will lay on his shoulder**: Because Eliakim is the LORD's servant, the LORD will give him great authority. In that day, the chief royal steward would have the large master key of the palace fastened to the shoulder of his tunic. The key was a picture and demonstration of the authority of the chief steward. Here, the LORD gives Eliakim the authority to **open** and **shut** as the LORD's representative, which no man can oppose.

i. In this, Eliakim becomes a prophecy of the Messiah, because Jesus told us this passage spoke of Himself: *These things says He who is holy, He who is true, "He who has the key of David, He who opens and no one shuts, and shuts and no one opens."* (Revelation 3:7) Jesus is the one with the keys of *Hades and of Death* (Revelation 1:18), who has all authority both in heaven and on earth. Jesus delegates this authority as it pleases Him (Matthew 16:19).

f. **He shall open, and no one shall shut; and he shall shut and no one shall open**: Eliakim would have this kind of authority from the LORD. Since he is a picture of Jesus, we know that Jesus has the authority to open and shut doors in our lives as He pleases. We need to accept both the open and the shut doors.

i. "Down a long corridor of closed doors we may sometimes have to pass. It seems heartbreaking to see doors labelled, Friendship, Love, Home shut against us; but beyond them there is the one unclosed door through which we shall enter into our true life. Oh do not lose heart and hope in useless weeping over the closed doors of the past. Follow Him, who has the keys." (Meyer)

g. **I will fasten him as a peg in a secure place**: Because the LORD established Eliakim's authority, it was secure. Shebna sought glory for himself but would find shame. But Eliakim was the LORD's servant and would **become a glorious throne to his father's house**.

i. In those days, houses didn't really have cupboards or storage closets as we think of them. Things were stored on *pegs* set up all around the room. If something was on its peg, it was safe and secure, stored properly and ready for use at the appropriate time.

h. **They will hang on him all the glory of his father's house, the offspring and the posterity**: The godly Eliakim was a secure peg and could spiritually support his **father's house** and his **offspring**. Since Eliakim is a picture of Jesus, we also see in this the believer's total dependence on Jesus.

i. Clarke on **they will hang on him all the glory of his father's house**: This "has been understood as the *dependence of all souls,* of *all capacities*, from the *lowest* in *intellect* to the most *exalted*, on the Lord Jesus, as the only Saviour of all lost human spirits."

ii. There are many different vessels in the LORD's house, with many different sizes and purposes. But they all must hang on the same peg! All will be equally wrecked if they drop from the peg. The safety isn't in the size or the quality of the vessel, but in its attachment to the peg.

3. (25) The removal of Shebna.

'In that day,' says the LORD of hosts, 'the peg that is fastened in the secure place will be removed and be cut down and fall, and the burden that was on it will be cut off; for the LORD has spoken.'"

a. **The peg that is fastened**: If Eliakim is yet to be promoted to the place of honor and responsibility pictured by the **peg** (*I will fasten him as a peg*, Isaiah 22:23), then Shebna is **the peg that is fastened** at the moment. Therefore, before Eliakim could be put in his rightful place, Shebna must **be removed and be cut down and fall**.

i. The LORD gave Shebna a place of honor and authority, but he didn't hold it as a faithful servant of the LORD. So, the LORD took the place of honor and authority away from Shebna. Even so, the great authority Jesus gave to His disciples was neither unlimited, nor unattached from Jesus' direction. Even though Jesus gave the promise of the keys to Peter (Matthew 16:19), Peter did not have unlimited authority. Instead, Peter was rightly challenged and rebuked by another apostle, Paul, when he was out of line (Galatians 2:11-21).

b. **And the burden that was on it will be cut off**: When Shebna was removed, all those who "hung" on him were also cut off. We have to make sure that we are resting on the right "peg."

Isaiah 23 – The Burden Against Tyre

A. The promise of coming judgment against Tyre.

1. (1-5) The sailors of Tyre agonize when they hear of the destruction of their home port.

The burden against Tyre.

Wail, you ships of Tarshish!
For it is laid waste,
So that there is no house, no harbor;
From the land of Cyprus it is revealed to them.
Be still, you inhabitants of the coastland,
You merchants of Sidon,
Whom those who cross the sea have filled.
And on great waters the grain of Shihor,
The harvest of the River, *is* her revenue;
And she is a marketplace for the nations.
Be ashamed, O Sidon;
For the sea has spoken,
The strength of the sea, saying,
"I do not labor, nor bring forth children;
Neither do I rear young men,
***Nor* bring up virgins."**
When the report *reaches* Egypt,
They also will be in agony at the report of Tyre.

a. **The burden against Tyre**: To the north of Israel, Tyre was the leading city of Phoenicia, the great maritime power of the ancient world. Because it was such an important harbor and center for shipping, Tyre was synonymous with commerce and materialism.

i. Tyre was the "Babylon of the Sea." Because of their excellent harbor and seamanship, they established a commercial empire far greater than one would expect given their size and military power.

ii. Tyre was a city in two parts – an inland city, and an island city. The inland city was conquered by the Assyrians and the Babylonians, just as Isaiah prophesied. The island city was conquered later by Alexander the Great in 332 B.C.

iii. The influence of Tyre was both good and bad for Israel. King Hiram of Tyre supplied David and Solomon great timbers for the building of the temple and other projects (2 Samuel 5:11, 1 Kings 5:1-11). Hiram also gave Solomon sailors, so Israel could build their commerce by sea (2 Chronicles 8:17-18). But later, Tyre gave Israel one of the worst rulers Israel ever had: Jezebel, the wife of King Ahab of Israel (1 Kings 16:31).

b. **There is no house, no harbor**: Isaiah pictures sailors from Tyre in **the land of Cyprus** and in **Egypt** hearing of the destruction of the harbor of Tyre. When they hear the news, they **wail** and are **in agony at the report of Tyre.**

2. (6-9) The proud city of Tyre is humbled.

Cross over to Tarshish;
Wail, you inhabitants of the coastland!
***Is* this your joyous *city*,**
Whose antiquity is from ancient days,
Whose feet carried her far off to dwell?
Who has taken this counsel against Tyre, the crowning city,
Whose merchants *are* princes,
Whose traders *are* the honorable of the earth?
The LORD of hosts has purposed it,
To bring to dishonor the pride of all glory,
To bring into contempt all the honorable of the earth.

a. **Wail, you inhabitants of the coastland**: Tyre was a city where money ruled. The **merchants are princes**, and the **traders are the honorable of the earth**. To be a leader or honorable, one didn't need to be of royal heritage, a good or an honest man. The only thing needed was success in business.

b. **The LORD of hosts has purposed it, to bring to dishonor the pride of all glory**: Because of its great success, Tyre had become proud and full of self-glory. But **the LORD of hosts has purposed** to judge and humble Tyre, and Isaiah announces it.

i. "Pride, pride, pride, is that basic sin to which God is ever opposed, and man is ever expressing." (Jennings)

3. (10-14) The destruction of the city of Tyre.

Overflow through your land like the River,
O daughter of Tarshish;
***There* is no more strength.**
He stretched out His hand over the sea,
He shook the kingdoms;
The Lord has given a commandment against Canaan
To destroy its strongholds.
And He said, "You will rejoice no more,
O you oppressed virgin daughter of Sidon.
Arise, cross over to Cyprus;
There also you will have no rest."
Behold, the land of the Chaldeans,
This people *which* was not;
Assyria founded it for wild beasts of the desert.
They set up its towers,
They raised up its palaces,
***And* brought it to ruin.**
Wail, you ships of Tarshish!
For your strength is laid waste.

a. **The Chaldeans...Assyria**: The mainland city of Tyre was defeated by both the Assyrians and the Babylonians. God used them to bring the city **to ruin**.

B. A promise of restoration to the city of Tyre.

1. (15-16) Seventy years of desolation for the city of Tyre.

Now it shall come to pass in that day that Tyre will be forgotten seventy years, according to the days of one king. At the end of seventy years it will happen to Tyre as *in* the song of the harlot:

"Take a harp, go about the city,
You forgotten harlot;
Make sweet melody, sing many songs,
That you may be remembered."

a. **Tyre will be forgotten seventy years**: God's judgments are so precise that He decrees the exact number of years **Tyre will be forgotten**.

b. **That you may be remembered**: Quoting what may have been a well-known song in his day, Isaiah makes the point that at the end of the seventy years appointed by God, Tyre will be remembered again.

2. (17-18) God's purpose in restoring the city of Tyre.

And it shall be, at the end of seventy years, that the LORD will deal with Tyre. She will return to her hire, and commit fornication with all the kingdoms of the world on the face of the earth. Her gain and her pay will be set apart for the LORD; it will not be treasured nor laid up, for her gain will be for those who dwell before the LORD, to eat sufficiently, and for fine clothing.

a. **She will return to her hire**: God will allow Tyre, symbolized by a prostitute, to continue her gross materialism **with all the kingdoms of the world**. But **Her gain and her pay will be set apart for the LORD**; ultimately, the riches Tyre so desperately sought will be given to the LORD anyway.

b. **The LORD will deal with Tyre**: Many commentators think this refers to the presence of Christianity in Tyre in the days of the early church.

i. "Tyre, after its destruction by Nebuchadnezzar, recovered, as it is here foretold, its ancient trade, wealth, and grandeur; as it did likewise after a second destruction by Alexander. It became Christian early with the rest of the neighbouring countries. St. Paul himself found many Christians there, Acts 21:4. It suffered much in the Diocletian persecution. It was an archbishopric under the patriarchate of Jerusalem, with fourteen bishoprics under its jurisdiction. It continued Christian till it was taken by the Saracens in 639; was recovered by the Christians in 1124; but in 1280 was conquered by the Mamelukes and afterwards taken from them by the Turks in 1517. Since that time it has sunk into utter decay; is now a mere ruin, a bare rock, 'a place to spread nets upon,' as the Prophet Ezekiel foretold it should be, chapter 26:14." (Clarke)

Isaiah 24 – The Character of the Judgment of the Lord

A. The scene of God's judgment.

1. (1-3) The scope of the judgment of the Lord.

Behold, the Lord makes the earth empty and makes it waste,
Distorts its surface
And scatters abroad its inhabitants.
And it shall be:
As with the people, so with the priest;
As with the servant, so with his master;
As with the maid, so with her mistress;
As with the buyer, so with the seller;
As with the lender, so with the borrower;
As with the creditor, so with the debtor.
The land shall be entirely emptied and utterly plundered,
For the Lord has spoken this word.

a. **Behold, the Lord makes the earth empty**: Isaiah invites us to **behold**, to look upon the scene of God's judgment. The principles revealed here apply universally to the judgment of the Lord, but the ultimate fulfillment of this will be in the ultimate period of judgment, the time of the Great Tribulation (Matthew 24:21-22), which will immediately precede the second coming of Jesus Christ (Matthew 24:29-30).

i. In the days of the Great Tribulation, the earth will not be literally **empty**, but Isaiah's poetic description applies because the earth will *seem* empty in many places. More than one-third of humanity will die in the judgments of the great tribulation (Revelation 9:15-21), making the areas hardest hit seem as if **the earth** were **empty**.

ii. "The *connection* between these chapters and the preceding ones appear to be as follows: the judgments pronounced upon the various countries and nations in those chapters are drawn together here into a focal point. The specific divine judgments described there become here the general judgment upon the nations, which will take place when the Lord Jesus Christ with His Church will return to this earth." (Bultema)

b. **As with the people, so with the priest; as with the servant, so with his master**: In these comparisons, Isaiah shows that a high station in life (**priest…master…mistress…seller**) will not protect one from the judgments of the LORD. As well, a low station of life (**borrower…debtor**) will not protect one either. When the judgment of the Great Tribulation comes, it will be complete in its scope.

i. Some who believe that the church will be left on the earth to endure the Great Tribulation believe that God will miraculously protect Christians during that time, so they face none of the judgments of the LORD, only perhaps persecution from the Antichrist. But this passage reinforces the idea that the judgments of the LORD during the Great Tribulation will be universal in their scope, and that no class of people will be immune from the general judgment of the LORD. Therefore, it makes sense for God to remove His redeemed before this period of Great Tribulation, so only those who do not trust in Him during the Great Tribulation have to suffer under these judgments.

2. (4-6) The reason for judgment.

The earth mourns *and* fades away,
The world languishes *and* fades away;
The haughty people of the earth languish.
The earth is also defiled under its inhabitants,
Because they have transgressed the laws,
Changed the ordinance,
Broken the everlasting covenant.
Therefore the curse has devoured the earth,
And those who dwell in it are desolate.
Therefore the inhabitants of the earth are burned,
And few men *are* left.

a. **The earth mourns and fades away**: Why does the earth mourn? Because in the Great Tribulation, the earth will be terribly afflicted by the judgments of the LORD. Revelation 8:7-13 describes the terrible effect of the judgments of the LORD upon the earth.

i. Is this God's fault? Does God hate the earth? No, this is the fault of man: **The earth is also defiled under its inhabitants**. Man has defiled the earth with his sin and great wickedness, so the earth must endure some of the righteous judgment of God also. In this sense, the most ecologically responsible thing anyone could do is to honor the LORD God, walk right with Him, and in obedience to Him.

ii. This passage is a good reminder of the principle that God is greater than His creation. The Bible never teaches the New Age idea of God that He is somehow bound up together with what He has created. God is separate from His creation, and when the earth **fades away**, when the world **fades away**, the LORD God will remain unchanged.

b. **Because they have transgressed the laws**: The idea of *transgression* is to step over the line that God has established. God has set boundaries for us, but many of us don't want to see or respect God's boundaries.

i. Transgression is the spirit of our age. We see this in the slogans from national advertising campaigns in decades past: Nothing is taboo.... Break all the rules.... To know no boundaries.... Relax: No rules here.... Peel off inhibitions. Find your own road.... We are all hedonists and want to do what feels good.... That's what makes us human.... Living without boundaries.... Just do it. The idea is constant: you don't have to respect God's boundaries, because you can make your own and live by them.

c. **Because they have...changed the ordinance**: The Hebrew word for **ordinance** here is *torah*, which often means *the law of God* and *the word of God*. Mankind is ripe for judgment because we have **changed** God's word into something "lighter," into something "more acceptable."

i. Mankind has changed the *law of God* in the sense of changing the basic moral code which men have recognized and lived by for centuries. When once it was universally recognized that it was wrong to lie, wrong to cheat, wrong to be sexually immoral, wrong to do so many other things, today all of that is approved and celebrated! We have **changed the ordinance** and are ripe for judgment.

ii. Mankind has changed the *word of God* by replacing it with substitutes, or by fashioning it into something more suitable to his liking. Every time a preacher soft-peddles the gospel, every time a politician twists the Scriptures to rise in the opinion polls, every time a counselor wrenches the context of God's word to make it fit a crazy psychological theory, they have **changed the ordinance**, and are ripe for judgment.

d. **Because they have...broken the everlasting covenant**: God has entered into covenant with man, and man has turned his back on His covenant.

Instead of receiving God's **everlasting covenant**, man wants to make up his own way with God.

i. There is no single covenant known as **the everlasting covenant** because the title applies to several different covenants.

- The covenant God made with mankind after the flood, never to judge the world again by water is called an *everlasting covenant* (Genesis 9:16).
- The covenant God made with Abraham and his descendants is called an *everlasting covenant* (Genesis 17:7, 13, 19).
- The covenant God made with Israel and the priesthood is called an *everlasting covenant* (Leviticus 24:8).
- The covenant God made with David, to bring the Messiah from his line, is called an *everlasting covenant* (2 Samuel 23:5).
- The New Covenant is called an *everlasting covenant*, both prophetically (Jeremiah 32:40) and after its establishment (Hebrews 13:20).

e. **The curse has devoured the earth**: There is a reason for this **curse**. Man's hardened, repeated rejection of God will bring the ultimate judgment: The Great Tribulation.

i. "Man has transgressed the laws, violated the statutes, and broken the covenant. For an interpretation of these words of

Isaiah, read Paul – Romans 1:18-32." (Morgan)

ii. "This is the interpretation of all disease, all insanity, all the things of waste, of disorder, of strife, of misery in human history and human experience. A polluted race pollutes the earth, and chaos is the result." (Morgan)

3. (7-13) The scene of judgment.

The new wine fails, the vine languishes,
All the merry-hearted sigh.
The mirth of the tambourine ceases,
The noise of the jubilant ends,
The joy of the harp ceases.
They shall not drink wine with a song;
Strong drink is bitter to those who drink it.
The city of confusion is broken down;
Every house is shut up, so that none may go in.
***There is* a cry for wine in the streets,**
All joy is darkened,

The mirth of the land is gone.
In the city desolation is left,
And the gate is stricken with destruction.
When it shall be thus in the midst of the land among the people,
It shall be **like the shaking of an olive tree,**
Like the gleaning of grapes when the vintage is done.

a. **All the merry-hearted sigh**: When the LORD brings the judgment of the Great Tribulation, there will be no more "partying as usual." The days for *eating and drinking, marrying and giving in marriage* (Matthew 24:38) are for before the Great Tribulation. When the Great Tribulation comes, **the noise of the jubilant ends, the joy of the harp ceases**.

b. **In the city desolation is left, and the gate is stricken with destruction**: During the Great Tribulation, God's judgment will bring destruction everywhere. The judgment will be so complete that the cities will look like bare olive trees (**like the shaking of an olive tree**) and grapevines stripped of everything (**like the gleaning of grapes when the vintage is done**).

4. (14-16) The glory of God and the woe of man.

They shall lift up their voice, they shall sing;
For the majesty of the LORD
They shall cry aloud from the sea.
Therefore glorify the LORD in the dawning light,
The name of the LORD God of Israel in the coastlands of the sea.
From the ends of the earth we have heard songs:
"Glory to the righteous!"
But I said, "I am ruined, ruined!
Woe to me!
The treacherous dealers have dealt treacherously,
Indeed, the treacherous dealers have dealt very treacherously."

a. **They shall lift up their voice, they shall sing**: Even in the midst of great judgment, God has His own who will praise Him. Before the Great Tribulation, God will remove all His people; but many come to trust in Jesus during the Great Tribulation, and these will praise Him in the midst of judgment (Revelation 7:9-14).

b. **Glory to the righteous**: They praise God because even in His judgments, or perhaps *especially* in His judgments, the LORD shows His **majesty** and He shows His **glory**. The godly can see the goodness, the greatness, and the glory of God even in judgment, even when **the treacherous dealers have dealt very treacherously**.

B. The character of God's judgment.

1. (17-18) The judgment of the LORD will always be completed.

Fear and the pit and the snare
***Are* upon you, O inhabitant of the earth.**
And it shall be
***That* he who flees from the noise of the fear**
Shall fall into the pit,
And he who comes up from the midst of the pit
Shall be caught in the snare;
For the windows from on high are open,
And the foundations of the earth are shaken.

a. **O inhabitant of the earth**: The Book of Revelation, writing of this time of Great Tribulation, makes constant reference to *those who dwell on the earth* (Revelation 3:10, 6:10, 11:10, 13:12, 13:14). This is in contrast to *those who dwell in heaven* (Revelation 13:6), who are seated with Jesus in the heavenly places (Ephesians 2:6).

i. It is fair for every disciple of Jesus Christ to ask themselves: Where do you sit? Where do you live? Are you an **inhabitant of the earth**, or do you sit with Jesus in heavenly places?

b. **Fear…pit…snare**: Simply put, the judgment of the LORD is inescapable. If you escape the fear, you will fall into the pit. If you escape the pit, you will fall into the snare. God's judgment has enough back-up plans to catch everyone. The only way to escape the judgment of God is to *satisfy* it, and the only place God's judgment was ever *satisfied* was on the cross.

i. "The images are taken from the different methods of hunting and taking wild beasts, which were anciently in use." (Clarke)

2. (19-20) The intensity of the judgment of the LORD touches everything.

The earth is violently broken,
The earth is split open,
The earth is shaken exceedingly.
The earth shall reel to and fro like a drunkard,
And shall totter like a hut;
Its transgression shall be heavy upon it,
And it will fall, and not rise again.

a. **The earth is violently broken, the earth is split open**: The Bible describes some of this judgment during the Great Tribulation (Revelation 6:13-14), and specifically mentions *a mighty and great earthquake as had not occurred since men were on the earth* (Revelation 16:18). No wonder Isaiah says, **the earth shall reel to and fro like a drunkard**.

3. (21-23) The judgment of the LORD will touch everyone.

It shall come to pass in that day
***That* the LORD will punish on high the host of exalted ones,**
And on the earth the kings of the earth.
They will be gathered together,
***As* prisoners are gathered in the pit,**
And will be shut up in the prison;
After many days they will be punished.
Then the moon will be disgraced
And the sun ashamed;
For the LORD of hosts will reign
On Mount Zion and in Jerusalem
And before His elders, gloriously.

a. **The LORD will punish on high the host of exalted ones**: One of the more frustrating aspects of life is to see the rich, powerful, and wicked escape the present consequences of their sin. But in His great judgment during the Great Tribulation, no one will be able to buy a high-priced lawyer to escape judgment or bribe a politician to come out without being hurt.

i. But Isaiah is probably speaking of something even higher than the **exalted ones** of this earth. Bultema and Wolf believe that the phrase **the host of exalted ones** refers to rebellious angels that are judged at the end of the age and imprisoned in the pit until the final rebellion at the end of the Millennium (Revelation 20:1-10). The NIV translates **the host of exalted ones** as *the powers in the heavens above.*

b. **The kings of the earth…. will be gathered together, as prisoners are gathered in the pit**: Under God's great and final judgment, their status on this earth will buy them nothing. Poetically speaking, even the moon will be disgraced and the sun ashamed. No degree of earthly greatness will help man on that day, and no degree of heavenly greatness will help an angelic being on that day.

i. "The image seems to be taken from the practice of the great monarchs of that time; who, when they had thrown their wretched captives into a dungeon, never gave themselves the trouble of inquiring about them; but let them lie a long time in that miserable condition, wholly destitute of relief, and disregarded." (Clarke)

c. **The LORD of hosts will reign on Mount Zion and in Jerusalem and before His elders, gloriously**: At the end of the Great Tribulation, God will usher in a thousand years of His glorious **reign** over all the earth on **Mount Zion and in Jerusalem**. God's purpose in judgment isn't simple vengeance or vindictiveness, it is to bring about a glorious new world.

Isaiah 25 – The Song of Joy from the Midst of Tribulation

A. Praising God for what He has done.

1. (1) Introduction: For You have done wonderful things.

O Lord, You are my God.
I will exalt You,
I will praise Your name,
For You have done wonderful *things*;
***Your* counsels of old *are* faithfulness *and* truth.**

a. **O Lord, You are my God**: Isaiah 24 spoke of the judgment to come upon the world, especially in the Great Tribulation. During that time, those who have come to trust in the Lord will praise Him, even in the midst of His righteous judgment. *They shall lift up their voice, they shall sing; for the majesty of the Lord they shall cry aloud from the sea* (Isaiah 24:14). This song shows the kind of heart that praises God in the midst of tribulation, even in the midst of the Great Tribulation.

b. **O Lord, You are my God**: Knowing that the **Lord** – the God of Abraham, Isaac, and Jacob, the God revealed in and by Jesus Christ – is our **God** makes us want to praise Him. When someone or something other than the **Lord** is our **God**, we are guilty of idolatry.

c. **I will exalt You, I will praise Your name**: The worshipper here makes a *decision* to praise God (**I will**). Worship is never to be just a feeling, even if it is an intense feeling. We are to worship God with a *decision.*

i. "If I did not praise and bless Christ my Lord, I should deserve to have my tongue torn out by its roots from my mouth. If I did not bless and magnify his name, I should deserve that every stone I tread on in the streets should rise up to curse my ingratitude, for I am a drowned debtor to the mercy of God – over head and ears – to infinite love and boundless compassion I am a debtor. Are you not the same? Then I charge you by the love of Christ, awake, awake your hearts now to magnify his glorious name." (Spurgeon)

d. **For You have done wonderful things**: When we think about all the **wonderful things** the LORD has done, it is pretty easy to make the decision to worship the LORD. God wants our worship to be filled with *thought* and *remembrance* of God's great works, not only an emotional response.

e. **Your counsels of old are faithfulness and truth**: When we remember the greatness and permanence of God's word, it makes us what to praise Him. What is more reliable, more everlasting, more enduring than the word of God?

2. (2-3) Praising God for His righteous judgment.

For You have made a city a ruin,
A fortified city a ruin,
A palace of foreigners to be a city no more;
It will never be rebuilt.
Therefore the strong people will glorify You;
The city of the terrible nations will fear You.

a. **For You have made a city a ruin**: We can worship God for His judgment because we have confidence in His fairness. As was the case with Sodom and Gomorrah, God will never make **a city a ruin** unless the judgment is deserved, and God has made provision for the righteous.

i. Which **city** is referred to? No specific city, but in reality, every city. "There is a complete lack of any specific national reference, and none of the activities which are pursued within the city differentiate it any special way. It can best be understood, therefore, as a pictorial description of the body of organised human society, a type of 'Vanity Fair,' which is to be subjected to the divine judgment. When God asserts his will in judgment he will bring to an end the existing human order, so that in a sense every city will be brought to chaos." (Clements, cited in Grogan)

b. **The strong people will glorify You**: The people of the LORD see His work and glorify Him. This is the first of two effects of the judgment of God. Second, **the city of the terrible nations will fear You**. The unrighteous fear God when they see His righteous judgment.

3. (4-5) Praising God for His goodness to the weak.

For You have been a strength to the poor,
A strength to the needy in his distress,
A refuge from the storm,

A shade from the heat;
For the blast of the terrible ones is as a storm *against* the wall.
You will reduce the noise of aliens,
As heat in a dry place;
***As* heat in the shadow of a cloud,**
The song of the terrible ones will be diminished.

a. **For You have been a strength to the poor, a strength to the needy**: God is worthy of our praise because He brings strength to the poor and needy.

b. **A refuge from the storm, a shade from the heat**: This is a wonderful reason to praise God, and even the strangers (**aliens**) are blessed by His goodness. God will even quiet **the song of the terrible ones**.

B. Praising God for what He will do.

1. (6) A glorious feast for God's people.

And in this mountain
The LORD of hosts will make for all people
A feast of choice pieces,
A feast of wines on the lees,
Of fat things full of marrow,
Of well-refined wines on the lees.

a. **In this mountain the LORD of hosts will make for all people a feast**: In several places, the Bible speaks of what is sometimes called *the Marriage Supper of the Lamb*. Revelation 19:9 says, *blessed are those who are called to the marriage supper of the Lamb!* According to Isaiah 25:6, we might say that this great feast takes place *on earth*, not in heaven.

b. **A feast of choice pieces, a feast of wines on the lees, of fat things full of marrow, of well-refined wines on the lees**. For God's people, this will be the "victory banquet" or the "awards banquet" when the final battle is over. What a **feast** that will be.

i. Jesus is really looking forward to this banquet. He said to His disciples at the Last Supper, *I will not drink of this fruit of the vine from now on until that day when I drink it new with you in My Father's kingdom* (Matthew 26:29). In this, Jesus spoke of His longing expectation for the day when He would take communion with His people at the Marriage Supper of the Lamb. Jesus is excited about this event; are you?

2. (7-8) The destruction of evil.

And He will destroy on this mountain
The surface of the covering cast over all people,
And the veil that is spread over all nations.
He will swallow up death forever,
And the Lord God will wipe away tears from all faces;
The rebuke of His people
He will take away from all the earth;
For the Lord has spoken.

a. **The veil that is spread over all nations**: This is what the Lord will **destroy**. The picture is that there is a **veil that is spread over all nations** that keeps them from seeing God, loving God, and obeying God. In this glorious day, the Lord will destroy that veil.

i. In the New Testament, Paul speaks of Israel being blinded by a veil: *But even to this day, when Moses is read, a veil lies on their heart* (2 Corinthians 3:15). In Isaiah's day, it was more apparent that the nations were veiled. In Paul's day, it was more apparent that Israel was veiled. But for both the nations and for Israel, the remedy is the same: *Nevertheless when one turns to the Lord, the veil is taken away* (2 Corinthians 3:16).

b. **He will swallow up death forever**: The Lord will also **destroy** death. The day will come when death is powerless. Death was introduced by Adam's rebellion (Genesis 2:16-17) and will one day be completely eliminated by God.

i. Paul knew this and looked forward to this day. He proclaimed in 1 Corinthians 15:54: *Death is swallowed up in victory*. This will be true for every believer when death is defeated by resurrection. A resurrected body is not a resuscitated corpse. It is a new order of life that will never die again.

ii. Freud was *wrong* when he said: "And finally there is the painful riddle of death, for which no remedy at all has yet been found, nor probably ever will be." Compare that sad statement with Isaiah's triumphant declaration, **He will swallow death up forever**.

iii. "Ever since death ran through the veins of Jesus Christ, who is life essential, it is destroyed or swallowed up; like as the bee dieth when she hath left her sting in the wound." (Trapp)

c. **And the Lord God will wipe away tears from all faces**: This is how glorious the tender mercy of God is. It isn't just that He takes away the things that made us sad, or even that He gives us a handkerchief to dry our eyes. Instead, He gently and lovingly **will wipe away tears from all faces**.

d. **The rebuke of His people He will take away from all the earth**: Now, we need God's **rebuke of His people**. If God did not rebuke and correct us, we could drift further and further from Him. But there will come a day when we are no longer troubled by sin, no longer in a place to rebel. In that glorious day, **the rebuke of His people He will take away**. We thank God for that coming day, and we also thank God for the faithful **rebuke of His people** until then.

3. (9) The testimony of God's people.

And it will be said in that day:
"Behold, this *is* our God;
We have waited for Him, and He will save us.
This *is* the Lord;
We have waited for Him;
We will be glad and rejoice in His salvation."

a. **Behold, this is our God**: We will proclaim it then because we have proclaimed it now. We are those who were unafraid to confess Jesus before men on earth, and we will be blessed to hear Him confess us before our Father in heaven (Luke 12:8).

b. **We have waited for Him, and He will save us**: It is a wonderful thing to wait on the Lord, and to see Him bring His salvation. God sometimes seems distant or cruel when we must wait on Him, but God's ways really are best, and will be shown to be the best.

c. **We will be glad and rejoice in His salvation**: If it is *our salvation* – in the sense of a salvation of our own making, of our own creation, then there is nothing to **be glad and rejoice in**. But since it is **His salvation**, there is everything to **be glad and rejoice in**.

d. **And it will be said in that day**: Each one of these things – confessing He is our God, the fulfillment of patient waiting, and rejoicing in His salvation – each of these will be ultimately fulfilled **in that day**. But they can be *substantially fulfilled* right now! We can praise God for these things *right now*! And as we do, we bring some of the glory of **that day** to pass in our lives *right now*.

i. "To be rapt in praise to God is the highest state of the soul. To receive the mercy for which we praise God for is something; but to be wholly clothed with praise to God for the mercy received is far more. Why, praise is heaven, and heaven is praise! To pray is heaven below, but praise is the essence of heaven above. When you bow in adoration, you are at your very highest." (Spurgeon)

4. (10-12) The LORD resolves all things.

For on this mountain the hand of the LORD will rest,
And Moab shall be trampled down under Him,
As straw is trampled down for the refuse heap.
And He will spread out His hands in their midst
As a swimmer reaches out to swim,
And He will bring down their pride
Together with the trickery of their hands.
The fortress of the high fort of your walls
He will bring down, lay low,
***And* bring to the ground, down to the dust.**

a. **For on this mountain the hand of the LORD will rest**: The LORD will settle His hand of favor, power, and glory on Mount Zion. After the Great Tribulation, when Jesus Christ reigns from Jerusalem, the whole creation will know that the **hand of the LORD** does **rest** on **this mountain**.

i. "The powerful and gracious presence of God (which is oft signified in Scripture by God's hand) shall have its constant and settled abode; it shall not move from place to place, as it did with the tabernacle; nor shall it depart from it, as it did from Jerusalem." (Poole)

b. **And Moab shall be trampled down**: In that day, Jesus will rule the nations with all authority and righteousness (Psalm 2:8-12). God will reach out (**As a swimmer reaches out to swim**) and bring low every proud, rebelling heart. Those who oppose His rule He will **bring to the ground, down to the dust**.

i. "In a powerful anthropomorphic figure, the prophet pictures the Lord's hand resting in blessing on Mount Zion and his feet trampling on Moab in judgment." (Grogan) So, which do we want – the touch of God's loving hand, or to be under His feet of judgment?

Isaiah 26 – Judah's Kingdom of God Song

A. The city of God and the city of Man.

1. (1-2) The strength of God's city

In that day this song will be sung in the land of Judah:
"We have a strong city;
***God* will appoint salvation *for* walls and bulwarks.**
Open the gates,
That the righteous nation which keeps the truth may enter in.

a. **In that day**: The context from Isaiah 24 and 25 points to the day of the Messiah's ultimate triumph, the day when the Messiah reigns over Israel, and over all the world. **In that day**, there will be a lot of joyful singing, such as this **song** that **will be sung in the land of Judah**.

b. **We have a strong city**: Since cities came into being after the fall of man in Genesis 3, mankind has never known a truly godly city, the *City of God* on earth. **In that day**, all will know the strength and glory of the city of God.

i. In the fifth century, the city of Rome was conquered by less civilized tribes from the north in Europe. In the west, the mighty Roman Empire was no more, and many blamed the fall of Rome on Christianity, the new religion she had officially embraced in the last 100 years. In this time of confusion, the greatest Christian theologian of the day wrote a book titled *The City of God*. In it, he tried to explain how the fall of the western Roman Empire related to the kingdom of God, and he made the contrast between the *city of man* (ultimately represented by Rome and the mighty Roman Empire) and the *City of God* (the kingdom of God). Augustine pointed out that though the fall of Rome was tragic for the *city of man*, it really only advanced the coming of the *City of God*. Speaking in Augustine's terms, Isaiah wrote about the *City of God* when he said, **we have a strong city**. The **strong city** is the Kingdom of God, the *city of man* is the world system.

ii. This is an important and often neglected idea. We often disapprove of the idea of the city, and romanticize the idea of man in isolation, in a rural or primitive setting. But in the Kingdom of Jesus Christ on this earth, there will be cities – but redeemed cities, glorious communities organized under the strength and salvation and righteousness and truth of the Lord. God's supreme ideal is not an escape from all community and a private communion with nature; the Kingdom of God will be realized in **a strong city**.

c. **God will appoint salvation for walls and bulwarks**: The city of God, from beginning to end, is all about **salvation**. Even the **walls** and the **bulwarks** of the city are saved.

d. **Open the gates, that the righteous nation which keeps the truth may enter it**: The city of God, with all its strength and salvation, is only for the **righteous**, and those who keep **the truth**. In the same principle, the New Jerusalem is a city filled with glory, which excludes the unrighteous (Revelation 21:22-27).

i. We should make a distinction between the Kingdom of the Messiah, the millennial reign of Jesus (described here in Isaiah 26), and the coming of the New Jerusalem (which comes when this earth passes away, Revelation 21:1-2). The cities are similar, because they are both from the Lord, but they come at different times in God's plan of the ages.

2. (3-4) The Lord is our source of strength.

You will keep *him* in perfect peace,
***Whose* mind is stayed *on You*,**
Because he trusts in You.
Trust in the Lord forever,
For in Yah, the Lord, is everlasting strength.

a. **You will keep him in perfect peace**: This is a wonderful promise: **perfect peace**. God promises that we can have **perfect peace**, and even be *kept* in a place of **perfect peace**.

i. In Hebrew, the term **perfect peace** is actually *shalom shalom*. This shows how in Hebrew, repetition communicates intensity. It isn't just *shalom*; it is *shalom shalom*, **perfect peace**.

ii. "Understand, dear soul, that it is thy privilege to live inside the double doors of God's loving care. He says to thee, 'Peace, peace.' If one assurance is not enough, He will follow it with a second and a third." (Meyer)

iii. Some can have this **perfect peace**, but it is fleeting, and they are never *kept* there. Others can be kept **in peace**, but it is not a **perfect peace**, it is the peace of the wicked, the peace of spiritual sleep and ultimate destruction. But there is a **perfect peace** that the LORD will **keep** us in.

b. **Whose mind is stayed on You**: This is the place of **perfect peace** and the source of it. When we keep our minds **stayed** – settled upon, established upon – the LORD Himself, then we can be kept in this **perfect peace**.

i. To be kept in this **perfect peace** is a matter of our **mind**. This isn't so much a matter of our *spirit* or of our *soul* or of our *heart*. It is a matter of our **mind**. We are to love the LORD our God with all of our *mind* (Matthew 22:37). We are transformed by the *renewing of your mind* (Romans 12:2). We can have the *mind of Christ* (1 Corinthians 2:16, Philippians 2:5). We are not to set our *mind on earthly things* (Philippians 3:19), but to *set* our *mind on things above* (Colossians 3:2). The Christian life is not an unthinking life of just *doing*, or *experiencing*, but it is also about *thinking*, and where we set our **mind** is essential in our walk before the LORD.

ii. To be kept in this **perfect peace**, our mind must be **stayed**. According to Strong's Dictionary, the Hebrew word *sawmak* comes from the root "to prop," and has the idea "to lean upon or take hold of...bear up, establish, uphold, lay, lean, lie hard, put, rest self, set self, stand fast, stay (self), sustain." In other places the same word is translated *sustained* (Genesis 27:37, Psalm 3:5), or when the priest would put their hands on the head of a sacrificial animal (Exodus 29:10, 15, 19), or of the laying on of hands in other circumstances (Numbers 27:18), of being *upheld* (Psalm 71:6), to *stand fast* upon (Psalm 111:8), of being *established* (Psalm 112:8), of leaning upon (Isaiah 36:6, 48:2). It is fair to ask the disciples of Jesus Christ: What *sustains* your mind? What do you *lay your mind* upon? What *upholds* your mind? What does your mind *stand fast* upon? What is your mind *established* upon? What does your mind *lean* upon? To have this **perfect peace**, your mind cannot occasionally come to and lean upon the LORD; it has to be **stayed on** Him.

iii. To be kept in this **perfect peace**, our **mind** must be **stayed** on *the LORD*. If our mind is **stayed** on ourselves, or our problems, or the problem people in our lives, or on anything else, we can't have this **perfect peace**. This is the heart that says with the Apostle Paul, *that I* *may know Him* (Philippians 3:10). In his spiritual attacks against us, Satan loves to get our minds set on *anything* except the Lord.

c. **Because he trusts in You**: This is another way of expressing the idea of keeping our minds **stayed on** Him. Almost always, you keep your mind **stayed on** whatever you are trusting. When we trust the Lord, we keep our mind **stayed on** Him.

i. Proverbs 3:5 expresses this same idea: *Trust in the Lord with all your heart, and lean not on your own understanding*. The word for *lean* in Proverbs 3:5 comes from the same root as the word **stayed** in Isaiah 26:3. When we *trust in the Lord*, we do not *lean on* our *own understanding*. To *lean on* the Lord is to trust Him. To be *sustained* by the Lord is to trust Him. To be *established* by the Lord is to trust Him. To be *upheld* by the Lord is to trust Him.

ii. The battle for trust in our lives *begins* in our minds. If we trust the Lord, it will show in our *actions*, but it will *begin* in our mind.

d. **Trust in the Lord forever**: Because of the promise of Isaiah 26:3, we are encouraged to **trust in the Lord forever** – and therefore to receive the blessing of the promise, **perfect peace**.

e. **For in Yah, the Lord, is everlasting strength**: If the Lord calls us to rely on Him completely with our mind, He appeals to our mind with a rational reason why we should trust the Lord – because He is **everlasting strength**. It isn't that the Lord *has* **everlasting strength**, He **is everlasting strength**.

i. Clarke's comment on Isaiah 12:2 applies here also: "The word *Yah* read here is probably a mistake; and arose originally from the custom of the Jewish scribes, who, when they found a line too short for the word, wrote as many letters as filled it, and then began the next line with the whole word."

3. (5-6) The destiny of the city of man.

For He brings down those who dwell on high,
The lofty city;
He lays it low,
He lays it low to the ground,
He brings it down to the dust.
The foot shall tread it down—
The feet of the poor
***And* the steps of the needy."**

a. **He brings down those who dwell on high, the lofty city**: The **city** of man is **lofty**, and the exalted ones of the city **dwell on high**. But the Lord will bring them **down** nonetheless. The city of man, the world system, is nothing to the LORD; **He lays it low**.

b. **He brings it down to the dust**: The city of man, the world system, is all about power and prestige, built on the backs of the weak and the poor. But when God brings the city of man **down to the dust**, He will turn all that around, and **the feet of the poor** shall **tread it down**.

i. Jesus expressed the same principle in Matthew 5:5: *Blessed are the meek, for they shall inherit the earth.* Jesus told us to oppose the power and prestige thinking of this world and to live with the thinking of His Kingdom right now (Matthew 20:25-28).

4. (7-9) The way of the upright.

The way of the just *is* uprightness;
O Most Upright,
You weigh the path of the just.
Yes, in the way of Your judgments,
O LORD, we have waited for You;
The desire of *our* soul *is* for Your name
And for the remembrance of You.
With my soul I have desired You in the night,
Yes, by my spirit within me I will seek You early;
For when Your judgments *are* in the earth,
The inhabitants of the world will learn righteousness.

a. **The way of the just is uprightness**: In the Kingdom of God, His righteous people walk in a **way** – the **way** of **uprightness**. Isaiah accurately gives the sense of order in this; the LORD makes His people **just** by a relationship of faith and trust in Him, then they walk in **the way of... uprightness**.

i. They walk in uprightness because they serve the LORD God, who is **Most Upright** Himself. As they trust the LORD, and are declared just by the LORD, they walk in His own way.

ii. **You weigh the path of the just**: The LORD looks at His righteous ones (**the just**) and He evaluates their path. The LORD cares about the walk of His just ones.

b. **The desire of our soul is for Your name**: In the Kingdom of God, His just people *love* Him and **desire** Him.

i. The **desire** is displayed in *waiting*: **O LORD, we have waited for You**. When you **desire** something, or someone, you will wait for them, and do it gladly because of your **desire**.

ii. The desire is displayed in *seeking*: **With my soul I have desired You in the night, yes, by my spirit within me I will seek You early**. When you **desire** something, or someone, you *seek* them all the time, both **early** and at **night**.

c. **The inhabitants of the world will learn righteousness**: The way of the upright will be one day vindicated.

5. (10-11) The way of the wicked.

Let grace be shown to the wicked,
***Yet* he will not learn righteousness;**
In the land of uprightness he will deal unjustly,
And will not behold the majesty of the LORD.
LORD, *when* Your hand is lifted up, they will not see.
But they will see and be ashamed
For *their* envy of people;
Yes, the fire of Your enemies shall devour them.

a. **Let grace be shown to the wicked, yet he will not learn righteousness**: The wicked are ungrateful for God's goodness.

b. **And will not behold the majesty of the LORD.... they will see and be ashamed...the fire of Your enemies shall devour them**: The wicked end in disaster.

B. Promises made to a humble heart.

1. (12-18) The prayer of a humble heart.

LORD, You will establish peace for us,
For You have also done all our works in us.
O LORD our God, masters besides You
Have had dominion over us;
***But* by You only we make mention of Your name.**
***They are* dead, they will not live;**
***They are* deceased, they will not rise.**
Therefore You have punished and destroyed them,
And made all their memory to perish.
You have increased the nation, O LORD,
You have increased the nation;
You are glorified;
You have expanded all the borders of the land.
LORD, in trouble they have visited You,
They poured out a prayer *when* Your chastening *was* upon them.
As a woman with child

Is in pain and cries out in her pangs,
***When* she draws near the time of her delivery,**
So have we been in Your sight, O Lord.
We have been with child, we have been in pain;
We have, as it were, brought forth wind;
We have not accomplished any deliverance in the earth,
Nor have the inhabitants of the world fallen.

a. **You have also done all our works in us**: Even though the Holy Spirit spoke through the Apostle Paul more than 500 years after Isaiah's time, one might feel that Isaiah must have read Ephesians 2:8-10: *For by grace you have been saved through faith, and that not of yourselves; it is the gift of God, not of works, lest anyone should boast. For we are His workmanship, created in Christ Jesus for good works, which God prepared beforehand that we should walk in them*. Even our good works are works that He has **done…in us**.

b. **Masters besides You have had dominion over us; but by You only we make mention of Your name**: The humble heart repents of past idolatry, and rejoices in the present freedom in the Lord.

i. The humble heart sees the folly of their past idolatry: **They are dead, they will not live**. The humble heart sees the victory of the Lord over all idols: **You have punished and destroyed them**. "Obviously this verse does not suggest that the 'other lords' had real existence as deities but simply that they were believed to have and that their rule was sinfully acknowledged by the people in past times." (Grogan)

ii. The Hebrew word for **dominion** is *baal*, which can mean *master* or *husband*. Of course, *Baal* was also the chief god of the native Canaanites, and a seductive idol for Israel. In this prayer, Judah essentially said, *O Lord our God, masters besides you have mastered us*.

c. **We have been with child, we have been in pain; we have, as it were, brought forth wind**: The humble heart knows the futility of working apart from the direction and blessing of God.

i. "We have had the torment of a woman in child-bearing, but not the comfort of a living child…for we have brought forth nothing but the wind; all our labours and hopes were vain and unsuccessful." (Poole)

d. **You have increased the nation**: The humble heart knows the Lord is responsible for increase and blessing.

e. **Lord, in trouble they have visited You**: The humble heart relies on the Lord in times of distress and futility.

2. (19) The promise of resurrection.

Your dead shall live;
***Together with* my dead body they shall arise.**
Awake and sing, you who dwell in dust;
For your dew *is like* the dew of herbs,
And the earth shall cast out the dead.

a. **Your dead shall live**: The Old Testament gave a shadowy understanding of the life to come, because the secrets of the life to come have *now been revealed by the appearing of our Savior Jesus Christ, who has abolished death and brought life and immortality to light through the gospel* (2 Timothy 1:10). But here is one Old Testament example of a confident expectation of resurrection and glory for the LORD's righteous ones.

3. (20-21) The promise of refuge in the time of great indignation.

Come, my people, enter your chambers,
And shut your doors behind you;
Hide yourself, as it were, for a little moment,
Until the indignation is past.
For behold, the LORD comes out of His place
To punish the inhabitants of the earth for their iniquity;
The earth will also disclose her blood
And will no more cover her slain.

a. **Come, my people, enter your chambers**: Isaiah, speaking for the LORD, prophesies a time when God's people are invited to come and find refuge **until the indignation is past**.

i. The refuge is secure. God's people are secure in **chambers**, with the **doors shut behind** them. They are hidden securely (**Hide yourself**).

b. **The LORD comes out of His place to punish the inhabitants of the earth for their iniquity**: The **indignation** God's people are hidden from is from the LORD Himself. This is not persecution from the wicked, but judgment from the LORD. This is not a local judgment, but something the LORD brings upon the **inhabitants of the earth** in general.

i. The devastation of the indignation of the LORD is seen all over the earth: **The earth will also disclose her blood, and will no more cover her slain.**

c. **Hide yourself, as it were**: When is this time when God's people are carried away, securely hidden, from a time of great indignation the LORD brings upon the earth? It could refer to the deliverance of the Jewish people from the fury of the Antichrist described in Revelation 12:6 and 12:13-16. But it is more likely that it speaks of the refuge, the safety, the security of God's people when they are caught up together with the Lord in the air (1 Thessalonians 4:16-17) and escape the horrific indignation of the Lord that He pours out upon the world in the Great Tribulation (Matthew 24:21-22, Revelation 9:15-21), which will immediately precede the second coming of Jesus Christ (Matthew 24:29-30).

i. Seen this way, this is a powerful passage supporting the teaching of the Pre-Tribulation Rapture, which says that Jesus Christ will remove His people from this earth before the time of Great Tribulation coming upon the earth immediately before His ultimate return.

Isaiah 27 – Ordering the Kingdom of the LORD

A. In His Kingdom, God blesses Israel.

1. (1) In the Kingdom of the Lord, Leviathan is defeated.

In that day the LORD with His severe sword, great and strong,
Will punish Leviathan the fleeing serpent,
Leviathan that twisted serpent;
And He will slay the reptile that *is* in the sea.

a. **In that day**: This brings us back to the theme of Isaiah 24 through 27 in general, the day when the Kingdom of the Messiah ultimately triumphs and rules.

b. **The LORD, with His severe sword, great and strong, will punish Leviathan the fleeing serpent**: The ultimate triumph of the LORD in the day of the Messiah is expressed in victory over Leviathan the fleeing serpent.

i. Some make the connection between **Leviathan** and ancient myths of nations near Israel. "The language used draws on mythology; but this need cause us no serious problem. Writers, whether of Scripture or otherwise, frequently use illustrative material, drawing that material from a wide variety of sources: nature, history, mythology, or literature. The use of mythology here simply shows that Isaiah and his readers knew the mythological stories, not that they believed them. If a modern historian referred to a fierce and aggressive nation as 'a great dragon,' would his readers assume he believed in the objective existence of such creatures? Surely not!" (Grogan)

ii. "The term as used here is normally linked with the Ugaritic Lotan, the chaos monster destroyed by Baal in the Canaanite creation myth... the term may be applied figuratively to monstrous enemies of Israel and of God." (Grogan)

iii. While there is an illustrative element here, Isaiah may be more literal than many would like to admit. If Satan could manifest himself as a serpent to Eve in the Garden of Eden, why not also manifest himself as a dreadful sea-dragon?

c. **Leviathan that twisted serpent**: What do we know about **Leviathan** from this passage? We know that Leviathan is identified with a **serpent**. We know that Leviathan is resisting God (**fleeing…twisting**; **twisting** has the idea of *coiling*, as if it were ready to strike). We know that Leviathan is connected with the **sea**. And we know that Leviathan's destiny is to be destroyed by the LORD.

i. What do we know about **Leviathan** from other passages of Scripture? Leviathan is referred to in passages like Job 3:8, Job 41, Psalm 74:14, and Psalm 104:26. These passages reinforce the idea of Leviathan as a mighty, serpent-like creature, connected with the sea, who resists God and will be crushed by the LORD.

ii. We are familiar with the reference to Satan as a serpent (Genesis 3:1-5), but here the picture is of a *sea-serpent* or perhaps what we would know as a *dragon*. This reference may be a *literal* reference, and at some point in history, either past or present, Satan may manifest himself as a monster connected with the sea. Certainly, Revelation uses this imagery in describing the emergence of the Antichrist (Revelation 13:1-4).

d. **He will slay the reptile that is in the sea**: Essentially, Isaiah prophesied the ultimate defeat of Satan when the Kingdom of the Messiah conquers all (**He will slay the reptile**).

2. (2-6) In the Kingdom of the LORD, Israel blossoms.

In that day sing to her,
"A vineyard of red wine!
I, the LORD, keep it,
I water it every moment;
Lest any hurt it,
I keep it night and day.
Fury is not in Me.
Who would set briers *and* thorns
Against Me in battle?
I would go through them,
I would burn them together.
Or let him take hold of My strength,
***That* he may make peace with Me;**
***And* he shall make peace with Me."**
Those who come He shall cause to take root in Jacob;

Israel shall blossom and bud,
And fill the face of the world with fruit.

a. **A vineyard of red wine! I, the LORD, keep it**: In the days of the Kingdom of the Messiah, the LORD will keep the vineyard of Israel with special care. He waters it (**I will water it every moment**), He protects it (**lest any hurt it**), He guards it constantly (**I keep it night and day**) against all enemies, forcing them to **make peace** with Him and His vineyard.

b. **Let him take hold of My strength**: We can only be fruitful when we take hold of the strength of the LORD. As long as we hold on to our own strength, what we really have is weakness.

i. Poole on **let him take hold of My strength**: "He seems to allude to that history of Jacob's wrestling with the angel of God...which he could never have done but by a strength received from God."

ii. "Verse 5 is a neglected Old Testament promise of forgiveness to the penitent. In verse 4 the God of battles is marching against the briers and the thorns with a flaming torch in his hand. He is about to set fire to this rank undergrowth, but before doing so he proclaims the alternative of peace." (Grogan)

c. **Israel shall blossom and bud, and fill the face of the world with fruit**: The result is blessing for the LORD's vineyard. This will be ultimately fulfilled in the Kingdom of the Messiah, but if we yield to the care of the LORD, He will care for us as His precious vineyard right now, and we will enjoy the blessings of that care (John 15:1-8).

i. "Whereas the vineyard in chapter 5 was overrun by thorns, not a brier or thorn can be found in this vineyard." (Wolf)

3. (7-9) In the Kingdom of the LORD, Israel receives mercy.

Has He struck Israel as He struck those who struck him?
Or has He been slain according to the slaughter of those who were slain by Him?
In measure, by sending it away,
You contended with it.
He removes *it* by His rough wind
In the day of the east wind.
Therefore by this the iniquity of Jacob will be covered;
And this is all the fruit of taking away his sin:
When he makes all the stones of the altar
Like chalkstones that are beaten to dust,
Wooden images and incense altars shall not stand.

a. **Has He struck Israel as He struck those who struck him?** The LORD shows His mercy to Israel, in that even though the LORD struck Israel when Israel went astray, He did not strike Israel as severely as He did the other nations that went astray.

b. **The iniquity of Jacob will be covered**: The LORD shows His mercy to Israel in that He covers their sin. This is ultimately fulfilled in the Kingdom of the Messiah when *all Israel will be saved* (Romans 11:26).

c. **When he makes all the stones of the altar like chalkstones that are beaten to dust**: The LORD shows His mercy to Israel in that He destroys their idolatrous altars and images, forcing them to worship the LORD only.

B. In His Kingdom, God makes the nations submit to Him.

1. (10-11) In the Kingdom of the LORD, the city of man lies desolate.

Yet the fortified city *will be* desolate,
The habitation forsaken and left like a wilderness;
There the calf will feed, and there it will lie down
And consume its branches.
When its boughs are withered, they will be broken off;
The women come *and* set them on fire.
For it *is* a people of no understanding;
Therefore He who made them will not have mercy on them,
And He who formed them will show them no favor.

a. **The fortified city will be desolate**: The city of man, representing the world system, will be made desolate by the judgment of the LORD. Knowing this, why would we put our hope, our confidence, or our expectation in the world system?

b. **The habitation forsaken and left like a wilderness**: The city of man, the world system, will be made so desolate that it will resemble a **wilderness** with bare **branches**, useful only for **fire**.

i. "In [Isaiah] 10:33-34, God goes into battle against the great trees, lopping the boughs from them with his axe. Here the undergrowth feels the shriveling heat of his anger." (Grogan)

c. **He who formed them will show them no favor**: This is the terrible judgment against the city of man, against the world system. We want the **favor** of the LORD, we long for His **favor**. But the world's system, the citizens of the city of man, will be shown **no favor**.

2. (12-13) In the Kingdom of the LORD, He is worshipped in Jerusalem.

And it shall come to pass in
***That* day that the LORD will thresh,**

From the channel of the River to the Brook of Egypt;
And you will be gathered one by one,
O you children of Israel.
So it shall be in that day:
The great trumpet will be blown;
They will come, who are about to perish in the land of Assyria,
And they who are outcasts in the land of Egypt,
And shall worship the LORD in the holy mount at Jerusalem.

a. **You will be gathered one by one, O you children of Israel**: The LORD will be worshipped by His own regathered people. They will come from the nations (**Assyria…. Egypt**), and they will come to **worship the LORD in the holy mount at Jerusalem**.

Isaiah 28 – A Word to Drunkards

Isaiah 28 begins an eight-chapter section (chapters 28-35) mostly directed to the southern kingdom of Judah. Since it is often most effective to address a sin present in a third party, and then apply it directly to the person, Isaiah will first speak of the sin of Israel, then switch the focus to Judah.

A. The sinful state of the drunkards of Ephraim.

1. (1-4) A flood of judgment upon the drunkards of Ephraim.

Woe to the crown of pride, to the drunkards of Ephraim,
Whose glorious beauty *is* a fading flower
Which *is* at the head of the verdant valleys,
To those who are overcome with wine!
Behold, the Lord has a mighty and strong one,
Like a tempest of hail and a destroying storm,
Like a flood of mighty waters overflowing,
Who will bring *them* down to the earth with *His* hand.
The crown of pride, the drunkards of Ephraim,
Will be trampled underfoot;
And the glorious beauty is a fading flower
Which *is* at the head of the verdant valley,
Like the first fruit before the summer,
Which an observer sees;
He eats it up while it is still in his hand.

a. **To the drunkards of Ephraim**: In **Ephraim** (another name for the northern nation of Israel because the tribe of Ephraim was a prominent tribe in that nation), drunkenness was a significant enough problem that the LORD directed Isaiah to directly address **the drunkards of Ephraim**.

i. This is one of several passages of Scripture that speaks to **drunkards**. Proverbs 23:29-35 speaks of the folly of drunkenness. Ephesians 5:18 tells us to be filled with the Spirit instead of being drunk. Romans

13:13, 1 Corinthians 5:11, 6:10, 11:21, Galatians 5:21, and 1 Peter 4:3 each contain commands against drunkenness. Jesus specifically warned against drunkenness in the last days (Luke 21:34-36).

ii. Spiritually, alcoholism and drug addiction have been the ruin of many a man and woman. The power of those addictions keeps many from coming to Jesus at all, and they severely stunt the spiritual growth of those who trust Jesus yet have to battle their addictions. We should listen to what Proverbs tells us about drunkenness in passages such as Proverbs 20:1 and 23:29-33.

iii. Practically, the world pays a high price for the ruin of alcoholism and drug addiction. To speak of alcohol alone, according to the United States Center for Disease Control, in 2010 88,000 people died of alcohol related causes in the USA, and excessive drinking cost the USA economy $249 billion dollars – almost a quarter of a trillion dollars.

iv. Drunkenness is behind many other crimes and sins. Many drunkards either commit violent or sexual crimes or become victims of violent or sexual crimes. According to some past statistics, 75% of the men and 55% of the women involved in date-rape situations had been drinking or taking drugs just before the attack. At one time the FBI said that 50% of all rapes involve alcohol.

b. **Woe to the crown of pride, to the drunkards of Ephraim**: Like any other sin, drunkenness is connected to **pride**, so much so that Isaiah likens the **drunkards of Ephraim** to a **crown of pride**. Much of the self-hatred and self-despising drunkards feel is rooted in *too much focus* upon one's self, which is the essence of pride.

c. **Whose glorious beauty is a fading flower**: Drunkenness makes everything beautiful and good in our lives fade away. Many men and women have gone from the top of success to homelessness because of drunkenness.

d. **To those who are overcome with wine**: When alcohol *overcomes* us, we are in sin. When it impairs our senses, our thinking, our judgment, or our reflexes, we are **overcome with wine** and it is sin.

i. One might wish that there was a strict prohibition against drinking alcohol in the Bible, but there isn't. Jesus made wine (John 2:1-10) and He drank wine (Mark 14:22-26). Jesus was even unjustly accused of being a drunkard (Matthew 11:19). Paul recommended the use of wine to Timothy, knowing that it was purer to drink than plain water (1 Timothy 5:23). The Bible regards drink, moderately used, as a gift from God (Psalm 104:15). So, while the Bible allows the moderate use of alcohol, *it strictly condemns drunkenness.*

ii. What is drunkenness? Some only consider a person drunk if they are "passed-out drunk." But whenever alcohol impairs our senses, our thinking, our judgment, or our reflexes, we are **overcome with wine** and it is sin. Whenever we feel *compelled* to drink, or have difficulty *not drinking*, we are **overcome with wine** and it is sin. If we have to *hide our drinking*, or are *secretly ashamed of our drinking*, we are **overcome with wine** and it is sin.

iii. **Overcome** is the Hebrew word *halam*, which literally means "to strike down" and by implication means "to hammer, to conquer, to beat down, to overcome, to hit with a hammer." The same word is translated *pounded* in Judges 5:26, describing when Jael pounded a tent peg through the head of Sisera. When you get drunk, that's what you are doing to yourself.

e. **Behold, the Lord has a mighty and strong one**: The drunkard needs to know that God is stronger than the drunkard, stronger than the power of alcohol, stronger than anything. If the drunkard is powerless to stop his drinking, God has the power to help him stop – or the power to judge him (**the drunkards of Ephraim will be trampled underfoot**).

f. **Like the first fruit before the summer, which an observer sees; he eats it up while it is still in his hand**: The drunkard needs to learn the value of *delayed gratification.* The gratification of drinking may be intense and immediate, but it fades quickly and crashes hard. The drunkard must learn the value delaying immediate gratification for a future benefit, instead of eating the **fruit...while it is still in his hand**.

i. The importance of appreciating the value of delayed gratification has been measured in what has been called the marshmallow test. A researcher gave this choice to a four-year-old: "I am leaving for a few minutes to run an errand and you can have this marshmallow while I am gone, but if you wait until I return, you can have two marshmallows." Researchers at Stanford did this test in the 1960s, and a dozen years later they found that the kids who grabbed the single marshmallow tended to be more troubled as adolescents, and the one-marshmallow kids also scored an average of 210 points less on SAT tests. Learning to delay gratification is important for human development and maturity.

2. (5-6) The beauty of the Lord replaces the faded beauty of Ephraim.

In that day the Lord of hosts will be
For a crown of glory and a diadem of beauty

To the remnant of His people,
For a spirit of justice to him who sits in judgment,
And for strength to those who turn back the battle at the gate.

a. **The LORD of hosts will be for a crown of glory and a diadem of beauty**: Sometimes when we see the faded glory that comes with sins like drunkenness, we can grow discouraged or depressed. But even if all the glory of man fades because of disobedience and sin, God's glory remains. When we are completely "unglorified" because of the wreckage of sin, we can set our focus on the glory of the LORD.

b. **For a spirit of justice to him who sits in judgment**: When our glory has faded because of our sin, we may lose our judgment and discernment. But then we can receive them from the LORD.

c. **And for strength to those who turn back the battle at the gate**: When our glory has faded because of our sin, we may lose our strength and ability to fight. But then we can receive them from the LORD.

3. (7-8) The corruption of drunkenness in Judah.

But they also have erred through wine,
And through intoxicating drink are out of the way;
The priest and the prophet have erred through intoxicating drink,
They are swallowed up by wine,
They are out of the way through intoxicating drink;
They err in vision, they stumble in judgment.
For all tables are full of vomit *and* filth;
No place *is clean*.

a. **They also**: Since Isaiah mentions the **priest** and the **prophet** in this section, it seems that **they also** refers to the people of Jerusalem and Judah. If the people of Ephraim had a problem with drunkenness, so did **they also**.

i. "Judah had caught this disease of Ephraim.... Sin is more contagious and catching than the plague." (Trapp)

b. **They also have erred through wine and through intoxicating drink are out of the way**: Drunkenness always leads to *error* and takes us out of the way – the way of wisdom and God's will.

c. **The priest and the prophet have erred through intoxicating drink**: Drunkenness is something that can touch any person, at any stage of life. Even the **priest and the prophet** can find themselves under the tyranny of drunkenness (**swallowed up by wine**).

d. **For all tables are full of vomit and filth; no place is clean**: Drunkenness leads to this kind of degradation and disgrace. This is because of the way alcohol works. Alcohol is a depressant; it "loosens" people because it depresses their self-control, their wisdom, their balance and judgment.

i. This makes the idea of being "drunk in the Holy Spirit" especially unbiblical and offensive. The Holy Spirit does not depress us; He has the exact opposite effect. The Holy Spirit is a stimulant, and He moves every aspect of our being to better and more perfect performance. Of those who act silly or crazy claiming to be "drunk in the Holy Spirit," the most charitable thing to say is that they are simply acting in their own flesh, because they *certainly* are not being led by the Holy Spirit of God.

B. God's message to those who are ripe for judgment.

1. (9-10) The simple message is mocked.

"Whom will he teach knowledge?
And whom will he make to understand the message?
Those *just* weaned from milk?
Those *just* drawn from the breasts?
For precept *must be* upon precept, precept upon precept,
Line upon line, line upon line,
Here a little, there a little."

a. **Whom will he teach knowledge?** These are the words of the drunk, ungodly prophets and priests described in Isaiah 28:7-8. They ask Isaiah, the godly prophet, **whom will he teach knowledge? And whom will he make to understand the message?** In their mocking minds, Isaiah's message is fit only for children (**Those just weaned from milk**).

i. "Verses 9 and 10 portray the sarcastic reaction these Judean leaders had to Isaiah's words of rebuke. They were tired of Isaiah's strictness and of his recurring application of God's laws. The string of monosyllables in verse 10 may mean that the Judean leaders regarded Isaiah's message as meaningless or as child's play." (Wolf)

ii. "Many commentators have been puzzled by verse 10 and have wrestled to make sense of the Hebrew. The truth of the matter seems to be, as the NIV margin suggests, that it is not meant to make sense. Isaiah's words had hardly penetrated the alcohol-impregnated atmosphere that surrounded his hearers." (Grogan)

iii. "Thus this good prophet became the drunkard's song. Any man may be witty in a biting way, and those that have the dullest brains have commonly the sharpest teeth to that purpose." (Trapp)

b. **Precept upon precept**: With this, the drunk, ungodly prophets and priests mock Isaiah's teaching. "It is too simple. It is simply **precept upon precept, line upon line…here a little, there a little**. We are so smart and spiritually sophisticated and advanced that we can go on to deeper things."

i. In their mocking of Isaiah's message, they actually pay him a great compliment. It is a beautiful thing for God's truth to be presented **precept upon precept, line upon line…here a little, there a little**. When the word of God is properly presented, there is something for both the simple and immature to receive, and also something for the great saint to rejoice in and be fed.

2. (11-13) Isaiah warns of the consequences of rejecting the simple message of the Lord.

For with stammering lips and another tongue
He will speak to this people,
To whom He said, "This *is* the rest *with which*
You may cause the weary to rest,"
And, "This *is* the refreshing";
Yet they would not hear.
But the word of the Lord was to them,
"Precept upon precept, precept upon precept,
Line upon line, line upon line,
Here a little, there a little,"
That they might go and fall backward, and be broken
And snared and caught.

a. **With stammering lips and another tongue He will speak to this people**: If the simple, straightforward message is rejected, God will find another way to communicate to the hard-hearted. He will send unusual messengers to bring the word.

b. **This is the rest…this is refreshing**: The message of rest and deliverance would be rejected (**they would not hear**). But it wasn't the fault of the word of the Lord – **the word of the Lord was to them, "Precept upon precept, precept upon precept, line upon line, line upon line, here a little, there a little."**

i. This is the blessed way to present God's word: **precept upon precept, line upon line**. Isaiah takes the taunt of the drunkards and receives it as a compliment. God's messengers are to present *all* of God's word (without skipping a line), and to present it *simply*.

ii. This also implies that we can't receive all aspects of God's message at once. "It is an excellent thing that the gospel is taught us by degrees. It is not forced home upon men's minds all at once, but it comes thus, 'Precept upon precept, line upon line, here a little and there a little.' God does not flash the everlasting daylight on weak eyes in one blaze of glory, but there is at first a dim dawn, and the soft incoming of a tender light for tender eyes, and so by degrees we see." (Spurgeon)

c. **That they might go and fall backward and be broken and snared and caught**: In fact, the result of the faithful presentation of the word of the LORD for those who reject isn't good for *them*. It will result in their destruction.

3. (14-15) The false confidence of sinful leaders.

Therefore hear the word of the LORD, you scornful men,
Who rule this people who *are* in Jerusalem,
Because you have said, "We have made a covenant with death,
And with Sheol we are in agreement.
When the overflowing scourge passes through,
It will not come to us,
For we have made lies our refuge,
And under falsehood we have hidden ourselves."

a. **You scornful men, who rule this people who are in Jerusalem**: Sadly, some of the simple and immature were those **who rule this people**. They needed to **hear the word of the LORD** just as everyone did.

i. There is no one too high, too exalted, too mature, too advanced for the word of the LORD, and to hear it *precept upon precept, line upon line, here a little and there a little*.

b. **We have made a covenant with death**: The rulers of Jerusalem were extreme in their rejection of God and felt they had an "agreement" with death and the grave (**Sheol**). They proudly believed **the overflowing scourge** of God's judgment and correction would not come against them.

i. They had no fear of death and thought they had made friends with death and the grave. This same way of thinking is common in our modern world. The ungodly *should* fear death, because with death ends all opportunity for repentance, and their eternal doom is sealed. Satan has a significant interest in making the wicked feel that death is their friend.

ii. Many of those who commit suicide are deceived into thinking that death is their friend. But without Jesus Christ, the moment those unfortunate people pass into eternity, they would give anything to go back to the world where faith and repentance are still possible.

c. **We have made lies our refuge**: This was their strength. This was their protection. **Lies** are a sad and useless **refuge**.

i. In his sermon on this verse titled *Refuges of Lies and What Will Become of Them*, Charles Spurgeon listed six lies that men attempt to make their refuge:

- The lie that we are good enough or can be good enough.
- The lie that fate or predestination determines everything, so there is nothing for us to do.
- The lie that places confidence in new, false teachings.
- The lie that mere religious profession is enough.
- The lie that one can have a saved soul and an unchanged life.
- The lie that trusts an old experience instead of an ongoing relationship.

4. (16-19) The security of the Messiah and the precarious place of sinners.

Therefore thus says the Lord God:
"Behold, I lay in Zion a stone for a foundation,
A tried stone, a precious cornerstone, a sure foundation;
Whoever believes will not act hastily.
Also I will make justice the measuring line,
And righteousness the plummet;
The hail will sweep away the refuge of lies,
And the waters will overflow the hiding place.
Your covenant with death will be annulled,
And your agreement with Sheol will not stand;
When the overflowing scourge passes through,
Then you will be trampled down by it.
As often as it goes out it will take you;
For morning by morning it will pass over,
And by day and by night;
It will be a terror just to understand the report."

a. **Behold, I lay in Zion a stone for a foundation**: In contrast to the weak, narrow foundation of the wicked (*we have made lies our refuge, and under falsehood we have hidden ourselves*), God has a solid foundation for those who trust in Him – **a stone for a foundation**.

i. What is this foundation? 1 Peter 2:6 applies this passage directly to the Messiah, Jesus Christ. He is the foundation for our lives, and only with a secure, stable foundation can anything lasting be built. Anything "added on" to the house, not built upon the foundation, is sure to end up in wreckage.

ii. Who lays this stone? **Behold, I lay in Zion.** It is God's work. We are unable to provide the right kind of foundation for our lives, but God can lay a foundation for us. We are asked to **behold** God's foundation, appreciate it, wonder at it, value it, and build our lives upon it.

b. **A tried stone**: Our Messiah was **tried**, was tested, and was proven to be the glorious, obedient Son of God in all things.

c. **A precious cornerstone**: Our Messiah is **precious**, and a **cornerstone.** The cornerstone provides the lines, the pattern for all the rest of the construction. The cornerstone is straight and true, and everything in the entire building lines up in reference to the cornerstone.

d. **A sure foundation**: Our Messiah is a **sure foundation**, and we can build everything on Him without fear.

e. **Justice the measuring line, and righteousness the plummet**: In God's building, it isn't just as if He established the cornerstone and then allows the building to be built as anyone pleases. Instead, God keeps the building straight with **justice** and **righteousness.**

f. **The hail will sweep away the refuge of lies, and the waters will overflow the hiding place**: The ungodly leaders of Jerusalem *made lies* their *refuge* and found a hiding place *under falsehood* (Isaiah 28:15). But the storms of life and God's judgment would **sweep away** their **refuge of lies** and their **hiding place.** They had built on the wrong foundation and would therefore be destroyed.

g. **Your covenant with death will be annulled**: The ungodly leaders of Jerusalem thought they made a "deal with death," but would find that God would cancel their **covenant with death**. When God's **scourge** of judgment comes, they will surely **be trampled down by it**.

i. And the whip of judgment will not touch them lightly. **Morning by morning** and **by day and by night** they will feel the sting of God's correction.

5. (20-22) Advice to those ripe for judgment.

For the bed is too short to stretch out *on*,
And the covering so narrow that one cannot wrap himself *in it*.
For the Lord will rise up as *at* Mount Perazim,

He will be angry as in the Valley of Gibeon;
That He may do His work, His awesome work,
And bring to pass His act, His unusual act.
Now therefore, do not be mockers,
Lest your bonds be made strong;
For I have heard from the Lord GOD of hosts,
A destruction determined even upon the whole earth.

a. **The bed is too short…the covering so narrow**: The rulers of Jerusalem had to realize that their present place was dangerous, and they could find no refuge where they were at right then.

i. Their rejection of God gave them no peace, no rest, and no warmth. What could be worse than trying to sleep in a **bed** that **is too short**? With trying to keep warm with something **so narrow that one cannot wrap himself in it**? Yet this is a picture of the world, working, striving, longing for their bed – and when they gain it, it is **too short** and has no proper blankets! The child of God, on the other hand, is given rest and peace and covering by Jesus Christ. We shouldn't long for the short beds and narrow coverings of the world; we should thank God for the place He gives us in Jesus Christ and enjoy it.

b. **For the LORD will rise up**: The rulers of Jerusalem had to realize that fighting against God was always a losing proposition. There was no way they could win that battle because God would always **do His work, His awesome work**.

c. **The LORD will rise up as *at* Mount Perazim**: At **Perazim**, the LORD accomplished a great victory for Israel in the days of David (2 Samuel 5:20). At **Gibeon**, the LORD accomplished a great victory for Israel in the days of Joshua (Joshua 10:11). In those cases, the LORD fought for Israel, but if her leaders did not repent, they would soon find the LORD fighting *against* Israel. This use of God's strength against His people is surely **His awesome work**, or as the King James Version puts it, *His strange work*.

d. **Now therefore, do not be mockers**: The rulers of Jerusalem had to realize the danger of mocking God with their "deals with death" and haughty words against God.

6. (23-29) The timing of the farmer and the timing of God.

Give ear and hear my voice,
Listen and hear my speech.
Does the plowman keep plowing all day to sow?
Does he keep turning his soil and breaking the clods?
When he has leveled its surface,

Does he not sow the black cummin
And scatter the cummin,
Plant the wheat in rows,
The barley in the appointed place,
And the spelt in its place?
For He instructs him in right judgment,
His God teaches him.
For the black cummin is not threshed with a threshing sledge,
Nor is a cartwheel rolled over the cummin;
But the black cummin is beaten out with a stick,
And the cummin with a rod.
Bread *flour* must be ground;
Therefore he does not thresh it forever,
Break it *with* his cartwheel,
Or crush it with his horsemen.
This also comes from the LORD of hosts,
***Who* is wonderful in counsel *and* excellent in guidance.**

a. **Give ear and hear my voice**: The rulers of Jerusalem had to listen to God's word and pay attention to His **voice**.

b. **Does the plowman keep plowing all day to sow?** The end of Isaiah 28 is a poem relating the work of God and the work of a farmer. A farmer doesn't *only* plow; he knows when to stop plowing and when to level the ground, when to plant, and what to plant where. A farmer uses different tools at different times and works them all together to produce crops. In the same way, God knows what instruments to use in our lives, and when to use them. We don't have to *doubt* or *despair* at what God is doing in our lives, because He is an expert farmer, working on us with all His wisdom.

i. "He used the proper instrument and procedure at the proper time to accomplish His purposes among His stubborn people." (Wolf)

c. **Who is wonderful in counsel and excellent in guidance**: The phrase **wonderful in counsel** is the same used to describe the Messiah in Isaiah 9:6 (*Wonderful Counselor*). It reminds us of the perfect timing and wisdom of God's work in our lives.

Isaiah 29 – The Cause and Cure of Spiritual Blindness

A. The coming distress upon Jerusalem.

1. (1-4) The LORD humbles a proud Jerusalem.

"Woe to Ariel, to Ariel, the city *where* David dwelt!
Add year to year;
Let feasts come around.
Yet I will distress Ariel;
There shall be heaviness and sorrow,
And it shall be to Me as Ariel.
I will encamp against you all around,
I will lay siege against you with a mound,
And I will raise siegeworks against you.
You shall be brought down,
You shall speak out of the ground;
Your speech shall be low, out of the dust;
Your voice shall be like a medium's, out of the ground;
And your speech shall whisper out of the dust.

a. **Woe to Ariel**: The name **Ariel** means *Lion of God*, and in this passage is used as a symbolic reference to Jerusalem (**the city where David dwelt**). The only place where **Ariel** is used as a name for Jerusalem is in this chapter of Isaiah, and the word only appears one other time in the Old Testament (as the name of a priest in Ezra 8:16).

i. There is some dispute as to if **Ariel** means *Lion of God* (the literal translation) or *an altar for burning*, which is a very similar word in Hebrew (used in passages like Ezekiel 43:15-16). If it is to be understood as *an altar for burning*, then the idea is that "The fighting and bloodshed around Jerusalem would make the city like a giant place of sacrifice." (Wolf) But, considering the context as a whole, it is best to see **Ariel** with its literal meaning – *Lion of God.*

ii. When we consider the way **Ariel** is used in these verses, and the context as a whole, the idea behind calling Jerusalem *Lion of God* is probably sarcastic. The repetition of the name (four times in two verses), and the context of God's judgment against Jerusalem, suggest the idea that Jerusalem may have thought of herself as the *Lion of God,* but God didn't share that lofty opinion of the city. It may be that the people of Jerusalem had taken to calling themselves by the name **Ariel**, to both express and strengthen their confidence.

b. **Add year to year; let feasts come around**: The feeling in Isaiah 29:1 is that Jerusalem is proud (**Ariel**), resting on its spiritual heritage instead of its present reality (**the city where David dwelt!**), and living for present pleasures without concern for God.

c. **Yet I will distress Ariel**: Jerusalem may have this high opinion of itself, but it is not out of the reach of God's hand of judgment. Instead of the routine of **year to year** and the **feasts**, God will send **heaviness and sorrow**. If Jerusalem sees itself as a *lion,* then God will fight against them with the same fury a man would have against a lion (**it shall be to Me as Ariel**).

d. **I will encamp against you all around**: Using the images of warfare for that day, God promises to battle against Jerusalem, and to conquer her (**You shall be brought down**).

e. **You shall be brought down**: In all of this, the LORD will bring down the lofty self-image Jerusalem has of itself. Instead of calling herself **Ariel**, and **the city where David dwelt**, their **speech shall be low, out of the dust**. Instead of loud boasts, their **speech shall whisper out of the dust**.

2. (5-8) The LORD protects and delivers a humbled Jerusalem.

"Moreover the multitude of your foes
Shall be like fine dust,
And the multitude of the terrible ones
Like chaff that passes away;
Yes, it shall be in an instant, suddenly.
You will be punished by the LORD of hosts
With thunder and earthquake and great noise,
***With* storm and tempest**
And the flame of devouring fire.
The multitude of all the nations who fight against Ariel,
Even all who fight against her and her fortress,
And distress her,

Shall be as a dream of a night vision.
It shall even be as when a hungry man dreams,
And look—he eats;
But he awakes, and his soul is still empty;
Or as when a thirsty man dreams,
And look—he drinks;
But he awakes, and indeed *he is* faint,
And his soul still craves:
So the multitude of all the nations shall be,
Who fight against Mount Zion."

a. **The multitude of your foes shall be like fine dust**: The closing image in the previous verses was Jerusalem groveling in the dust. Now, the Lord uses another image, spun off of the idea of **dust** – Jerusalem's enemies will be scattered as **fine dust**. God will humble Jerusalem in the dust, and then scatter her enemies like **fine dust**, like **chaff that passes away**.

b. **You will be punished**: This seems to be directed against the nations that come against Jerusalem. God will allow them to come against the city, and to humble it, but God will punish the nations that have come against His city.

c. **It shall even be as when a hungry man dreams**: Because the Lord will protect Jerusalem, the nations that come against her will ultimately be frustrated. They will be like a man who dreams of food but wakes up hungry. They will dream of fulfillment but be unfulfilled.

B. The spiritual blindness of Jerusalem.

1. (9-10) The spiritual stupor of Jerusalem.

Pause and wonder!
Blind yourselves and be blind!
They are drunk, but not with wine;
They stagger, but not with intoxicating drink.
For the Lord has poured out on you
The spirit of deep sleep,
And has closed your eyes, namely, the prophets;
And He has covered your heads, *namely*, the seers.

a. **Pause and wonder! Blind yourselves and be blind**: Jerusalem's pride (as expressed in Isaiah 29:1) has made them spiritually **blind**, and spiritually **drunk**. The Lord tells Jerusalem to **pause and wonder** at this, because though they do it to themselves, they lack the self-awareness to see their condition.

b. **They stagger, but not with intoxicating drink**: This *was not* a blessing from the Spirit of the LORD. This was a *curse*, both self-induced and sent from the LORD. This speaks powerfully to those today who wrongly promote the idea of God "blessing" His people with being "drunk in the Spirit." This is no blessing.

c. **For the LORD has poured out on you**: Because Jerusalem chose blindness, and chose spiritual drunkenness, God *sent* something: the LORD **poured out on** them **the spirit of deep sleep**. As drunks will "sleep it off," so the LORD will send blind, proud, drunk Jerusalem into the lethargy and vulnerability of spiritual sleep. But a drunk can become sober after sleep; for those who are spiritually drunk, sleep worsens their condition.

i. When we are asleep, we are doing nothing *productive*. When we are asleep, we are *vulnerable*. When we are asleep, we are *insensitive*. God sent these things to a blind, proud, drunk Jerusalem.

ii. The problem of spiritual sleep didn't end with the Jerusalem of Isaiah's day. Romans 13:11 was written to Christians: *And do this, knowing the time, that now it is high time to awake out of sleep; for now our salvation is nearer than when we first believed.* Christians need to be *awake*, especially knowing the time.

d. **For the LORD has poured out on you**: Because Jerusalem chose blindness, and chose spiritual drunkenness, God *took away* something: He **has closed your eyes, namely, the prophets**. As a drunk has blurred vision and poor perception, so God **closed** the spiritual **eyes** of the nation – **namely, the prophets**.

i. The prophets were silent, and the word of God was neglected because the people *wanted* it that way. In silencing the **prophets** and the **seers**, God simply gave Jerusalem what she wanted.

ii. The prophet Amos spoke of the same idea: *"Behold, the days are coming," says the Lord GOD, "That I will send a famine on the land, not a famine of bread, nor a thirst for water, but of hearing the words of the LORD. They shall wander from sea to sea, and from north to east; they shall run to and fro, seeking the word of the LORD, but shall not find it."* (Amos 8:11-12)

2. (11-12) The spiritual illiteracy of Jerusalem.

The whole vision has become to you like the words of a book that is sealed, which *men* deliver to one who is literate, saying, "Read this, please." And he says, "I cannot, for it is sealed." Then the book is delivered to one who is illiterate, saying, "Read this, please." And he says, "I am not literate."

a. **A book that is sealed, which men deliver to one who is literate**: Isaiah had likened Jerusalem to the *blind* and to the *drunk*. Here, he likened them to the *illiterate*. But this wasn't a literal literacy, because the **literate** man received the **vision** of God, but to him it was like a **sealed** book. When the book of the vision was brought to the **illiterate** man, he did no better (**I am not literate**).

b. **Read this, please**: Many today read or receive God's word like an illiterate man "reads" the newspaper. They can pick out a few words here and there, and they can certainly look at the pictures. They can sit with an open newspaper, enjoy themselves to some degree, and *appear* to be reading. But the true content of what is written has no impact on them.

3. (13-16) Why the Lord sends spiritual blindness upon Jerusalem.

Therefore the Lord said:
"Inasmuch as these people draw near with their mouths
And honor Me with their lips,
But have removed their hearts far from Me,
And their fear toward Me is taught by the commandment of men,
Therefore, behold, I will again do a marvelous work
Among this people,
A marvelous work and a wonder;
For the wisdom of their wise *men* shall perish,
And the understanding of their prudent *men* shall be hidden."
Woe to those who seek deep to hide their counsel far from the Lord,
And their works are in the dark;
They say, "Who sees us?" and, "Who knows us?"
Surely you have things turned around!
Shall the potter be esteemed as the clay;
For shall the thing made say of him who made it,
"He did not make me"?
Or shall the thing formed say of him who formed it,
"He has no understanding"?

a. **These people draw near to Me with their mouths and honor Me with their lips, but have removed their hearts far from Me**: Jerusalem knew how to *talk the spiritual talk*, but their **hearts** were **far from** God. You can't always tell a person's heart by what they *say*. You can't always tell a person's heart by what they *do*. Though only God can really know the heart, the closest we can come is by looking at the *whole of their life* – not only what they say or do, and especially not only at how they act at church or among Christians.

i. Jesus said, *for out of the abundance of the heart the mouth speaks* (Matthew 12:34). This is a true – but not absolute – principle, because people can **draw near to** God **with their mouths and honor** the LORD **with their lips**, and their hearts can still be **far from** God. Of course, their speech will betray them at one time or another – but just maybe never at church.

ii. This manner of talking the talk, but not having the heart, didn't end in Isaiah's day. Jesus quoted this passage from Isaiah when He rebuked the religious leaders of His day for their hypocrisy (Matthew 15:7-9, Mark 7:6-7). It didn't end in Jesus' day either.

iii. God tells us how their hearts got far from Him – they **have removed their hearts far from Me**. God didn't move away from His people; they removed their hearts from Him.

b. **And their fear toward Me is taught by the commandment of men**: The people of Jerusalem had no fear of God in themselves; it had to be *commanded* by others. Their hearts did not respond to God, but only to men.

c. **The wisdom of their wise men shall perish**: Because Jerusalem's pride had led them into spiritual blindness, sleep, drunkenness, illiteracy, and hypocrisy, God will destroy the **wisdom of their wise men**. Their **wise men** promoted the pride that led to all these evils.

i. Isaiah calls this **a marvelous work and a wonder**, for God to reject the wisdom of man and to display His wisdom. Paul was also amazed at the so-called wisdom" of man, and how it compared to what was thought to be the foolishness of God: *For since, in the wisdom of God, the world through wisdom did not know God, it pleased God through the foolishness of the message preached to save those who believe. For Jews request a sign, and Greeks seek after wisdom; but we preach Christ crucified, to the Jews a stumbling block and to the Greeks foolishness, but to those who are called, both Jews and Greeks, Christ the power of God and the wisdom of God. Because the foolishness of God is wiser than men, and the weakness of God is stronger than men* (1 Corinthians 1:21-25).

d. **Who sees us?** In their false wisdom, the proud people of Jerusalem thought they could hide their thoughts (**hide their counsel**) and their deeds (**their works are in the dark**) from the LORD.

e. **Surely you have things turned around!** The proud people of Jerusalem thought they could hide from the LORD, and that they had Him all figured out. God told them here that they had actually **turned around** the true state of things. In truth, the LORD had *them* all figured out, and they really don't know God at all.

f. **Shall the potter be esteemed as the clay**: The people of Jerusalem made the terrible mistake of *raising* themselves up and *lowering* God at the same time. So, for them, the **clay** was just as worthy, just as intelligent, just as powerful, as the **potter** was.

g. **For shall the thing made say of him who made it, "He did not make me"?** Indeed, man says exactly this today. Man looks at God our Creator, and says, **"He did not make me."** For the LORD and His prophet, this was absolutely absurd, but today it passes for high science.

h. **Or shall the thing formed say of him who formed it, "He has no understanding"?** Indeed, man says exactly this today. Instead of seeing the absolute need for an Intelligent Designer who created all things, many believe that chance – absolute blind, random, purposeless chance, having no **understanding** at all – brought all things into being.

i. Some intelligent people may fall into this delusion. Jacques Monod, a biochemist, wrote: "Chance *alone* is at the source of every innovation, of all creation in the biosphere. Pure chance, absolutely free but blind, at the very root of the stupendous edifice of evolution."

ii. But assigning such power to *chance* is doesn't make sense. Chance has no power. For example, when a coin is flipped, the chance it will land "heads" is 50%; however, *chance* does not make it land heads. Whether or not it lands heads or tails is due to the strength with which the coin is flipped, the strength of air currents and air pressure as it flies through the air, where it is caught, and if it is flipped over once it is caught. *Chance* doesn't do anything but describe a probability.

iii. Many years ago a scientist named Carl Sagan petitioned the U.S. government for a grant to fund the search for intelligent life in outer space. He hoped to find evidence of life by using a super-sensitive instrument to pick up radio signals from distant space. When he received those radio signals, he looked for *order* and *pattern*, which demonstrated the signals were transmitted by intelligent life. In the same way, the order and pattern of the whole universe demonstrate that it was fashioned by intelligent life, not by *chance*. Scientists detect chance in the radio signals constantly (in the form of static with no pattern), but it tells them *nothing*.

iv. Therefore, when someone says the universe or anything else came about by *chance*, one may say that despite their expertise or skill in other areas, when it comes to this subject, they are ignorant, superstitious, or simply repeating a tired theory presented and disproved before, yet is often unthinkingly accepted.

i. **He did not make me**: We need to remember the context of the whole chapter – the pride and blindness of Jerusalem. It is perhaps the height of man's pride and blindness to reject the LORD as our creator.

C. A promise of restoration.

1. (17-21) Sight for the spiritually blind, justice for the wicked.

***Is* it not yet a very little while**
Till Lebanon shall be turned into a fruitful field,
And the fruitful field be esteemed as a forest?
In that day the deaf shall hear the words of the book,
And the eyes of the blind shall see out of obscurity and out of darkness.
The humble also shall increase *their* joy in the LORD,
And the poor among men shall rejoice
In the Holy One of Israel.
For the terrible one is brought to nothing,
The scornful one is consumed,
And all who watch for iniquity are cut off—
Who make a man an offender by a word,
And lay a snare for him who reproves in the gate,
And turn aside the just by empty words.

a. **Is it not yet a very little while**: God's restoration will come, and all things considered, it is in **a very little while**. It may not seem so to us when we are in the midst of a trial, but it is true.

b. **Till Lebanon shall be turned into a fruitful field, and the fruitful field be esteemed as a forest**: The land of **Lebanon** was known for its mighty forests, which would be brought low and **turned into a fruitful field**. On the other hand, the **fruitful field** would become **as a forest**. God would cut one down and raise another up.

i. This was a "proverbial saying, expressing any great revolution of things; and, when respecting two subjects, and entire reciprocal change." (Clarke)

c. **The deaf shall hear…the eyes of the blind shall see**: When God's people are restored, pride no longer prevents them from hearing God's word or seeing God's work. Just as much as these are miracles in the natural realm, they are miracles in the spiritual realm also. We need to humbly seek God for ears to hear and eyes to see.

d. **The humble also shall increase their joy in the Lord**: This **joy** is the proper reward for **the humble**. When we are **humble** – having an accurate estimation of ourselves, and a proper perspective of ourselves in relation to God and others – our lives are filled with the most **joy**.

i. The **humble** and the **poor** have their joy **in the Lord**. He is a constant source of joy that can never be taken away.

ii. Pride is the enemy of joy. We can be proud and have *fun*, we can be proud and have *success*, we can be proud and experience *excitement*, and we can be proud and be *happy* because of happy circumstances. But we cannot be proud and have **joy in the Lord**, or to whatever degree we are proud, we are missing **joy in the Lord**. The proud can never have **joy in the Lord** if they are in humble or poor circumstances.

e. **The terrible one is brought to nothing**: The work of the Lord does not stop at restoring His corrected people. It extends to bringing justice upon the wicked. Singled out for judgment by the prophet are those who have no sense of proportion or justice: **Who make a man an offender by a word...turn aside the just by empty words**.

2. (22-24) The restoration of God's people.

Therefore thus says the Lord, who redeemed Abraham, concerning the house of Jacob:

"Jacob shall not now be ashamed,
Nor shall his face now grow pale;
But when he sees his children,
The work of My hands, in his midst,
They will hallow My name,
And hallow the Holy One of Jacob,
And fear the God of Israel.
These also who erred in spirit will come to understanding,
And those who complained will learn doctrine."

a. **Jacob shall not now be ashamed**: Significantly, God addresses His people as **Jacob** in this promise of restoration. The name **Jacob**, given to the father of the 12 tribes, is not complimentary. It has the idea of a "con-man" or a "trickster." Anyone who is really a **Jacob**, has good reason to **be ashamed**, but when God restores His people, even the "Jacobs" **shall not now be ashamed**.

b. **When he sees his children, the work of My hands, in his midst, they will hallow My name**: The picture is of the patriarch Jacob looking over his descendants, and no longer being **ashamed** of them, because they now **hallow** the name of the Lord, and respect the holiness of the Lord.

c. **These also who erred in spirit will come to understanding, and those who complained will learn doctrine**: Finally, in God's day of restoration, the truth is taught and known and exalted. Those **who erred in spirit** now have **understanding**, and those who **complained** know better because they know the truth.

i. This chapter says a great deal about spiritual blindness:

- Spiritual blindness is caused by pride.
- Spiritual blindness will bring us low.
- Spiritual blindness leads to spiritual drunkenness.
- Spiritual blindness leads to spiritual sleep.
- Spiritual blindness leads to spiritual illiteracy.
- Spiritual blindness causes hypocrisy.
- Spiritual blindness makes men believe God cannot know what they think or see what they do.
- Spiritual blindness makes men deny God as Creator.
- Spiritual blindness is cured through humility.
- Spiritual blindness can only be healed through the LORD's restoration.

Isaiah 30 – Trust In the Lord*, Not In Egypt*

A. A rebuke to those in Judah who looked to Egypt for deliverance.

1. (1-2) God exposes the sin of those who put their trust in Egypt.

"Woe to the rebellious children," says the Lord,
"Who take counsel, but not of Me,
And who devise plans, but not of My Spirit,
That they may add sin to sin;
Who walk to go down to Egypt,
And have not asked My advice,
To strengthen themselves in the strength of Pharaoh,
And to trust in the shadow of Egypt!"

a. **Who walk to go down to Egypt…. To strengthen themselves in the strength of Pharaoh**: This prophecy was given at a time when the Assyrian army was attacking Israel and Judah. The northern kingdom of Israel would soon be conquered by Assyria, and the people of Israel would be taken into exile. The Assyrians would then come against the southern kingdom of Judah, and because of this threat the leaders of Judah looked to Egypt for protection against the Assyrian invasion.

b. **Who take counsel, but not of Me, and who devise plans, but not of My Spirit**: In looking to Egypt, Judah forsook the Lord. In one sense, it was wise and good for Judah to understand that they needed help and were willing to look outside of themselves for help. In the larger sense, it was foolish and evil of Judah to look to others – especially Egypt – for help, instead of looking to the Lord.

i. You **take counsel** – but is it of the Lord? You **devise plans** – but are they of God's Spirit? It is one sin to reject the Lord, and another sin altogether to trust in something else. Therefore, to do what Judah did in this situation is to **add sin to sin**.

2. (3-5) The folly of trusting in Egypt.

Therefore the strength of Pharaoh
Shall be your shame,
And trust in the shadow of Egypt
Shall be *your* humiliation.
For his princes were at Zoan,
And his ambassadors came to Hanes.
They were all ashamed of a people *who* could not benefit them,
Or be help or benefit,
But a shame and also a reproach.

a. **Therefore the strength of Pharaoh shall be your shame, and trust in the shadow of Egypt shall be your humiliation**: From the perspective of heaven, the **strength of Pharaoh** was nothing. As the LORD saw it, Egypt was no substance, just a **shadow**.

b. **They were all ashamed of a people who could not benefit them**: The ambassadors of Egypt came to Judah and saw that Judah had nothing to "give" them. It was foolish for the leaders of Judah to trust in a nation that looked at them this way.

B. The burden against Judah for their trust in Egypt.

1. (6-7) Their trust in Egypt will gain them nothing.

The burden against the beasts of the South.
Through a land of trouble and anguish,
From which *came* the lioness and lion,
The viper and fiery flying serpent,
They will carry their riches on the backs of young donkeys,
And their treasures on the humps of camels,
To a people *who* shall not profit;
For the Egyptians shall help in vain and to no purpose.
Therefore I have called her
Rahab-Hem-Shebeth.

a. **The burden against the beasts of the South**: Isaiah proclaimed a burden against the pack animals of Judah, which would carry the riches of Judah down to Egypt, through the wilderness, in a foolish attempt to purchase protection against the Assyrians.

b. **The Egyptians shall help in vain and to no purpose**. No wonder Isaiah felt sorry for the donkeys that would carry the treasure of Judah down to Egypt. Despite the riches that the pack animals bring across the desert, Egypt would not help Judah at all, so one could call Egypt

Rahab-Hem-Shebeth, which means "Rahab Sits Idle" or "Rahab the Do-Nothing." **Rahab** is a name, but it is also the Hebrew word for *pride*, and is sometimes used as a title for Egypt (Psalm 87:4). Egypt would sit idly by as the Assyrians trouble Judah.

i. "It is all *useless*, bringing *neither help nor advantage*. 'Well, of course!' Isaiah might have said, for from the feared killer (Assyria) they were seeking help from the proved killer (Egypt)!" (Motyer)

2. (8-11) The LORD documents Judah's rejection of His message.

Now go, write it before them on a tablet,
And note it on a scroll,
That it may be for time to come,
Forever and ever:
That this is a rebellious people,
Lying children,
Children *who* will not hear the law of the LORD;
Who say to the seers, "Do not see,"
And to the prophets, "Do not prophesy to us right things;
Speak to us smooth things, prophesy deceits.
Get out of the way,
Turn aside from the path,
Cause the Holy One of Israel
To cease from before us."

a. **Now go, write it before them on a tablet…that it may be for a time to come, forever and ever**: God told Judah this before it happened, and wanted it documented. This was so when it all unfolded exactly as the LORD had spoken, Judah could have greater trust in the LORD.

b. **That this is a rebellious people, lying children…who say to the seers, "Do not see"**: God wanted Judah's rejection of His message, and His messengers, to be documented. Judah wanted to hear from the prophets and God's messengers, but they did not want to hear the truth from them. They wanted religion, but they didn't want the living God of heaven to have a real presence in their lives (**Cause the Holy One of Israel to cease from before us**).

i. The problem God confronted in Judah didn't end in the days of Judah. Paul describes the same kind of heart in 2 Timothy 4:3-4: *For the time will come when they will not endure sound doctrine, but according to their own desires, because they have itching ears, they will heap up for themselves teachers; and they will turn their ears away from the truth, and be turned aside to fables.*

3. (12-14) The judgment to come upon Judah for their trust in Egypt and for their rejection of His message.

Therefore thus says the Holy One of Israel:
"Because you despise this word,
And trust in oppression and perversity,
And rely on them,
Therefore this iniquity shall be to you
Like a breach ready to fall,
A bulge in a high wall,
Whose breaking comes suddenly, in an instant.
And He shall break it like the breaking of the potter's vessel,
Which is broken in pieces;
He shall not spare.
So there shall not be found among its fragments
A shard to take fire from the hearth,
Or to take water from the cistern."

a. **Because you despise this word…Therefore this iniquity shall be to you like a breach ready to fall**: God promised that because Judah trusted in Egypt instead of Him, everything would be broken and collapsed. Judah would be like a collapsed wall, **whose breaking comes suddenly, in an instant**. Judah would be like a shattered clay pot, **which is broken in pieces**.

4. (15-17) Judah brought low because of their self-reliance and rejection of God's message.

For thus says the Lord GOD, the Holy One of Israel:
"In returning and rest you shall be saved;
In quietness and confidence shall be your strength."
But you would not,
And you said, "No, for we will flee on horses"—
Therefore you shall flee!
And, "We will ride on swift *horses*" —
Therefore those who pursue you shall be swift!
One thousand *shall flee* at the threat of one,
At the threat of five you shall flee,
Till you are left as a pole on top of a mountain
And as a banner on a hill.

a. **In returning and rest you shall be saved; in quietness and confidence shall be your strength**: God offered to Judah the promise of protection from Assyria. They didn't need to look to Egypt to help at all. They could have trusted God for His promise.

i. Trusting God's promise means **returning**. If there is conspicuous disobedience in our lives, we must return to the LORD's ways. Outright disobedience is never consistent with real trust in God's promise. **Returning** also has the idea of drawing close to the LORD.

ii. Trusting God's promise means **rest**. When we trust God, we don't have to strive for ourselves. We don't have to run all about trying to protect or guard ourselves. We have the best Protector, the best Guard in God. We can **rest** in Him, and when we do, it shows we are really trusting in God's promise.

iii. Trusting God's promise means **quietness**. You don't need to argue for your side when God is on your side. Be quiet before Him and before others. It shows that you really trust Him.

iv. Trusting God's promise means **confidence**. You aren't given to despair or fear because you trust God's promise. You know He can and will come through, and you have a profound confidence in the God who loves you.

v. All of these things together mean a real trust in God's promise, and it means that we **shall be saved**, and it means that we will find **strength**. There is no person walking this earth more powerful than a child of God boldly and properly trusting the promise of the living God.

b. **But you would not, and you said, "No, for we will flee on horses" – Therefore you shall flee**: Because Judah rejected God's promise, and trusted in **horses** and other such things instead, they would need to flee! If they would have trusted God's promise instead, they would never have had reason to flee, and would have seen the LORD's salvation and strength instead.

c. **One thousand shall flee at the threat of one**: This is a reversal of the promise of Leviticus 26:8, and a fulfillment of the curse promised in Leviticus 26:17: *I will set My face against you, and you shall be defeated by your enemies. Those who hate you shall reign over you, and you shall flee when no one pursues you.*

C. The blessing of restoration for Judah.

1. (18) A call to trust in God's timing.

Therefore the LORD will wait, that He may be gracious to you;
And therefore He will be exalted, that He may have mercy on you.
For the LORD *is* a God of justice;
Blessed *are* all those who wait for Him.

a. **Therefore the Lord will wait, that He may be gracious to you**: We often wonder why the Lord waits to do things in our lives. Isaiah tells us plainly that it is so **He may be gracious to you**. Whenever the Lord waits or seems to delay, it always has a loving purpose behind it. We can trust that even when we don't understand it.

b. **And therefore He will be exalted, that He may have mercy on you**: When God has mercy on us, it exalts Him. Mercy does nothing to exalt the person who receives it; mercy recognizes the *guilt* of the one who deserves the punishment. But mercy exalts the goodness of the person who gives it. It shows them to be loving, generous, and full of mercy.

c. **For the Lord is a God of justice**: On the surface, **mercy** and **justice** seem to oppose each other. If some guilty criminal stands before the judge, he has the choice to show either **mercy** or **justice**. But God is so great, He can show both at the same time.

i. This was shown at the cross, where Jesus took the punishment we deserve and God's **justice** was satisfied. At the same time, God shows **mercy** by extending the work of Jesus to us as payment for our sins. Only God can reconcile **mercy** and **justice**, *that He might be just and the justifier of the one who has faith in Jesus* (Romans 3:26).

d. **Blessed are all those who wait for Him**: Because God is so great, there is a built-in blessing for **those who wait for Him**. Isaiah doesn't mean **wait** just in the sense of passing time but in the sense of patiently waiting for and trusting God's promise.

i. "Certain of God's people are in trouble and distress, and they are eager for immediate rescue. They cannot wait God's time, nor exercise submission to his will. He will surely deliver them in due season; but they cannot tarry till the hour cometh; like children, they snatch at unripe fruit. 'To everything there is a season, and a time to every purpose under the heaven'; but their one season is the present; they cannot, they will not wait. They must have their desire instantaneously fulfilled, or else they are ready to take wrong means of attaining it. If in poverty, they are in haste to be rich; and they shall not long be innocent. If under reproach, their heart ferments towards revenge. They would sooner rush under the guidance of Satan into some questionable policy, than in childlike simplicity trust in the Lord and do good. It must not be so with you, my brethren, you must learn a better way." (Spurgeon)

2. (19) God promises to bless His people by responding to their cry.

For the people shall dwell in Zion at Jerusalem;
You shall weep no more.
He will be very gracious to you at the sound of your cry;
When He hears it, He will answer you.

a. **You shall weep no more…. He will be very gracious to you at the sound of your cry**: When God's people wait on Him and patiently trust His promise, God pours out His grace at the cry of their heart. Even if it feels God is distant, He hears and promises to answer.

3. (20-21) God promises to bless His people with guidance.

And *though* the Lord gives you
The bread of adversity and the water of affliction,
Yet your teachers will not be moved into a corner anymore,
But your eyes shall see your teachers.
Your ears shall hear a word behind you, saying,
"This *is* the way, walk in it,"
Whenever you turn to the right hand
Or whenever you turn to the left.

a. **Though the Lord gives you the bread of adversity and the water of affliction…your eyes shall see your teachers**: When Judah was prosperous and comfortable, they wouldn't listen to God. Now, God gave them the **bread of adversity and water of affliction**, but they could hear God and be guided by Him again. It's always better to be uncomfortable and in tune with the Lord than to be comfortable and out of step with God.

4. (22) God promises to bless His people with the desire for purity.

You will also defile the covering of your images of silver,
And the ornament of your molded images of gold.
You will throw them away as an unclean thing;
You will say to them, "Get away!"

a. **You will also defile the covering of your images of silver**: The people of Judah kept household idols that they used to honor or worship other gods. The Lord promises a day when they will **defile** those images and **throw them away as an unclean thing**. What a wonderful thing it is when God's people say to wicked and idolatrous things, **"Get away!"**

b. **You will throw them away as an unclean thing**: The literal Hebrew for **unclean thing** is literally a *menstrual cloth*. The people of God would come to hate their idols so much that they would throw them away as readily as they would throw away a used menstrual cloth. Interestingly, the King James Version and the New International Version both translate these words as *menstrual cloth,* but the New King James Version uses the euphemistic **unclean thing**.

5. (23-26) God promises to bless nature with abundance.

Then He will give the rain for your seed
With which you sow the ground,
And bread of the increase of the earth;
It will be fat and plentiful.
In that day your cattle will feed
In large pastures.
Likewise the oxen and the young donkeys that work the ground
Will eat cured fodder,
Which has been winnowed with the shovel and fan.
There will be on every high mountain
And on every high hill
Rivers *and* streams of waters,
In the day of the great slaughter,
When the towers fall.
Moreover the light of the moon will be as the light of the sun,
And the light of the sun will be sevenfold,
As the light of seven days,
In the day that the LORD binds up the bruise of His people
And heals the stroke of their wound.

a. **Then He will give the rain for your seed**: When Judah puts away their idols, boldly trusting God's promise, then God will send material blessings on Judah. For a nation of farmers, it was a wonderful promise to make them **fat and plentiful**. In a naturally dry land, it was a wonderful promise to give abundant **rivers and streams of waters**.

b. **In the day that the LORD binds up the bruise of His people and heals the stroke of their wound**: Better than the material blessing of the LORD is His loving care.

6. (27-29) God promises His people will have gladness in the day of judgment.

Behold, the name of the LORD comes from afar,
Burning *with* His anger,
And *His* burden is heavy;
His lips are full of indignation,
And His tongue like a devouring fire.
His breath is like an overflowing stream,
Which reaches up to the neck,
To sift the nations with the sieve of futility;
And *there shall be* a bridle in the jaws of the people,

Causing *them* to err.
You shall have a song
As in the night *when* a holy festival is kept,
And gladness of heart as when one goes with a flute,
To come into the mountain of the LORD,
To the Mighty One of Israel.

a. **Behold, the name of the LORD comes from afar, burning with His anger**: Isaiah sees the judgment of the LORD quickly coming, **to sift the nations with the sieve of futility**. However, God's people do not need to fear: **You shall have a song…and gladness of heart as when one goes with a flute, to come into the mountain of the LORD**. What a contrast!

i. "The truth is that God's people are here portrayed rejoicing at his judgment on sin because they must take his point of view on everything, and because this judgment is at the same time their salvation." (Grogan)

b. **You shall have a song**: 1 John 4:17 expresses the same idea: *Love has been perfected among us in this: that we may have boldness in the day of judgment; because as He is, so are we in this world.* Boldness and joy in the day of judgment are precious gifts from God.

7. (30-33) The glory of the judgment of the LORD.

The LORD will cause His glorious voice to be heard,
And show the descent of His arm,
With the indignation of *His* anger
And the flame of a devouring fire,
***With* scattering, tempest, and hailstones.**
For through the voice of the LORD
Assyria will be beaten down,
As He strikes with the rod.
And *in* every place where the staff of punishment passes,
Which the LORD lays on him,
***It* will be with tambourines and harps;**
And in battles of brandishing He will fight with it.
For Tophet was established of old,
Yes, for the king it is prepared.
He has made *it* deep and large;
Its pyre is fire with much wood;
The breath of the LORD, like a stream of brimstone,
Kindles it.

a. **The LORD will cause His glorious voice to be heard**: Isaiah wanted God's people to see the *glory* of God's judgments. When we understand how God's perfect judgment exalts His justice and His righteousness, we see the *glory* of the judgment of the LORD.

b. **Assyria will be beaten down**: In the near view, Isaiah saw the judgment of the LORD against Assyria. Judah had no business trusting in Egypt for help against the Assyrians, but they should have trusted the LORD instead, because the LORD would take care of the Assyrians

i. As it happened, this was exactly the case. 2 Kings 19:35 describes how God sent the angel of the LORD and killed 185,000 Assyrians in one night. When the people woke up, there were 185,000 dead Assyrian soldiers.

c. **For Tophet was established of old, yes for the king it is prepared**: **Tophet** was a place in the Valley of Hinnom, just outside of Jerusalem's walls (Jeremiah 7:31). The Valley of Hinnom served as Jerusalem's garbage dump, and the combination of disgusting rubbish and smoldering fires made it a picture of hell. The Hebrew word for hell (*gehenna*) comes from the word for the Valley of Hinnom. Therefore, God says He has a special place in hell for the Assyrian king.

i. Trapp on **Tophet**: "Hence it is here used for *hell*, together with that eternity of extremity which the damned there endure; and this the Assyrians are here threatened with, yea, their very king, whose preservation from the stroke of the angel was but a reservation to a worse mischief here and hereafter."

ii. God had an eternal place for the Assyrian king who attacked Judah and Jerusalem (**He has made it deep and large; its pyre is fire with much wood**). But God also had a special judgment for that king on earth. 2 Kings 19:36-37 describes how when the king of the Assyrians returned home after attacking Judah, his own sons murdered him as he worshipped in the temple of Nisroch his god. "Great men, if not good, shall be greatly tormented; and the more they have of the fat of the earth, the more they are sure to fry in hell." (Trapp)

iii. "Isaiah starts with the 'real' day of the Lord. He is Lord over all the nations. (By implication, what is Assyria, compared with such a God!) The Lord's people will be safe in his Day: their part will be to sing amid the judgments of God. So then, regarding Assyria in the here and now, they will be shattered, Judah will sing, the funeral pyre is ready and so is the fire." (Motyer)

Isaiah 31 – The LORD *Will Give Victory, Not Egypt*

A. The folly of trusting in Egypt.

1. (1) Woe to those who look to Egypt, not the LORD.

Woe to those who go down to Egypt for help,
***And* rely on horses,**
Who trust in chariots because *they are* many,
And in horsemen because they are very strong,
But who do not look to the Holy One of Israel,
Nor seek the LORD!

a. **Woe to those who go down to Egypt for help**: Isaiah confronted Judah with two sins: the sin of trusting in Egypt and their military might, and the sin of not looking **to the Holy One of Israel**. Judah felt they had a *reason* to trust in chariots (**because they are many**). Judah felt they had a *reason* to trust in horsemen (**because they are very strong**). But they couldn't seem to find a *reason* to trust in the LORD.

i. "They did not, of course, abandon faith *per se.* Everybody lives by faith. It is part of the human condition. Financiers trust market forces, militarists trust bombs, scientists trust nature's regularities. Jerusalem's leaders trusted Egypt." (Motyer)

b. **Nor seek the LORD**: How much better it is to have the heart of the Psalmist in Psalm 20:7: *Some trust in chariots, and some in horses; but we will remember the name of the LORD our God.* And our trust should *only* be in the LORD.

i. "He that stands with one foot on a rock, and another foot upon a quicksand, will sink and perish as certainly as he that stands with both feet on a quicksand." (Trapp)

2. (2-3) The LORD is mightier than the Egyptians.

**Yet He also *is* wise and will bring disaster,
And will not call back His words,
But will arise against the house of evildoers,
And against the help of those who work iniquity.
Now the Egyptians *are* men, and not God;
And their horses are flesh, and not spirit.
When the LORD stretches out His hand,
Both he who helps will fall,
And he who is helped will fall down;
They all will perish together.**

a. **Yet He also is wise and will bring disaster**: Though Judah couldn't seem to find a reason to trust God, the reasons were there, and Isaiah called them to remember the reasons. They should trust God more than the Egyptians or their armies because **He also is wise and will bring disaster...**He **will arise against the house of evildoers**.

b. **Now the Egyptians are men, and not God; and their horses are flesh, and not spirit**: Judah was also wrong about their trust in Egypt. The Egyptians and their armies were not as mighty as they seemed to be. All the LORD must do to topple them, along with all who trust in them, was to stretch **out His hand**.

B. The LORD will defend Judah and Jerusalem.

1. (4-5) The LORD defends Mount Zion.

For thus the LORD has spoken to me:

**"As a lion roars, and a young lion over his prey
(When a multitude of shepherds is summoned against him,
He will not be afraid of their voice
Nor be disturbed by their noise),
So the LORD of hosts will come down
To fight for Mount Zion and for its hill.
Like birds flying about,
So will the LORD of hosts defend Jerusalem.
Defending, He will also deliver *it*;
Passing over, He will preserve *it*."**

a. **As a lion roars...So the LORD of hosts will come down to fight for Mount Zion**: Again, their trust in Egypt for protection against the Assyrian invasion was *both* foolish and unnecessary. God would protect **Mount Zion** if Judah trusted Him or not.

b. **Like birds flying about, so will the Lord of hosts defend Jerusalem**: The picture is of a mother bird protecting her young. So, God will defend Jerusalem with the ferocity of a lion, and also with the tender care of a bird. The combination of the two images is powerful.

i. "*As birds flying*; which come from above, and so cannot be kept off; which fly swiftly and engage themselves valiantly and resolutely, when they perceive that their young ones are in eminent danger." (Poole)

ii. "The Lord of Hosts will be strong as the lion that growls over his prey…and He will be sweet and soft and gentle as a mother-bird." (Meyer)

2. (6-9) An invitation to repent to the God who will deliver.

Return to Him against whom the children of Israel have deeply revolted. For in that day every man shall throw away his idols of silver and his idols of gold—sin, which your own hands have made for yourselves.

"Then Assyria shall fall by a sword not of man,
And a sword not of mankind shall devour him.
But he shall flee from the sword,
And his young men shall become forced labor.
He shall cross over to his stronghold for fear,
And his princes shall be afraid of the banner,"
Says the Lord,
Whose fire *is* in Zion
And whose furnace *is* in Jerusalem.

a. **Return to Him**: Because of how great God is, because of how terrible the alternatives to serving Him are, we should feel compelled to **return to Him**. Repentance means turning towards God, and away from anything we have put in God's place (**idols of silver and idols of gold–sin, which your own hands have made**).

b. **Then Assyria shall fall by a sword not of man**: This was fulfilled exactly. The Assyrian army devastated almost the entire land of Judah, and camped on the outskirts of Jerusalem, waiting to conquer the nation by defeating the capital city. But 2 Kings 19:35 describes how God simply sent the angel of the Lord and killed 185,000 Assyrians in one night. When the people woke up, there were 185,000 dead Assyrian soldiers. It was a victory that had nothing to do with the **sword…of man**. God was more than able to protect Judah and Jerusalem.

Isaiah 32 – A King's Reign of Righteousness

A. Blessings from the coming king.

1. (1) In the aftermath of Jerusalem's deliverance, a king comes.

Behold, a king will reign in righteousness,
And princes will rule with justice.

a. **Behold, a king will reign in righteousness**: This promise was made in a certain context. In the previous chapter, God assured that the Assyrians would be judged, and Judah would be delivered. But God didn't want only to remove the threat; He also wanted to bless Judah with a righteous king, so the promise was made.

i. However, it is likely that the prophecy of Isaiah 32 and 33 was given before the time of the prophecy of Isaiah 30 and 31. Both look to the time of the Assyrian invasion of Judah, but Isaiah 30 and 31 are set in the time of Hezekiah, as the invasion neared Jerusalem. Most commentators believe that the **king** who **will reign in righteousness** mentioned here was Hezekiah, and since it says that he **will reign**, this prophecy may have been given at the beginning of Isaiah's prophetic career, during the reign of King Ahaz, the predecessor to King Hezekiah.

ii. It is possible that the prophecy of Isaiah 32 and 33 was given during the reign of Hezekiah, and this announcement refers to the latter part of his reign. It is also possible that it was given during the time of Hezekiah, and it prophesies the coming of King Josiah, the great-grandson of the present king of Judah, Hezekiah, who reigned during the Assyrian threat. Josiah was a righteous king (2 Kings 22:2).

b. **A king will reign in righteousness**: In some sense, Hezekiah certainly fulfilled this prophecy. It was written of him, *and he did what was right in the sight of the LORD, according to all that his father David had done.... He trusted in the LORD God of Israel, so that after him was none like him among* *all the kings of Judah, nor any who were before him. For he held fast to the* LORD*; he did not depart from following Him, but kept His commandments, which the* LORD *had commanded Moses* (2 Kings 18:3, 5-6).

c. **A king will reign in righteousness**: Yet ultimately, Hezekiah was a picture of the King of Kings, Jesus Christ. Jeremiah 23:5 announces this about our Messiah: *"Behold, the days are coming," says the* LORD*, "That I will raise to David a Branch of righteousness; a King shall reign and prosper, and execute judgment and righteousness in the earth.*

i. "This seems to have been delivered in the time of Ahaz, and to speak of Hezekiah, and of his righteousness and happy government. But withal, as Hezekiah and his reign was an eminent type of Christ and of his kingdom; so this prophecy looks through Hezekiah unto Christ." (Poole)

d. **And princes will rule with justice**: It wasn't enough – it is never enough – to have a righteous king. The king must have helpers, **princes** under him, who will also **rule with justice**. Hezekiah had such loyal **princes**, such as Eliakim, Shebna the scribe, the elders of the priests, and Isaiah himself (2 Kings 19:2).

i. These weren't **princes** in the literal sense of being sons of King Hezekiah. The Hebrew word for **princes** can mean any ruler under a king.

ii. If Hezekiah, the righteous king, points to Jesus, then who are Jesus' **princes**? His people are His princes, as 1 Peter 2:9 later explains: *But you are a chosen generation, a royal priesthood, a holy nation, His own special people, that you may proclaim the praises of Him who called you out of darkness into His marvelous light.* Revelation 5:10 also has this proclamation from God's people: *And* [You] *have made us kings and priests to our God; and we shall reign on the earth.* Many of the seemingly unnecessary trials and pains of this life have a wonderful purpose in the world beyond: training us to be princes, faithfully ruling with King Jesus.

2. (2-4) The blessings of restoration from the king.

A man will be as a hiding place from the wind,
And a cover from the tempest,
As rivers of water in a dry place,
As the shadow of a great rock in a weary land.
The eyes of those who see will not be dim,
And the ears of those who hear will listen.

Also the heart of the rash will understand knowledge,
And the tongue of the stammerers will be ready to speak plainly.

a. **Rivers of water in a dry place**: This described how wonderful the spiritual renewal during the reign of Hezekiah was, like the **shadow of a great rock in a weary land**. By God's blessing, **those who see** could see better than ever, and **those who hear will listen**.

i. The more glorious reign of Jesus is all these things for us as well. He is a shelter from the storm (**a cover from the tempest**), **as rivers of water in a dry place**, and like **the shadow of a great rock in a weary land**.

ii. "If King Hezekiah were a type of Christ, then this prophecy may refer to his time; but otherwise it seems to have Hezekiah primarily in view. It is evident, however, that in the fullest sense these words cannot be applied to any man; God alone can do all that is promised here." (Clarke)

b. **The heart of the rash will understand knowledge**: The spiritual renewal during the reign of Hezekiah promoted trust in God's word, and because of that, hearts were changed. God also would bless in miraculous ways (**the tongue of the stammerers will be ready to speak plainly**).

3. (5-8) The blessings of righteousness and integrity from the king.

The foolish person will no longer be called generous,
Nor the miser said *to be* bountiful;
For the foolish person will speak foolishness,
And his heart will work iniquity:
To practice ungodliness,
To utter error against the Lord,
To keep the hungry unsatisfied,
And he will cause the drink of the thirsty to fail.
Also the schemes of the schemer *are* evil;
He devises wicked plans
To destroy the poor with lying words,
Even when the needy speaks justice.
But a generous man devises generous things,
And by generosity he shall stand.

a. **The foolish person will no longer be called generous…the foolish person will speak foolishness**: The spiritual renewal during the reign of Hezekiah meant that spiritual reality would be exposed for all to see. No more would there be deception by appearances; if a man were foolish, he would be exposed as foolish.

i. **Wicked plans**: "Apart from Job 17:11, has a uniformly bad meaning. It occurs nineteen times of sexual misconduct (*e.g.* Leviticus 18:17). It is planning for one's own advantage at whatever cost to others." (Motyer)

b. **But a generous man devises generous things**: Not only would the foolishness of the foolish be exposed, but so would the generosity of the generous. Righteousness and wickedness would each be seen for what they were and regarded accordingly.

i. "Wickedness shall be discovered and punished wheresoever it is, and virtue shall be manifested and rewarded, and all things shall be managed with sincerity and simplicity." (Poole)

B. A call to prepare for the coming of the Spirit.

1. (9-11) The women at ease are called to repent.

Rise up, you women who are at ease,
Hear my voice;
You complacent daughters,
Give ear to my speech.
In a year and *some* days
You will be troubled, you complacent women;
For the vintage will fail,
The gathering will not come.
Tremble, you *women* who are at ease;
Be troubled, you complacent ones;
Strip yourselves, make yourselves bare,
And gird *sackcloth* on *your* waists.

a. **Rise up, you women who are at ease**: Before the righteous king would come, the people had to prepare themselves. The **women who are at ease** and the **complacent daughters** had to get ready for the righteous king.

i. **At ease** is the same word used later in the chapter, where God promises *secure dwelling places* (Isaiah 32:18). **Complacent** is the same word used later in the same chapter, where God promises *peaceful habitation*. "According to Isaiah, there is nothing wrong with feeling secure and undisturbed as long as one's trust is solidly based on the Lord." (Wolf)

b. **Tremble, you women who are at ease**: Instead of an indulgent, self-focused life, they would be required to **tremble**, **be troubled**, and put on the clothing of mourning. This would show repentance and readiness for the righteous king.

2. (12-14) The whole land mourns.

People shall mourn upon their breasts
For the pleasant fields, for the fruitful vine.
On the land of my people will come up thorns *and* briers,
Yes, on all the happy homes *in* the joyous city;
Because the palaces will be forsaken,
The bustling city will be deserted.
The forts and towers will become lairs forever,
A joy of wild donkeys, a pasture of flocks—

a. **People shall mourn upon their breasts for the pleasant fields, for the fruitful vine**: Because of the Assyrian invasion to come, God would use the tough economic times to wake Judah up. *For the vintage will fail, the gathering will not come* (Isaiah 32:10). The tough times touched everyone (**all the happy homes in the joyous city…the palaces will be forsaken**).

3. (15) The Spirit is poured out upon a humbled people.

Until the Spirit is poured upon us from on high,
And the wilderness becomes a fruitful field,
And the fruitful field is counted as a forest.

a. **Until the Spirit is poured upon us from on high**: God used the invasion from Assyria, the tough times, and the humble mourning of the people to prepare them for an outpouring of His Spirit.

i. **Until**: It was only the **Spirit** of God that could make the difference; the tough times would last **until** the Spirit was poured out.

ii. **Is poured upon us**: God wanted to do more than scatter a few drops of His mercy and blessing; He wanted His Spirit to be **poured upon** His people.

iii. **From on high**: This is the source of the true outpouring of the Holy Spirit. It doesn't come from among men, or because of men's efforts. It comes from heaven, **from on high**.

b. **The wilderness becomes a fruitful field**: When the Holy Spirit is poured out, what was barren and desolate before is now full of life and fruitfulness. True fruitfulness comes from the outpouring of the Holy Spirit.

c. **And the fruitful field is counted as a forest**: When the Holy Spirit is poured out, what was good before (**a fruitful field**) miraculously becomes even better (**a forest**).

4. (16-20) Blessings brought by the Spirit.

Then justice will dwell in the wilderness,
And righteousness remain in the fruitful field.

The work of righteousness will be peace,
And the effect of righteousness, quietness and assurance forever.
My people will dwell in a peaceful habitation,
In secure dwellings, and in quiet resting places,
Though hail comes down on the forest,
And the city is brought low in humiliation.
Blessed *are* you who sow beside all waters,
Who send out freely the feet of the ox and the donkey.

a. **Justice…righteousness…. peace…quietness and assurance forever**: When God's Spirit is poured out among His people, this is what it is like. This means that we shouldn't be satisfied with what claims to be of the Spirit but isn't marked by the fruit of the Spirit. This means that if we lack these things, we can come and ask the LORD to pour out His Spirit upon us.

b. **My people will dwell in a peaceful habitation, in secure dwellings… though hail comes down on the forest, and the city is brought low in humiliation**: When God's Spirit is poured out, we live on a principle higher than circumstances. If others feel the pelting **hail**, or are **brought low in humiliation**, it doesn't affect those blessed by the poured-out Spirit of God.

Isaiah 33 – The LORD Delivers Zion

A. The LORD comes in judgment and graciousness.

1. (1) Woe to plundering Assyria.

Woe to you who plunder, though you *have* not *been* plundered;
And you who deal treacherously, though they have not dealt treacherously with you!
When you cease plundering,
You will be plundered;
When you make an end of dealing treacherously,
They will deal treacherously with you.

a. **Woe to you who plunder**: This prophecy, spoken before the Assyrian invasion, shows that this seemingly unstoppable army will in fact be stopped. Those who did the plundering **will be plundered** and will be dealt with **treacherously** by others.

b. **They will deal treacherously with you**: Jesus spoke of this same principle in Matthew 7:1-2: *Judge not, that you not be judged. For with what judgment you judge, you will be judged; and with the same measure you use, it will be measured back to you.* God has every right to deal with us as we have dealt with others.

2. (2-4) The prayer of God's people.

O LORD, be gracious to us;
We have waited for You.
Be their arm every morning,
Our salvation also in the time of trouble.
At the noise of the tumult the people shall flee;
When You lift Yourself up, the nations shall be scattered;
And Your plunder shall be gathered
***Like* the gathering of the caterpillar;**

As the running to and fro of locusts,
He shall run upon them.

a. **O Lord, be gracious to us**: In light of the Assyrian threat and the longed-for deliverance of a righteous king, God's people no longer look to the Egyptians, they no longer look to themselves. Now, they look to the Lord, and cry out, "**O Lord, be gracious to us**."

b. **We have waited for You. Be their arm every morning**: God's people aren't trusting in themselves anymore. They are waiting on the Lord and looking to *His* **arm every morning**.

c. **When You lift Yourself up, the nations shall be scattered**: God's people have a *confident* expectation in the Lord. Their prayer is filled with wonderful expectancy.

i. **Like the gathering of the caterpillar**: "Verse four may already have had an initial fulfillment after the death of the Assyrian soldiers, for undoubtedly the inhabitants of Jerusalem congregated like caterpillars around the corpses and the implements of war." (Bultema)

3. (5-6) The praise of God's people.

The Lord is exalted, for He dwells on high;
He has filled Zion with justice and righteousness.
Wisdom and knowledge will be the stability of your times,
***And* the strength of salvation;**
The fear of the Lord *is* His treasure.

a. **The Lord is exalted**: The tough times were hard, but they brought God's people to a different, better view of who He is. Because they have been brought low, they see that **the Lord is exalted**.

b. **He has filled Zion with justice and righteousness**: God's people pray this in *anticipation* of the answer. You don't have to wait until God does it all to give Him thanks. You can, by faith, give Him thanks ahead of time.

c. **The fear of the Lord is His treasure**: Honor, respect, and reverence towards the Lord is **His treasure**. It is a gift God gives us, not so we will cower in fear, but so we will rightly honor Him.

4. (7-9) The Lord's judgment brings the earth low.

Surely their valiant ones shall cry outside,
The ambassadors of peace shall weep bitterly.
The highways lie waste,
The traveling man ceases.
He has broken the covenant,
He has despised the cities,

He regards no man.
The earth mourns *and* languishes,
Lebanon is shamed *and* shriveled;
Sharon is like a wilderness,
And Bashan and Carmel shake off *their fruits*.

a. **Their valiant ones shall cry outside…. The earth mourns and languishes**: When the judgment of the LORD comes to the earth, everyone is brought low before Him. The **valiant ones shall cry**, and the **ambassadors of peace** – who trusted in other nations instead of the LORD – **shall weep bitterly**. Even the mighty **Lebanon**, with her majestic forests of cedar, **is shamed and shriveled**.

b. **Their valiant ones**: The Hebrew word translated **valiant ones** appears only this one time in the Bible.

i. "The word *erellam*, which we translate *valiant ones*, is very difficult; no man knows what it means. *Kimchi* supposes that it is the name of the angel that smote the Assyrian camp! The *Vulgate*, and my old manuscript translate it *seers*; and most of the Versions understand it this way. None of the manuscripts give us any help." (Clarke)

B. The fire of the LORD.

1. (10-13) The LORD announces His fire of judgment.

"Now I will rise," says the LORD;
"Now I will be exalted,
Now I will lift Myself up.
You shall conceive chaff,
You shall bring forth stubble;
Your breath, *as* fire, shall devour you.
And the people shall be *like* the burnings of lime;
***Like* thorns cut up they shall be burned in the fire.**
Hear, you *who are* afar off, what I have done;
And you *who are* near, acknowledge My might."

a. **Now I will rise**: As the whole earth is brought low by the judgment of the LORD, at the same time, the LORD lifts Himself up.

b. **And the people shall be like the burnings of lime; like thorns cut up they shall be burned in the fire**: God's judgment will come like fire, and the wicked and worthless works of man will be like **chaff** and **stubble** that is quickly and ferociously burned in the fire.

i. "*To lime* stresses the intensity of the blaze." (Motyer)

2. (14-19) Fearful sinners and blessed saints.

The sinners in Zion are afraid;
Fearfulness has seized the hypocrites:
"Who among us shall dwell with the devouring fire?
Who among us shall dwell with everlasting burnings?"
He who walks righteously and speaks uprightly,
He who despises the gain of oppressions,
Who gestures with his hands, refusing bribes,
Who stops his ears from hearing of bloodshed,
And shuts his eyes from seeing evil:
He will dwell on high;
His place of defense *will be* the fortress of rocks;
Bread will be given him,
His water *will be* sure.
Your eyes will see the King in His beauty;
They will see the land that is very far off.
Your heart will meditate on terror:
"Where *is* the scribe?
Where *is* he who weighs?
Where *is* he who counts the towers?"
You will not see a fierce people,
A people of obscure speech, beyond perception,
Of a stammering tongue *that you* cannot understand.

a. **The sinners in Zion are afraid**: Of course they were **afraid**. They were **afraid** because judgment of the LORD was coming. Those who were not afraid to practice their sin were now **afraid** when righteous judgment comes upon their sin.

b. **He who walks righteously and speaks uprightly…He will dwell on high**: Though the **sinners** and **hypocrites** are terrified at the coming judgment of the LORD, the LORD's righteous ones are comforted that God is coming to set things right.

c. **Your eyes will see the King in His beauty**: The LORD will bless His righteous ones. They will have a **place of defense**, a **fortress**, and **bread** and **water** will not fail them. But far above these material blessings, they will **see the King in His beauty**. In the most immediate sense, this referred to Hezekiah; but in the ultimate sense, to our Beautiful Savior Jesus Christ.

i. Beyond all the material glory, splendor, and comfort of heaven, this is the greatest glory of heaven: not to be personally glorified, but to **see the King in His beauty**.

ii. It isn't only seeing **the King**; it is seeing Him **in His beauty**. It can be said that we occasionally catch a "glimpse" of our King Jesus, and even sometimes have a glance at **His beauty**. But the highest experience we could have now is like nothing compared to what we will experience when we **see the King in His beauty**. Paul said of our present walk, *For now we see in a mirror, dimly, but then face to face. Now I know in part, but then I shall know just as I also am known* (1 Corinthians 13:12). Today, when we look in a good mirror, the image is clear. But in the ancient world, mirrors were made out of polished metal, and the image was always unclear and somewhat distorted. We see Jesus now only in a dim, unclear way, but one day we will see Him with perfect clarity.

iii. Heaven is precious to us for many reasons. We long to be with loved ones who have passed before us and whom we miss so dearly. We long to be with the great men and women of God who have passed before us in centuries past. We want to walk the streets of gold, see the pearly gates, see the angels round the throne of God worshipping Him day and night. However, none of those things, precious as they are, make heaven really "heaven." What makes heaven really heaven is the unhindered, unrestricted, presence of our Lord, and to **see the King in His beauty** will be the greatest experience of your eternal existence.

iv. Part of the **beauty** of **the King** in heaven will be the scars He retains from His suffering for our sake on this earth. After Jesus rose from the dead in His glorified body, His body uniquely retained the nail prints in His hands and the scar on His side (John 20:24-29). In Zechariah 12:10, Jesus speaks prophetically of the day when the Jewish people, turned to Him, see Him in glory: *then they will look on Me whom they pierced. Yes, they will mourn for Him as one mourns for his only son, and grieve for Him as one grieves for a firstborn.* Zechariah 13:6 continues the thought: *And one will say to him, "What are these wounds between your arms?" Then he will answer, "Those with which I was wounded in the house of my friends."*

d. **Your heart will meditate on terror**: The revealing of the King will be the greatest glory for the child of God, but it will be the greatest terror for the one who has set their heart against or apart from God. In vain, they will look to the **scribe** or **he who weighs** or **he who counts the towers** for help, but there will be none.

e. **You will not see a fierce people, a people of obscure speech**: Though the northern nation of Israel was demolished by the Assyrians (**a people of obscure speech, beyond perception**), the southern nation of Judah would be delivered (**you will not see**). Isaiah mixes the pictures of the LORD's ultimate deliverance on the day of judgment, and the soon coming deliverance from the Assyrians.

3. (20-24) Zion is delivered and blessed.

Look upon Zion, the city of our appointed feasts;
Your eyes will see Jerusalem, a quiet home,
A tabernacle *that* will not be taken down;
Not one of its stakes will ever be removed,
Nor will any of its cords be broken.
But there the majestic LORD *will be* for us
A place of broad rivers *and* streams,
In which no galley with oars will sail,
Nor majestic ships pass by
(For the LORD *is* our Judge,
The LORD *is* our Lawgiver,
The LORD *is* our King;
He will save us);
Your tackle is loosed,
They could not strengthen their mast,
They could not spread the sail.
Then the prey of great plunder is divided;
The lame take the prey.
And the inhabitant will not say, "I am sick";
The people who dwell in it *will be* forgiven *their* iniquity.

a. **Look upon Zion…Your eyes will see Jerusalem, a quiet home**: In the midst of the Assyrian threat, God will preserve Jerusalem. **Not one of its stakes will ever be removed**.

b. **A place of broad rivers and streams**: God's blessing on Zion would bring **broad rivers and streams** to this once barren, desert land.

i. "This chapter, so full of compelling imagery, presents a picture of Jerusalem as a kind of Near Eastern Venice or Amsterdam, or, to place it in its historical context, like the great cities of Egypt or Mesopotamia. Most great civilisations have grown up around important rivers. Israel, in general, and Jerusalem, in particular, were exceptions to this." (Grogan)

c. **There the majestic LORD will be for us…no galley with oars will sail, nor majestic ships pass by. For the LORD is our Judge…He will save us**: A wide river will not give a path to an enemy coming on a ship. God will **save** and protect.

i. Those **majestic ships** turned out to be not so **majestic** after all. **Your tackle is loosed, they could not strengthen their mast, they could not spread the sail**. It was foolish to ever fear the **majestic ships** instead of trusting the **majestic LORD**.

ii. "Although they shall have from God the security of a great river, yet they shall be freed from the disadvantage of it; which is, that the enemies may come against them in ships; for no galleys nor ships of the enemy's shall be able to come into this river to annoy them." (Poole)

d. **The lame take the prey…. The people who dwell in it will be forgiven their iniquity**: When God saves, He does it in unlikely ways. It is an unexpected blessing that the **lame take the prey**. It is an unexpected blessing that people can be **forgiven their iniquity**. The **majestic LORD** brings unexpected blessing.

i. "They shall not only receive from me a glorious temporal deliverance; but, which is infinitely better, the pardon of all their sins, and all those spiritual and everlasting blessings which attend upon that mercy." (Poole)

Isaiah 34 – The Indignation of the LORD Against All Nations

A. The indignation of the LORD against the peoples of the nations.

1. (1-4) The fury and the completeness of the judgment of the LORD.

Come near, you nations, to hear;
And heed, you people!
Let the earth hear, and all that is in it,
The world and all things that come forth from it.
For the indignation of the LORD is against all nations,
And *His* fury against all their armies;
He has utterly destroyed them,
He has given them over to the slaughter.
Also their slain shall be thrown out;
Their stench shall rise from their corpses,
And the mountains shall be melted with their blood.
All the host of heaven shall be dissolved,
And the heavens shall be rolled up like a scroll;
All their host shall fall down
As the leaf falls from the vine,
And as *fruit* falling from a fig tree.

a. **The indignation of the LORD**: In the immediate context, Isaiah continues the thought of the coming judgment against the Assyrians. But in the larger context, we can see this passage as an announcement of the judgment to come upon the **nations** during the Great Tribulation.

i. Jesus, and many Old Testament prophets, plainly told us of a coming time He called the *great tribulation* (Matthew 24:21), when because of the judgment of God, conditions on earth would be the worst human history had ever seen. Revelation chapters 6, 8-9, and 16-18 describe this horrific time when there will be widespread ecological, economic, cosmic, and human catastrophe on a level never before known in history.

ii. The idea that this chapter relates to the very end times goes back a long time among Christian teachers. "Eusebius, with many other ancients, will have this chapter to be understood of the end of the world and the last judgment." (Trapp)

b. **Come near, you nations, to hear; and heed, you people**: It made sense for Isaiah to address the **nations.** In light of how terrible the great tribulation will be, when we consider how prophecy has been fulfilled, and how the stage is set for even more fulfilled prophecy, we should **hear** and take **heed**.

- The stage is set for a rebuilt temple that will come in the last days, necessary to fulfill the prophecies of the abomination of desolation (Matthew 24:15; Mark 13:14; 2 Thessalonians 2:3-4).
- The stage is set for the sort of world-dominating confederation of nations, heir to the Roman Empire, to arise (Daniel 2:36-45; Revelation 13:1-8; 17:10-14).
- The stage is set for a political and economic "superman" to arise, the sort of single political leader who will lead this world-dominating confederation of nations (2 Thessalonians 2:3-12; Revelation 13:4-7).
- The stage is set for the kind of false religion the Bible says will characterize the very last days (2 Thessalonians 2:4, 9-12; Revelation 13:11-15; 17:1-6).
- The stage is set for the kind of economic system predicted for the very last days (Revelation 13:15-17).
- The stage is set for the end-times scenario the Bible says will happen between Russia and Israel in Ezekiel 38-39.

c. **For the indignation of the LORD is against all nations**: The warning regarding this time of the **indignation of the LORD** is directed not to God's people, but to the **nations**. This is because God's people will escape the terrors of the great tribulation, though they may experience great hardship in the time leading up to it. Jesus said we should pray that we would be counted worthy to escape that time of terrors (Luke 21:36) and be taken to heaven in the great catching away of the church (1 Thessalonians 4:16-18).

2. (5-7) The great bloodshed at the judgment of the LORD.

"For My sword shall be bathed in heaven;
Indeed it shall come down on Edom,
And on the people of My curse, for judgment.

The sword of the LORD is filled with blood,
It is made overflowing with fatness,
With the blood of lambs and goats,
With the fat of the kidneys of rams.
For the LORD has a sacrifice in Bozrah,
And a great slaughter in the land of Edom.
The wild oxen shall come down with them,
And the young bulls with the mighty bulls;
Their land shall be soaked with blood,
And their dust saturated with fatness."

a. **Indeed it shall come down on Edom**: The Edomites were near neighbors to Israel, and often bitter rivals. The Edomites rejoiced whenever the people of Judah or Israel were afflicted, so Isaiah focuses on the judgment that will come against Edom, using them as a single example of the large judgment that will come upon all the *nations* (as in Isaiah 34:1-2).

i. "Edom was a sister nation to Israel, but it hated Israel more than any other nation. Throughout all of history we see a burning hatred of Edom against Israel. It is for this reason that Edom is frequently presented as a representative of all the nations that hated the Jews." (Bultema)

ii. "Edom had derided and attacked Judah for centuries, but now God would avenge this hateful attitude that is so characteristic of the world's ways." (Wolf)

b. **The sword of the LORD is filled with blood…their land shall be soaked with blood**: The *indignation of the LORD* finds its final fulfillment in the battle of Armageddon, which will be a terribly bloody affair (Revelation 14:20).

c. **Overflowing with fatness, and with the blood of lambs and goats, with the fat of the kidneys of rams, for the LORD has a great sacrifice… and a great slaughter**: In associating this time of judgment with the image of sacrifice, Isaiah tells us that this is payment for the penalty of sin. Even as a sacrificial victim paid for the sin of the one bringing the sacrifice, so the bloody judgment of sin at Armageddon will be a payment for the penalty of sin. It will be an imperfect, incomplete payment, but it will be a payment of some kind.

i. "The mention of sacrificial animals is primarily intended to refer to the slaughter of people." (Wolf)

d. **The wild oxen shall come down with them**: The King James Version translates **wild oxen** as *unicorns.* **Wild oxen** is the preferred translation.

i. "There used to be quite a difference of opinion regarding the word *unicorns*, but today the general opinion is that it does not mean rhinoceros but aurochs, or wild bison. According to Deuteronomy 33:17, this animal did not have one but two horns." (Bultema)

ii. "*Wild oxen* were not used in the sacrifices. Possibly therefore Isaiah is using animal metaphors for the important people and leaders of Edom." (Motyer)

B. The indignation of the LORD against the land of the nations.

1. (8-10) The land is made desolate.

For *it* is the day of the LORD's vengeance,
The year of recompense for the cause of Zion.
Its streams shall be turned into pitch,
And its dust into brimstone;
Its land shall become burning pitch.
It shall not be quenched night or day;
Its smoke shall ascend forever.
From generation to generation it shall lie waste;
No one shall pass through it forever and ever.

a. **Its streams will be turned into pitch, and its dust into brimstone**: In this **day of the LORD's vengeance** known as the great tribulation, there will be unparalleled ecological disaster. Before Jesus Christ returns at the end of the great tribulation, one-third of the earth's vegetation, one-third of the oceans, and one-third of fresh waters will be destroyed and unusable (Revelation 8 and 16).

2. (11-15) The land is inhabited only by animals of the wilderness.

But the pelican and the porcupine shall possess it,
Also the owl and the raven shall dwell in it.
And He shall stretch out over it
The line of confusion and the stones of emptiness.
They shall call its nobles to the kingdom,
But none *shall be* there, and all its princes shall be nothing.
And thorns shall come up in its palaces,
Nettles and brambles in its fortresses;
It shall be a habitation of jackals,
A courtyard for ostriches.
The wild beasts of the desert shall also meet with the jackals,
And the wild goat shall bleat to its companion;
Also the night creature shall rest there,
And find for herself a place of rest.

There the arrow snake shall make her nest and lay *eggs*
And hatch, and gather *them* under her shadow;
There also shall the hawks be gathered,
Every one with her mate.

a. **But the pelican and the porcupine shall possess it**: Much of the earth will be so destroyed that in many places, only wild animals will be able to live.

b. **The wild goat shall bleat to its companion**: The King James Version translates **wild goat** as *satyr*, which was a mythical demonic creature. The Hebrew word here is *sair*, which as an adjective means *hairy* (Genesis 27:11) and as a noun refers to a male goat (Genesis 37:31 and Leviticus 4:23). It is possible that Isaiah meant that wild goats would inhabit the desolate regions of Edom, or he may mean that it will be the haunt of demonic spirits.

i. Bultema suggested that the best translation "is satyrs, demons, or field devils."

c. **Also the night creature shall rest there**: The Hebrew word for **night creature** is *lilith*, which is the feminine form of the word "night." Old Jewish superstitions make *Lilith* a person who was a beautiful demon of the night, who seduced men and killed children. It is possible that Isaiah used the term to describe the demonic habitation of Edom after God's judgment.

3. (16-17) The surety of the judgments of the Lord.

"Search from the book of the Lord, and read:
Not one of these shall fail;
Not one shall lack her mate.
For My mouth has commanded it, and His Spirit has gathered them.
He has cast the lot for them,
And His hand has divided it among them with a measuring line.
They shall possess it forever;
From generation to generation they shall dwell in it."

a. **Search from the book of the Lord, and read: not one of these shall fail**: This remarkable statement tells us that Isaiah *understood that his words were the words of the Lord*. It also tells us that Isaiah meant that *his prophecy should be understood literally* – poetically, but *literally*. It also means that Isaiah clearly challenged doubters to "look it up" once the prophecy was fulfilled.

i. "After Edom has become a wasteland, men will take out the scroll and verify that Isaiah's predictions came true." (Wolf)

b. **Search from the book of the Lord, and read: not one of these shall fail**: This time of great tribulation is certainly coming upon the earth. This is beyond all doubt; our part isn't to bring it or to prevent it, but simply to be ready, and to *pray always that you may be counted worthy to escape all these things that will come to pass, and to stand before the Son of Man* (Luke 21:36).

Isaiah 35 – The Highway of Holiness

A. The restoration of the land and of the people.

1. (1-2) The land is restored.

The wilderness and the wasteland shall be glad for them,
And the desert shall rejoice and blossom as the rose;
It shall blossom abundantly and rejoice,
Even with joy and singing.
The glory of Lebanon shall be given to it,
The excellence of Carmel and Sharon.
They shall see the glory of the LORD,
The excellency of our God.

a. **The wilderness and the wasteland shall be glad for them, and the desert shall rejoice and blossom as the rose**: After the judgment on the nations described in Isaiah 34, God will bring a beautiful restoration.

b. **It shall blossom abundantly and rejoice**: This promise was proved true in many ways, and in some sense will yet be fulfilled.

- This promise *was* true in the immediate term when Judah was restored after the invasion of the Assyrians was turned back.
- This promise *is* true in the longer term as modern-day Israel has turned **the wilderness and the wasteland** into productive farms, and truly has made **the desert...blossom as the rose**.
- This promise *will be* true in the ultimate fulfillment of this prophecy when God restores the ecology of the world after the end of the great tribulation and the battle of Armageddon (Isaiah 11:6-9).

i. Romans 8:19-22 says: *The earnest expectation of the creation eagerly waits for the revealing of the sons of God. For the creation was subjected to futility, not willingly, but because of Him who subjected it in hope; because the creation itself also will be delivered from the bondage of corruption into the glorious liberty of the children of God. For we know that the whole creation groans and labors with birth pangs together until now.* Nature is waiting for the transformation that will come when the Messiah reigns and believers are glorified.

2. (3-4) Weak people are strengthened.

Strengthen the weak hands,
And make firm the feeble knees.
Say to those *who* are fearful-hearted,
"Be strong, do not fear!
Behold, your God will come *with* vengeance,
***With* the recompense of God;**
He will come and save you."

a. **Strengthen the weak hands, and make firm the feeble knees**: The coming judgment would be enough to make the hands of anyone weak, and knees of anyone feeble. But in light of the glorious restoration God will bring from that time, it would be no time to have **weak hands** or **feeble knees**. God wanted His people to get strong and get going.

i. We use our **hands** to work with; those with **weak hands** are not working for the Lord as they should. We use our **knees** both to progress with and to pray with. Those with **feeble knees** are not progressing with the Lord and praying as they should.

ii. Hebrews 12:12 quotes this verse from Isaiah to make the point that even in a time of chastening from the Lord, we should take strength and courage in the Lord, knowing that it is His Fatherly love and care that has allowed and directed the chastening. It's time to get strong in the Lord and move on.

iii. But the passage both here in Isaiah and Hebrews 12 indicates that there are some among God's people who indeed have **weak hands** and **feeble knees**. What is the cause of it? If we are not making progress in our walk with Jesus, fault can surely be found with **weak hands** and **feeble knees**.

b. **Say to those who are fearful-hearted, "Be strong, do not fear…. He will come and save you"**: In our present trials, we need the strong hope of the Lord to overcome our fearful hearts. Our fearful hearts are not helped by a vain, vague optimism; they are helped by the assured confidence that **He will come and save**.

3. (5-6a) The sick and the diseased are healed.

Then the eyes of the blind shall be opened,
And the ears of the deaf shall be unstopped.

Then the lame shall leap like a deer,
And the tongue of the dumb sing.

a. **Then the eyes of the blind shall be opened**: When God's salvation comes, miraculous *power* comes with it. It is a miracle for the blind to see, for the deaf to hear, for the lame to run, and for the mute to speak. But when *He will come and save you*, He does it with miraculous power.

b. **Shall be opened**: When John the Baptist was in prison, he became discouraged, and began to wonder if Jesus really was the Messiah he had proclaimed Him to be. When John's disciples brought this question to Jesus, He replied: *Go and tell John the things which you hear and see: The blind see and the lame walk; the lepers are cleansed and the deaf hear; the dead are raised up and the poor have the gospel preached to them. And blessed is he who is not offended because of Me.* (Matthew 11:4-6). If Jesus didn't use the exact words of Isaiah 35, He certainly used the idea. Jesus, the Messiah, had come to bring God's salvation, and that would be accompanied by miraculous power.

4. (6b-7) Abundance replaces lack.

For waters shall burst forth in the wilderness,
And streams in the desert.
The parched ground shall become a pool,
And the thirsty land springs of water;
In the habitation of jackals, where each lay,
***There shall be* grass with reeds and rushes.**

a. **For waters shall burst forth in the wilderness, and streams in the desert**: When God's salvation comes, miraculous *provision* comes with it. What was dry and useless before becomes well-watered and fruitful.

b. **Streams in the desert**: Jesus said He would bring this kind of beautiful provision in the lives of His people: "He who believes in Me, as the Scripture has said, out of his heart will flow rivers of living water." But this He spoke concerning the Spirit, whom those believing in Him would receive (John 7:38-39). There is no reason for a Christian to endure a "dry time," not when the miraculous power of Jesus Christ to provide is present.

i. **The parched ground shall become a pool**: "The word translated *parched ground* actually means *mirage*, air reflection, an atmospheric phenomenon frequently seen in Eastern deserts which is caused by the reflection of the hot rays of the sun.... Now the prophet brings the glad tiding that what used to be a mere semblance and an illusion will one day become a glorious reality." (Bultema)

B. The Highway of Holiness.

1. (8) A **Highway of Holiness** is made for God's people.

A highway shall be there, and a road,
And it shall be called the Highway of Holiness.
The unclean shall not pass over it,
But it *shall be* for others.
Whoever walks the road, although a fool,
Shall not go astray.

a. **A Highway of Holiness**: Today, we take good roads for granted. But in the ancient world, a good road – a **highway** – was an amazing blessing for travel, progress, and business. Isaiah announces that in the ministry of the Messiah, there will be a wonderful **highway**, a **road**, known as the **Highway of Holiness**.

i. The Hebrew word for **highway** indicates what our English word literally says: "a high-way." It speaks of a raised road, lifted above the ground. It is a high, glorious road to travel on.

ii. The construction of this **Highway of Holiness** was the greatest engineering feat ever accomplished. "Engineering has done much to tunnel mountains, and bridge abysses; but the greatest triumph of engineering is that which made a way from sin to holiness, from death to life, from condemnation to perfection. Who could make a road over the mountains of our iniquities but Almighty God? None but the Lord of love would have wished it; none but the God of wisdom could have devised it; none but the God of power could have carried it out." (Spurgeon)

b. **The unclean shall not pass over it**: This highway isn't for everyone. It has a "toll booth," but you can't make it on this highway by paying your way. You are only allowed on this highway if you are cleansed by the great work of the Messiah.

c. **Whoever walks the road, although a fool, shall not go astray**: When we stick on God's **Highway of Holiness**, even though His work in us isn't complete yet – we may still be in some ways **a fool** – yet we are safe because we are on His highway! There are guardrails on the dangerous curves, and He keeps us from falling off as He develops the wisdom and maturity in us that will also keep us on the highway.

2. (9) The safety of the Highway of Holiness.

No lion shall be there,
Nor shall *any* ravenous beast go up on it;

It shall not be found there.
But the redeemed shall walk *there*.

a. **No lion shall be there**: As we stay on God's *Highway of Holiness*, we are protected from the attacks of the lion. Though *your adversary the devil walks about like a roaring lion, seeking whom he may devour* (1 Peter 5:8), that lion has never yet devoured anyone who stayed on the road. The promise is sure, **no lion shall be there**! **It shall not be found there**.

3. (10) The travelers on the Highway of Holiness.

And the ransomed of the LORD shall return,
And come to Zion with singing,
With everlasting joy on their heads.
They shall obtain joy and gladness,
And sorrow and sighing shall flee away.

a. **And the ransomed of the LORD shall return, and come to Zion with singing**: We use this *Highway of Holiness* to come to where God lives and reigns – **Zion** – and we come there **with singing**. God can put a song in our hearts as we travel on His *Highway of Holiness*.

i. **The ransomed of the LORD**: The word **ransomed** is related to the word *goel* and refers to the one who has been rescued by the *goel* – the kinsman-redeemer.

b. **With everlasting joy on their heads.... And sorrow and sighing shall flee away**: We can know some of this now, but we aren't at our destination on the *Highway of Holiness* yet. But when we arrive there, *God will wipe away every tear from their eyes; there shall be no more death, nor sorrow, nor crying. There shall be no more pain, for the former things have passed away.* (Revelation 21:4)

i. Using the pictures of this chapter, it is as if we come to God barren, dry, blind, deaf, weak, and crippled. Then the miraculous power of Jesus comes to change us, heal us, and provide for us. That isn't the end of God's work though; He then goes on to make a **Highway of Holiness** that the transformed man can walk on. The highway would be helpful to one who was barren, dry, blind, deaf, weak, and crippled; but when the highway is provided for the one who is healed and provided for as we are in Jesus, the blessing is even more amazing.

- Are you on that Highway?
- Are you making progress on it?
- Are you enjoying the travel?
- Are you inviting others to join you?

Isaiah 36 – A Demoralizing Attack on Faith

A. Rabshakeh speaks to leaders in King Hezekiah's government.

1. (1-3) Officials from King Hezekiah's government meet Rabshakeh, general of the armies of Assyria.

Now it came to pass in the fourteenth year of King Hezekiah *that* Sennacherib king of Assyria came up against all the fortified cities of Judah and took them. Then the king of Assyria sent *the* Rabshakeh with a great army from Lachish to King Hezekiah at Jerusalem. And he stood by the aqueduct from the upper pool, on the highway to the Fuller's Field. And Eliakim the son of Hilkiah, who was over the household, Shebna the scribe, and Joah the son of Asaph, the recorder, came out to him.

a. **In the fourteenth year of King Hezekiah**: This was about the year 700 B.C., during the reign of the godly King Hezekiah of Judah. The events of this chapter are also recorded in 2 Kings 18:13-27 and 2 Chronicles 32:1-19.

i. This begins a four-chapter section different than the prophecies recorded before or after. Isaiah 36 and 37 describe the LORD's work against the Assyrian threat. Isaiah 38 and 39 describe the response to the Babylonian threat.

ii. "This is history at its best, not dull recital of statistics and dates but an account which enables us to sense the haughty arrogance of the Assyrian and the chilling clutch of despair at the hearts of the Israelites." (Cundall, cited in Grogan)

b. **Sennacherib King of Assyria came up against all the fortified cities of Judah and took them**: This Assyrian invasion has been the broad background for much of Isaiah's prophecy in Isaiah chapters 1 through 35. Now, Isaiah gives us a historical record of what happened during the time he prophesied about.

i. The Assyrian army swept down from the north, conquering Syria and Israel, as Isaiah prophesied in Isaiah 8:3-4 and many other passages. The Assyrian army then **came up against all the fortified cities of Judah and took them**, as Isaiah prophesied in Isaiah 7:16-17 and many other passages.

c. **Then the king of Assyria sent the Rabshakeh with a great army from Lachish to King Hezekiah at Jerusalem**: At the time of Isaiah 36:1-3, the Assyrian army has conquered both Syria and the northern kingdom of Israel and has devastated the countryside and **fortified cities** of Judah. All that remains is Jerusalem, and if the Assyrians conquer her, then Judah is destroyed as a nation just as Syria and Israel were. These were the desperate times of King Hezekiah.

i. Who was **the Rabshakeh**? Actually, it is a title, not a name. It describes the "field commander" for the Assyrian army, who represented the Assyrian King Sennacherib. "Rab-shakeh, an Assyrian title, possibly originally 'chief cup-bearer' but by this time some high officer of state." (Motyer)

ii. The mention of **Lachish** is important historically. Lachish was thirty miles south-west of Jerusalem. Archaeologists have discovered a pit there with the remains of about 1,500 casualties of Sennacherib's attack. In the British Museum, you can see the Assyrian carving depicting their siege of the city of Lachish, which was an important fortress city of Judah.

d. **He stood by the aqueduct from the upper pool.... Eliakim... Shebna...Joah...came out to him**: Rabshakeh seems to be in complete command of the situation. He can walk right into the city of Jerusalem and stand at the crucial water supply – which would be Jerusalem's lifeline in a siege attack. As he stands there, three officials from Hezekiah's government come to meet him.

2. (4-6) Rabshakeh speaks against Judah's trust in an alliance with Egypt.

Then *the* Rabshakeh said to them, "Say now to Hezekiah, 'Thus says the great king, the king of Assyria: "What confidence is this in which you trust? I say you speak of having plans and power for war; but *they are* mere words. Now in whom do you trust, that you rebel against me? Look! You are trusting in the staff of this broken reed, Egypt, on which if a man leans, it will go into his hand and pierce it. So *is* Pharaoh king of Egypt to all who trust in him.

a. **What confidence is this in which you trust?** One of the great battles for Hezekiah during this time was the temptation to make a defensive alliance with Egypt, which seemed to be the only nation strong enough to protect Judah against the mighty Assyrians.

i. As a prophet, Isaiah did everything he could to discourage Hezekiah and the leaders of Judah from putting their trust in Egypt (Isaiah 19:11-17, 20:1-6, 30:1-7). The Lord wanted Judah to trust Him instead of Egypt.

ii. In this sense, Rabshakeh is speaking the truth! God wanted Judah to have no **confidence** in Egypt at all. But Rabshakeh isn't doing it to bring Judah to a firm trust in the Lord God, who can and will deliver them from the Assyrians. He does it to completely demoralize Judah and drive them to despair.

iii. Satan attacks us the same way! Often, even when he tells the truth ("You are such a rotten sinner!"), he never does it to lead us to a firm trust in the Lord our God ("Jesus died for sinners, so if I am a rotten sinner, Jesus died to forgive and free me!"). Instead, Satan's strategy – even if he tells us the truth – is always to demoralize us and drive us to despair.

b. **You are trusting in the staff of this broken reed, Egypt**: Strangely, Rabshakeh could see the truth of Egypt's weakness better than many of the leaders of Judah could.

i. "*Egypt* had made its one attempt to redeem its promises (28:14) and its army had been beaten at El Tekeh. The Rab-shakeh had himself seen this, but his words are more far-reaching and damaging, exposing the criminal stupidity of Judah's leaders: surely, he said, they knew that anyone who ever trusted Egypt suffered for it." (Motyer)

3. (7) Rabshakeh speaks against Judah's trust in God.

"But if you say to me, 'We trust in the Lord our God,' *is it* not He whose high places and whose altars Hezekiah has taken away, and said to Judah and Jerusalem, 'You shall worship before this altar'?"'

a. **If you say to me, "We trust in the Lord our God"**: Rabshakeh anticipated the response of the leaders of Judah. "Rabshakeh, you say that we can't trust in Egypt. All right, we won't. But we can trust in the Lord our God."

b. **Is it not He whose high places and whose altars Hezekiah has taken away?** Rabshakeh knew that King Hezekiah had implemented broad reforms in Judah, including the removal of the *high places* (2 Kings 18:3-4).

i. The **high places** were spots of "individual worship" which were prohibited by God's law (Leviticus 17:1-4). Israel was commanded to bring their sacrifices to the official center for sacrifice (the tabernacle or later, the temple). In the pagan world at that time, it was customary to offer sacrifice wherever one pleased – altars would customarily be built on high hills, in forested areas, or at other special places.

ii. That practice may have been fine for the time of the patriarchs. But now, God regarded sacrifice at **high places** as an offense. Hezekiah did right when he took away the **high places** and the **altars**, demanding that people come to the temple in Jerusalem to offer sacrifice.

iii. This command runs completely contrary to the way most people come to God in our culture. For the most part, Americans have an entirely individualistic way of coming to God, where each person makes up their own rules about dealing with God as they see Him. In the book *Habits of the Heart*, Robert Bellah and his colleagues interview a young nurse named Sheila Larson, whom they describe as representing many Americans' experience and views on religion. Speaking about her own faith and how it operates in her life, she says: "I believe in God. I'm not a religious fanatic. I can't remember the last time I went to church. My faith has carried me a long way. It is 'Sheilaism.' Just my own little voice." This "pick-and-choose-as-I-go-along-according-to-my-inner-voice" approach is just like picking your own high place and altar to sacrifice to God the way *you* want to instead of the way *God* wants you to.

c. **Is it not He whose high places and whose altars Hezekiah has taken away?** In Rabshakeh's thinking, Hezekiah's reforms have really *displeased* God, so he should not expect help from the Lord God of Israel. Rabshakeh would say, "Look at all the places there used to be where people would worship the Lord God of Israel. Now, since Hezekiah came in, there is only one place. More is always better, so the Lord God of Israel must be pretty sore at Hezekiah!"

i. The enemy of our souls has an amazing way of discouraging our obedience. If Hezekiah was not careful, this argument of Rabshakeh would start to make sense, when really it was demonic logic through and through.

ii. "The theological misunderstanding shown by the field commander at this point argues for the authenticity of the speech, which many critics have dubbed a free creation by the author of the narrative." (Grogan)

4. (8-9) Rabshakeh speaks against the army of Judah.

Now therefore, I urge you, give a pledge to my master the king of Assyria, and I will give you two thousand horses—if you are able on your part to put riders on them! How then will you repel one captain of the least of my master's servants, and put your trust in Egypt for chariots and horsemen?

a. **Give a pledge to my master the king of Assyria**: This reminds us of Rabshakeh's whole strategy, which is to *make Judah give up*. This is the *entire reason* Rabshakeh is at the aqueduct, speaking to these leaders of Hezekiah's government. He had the vastly superior armies; he could have just attacked Jerusalem without this little speech. But Rabshakeh would prefer it if Judah would simply *give up*, out of fear, discouragement, or despair.

i. The enemy of our soul uses the exact same approach. Many of us picture Satan as "itching for a fight" with us. Really, Satan doesn't want to do battle with you. First of all, there is the strong chance you will win. Second of all, win or lose, the battle can draw you closer to the Lord. Thirdly, what the Lord does in your life through the battle can be a great blessing for other people. No, Satan would much rather not fight you at all! He would much rather try to *talk you into giving up.*

ii. We see this exact strategy used against Jesus during His temptation in the wilderness. When Satan promised Jesus all the kingdoms of the world in exchange for Jesus' worship, Satan was trying to *avoid* the fight, and trying to *talk Jesus into giving up* (Luke 4:5-8). It didn't work with Jesus, and it shouldn't work with us.

b. **I will give you two thousand horses–if you are able on your part to put riders on them**: Here, Rabshakeh mocked Judah's weak army. He said, "Even if we helped you with 2,000 horses, it wouldn't do you any good." His basic message was, "We could beat you with one hand tied behind our backs!" (**How then will you repel one captain of the least of my master's servants**).

5. (10) Rabshakeh tells them that the Lord God of Israel is on *his* side.

Have I now come up without the Lord against this land to destroy it? The Lord said to me, 'Go up against this land, and destroy it.'"

a. **Have I now come up without the Lord against this land to destroy it?** Rabshakeh saved his best thrust for last: "Admit it, Hezekiah. You know that your God is on my side."

i. Like all good deception, it would have been easy for Hezekiah and his men to believe this one. After all, hadn't the Assyrians been *wildly successful*? Surely, God must be on their side. Didn't they have the *most powerful army*? Surely, God must be on their side.

b. **The Lord said to me, "Go up against this land, and destroy it"**: This was the finishing blow of a brilliant attack. "Hezekiah, *God told me* to destroy you. I'm just doing His will, and there is nothing you can do to stop it, so you may as well surrender."

i. Significantly, we can say that *Rabshakeh was partially correct!* God was with him, and his attack on Judah fulfilled God's prophesied plan! In conquering Syria, in conquering Israel, and in bringing Judah to the brink, the Assyrians *did the will of God!* God prophesied that all this would happen (Isaiah 8:3-4, 7:16-17 and many other passages in Isaiah). He allowed it to happen so His prophesied plan would be fulfilled.

ii. However, we should never think that God tempted an *innocent man* with an *evil plan*. In fact, even though God predicted and planned this invasion of the Assyrians, Rabshakeh may have been lying indeed when he said, **"The Lord said to me."** God did not have to do *anything special* to direct the bloodthirsty, conquest-hungry Assyrians to attack Syria, Israel, and Judah. He simply allowed the Assyrians to carry out the corrupt desires of their evil hearts. Therefore, the Assyrians could *never* excuse themselves by saying, "We were doing the Lord's will!" even as Judas could never make that excuse regarding his wicked betrayal of Jesus.

B. Rabshakeh speaks directly to the people of Jerusalem.

1. (11-12) Hezekiah's men ask Rabshakeh to speak only to them.

Then Eliakim, Shebna, and Joah said to *the* Rabshakeh, "Please speak to your servants in Aramaic, for we understand *it*; and do not speak to us in Hebrew in the hearing of the people who *are* on the wall." But *the* Rabshakeh said, "Has my master sent me to your master and to you to speak these words, and not to the men who sit on the wall, who will eat and drink their own waste with you?"

a. **Please speak to your servants in Aramaic, for we understand it**: We can just imagine how difficult this was for these leaders in Hezekiah's government. They must have thought, "It's bad enough we have to hear this. But since he is speaking in Hebrew, *everyone* will hear, and soon the people will become so discouraged they will rise up against us and make us surrender!"

b. **Has my master sent me to your master and to you to speak these words, and not to the men who sit on the wall**: Rabshakeh doesn't care if the common citizens of Jerusalem hear him. That's how he wants it! The more fear, discouragement, and despair he can spread, the better.

c. **Who will eat and drink their own waste**: Rabshakeh pointed forward to what conditions would be like in Jerusalem after an extended siege. He wanted this to disgust everyone who heard it, and he wanted to magnify the sense of fear, discouragement, and despair.

2. (13-20) Rabshakeh's speech to the people of Jerusalem.

Then *the* Rabshakeh stood and called out with a loud voice in Hebrew, and said, "Hear the words of the great king, the king of Assyria! Thus says the king: 'Do not let Hezekiah deceive you, for he will not be able to deliver you; nor let Hezekiah make you trust in the Lord, saying, "The Lord will surely deliver us; this city will not be given into the hand of the king of Assyria."' Do not listen to Hezekiah; for thus says the king of Assyria: 'Make *peace* with me *by* a present and come out to me; and every one of you eat from his own vine and every one from his own fig tree, and every one of you drink the waters of his own cistern; until I come and take you away to a land like your own land, a land of grain and new wine, a land of bread and vineyards. Beware lest Hezekiah persuade you, saying, "The Lord will deliver us." Has any one of the gods of the nations delivered its land from the hand of the king of Assyria? Where *are* the gods of Hamath and Arpad? Where *are* the gods of Sepharvaim? Indeed, have they delivered Samaria from my hand? Who among all the gods of these lands have delivered their countries from my hand, that the Lord should deliver Jerusalem from my hand?'"

a. **Then Rabshakeh stood and called out with a loud voice in Hebrew**: Saying "don't do that" to Rabshakeh was like saying it to a naughty child. He *couldn't wait* to speak to the people of Jerusalem.

b. **Hear the words of the great king**: Rabshakeh's speech was intended to *glorify the enemy facing God's people.*

c. **Do not let Hezekiah deceive you**: Rabshakeh's speech was intended to *make God's people doubt their leaders.*

d. **Nor let Hezekiah make you trust in the Lord**: Rabshakeh's speech was intended to *build fear and unbelief in God's people.*

e. **For thus says the king of Assyria: "Make peace with me by a present and come out to me, and everyone one of you will eat from his own**

vine": Rabshakeh's speech was intended to make *surrender an attractive option.*

f. **Until I come and take you away to a land like your own land**: Here, Rabshakeh refers to the policy of "ethnic cleansing" and "forced resettlement" practiced by the Assyrians. When they conquered a people, they forcibly resettled them in faraway places, to keep their spirits broken and their power weak. Rabshakeh's speech was intended to make this terrible fate *seem attractive.*

g. **Has any one of the gods of the nations delivered its land from the hand of the king of Assyria?** Rabshakeh's speech was intended to *destroy their trust in God.* His message is simple, and cunning in its Satanic logic: "The gods of other nations have not been able to protect them against us. Your God is just like one of them and can't protect you either."

i. For anyone who had the spiritual understanding to see it, Judah could have started planning the victory party right then. It is one thing to speak against Judah, its people and leaders. It was another thing altogether to mock the LORD God of Israel this way and count Him as "just another god."

ii. Typical of the work of the enemy of our souls, Rabshakeh was going well until he simply overstepped his bounds. There was no way God would let him off the hook for this one. He has offended the LORD God in a way he will soon regret.

3. (21-22) The response of the leaders in Hezekiah's government and the citizens of Jerusalem.

But they held their peace and answered him not a word; for the king's commandment was, "Do not answer him." Then Eliakim the son of Hilkiah, who *was* over the household, Shebna the scribe, and Joah the son of Asaph, the recorder, came to Hezekiah with *their* clothes torn, and told him the words of *the* Rabshakeh.

a. **But they held their peace and answered him not a word**: They didn't try to argue with Rabshakeh. Often, it is useless – if not dangerous – to try and match wits with this demonic logic. How much better to keep silent and trust God, instead of trying to win an argument.

i. "Silence is our best reply to the allegations and taunts of our foes. Be still, O persecuted soul! Hand over thy cause to God. It is useless to argue, even in many cases to give explanations. Be still, and commit thy cause to God." (Meyer)

b. **For the king's commandment was, "Do not answer him"**: King Hezekiah was wise enough to make this command, and his officials and the people were wise enough to obey him.

c. **Came to Hezekiah with their clothes torn**: Though they were silent, they were still deeply affected by this attack. It didn't just roll off their backs as if it were nothing. They have the same experience Paul described in 2 Corinthians 4:8-9: *We are hard pressed on every side, yet not crushed; we are perplexed, but not in despair; persecuted, but not forsaken; struck down, but not destroyed.* Things were hard, but the battle was not lost yet.

Isaiah 37 – Assyria Destroyed, God Glorified

A. King Hezekiah seeks the Lord.

1. (1-5) Hezekiah's immediate reaction upon hearing the words of Rabshakeh.

And so it was, when King Hezekiah heard *it*, that he tore his clothes, covered himself with sackcloth, and went into the house of the Lord. Then he sent Eliakim, who *was* over the household, Shebna the scribe, and the elders of the priests, covered with sackcloth, to Isaiah the prophet, the son of Amoz. And they said to him, "Thus says Hezekiah: 'This day *is* a day of trouble and rebuke and blasphemy; for the children have come to birth, but *there is* no strength to bring them forth. It may be that the Lord your God will hear the words of *the* Rabshakeh, whom his master the king of Assyria has sent to reproach the living God, and will rebuke the words which the Lord your God has heard. Therefore lift up *your* prayer for the remnant that is left.'" So the servants of King Hezekiah came to Isaiah.

a. **When King Hezekiah heard it…he tore his clothes, covered himself with sackcloth**: The tearing of clothes and the wearing of **sackcloth** (a rough, burlap-type material) were expressions of deep mourning, usually for the death of a loved one. Hezekiah took this report regarding Rabshakeh seriously, knowing how dedicated they were to the complete conquest of Jerusalem.

i. Hezekiah's initial reaction is good. *He sees the situation for what it really is*. Often, when we are in some kind of trial or difficulty, we handle it poorly because we never see the situation accurately. Jerusalem's situation is desperate, and Hezekiah knows it.

ii. There was good reason for Hezekiah to be so humble before the Lord. "City after city has fallen to Sennacherib and long lines of deportees are already snaking their bitter way into exile – and it is all Hezekiah's fault! He followed the lunatic policy of rebellion and was bewitched by Egyptian promises. He might as well have sold his people himself. But even when a matter is our own fault we can still pray about it. And the Lord can always be trusted to pity his people." (Motyer)

b. **And went into the house of the Lord**: Hezekiah's second reaction was even better. He did not allow his mourning and grief to spin him into a rejection of the Lord's power and help. He knew this was a more necessary time than ever to seek the Lord.

i. When it says, **went into the house of the Lord**, we should not think that it means that King Hezekiah went into the holy place itself, which was forbidden for all except priests. It simply means that Hezekiah went to the courts of the house of the Lord, to seek God in the place which was open to him as a man of Israel.

ii. A previous king of Judah, King Uzziah, saw his life tragically struck when he broke this command of the Lord to stay out of the holy place of the temple. 2 Chronicles 26:16 says, *But when he was strong his heart was lifted up, to his destruction, for he transgressed against the Lord his God by entering the temple of the Lord to burn incense on the altar of incense.* In response, God struck Uzziah with leprosy, and he was an isolated leper until his death.

c. **Then he sent Eliakim…Shebna…and the elders of the priests…to Isaiah the prophet**: The third thing Hezekiah did was also good. The king sought out the word of the Lord, given through the prophet of the Lord.

d. **The children have come to birth, but there is no strength to bring them forth**: Hezekiah put these words in the mouth of his messengers to Isaiah to express the total calamity of the situation. This was a proverbial expression for a disaster – a woman so exhausted by labor that she could not complete the birth, so it was likely that both mother and child would die.

e. **It may be that the Lord your God will hear the words of the Rabshakeh**: Hezekiah knew that their only hope was that God would take offense at the blasphemies of Rabshakeh and rise up against him.

f. **Therefore lift up your prayer for the remnant that is left**: It was as if Hezekiah said, "Isaiah, pray for us. Our nation is devastated by this Assyrian invasion, and Jerusalem alone is left standing. Pray **for the remnant that is left**."

2. (6-7) Isaiah's words of assurance to King Hezekiah.

And Isaiah said to them, "Thus shall you say to your master, 'Thus says the Lord: "Do not be afraid of the words which you have heard, with

which the servants of the king of Assyria have blasphemed Me. Surely I will send a spirit upon him, and he shall hear a rumor and return to his own land; and I will cause him to fall by the sword in his own land.”””

a. **Thus says the Lord**: Isaiah was aware he spoke as a prophet of the Lord. Without hesitation, he speaks as if he were speaking for the Lord God of heaven. We can be sure Isaiah did not take this lightly. The fate of the nation, and his entire credibility as a prophet, was riding on what he said.

i. Isaiah, speaking for the Lord, was about to make a bold prediction. His prophecy would be entirely “provable.” It would either happen or it would not happen; Isaiah would soon be known as a true prophet or a false prophet.

b. **Do not be afraid of the words which you have heard**: Perhaps we can sense the gentlest rebuke in these words from the Lord. “Hezekiah, it is good for you to seek Me so passionately. But the **words** of Rabshakeh are only **words. Do not be afraid of** them.”

c. **With which the servants of the king of Assyria have blasphemed Me**: How these words must have cheered Hezekiah! Before, he had hoped *it may be that the Lord your God will hear the words of the Rabshakeh...to reproach the living God* (Isaiah 37:4). Here, the Lord spoke through the prophet Isaiah, saying He had indeed heard these words. Now, God was taking it personally.

i. **The servants of the king of Assyria**: **Servants** is “a deliberately belittling expression, ‘the king of Assyria’s lads/flunkies’.” (Motyer)

ii. “He calls Rabshakeh and the other officers of the army the *slaves* or *servant boys* – we could say the *errand boys* – of the king of Assyria.” (Bultema)

d. **Surely I will send a spirit upon him, and he shall hear a rumor and return to his own land; and I will cause him to fall by the sword in his own land**: Here, the Lord God assures Hezekiah that He will indeed deal with Rabshakeh. He has heard his blasphemy and will bring judgment against him.

i. Significantly, in this initial word from the prophet Isaiah, there is no mention of Jerusalem’s deliverance or the defeat of the Assyrian army. God focuses this word against Rabshakeh *personally*.

3. (8-13) Rabshakeh’s letter to Hezekiah.

Then *the* Rabshakeh returned, and found the king of Assyria warring against Libnah, for he heard that he had departed from Lachish. And the king heard concerning Tirhakah king of Ethiopia, “He has come

out to make war with you." So when he heard *it*, he sent messengers to Hezekiah, saying, "Thus you shall speak to Hezekiah king of Judah, saying: 'Do not let your God in whom you trust deceive you, saying, "Jerusalem shall not be given into the hand of the king of Assyria." Look! You have heard what the kings of Assyria have done to all lands by utterly destroying them; and shall you be delivered? Have the gods of the nations delivered those whom my fathers have destroyed, Gozan and Haran and Rezeph, and the people of Eden who *were* in Telassar? Where *is* the king of Hamath, the king of Arpad, and the king of the city of Sepharvaim, Hena, and Ivah?'"

a. **Then the Rabshakeh returned, and found the king of Assyria warring against Libnah**: This must have seemed to Hezekiah to be the fulfillment of the LORD's promise through the prophet Isaiah. Rabshakeh left Jerusalem, and Hezekiah must have thought "Now he'll go back to his own land and be killed, just like the LORD promised. Good riddance! Thank You LORD!"

b. **The king heard concerning Tirhakah king of Ethiopia, "He has come out to make war with you"**: While Rabshakeh was away, the Assyrians learned that Egyptian troops (under an Ethiopian king) were advancing from the south. This would be the Egyptian intervention Assyria feared, and that many in Judah trusted in. But as Isaiah prophesied, it would amount to nothing (Isaiah 20:1-6 and 30:1-7).

i. "Actually Tirhakah was only a prince at the time, but because he assumed the throne in 690 B.C., the title 'king' is used proleptically [in advance]." (Wolf)

c. **Do not let your God in whom you trust deceive you**: Rabshakeh is not in Jerusalem, but that didn't stop him from trying to build fear, discouragement, and despair in King Hezekiah. He sent a letter to the king of Judah, hoping to defeat him from a distance.

d. **Have the gods of the nations**: If read with an eye of faith, these must have been trust-building words of Rabshakeh to Hezekiah. In counting the LORD God of Israel among the gods of the nations, Rabshakeh blasphemes the LORD and invites judgment.

4. (14-20) Hezekiah's prayer.

And Hezekiah received the letter from the hand of the messengers, and read it; and Hezekiah went up to the house of the LORD, and spread it before the LORD. Then Hezekiah prayed to the LORD, saying: "O LORD of hosts, God of Israel, *the One* who dwells *between* the cherubim, You *are* God, You alone, of all the kingdoms of the earth. You have made heaven and earth. Incline Your ear, O LORD, and hear; open Your eyes,

O Lord, and see; and hear all the words of Sennacherib, which he has sent to reproach the living God. Truly, Lord, the kings of Assyria have laid waste all the nations and their lands, and have cast their gods into the fire; for they *were* not gods, but the work of men's hands—wood and stone. Therefore they destroyed them. Now therefore, O Lord our God, save us from his hand, that all the kingdoms of the earth may know that You *are* the Lord, You alone."

a. **Hezekiah went up to the house of the Lord, and spread it before the Lord**: Hezekiah did exactly what any child of God should do with such a letter. He took it **to the house of the Lord** (to the outer courts, not the holy place), and he **spread it before the Lord**. In this, Hezekiah boldly and effectively fulfilled the later command of 1 Peter 5:7: *casting all your care upon Him, for He cares for you.*

i. To be in the ministry means that from time to time, you will receive nasty messages from others. What should one do with them? Often, the best thing to do is to simply throw them away, especially if they are anonymous. But if they are to be read and kept, they should be **spread…before the Lord**. "Lord, show me what there is in this letter that I need to hear. Show me what I need to disregard. Help me to see beyond this person's sinful manner or tone and see if You have something in this for me."

ii. One old preacher received a letter with no sender or return address on the envelope. When he opened it, he saw a single piece of paper with only one word: "Fool!" He took it to the pulpit the next Sunday, and said: "I received an unusual letter this week. Never before have I received a letter where the writer signed his name, but forgot to write anything else."

b. **O Lord of hosts**: This title for our God essentially means, "Lord of armies." Hezekiah was in a crisis that was primarily *military* in nature, so it made sense for him to address the Lord first according to the aspect of God's nature that was most needful for him. "Lord of armies, send some troops to help us!"

c. **God of Israel**: This title for God reminded Hezekiah – and the Lord also, in our human way of understanding – that the Lord God was the covenant God of Israel, and that He should not forsake His people.

d. **The One who dwells between the cherubim**: Here, Hezekiah sees the great majesty of God. Surely, **the One who dwells between the cherubim** would never allow Rabshakeh's blasphemies to go unpunished.

e. **You are God, You alone**: **God** is a simple title for our LORD, but perhaps the most powerful. If He is **God**, then what can He *not* do? If He is **God**, then what is *beyond* His control? Hezekiah realizes the most fundamental fact of all theology: God is **God**, and we *are not!* God is **God**, and Rabshakeh or the Assyrians *are not!*

f. **You have made heaven and earth**: In recognizing the LORD God as Creator, Hezekiah saw that the LORD had all *power* and all *rights* over every created thing. We can almost feel Hezekiah's faith rising as he prayed this.

g. **Incline Your ear, O LORD, and hear; open Your eyes, O LORD, and see**: Hezekiah knew very well that the LORD did in fact hear and see the blasphemies of Rabshakeh. This is a poetic way of asking God to *act upon* what He has seen and heard, assuming that if God *has seen* such things, He will certainly act.

h. **All the words of Sennacherib, which he has sent to reproach the living God**: In his prayer, King Hezekiah draws the contrast between **the living God** and the false gods of the nations the Assyrians have already conquered. Those false gods were **not gods, but the work of men's hands – wood and stone**, so they were not able to save them from the Assyrians. But Hezekiah prays confidently that the **living God** will save them, **that all the kingdoms of the earth may know that You are the LORD, You alone**.

B. Isaiah brings the LORD's answer to King Hezekiah's prayer and a word to Rabshakeh.

1. (21) The power of Hezekiah's prayer.

Then Isaiah the son of Amoz sent to Hezekiah, saying, "Thus says the LORD God of Israel, 'Because you have prayed to Me against Sennacherib king of Assyria,

a. **Because you have prayed to Me**: The glorious answer which fills the rest of the chapter came because Hezekiah prayed. What if he would not have prayed? Then we are to think that no answer would have come, and Jerusalem would have been conquered. Hezekiah's prayer really mattered. How many blessings, how many victories, how many souls saved for Jesus' glory, lie unclaimed in heaven until the LORD can say, **because you have prayed to Me**?

2. (22-35) The LORD's word to Rabshakeh.

This is the word which the LORD has spoken concerning him:

"The virgin, the daughter of Zion,
Has despised you, laughed you to scorn;

The daughter of Jerusalem
Has shaken *her* head behind your back!
Whom have you reproached and blasphemed?
Against whom have you raised *your* voice,
And lifted up your eyes on high?
Against the Holy One of Israel.
By your servants you have reproached the Lord,
And said, 'By the multitude of my chariots
I have come up to the height of the mountains,
To the limits of Lebanon;
I will cut down its tall cedars
***And* its choice cypress trees;**
I will enter its farthest height,
To its fruitful forest.
I have dug and drunk water,
And with the soles of my feet I have dried up
All the brooks of defense.'
Did you not hear long ago
***How* I made it,**
From ancient times that I formed it?
Now I have brought it to pass,
That you should be
For crushing fortified cities *into* heaps of ruins.
Therefore their inhabitants *had* little power;
They were dismayed and confounded;
They were *as* the grass of the field
And the green herb,
***As* the grass on the housetops**
And grain blighted before it is grown.
But I know your dwelling place,
Your going out and your coming in,
And your rage against Me.
Because your rage against Me and your tumult
Have come up to My ears,
Therefore I will put My hook in your nose
And My bridle in your lips,
And I will turn you back
By the way which you came."'

This *shall be* a sign to you:
You shall eat this year such as grows of itself,
And the second year what springs from the same;

Also in the third year sow and reap,
Plant vineyards and eat the fruit of them.
And the remnant who have escaped of the house of Judah
Shall again take root downward,
And bear fruit upward.
For out of Jerusalem shall go a remnant,
And those who escape from Mount Zion.
The zeal of the LORD of hosts will do this."

Therefore thus says the LORD concerning the king of Assyria:
"He shall not come into this city,
Nor shoot an arrow there,
Nor come before it with shield,
Nor build a siege mound against it.
By the way that he came,
By the same shall he return;
And he shall not come into this city,"
Says the LORD.
"For I will defend this city, to save it
For My own sake and for My servant David's sake."

a. **The virgin, the daughter of Zion, has despised you, laughed you to scorn**: The idea is that the Assyrians have come to ravish the **daughter of Zion**, the city of Jerusalem. But God won't allow it.

i. "Jerusalem is represented as a young girl rebuffing with contempt the unwelcome advances of a churl." (Grogan)

ii. "*Virgin* is used here in the sense of being untouched by the marauder. The Assyrian came intent on rape but his victim remains unharmed *because you have prayed*." (Motyer)

b. **Whom have you reproached and blasphemed? Against whom have you raised your voice, and lifted up your eyes on high? Against the Holy One of Israel**: The LORD, speaking through Isaiah, simply says to Rabshakeh, "Do you know whom you are dealing with?" Rabshakeh obviously did not know.

i. Curiously, this prophecy may have never reached the ears of Rabshakeh. After all, Isaiah didn't exactly have free access to him. But perhaps before his terrible end, God found a way to get this prophecy to him. Or, perhaps God had it for this blasphemer as a special message in hell. At the very least, this prophecy would have been hugely encouraging to Hezekiah and all of Judah, even if Rabshakeh never heard it on this earth.

c. **By the multitude of my chariots, I have come up to the height of the mountains**: Here, the LORD describes the great pride the Assyrians had in their own conquests. But they forgot that the LORD was really in charge (**Now I have brought it to pass, that you should be for crushing fortified cities into heaps of ruins. Therefore their inhabitants had little power**). Even if the Assyrians didn't know it, they owed their success to the LORD.

i. How humbling this must have been for the Assyrians! All along, they thought it was because of their mighty power they had accomplished so much. Here, God makes it plain that it was His power that did it.

d. **I know your dwelling place, your going out and your coming in**: God knew everything about this enemy, and because Assyria went too far in blaspheming the One who made all their success possible, **therefore I will put My hook in your nose…and I will turn you back by the way which you came**. This was an especially dramatic statement, because this is exactly how the Assyrians would cruelly march those whom they forced to relocate out of their conquered lands. They would line up the captives, and drive a large fishhook through the lip or the nose of each captive, string them all together and march them. God said to Assyria, "I'm going to do the same thing to you."

i. **You shall eat this year such as grows of itself**: "The invasion prevented sowing in 702 B.C., but when the threat lifted in 701 they would find sufficient growth to preserve life; in 701 the withdrawing Assyrians still inhibited agriculture, yet in 700 there would still be enough through 'chance growth'. Thus the Lord would confirm retrospectively that it was his hand that dispersed the threat." (Motyer)

e. **For out of Jerusalem shall go a remnant**: As much as the Assyrians would like to crush Jerusalem and Judah, they will not be able to. God will preserve His remnant.

f. **He shall not come into this city, nor shoot an arrow there…. For I will defend this city, to save it for My own sake and for My servant David's sake**: God plainly and clearly draws a line. Although the Assyrian military machine is poised to lay siege to Jerusalem, and ultimately crush them, they won't. The king of Assyria will **not come into this city**, because God is defending it.

i. Why does God defend the city? **For My own sake**. God will defend His own glory. Often, we unnecessarily think that we must defend the glory of the LORD. But that isn't really the case. God is more than able to defend His own glory.

ii. Why does God defend the city? **For My servant David's sake**. King David had died almost 300 years before this, but God still honored His promise to David (2 Samuel 7:10-17). God would defend Jerusalem, not for the city's sake at all – Jerusalem *deserved* judgment! But He does it for His own sake, and for the sake of David. In the same way, God the Father defends and blesses us, not for our own sake – we often *deserve* His judgment! But He often does it for His own sake, and for the sake of Jesus Christ our Lord.

3. (36) God strikes down the mighty army of Assyria.

Then the angel of the LORD went out, and killed in the camp of the Assyrians one hundred and eighty-five thousand; and when *people* arose early in the morning, there were the corpses—all dead.

a. **The angel of the LORD went out**: Simply and powerfully, God destroys this mighty nation in one night. 185,000 died at the hand of **the angel of the LORD**. Against all odds, and against every expectation except the expectation of faith, the Assyrian army was turned back without having even shot an arrow into Jerusalem. The unstoppable was stopped, the undefeated was defeated.

i. The prophet Hosea made this same prediction: *Yet I will have mercy on the house of Judah, will save them by the LORD their God, and will not save them by bow, nor by sword or battle, by horses or horsemen.* (Hosea 1:7)

ii. "Herodotus, the Greek historian, recorded that one night Sennacherib's army camp was infested with mice (or rats) that destroyed the arrows and shield-thongs of the soldiers. He probably got this tradition from Egyptian sources, and it could well be a somewhat garbled version of the event recorded here." (Grogan)

b. **All dead**: This was not difficult for God to do. Far "harder" for the LORD was getting the hearts and minds of His people in the right place. Once they were there, it was nothing for God to dispatch *one angel* to do this.

4. (37-38) The end of Sennacherib, king of Assyria.

So Sennacherib king of Assyria departed and went away, returned *home*, and remained at Nineveh. Now it came to pass, as he was worshiping in the house of Nisroch his god, that his sons Adrammelech and Sharezer struck him down with the sword; and they escaped into the land of Ararat. Then Esarhaddon his son reigned in his place.

a. **Departed and went away**: This was exactly as God said he would. But Sennacherib left still full of pride. After this retreat from Judah, Sennacherib commissioned a record, which is preserved in the spectacular Annals of

Sennacherib (the Taylor Prism), which can be seen in the British Museum. It shows how full of pride Sennacherib's heart still was, even if he did not conquer Jerusalem.

i. "I attacked Hezekiah of Judah who had not subjected himself to me, and took forty-six fortresses, forts and small cities. I carried away captive 200,150 people, big and small, both male and female, a multitude of horses, young bulls, asses, camels, and oxen. Hezekiah himself I locked up in Jerusalem like a bird in its cage. I put up banks against the city. I separated his cities whose inhabitants I had taken prisoners from his realm and gave them to Mitiniti, king of Ashdod, Padi, king of Ekron, and Zilbel, king of Gaza and thus diminished his country. And I added another tax to the one imposed on him earlier." (Cited in Bultema)

ii. "The Biblical account concludes with the much-debated statement that the Assyrian army was struck down in some way during the night with considerable loss of life, following which the siege was called off.... The Assyrian Annals tacitly agree with the Biblical version by making no claim that Jerusalem was taken, only describing tribute from Hezekiah." (T.C. Mitchell, *The Bible in the British Museum*)

b. **Now it came to pass**: Between Isaiah 37:37 and Isaiah 37:38, some 20 years passed. Perhaps Sennacherib thought he had escaped the judgment of God, but he hadn't. He met the bitter end of death at the end of swords held by his own sons.

i. An old Jewish legend – and nothing more than a legend – says how it was that Sennacherib's sons came to kill him. Sennacherib was troubled at how God seemed to bless the Jews so much and tried to find out why. Someone told him it was because Abraham had loved God so much that he was willing to sacrifice his son to the Lord. Sennacherib thought he would be even more favored by God, and decided to kill two of his sons in sacrifice to the Lord, becoming even more blessed than Abraham and his descendants. But his two sons learned of the plan, and killed him before he could kill them, thus fulfilling the word of the Lord.

Isaiah 38 – King Hezekiah's Life is Spared

A. The mercy of God to Hezekiah.

1. (1) Isaiah's announcement to Hezekiah.

In those days Hezekiah was sick and near death. And Isaiah the prophet, the son of Amoz, went to him and said to him, "Thus says the LORD: 'Set your house in order, for you shall die and not live.'"

a. **In those days**: This happened at the time of the Assyrian invasion of Judah, because Jerusalem had not been delivered from the Assyrian threat yet (Isaiah 38:6). The events of this chapter are also recorded in 2 Kings 20:1-11.

i. "Interpreters agree that the events described in chapters 38 and 39 preceded the invasion of 701 B.C..... Many date these events in 703 B.C., but the evidence more strongly suggests a date of about 712 B.C." (Wolf)

b. **Was sick and near death**: We are not told how Hezekiah became sick. It may have been through something obvious to all, or it may have been through something known only to God. However Hezekiah became sick, it was certainly permitted by the LORD.

c. **Set your house in order, for you shall die and not live**: God was remarkably kind to Hezekiah, telling him that his death was near. Not all people are given the time to set their house in order.

i. We know from comparing 2 Kings 18:2 with 2 Kings 20:6, that Hezekiah was 39 years old when he learned he would soon die.

2. (2-3) Hezekiah's prayer.

Then Hezekiah turned his face toward the wall, and prayed to the LORD, and said, "Remember now, O LORD, I pray, how I have walked before You in truth and with a loyal heart, and have done *what is* good in Your sight." And Hezekiah wept bitterly.

a. **Hezekiah turned his face toward the wall**: This shows how earnest Hezekiah was in his prayer. He directed his prayer in privacy to God, and not to any man.

b. **Remember now, O LORD**: To our ears, Hezekiah's prayer might almost sound ungodly. In it, his focus is on self-justification and his own merits. It is pretty much as if Hezekiah prayed, "LORD, I've been such a good boy and You aren't being fair to me. Remember what a good boy I've been and rescue me."

i. But under the Old Covenant, this was a valid principle on which to approach God. Passages like Leviticus 26 and Deuteronomy 28 show that under the Old Covenant, blessing and cursing were sent by God on the basis of obedience or disobedience. On that principle, David could write in Psalm 15: *LORD, who may abide in Your tabernacle? Who may dwell in Your holy hill? He who walks uprightly, and works righteousness, and speaks the truth in his heart.* (Psalm 15:1-2)

ii. But under the New Covenant, we are blessed on the principle of faith in Jesus (Galatians 3:13-14). Hezekiah's principle of prayer isn't fitting for a Christian today. We pray in the name of Jesus (John 16:23-24), not in the name of who we are or what we have done.

iii. "We come across similar pleas again and again in the prayers of God's children of old. The Psalms abound with them. But we do not find them in the New Testament. The Church bases its pleas on Christ's righteousness." (Bultema)

c. **And Hezekiah wept bitterly**: Why was Hezekiah so undone at the prospect of death? Many Christians today would say, "Take me home, LORD!" But Hezekiah lived under the Old Covenant, and at that time there was not a confident assurance of the glory in the life beyond. Instead, Jesus brought life and immortality to light through the gospel (2 Timothy 1:10). Also, under the Old Covenant Hezekiah would have regarded this as evidence that God was very displeased with him.

3. (4-5) Isaiah brings God's answer to Hezekiah's prayer.

And the word of the LORD came to Isaiah, saying, "Go and tell Hezekiah, 'Thus says the LORD, the God of David your father: "I have heard your prayer, I have seen your tears; surely I will add to your days fifteen years.

a. **I will add to your days fifteen years**: In response to Hezekiah's prayer, God granted Hezekiah **fifteen years** more.

i. Because Hezekiah recovered, was God's word (*You shall die and not live*, Isaiah 38:1) proved false? No; first, Hezekiah did in fact die, just not as soon as God first announced. Second, when God announces judgment it is almost always an invitation to repent and to receive mercy.

b. **I have heard your prayer**: Hezekiah's prayer was important. By all indications, if Hezekiah had not made his passionate prayer, then his life would not have been extended. Prayer matters.

i. In fact, God gave two gifts to Hezekiah. First, He gave the gift of an extended life. Second, He gave the gift of knowing he only had fifteen years left. If he were wise, this would still give King Hezekiah the motivation to walk right with God and to set his house in order.

4. (6) The promise of deliverance from the Assyrian threat.

I will deliver you and this city from the hand of the king of Assyria, and I will defend this city."'

a. **I will deliver you and this city from the hand of the king of Assyria**: This promise is in accord with the LORD's previous prophecies of deliverance, and dates this chapter as being before God destroyed the Assyrian army (Isaiah 37:36-37).

b. **I will deliver you…and I will defend this city**: The connection of the two promises indicates that one would confirm the other. When Hezekiah recovered his health, he could know that God would also deliver him from the Assyrians.

5. (7-8) A sign to confirm the promise.

And this is the sign to you from the LORD, that the LORD will do this thing which He has spoken: Behold, I will bring the shadow on the sundial, which has gone down with the sun on the sundial of Ahaz, ten degrees backward." So the sun returned ten degrees on the dial by which it had gone down.

a. **This is the sign…that the LORD will do this thing which He has spoken**: God showed even more mercy to Hezekiah. God was under no obligation to give this sign. In fact, God would have been justified in saying, "Hey Hezekiah, I said it and you believe it. How dare you not take My word for true?" But in real love, God gave Hezekiah more than he needed or deserved.

i. God shows the same mercy to us. It should be enough for God to simply say to us, "I love you." But God did so much to *demonstrate* His love to us (John 3:16, Romans 5:8).

b. **Behold, I will bring the shadow of the sundial…ten degrees backward**: God promised to do something completely miraculous for the confirming sign. And it happened just as God promised: **So the sun returned ten degrees on the dial by which it had gone down**.

i. This was a wonderfully appropriate sign for Hezekiah. By having the shadow of the sundial move backward, it gave *more time* in a day – just as God gave Hezekiah *more time*.

ii. How was this miracle accomplished? We don't know. God could have simply "moved the sun back." Or, He may have provided the miraculous appearance of time moving back on the sundial of Ahaz. It doesn't really matter how God did it; He has miraculous resources and ways we know nothing about.

B. King Hezekiah's statement regarding his healing.

1. (9-14) Hezekiah's lament.

This is the writing of Hezekiah king of Judah, when he had been sick and had recovered from his sickness:

I said,
"In the prime of my life
I shall go to the gates of Sheol;
I am deprived of the remainder of my years."
I said,
"I shall not see Yah,
The Lord in the land of the living;
I shall observe man no more among the inhabitants of the world.
My life span is gone,
Taken from me like a shepherd's tent;
I have cut off my life like a weaver.
He cuts me off from the loom;
From day until night You make an end of me.
I have considered until morning—
Like a lion,
So He breaks all my bones;
From day until night You make an end of me.
Like a crane *or* a swallow, so I chattered;
I mourned like a dove;
My eyes fail *from looking* upward.
O Lord, I am oppressed;
Undertake for me!

a. **In the prime of my life I shall go to the gates of Sheol**: The Hebrew word **Sheol** refers to "the grave" or "the place of the dead." Here, Hezekiah laments the news of his impending death.

b. **I shall not see YAH, the LORD in the land of the living**: Hezekiah's pain at his approaching death is increased as he believes that in the grave, he will no longer see the LORD.

i. Again, Hezekiah's thinking is based in the cloudy understanding of the world beyond, before life and immortality were brought to life through the gospel of Jesus Christ (2 Timothy 1:10). Though there are occasional glimpses of hope into the world beyond (such as in Job 19:25-27), for the most part there is no clear understanding of the nature of life after death (Psalm 6:5, Psalm 88:3-5, 11).

ii. This explains why Hezekiah does not welcome death as a certain pathway to the presence of the LORD. For these Old Testament saints like Hezekiah and David, the grave (**Sheol**) was an uncertain place. They knew the LORD was there (Psalm 139:8), but they didn't know much more than that. For these Old Testament saints, going to the world beyond was exchanging this world's certainty for the uncertainty of the world beyond.

c. **O LORD, I am oppressed**: Since Hezekiah lived before the finished work of Jesus, he lived under the bondage of the fear of death (Hebrews 2:14-15). How different for the believer in Jesus Christ, for whom death has no victory or sting (1 Corinthians 15:53-55).

i. "Hezekiah has been compared with Paul who desired to depart and be with Christ, but this comparison is unfair, for Hezekiah still lived under the shadow of the Old Dispensation. Israel knew of an immortal life but did not quite have the glorious hope the Church now has." (Bultema)

d. **Like a crane or a swallow, so I chattered; I mourned like a dove**: "The varied cries of Palestine's birds express the varied nature of Hezekiah's many cries to God, now quiet, now shrill, now mournful." (Grogan)

2. We can have a clearer understanding of the world beyond than King Hezekiah did.

a. The Bible uses several different words in the Old and New Testaments to describe the world beyond, and where people go when they die.

- *Sheol* is a Hebrew word with the idea of the "place of the dead." It has no direct reference to either torment or eternal happiness. The idea of *Sheol* is often accurately expressed as "the grave."
- *Hades* is a Greek word used to describe the "world beyond." In the Bible, it has generally the same idea as *Sheol*.

- Revelation 9:1 speaks of the *bottomless pit*; this place called the *abyssos* is a prison for certain demons (Luke 8:31; 2 Peter 2:4; Jude 6). Or more generally, it is considered part of the realm of the dead (Romans 10:7 uses it in the sense of *Hades*).
- *Gehenna* is a Greek word borrowed from the Hebrew language. In Mark 9:43-44, Jesus speaks of *hell* (*gehenna*). *Hell is a* Greek translation of the Hebrew "Valley of Hinnom," a place outside Jerusalem's walls desecrated by Molech worship and human sacrifice (2 Chronicles 28:1-3; Jeremiah 32:35). It was also a garbage dump where rubbish and refuse were burned. The smoldering fires and festering worms of the Valley of Hinnom made it a graphic and effective picture of the fate of the damned. This place is also called the "lake of fire" in Revelation 20:13-15, prepared for the devil and his angels (Matthew 25:41).

b. The place known as *Sheol* and *Hades* is not what we normally think of as "Hell." It was, before the finished work of Jesus, the place where the dead awaited judgment or final justification (as illustrated by Jesus in the story of the rich man and Lazarus in Luke 16:19-31). Jesus was in Hades after His death on the cross, but did not (and *could* not) remain there (Acts 2:25-32). It seems that Jesus preached in Hades (1 Peter 3:18-19) and there is a sense in which Jesus set the captives in Hades free (Ephesians 4:8-9 and Isaiah 61:1). Jesus *made no atonement* in Hades; the price was already paid on the cross (John 19:30) when Jesus suffered in His *physical body* (Colossians 1:19-22). Jesus went to Hades as a *victor* not as a *victim.* Jesus' work and preaching offered salvation for the believing dead who in faith waited in Hades (Hebrews 11:39-40), and His work sealed the condemnation of the wicked and unbelieving. Since Jesus' work on the cross is finished, there is no "waiting" for believers who die, who go straight to heaven (2 Corinthians 5:6-8, Philippians 1:21-23). In that sense, Jesus "shut down" the part of Hades known as "Abraham's Bosom"; but the portion of Hades reserved for torment is occupied until the final judgment, when those who are there will be sent to what we normally think of as "Hell." *Gehenna* is what we normally think of as "Hell," the *Lake of Fire* (Revelation 19:20, 20:10-15, and 21:6-8). Actually, *Gehenna* or hell has many names or titles in the Bible, including *lake of fire* (Revelation 19:20), *everlasting fire* (Matthew 25:41), *everlasting punishment* (Matthew 25:46), and *outer darkness* (Matthew 8:12).

c. The Old Testament has little clear revelation about the afterlife; confident statements like Job 19:25-26 are countered by unsure passages like Ecclesiastes 3:19-20 and Psalm 6:4-5. However, the New Testament gives much more specific revelation regarding the afterlife; these are things that have *now been revealed by the appearing of our Savior Jesus Christ, who has abolished death and brought life and immortality to light through the gospel.* (2 Timothy 1:10) Significantly, most people who teach wrong doctrines about the afterlife (such as "soul sleep" or annihilationism) base their arguments on these "unsure" passages from the Old Testament, instead of the much clearer passages in the New Testament. In doing this, they reject the clear principle of 2 Timothy 1:10.

3. (15-20) Hezekiah praises God for sparing his life.

"What shall I say?
He has both spoken to me,
And He Himself has done *it*.
I shall walk carefully all my years
In the bitterness of my soul.
O LORD, by these *things men* live;
And in all these *things is* the life of my spirit;
So You will restore me and make me live.
Indeed *it was* for *my own* peace
***That* I had great bitterness;**
But You have lovingly *delivered* my soul from the pit of corruption,
For You have cast all my sins behind Your back.
For Sheol cannot thank You,
Death cannot praise You;
Those who go down to the pit cannot hope for Your truth.
The living, the living man, he shall praise You,
As I *do* this day;
The father shall make known Your truth to the children.
"The LORD *was ready* to save me;
Therefore we will sing my songs with stringed instruments
All the days of our life, in the house of the LORD."

a. **What shall I say? He has both spoken to me, and He Himself has done it**: When God answered his prayer, all Hezekiah could do was praise God. He knew that it was all the LORD's work, both in word (**spoken to me**) and deed (**done it**). So, Hezekiah was speechless (**What shall I say?**).

b. **I shall walk carefully all my years**: This is a good promise Hezekiah makes, and one often on the lips of the person God has spared. But in the end, it was only a good promise if Hezekiah *made* it good.

i. What did Hezekiah do with these added 15 years? One thing he did was father a son who would succeed him on the throne of Judah. Of the next king of Judah, Manasseh, the son of Hezekiah, it is written that he was 12 years old when he became king (2 Kings 21:1). This means he must have been born in the last 15 years of Hezekiah's life. Sadly, fathering Manasseh was not a worthy achievement. It was written of him, *And he did evil in the sight of the LORD, according to the abominations of the nations whom the LORD had cast out before the children of Israel* (2 Kings 21:2). In fact, God specifically targeted Judah for judgment because of the terrible sins of Manasseh (2 Kings 21:10-15).

ii. In this, we may see that the LORD had a better plan than Hezekiah did in calling him home at the earlier time. God knew that if Hezekiah lived, he would give birth to this wicked successor. Sometimes it is best to simply leave our lot with the LORD, and leave what even seems to be clearly good up to His wisdom.

c. **It was for my own peace that I had great bitterness**: Hezekiah is to be admired for his accurate self-knowledge, and his honesty. He admits that it was not for God's glory or honor, or even for the glory or honor of his kingdom that he was troubled over his impending death and that he wanted his life spared. It was for his **own peace**.

d. **For Sheol cannot thank You, death cannot praise You; those who go down to the pit cannot hope for Your truth. The living, the living man, he shall praise You, as I do this day**: Again, this passage reflects the uncertain understanding of the "world beyond" before the finished work of Jesus Christ. Hezekiah *knew* he could praise God while he walked this earth, but he wasn't so sure about the world beyond.

e. **Therefore we will sing my songs with stringed instruments all the days of our life, in the house of the LORD**: Hezekiah shows the logical response to God's great deliverance – praise.

4. (21-22) How the LORD healed Hezekiah.

Now Isaiah had said, "Let them take a lump of figs, and apply *it* as a poultice on the boil, and he shall recover." And Hezekiah had said, "What *is* the sign that I shall go up to the house of the LORD?"

a. **Let them take a lump of figs, and apply it as a poultice on the boil, and he shall recover**: Apparently, God used this medical treatment – at the very least, He used it as a **sign** – to bring Hezekiah's healing. God can, and often does, bring healing through medical treatments, and apart from an unusual direction from God, medical treatment should never be rejected in the name of "faith."

i. "The patient must pray, but withal make use of means; trust God, but not tempt him." (Trapp)

b. **What is the sign that I shall go up to the house of the LORD?** Hezekiah wanted a sign, but why a sign that would allow him to **go up to the house of the LORD**? Because he could not and would not **go up to the house of the LORD** until he was healed, so the two were connected.

Isaiah 39 – Showing Off the LORD's Treasure

A. King Hezekiah shows off the treasures of his house to envoys from Babylon.

1. (1) A letter from the king of Babylon.

At that time Merodach-Baladan the son of Baladan, king of Babylon, sent letters and a present to Hezekiah, for he heard that he had been sick and had recovered.

a. **At that time**: This was after the miraculous recovery of Hezekiah. The LORD was good enough to give King Hezekiah 15 years more of life, but it was up to Hezekiah if those years would be lived in wisdom and to the glory of God.

b. **Sent letters and a present to Hezekiah, for he heard that he had been sick and had recovered**: Apparently this was a gesture of kindness from the king of Babylon, showing concern to Hezekiah as fellow royalty.

c. **Merodach-Baladan**: His presence showed this was more than a courtesy call. This was an attempt to bring the kingdom of Judah on to the side of the Babylonians against the Assyrians.

i. "To the Assyrians Merodach-Baladan was a terrorist; to himself he was a freedom-fighter with his life devoted to the liberation of his beloved Babylon from Assyrian tyranny." (Motyer)

ii. "Hezekiah was deeply worried about Assyria. Feeling honored by the embassy, he gladly welcomed the envoys of this archenemy of Assyria. Without consulting either the Lord or Isaiah, he showed them his vast treasures, his abundant supplies of food, and his military armaments. God had given Hezekiah great wealth, so the visitors were duly impressed (2 Chron. 32:27-29)." (Wolf)

iii. The first part of Isaiah (chapters 1 through 38) mainly dealt with the present threat from the Assyrian Empire. The rest of Isaiah (chapters 39 through 66) will prophetically speak to the threat of the coming Babylonian Empire. Therefore, "This brief chapter is actually an introduction to the second half of Isaiah." (Bultema)

2. (2) Hezekiah entertains the envoys from the king of Babylon.

And Hezekiah was pleased with them, and showed them the house of his treasures—the silver and gold, the spices and precious ointment, and all his armory—all that was found among his treasures. There was nothing in his house or in all his dominion that Hezekiah did not show them.

a. **And Hezekiah was pleased with them**: We can imagine that this was flattering for King Hezekiah. After all, Judah was a lowly nation with little power, and Babylon was a junior superpower. To receive this notice and recognition from the king of Babylon must have really made Hezekiah feel he was important.

b. **Showed them the house of his treasures**: We can imagine Hezekiah wanting to please these envoys from Babylon and wanting to show them that they had good reason to be impressed with him and his kingdom. So, he did everything he could to impress them, and showed them the very best riches of the royal household – and he showed them everything.

c. **There was nothing in his house or in all his dominion that Hezekiah did not show them**: As the coming rebuke from Isaiah will demonstrate, this was nothing but proud foolishness on Hezekiah's part. He is in the dangerous place of wanting to please and impress men, especially ungodly men.

i. It was a genuine compliment for Hezekiah to receive this recognition from the king of Babylon. But Hezekiah received it wrongly, and let it go to his head. It is easy to get too puffed up when people compliment or recognize us, and to begin to take their praise – and ourselves – too seriously.

ii. In this place of wanting to please men, Hezekiah is no longer a true servant of God. Paul wrote in Galatians 1:10, *For if I still pleased men, I would not be a bondservant of Christ.* When we live to please men, we cannot at the same time live to please and serve God. When we live to please men, we are really living to serve ourselves, because what we value from men is the praise and honor and recognition they may give us. It is a glorious thing to live to *serve* men, but not to live to *please* them.

iii. "Just as Samson revealed his strength to the whore, so Hezekiah revealed God's glory to the devils as though he were their companion and had received favors from Babylon." (Kohlbrugge, cited in Bultema)

iv. "'What should Hezekiah have said to the envoys?' The answer is plain: 'Thank you for coming and thank Merodach for his gift and invitation, but the fact is I have a divine promise to lean on; it has been confirmed personally in my return to health and cosmically in the sign of the sun. I cannot turn from faith in the promises of God.'" (Motyer)

B. Isaiah reproves Hezekiah.

1. (3-4) Isaiah questions Hezekiah regarding the visit of the Babylonian envoys.

Then Isaiah the prophet went to King Hezekiah, and said to him, "What did these men say, and from where did they come to you?" So Hezekiah said, "They came to me from a far country, from Babylon." And he said, "What have they seen in your house?" So Hezekiah answered, "They have seen all that *is* in my house; there is nothing among my treasures that I have not shown them."

a. **What did these men say, and from where did they come to you?** Isaiah probably already knew the answer to these questions. It is likely that his questions were guided by God to allow Hezekiah the opportunity to answer honestly (which he did) and to see his error himself (which he apparently did not).

b. **They have seen all that is in my house**: There is the sense that Hezekiah was *proud* to tell Isaiah this. He is like a small-town boy who is awed by the attention of a big-city man. "Isaiah, you should have seen how impressed those Babylonians were by all I have. They really know we are something here in Judah!" Hezekiah's pride and inflated ego have made him *blind*.

2. (5-7) The word of the LORD to Hezekiah through Isaiah.

Then Isaiah said to Hezekiah, "Hear the word of the LORD of hosts: 'Behold, the days are coming when all that is in your house, and what your fathers have accumulated until this day, shall be carried to Babylon; nothing shall be left,' says the LORD. 'And they shall take away some of your sons who will descend from you, whom you will beget; and they shall be eunuchs in the palace of the king of Babylon.'"

a. **All that is in your house...shall be carried to Babylon**: Hezekiah thought that this display of wealth would impress the Babylonians. All it did was show them what the kings of Judah had, and what they could get from them. One day the kings of Babylon would come and take it all away. This was fulfilled in 2 Kings 24:10-13 and 2 Kings 25:11-17, under the Babylonian king Nebuchadnezzar.

i. It would be more than a hundred years before Babylon carried away the royal treasures of Judah, but they did come, just as Isaiah prophesied. This prophecy is so remarkably accurate that many skeptics insist – without grounds other than unbelief – a later "Isaiah" must have written it after the fact.

b. **And they shall take away some of your sons...and they shall be eunuchs in the palace of the king of Babylon**: Worse than taking the material *riches* of the kings of Judah, the king of Babylon would take the **sons** of the king of Judah – his true riches.

i. One fulfillment of this was the taking of Daniel and his companions into captivity. Daniel was one *of the king's descendants* taken into the **palace of the king of Babylon** (Daniel 1:1-4). Because of this promise of God through Isaiah, many think that Daniel and his companions were made **eunuchs** when they were taken to serve in the palace.

3. (8) King Hezekiah's response.

So Hezekiah said to Isaiah, "The word of the LORD which you have spoken is good!" For he said, "At least there will be peace and truth in my days."

a. **"The word of the LORD which you have spoken is good!" For he said, "At least there will be peace and truth in my days"**: This is a sad state of heart in the king of Judah. God announces coming judgment, and all he can respond with is relief that it will not happen in his lifetime.

i. In this, Hezekiah shows himself to be almost the exact opposite of an "others-centered" person. He is almost totally self-centered. All he cares about is his own personal comfort and success.

b. **For he said, "At least there will be peace and truth in my days"**: There is no doubt that Hezekiah started out as a godly king, and overall his reign was one of outstanding godliness (2 Kings 18:3-7). Yet his beginning was much better than his end; Hezekiah did not finish well. God gave Hezekiah the gift of 15 more years of life, but the added years did not make him a better or more godly man.

i. Time or age doesn't necessarily make us any better. Consider that time does nothing but pass away. We sometimes say, "time will tell," "time will heal," or "time will bring out the potential in me." But time will do nothing of the sort! Time will only come and go. It is only how we *use* time that matters. Hezekiah didn't make good use of the extra time the LORD gave him.

Isaiah 40 – Comfort and Strength for God's People

A. The Word of the LORD prepares the way of the LORD.

1. (1-2) Comfort for the afflicted people of God.

"Comfort, yes, comfort My people!"
Says your God.
"Speak comfort to Jerusalem, and cry out to her,
That her warfare is ended,
That her iniquity is pardoned;
For she has received from the LORD's hand
Double for all her sins."

a. **"Comfort, yes, comfort My people!" Says your God**: The previous 39 chapters of Isaiah certainly had passages of comfort and hope, but there was a strong tone of judgment and warning throughout the section. Now, beginning with Isaiah 40, the tone shifts to being predominantly full of comfort and blessing, full of the glory of God.

i. Remember where Isaiah 39 just ended: announcing the coming Babylonian conquest of Jerusalem, and the exile of the nation. "The announcement that the Babylonians would someday capture Jerusalem and take the people into exile was a bitter blow. How could Judah celebrate the downfall of Assyria when everyone knew that a more powerful invader was on the way?" (Wolf)

ii. Isaiah is a book in three sections. Chapters 1-35 are prophetic, with the theme of *condemnation.* Chapters 36-39 are historic, and the theme is *confiscation.* Chapters 40-66 are messianic, and the theme is *consolation.*

b. **Comfort, yes, comfort My people**: Isaiah knew what it was to warn and instruct God's people, but the LORD also wanted His people to receive His

comfort. 2 Corinthians 1:3 speaks of our Lord as *the God of all comfort*; God wants His messengers to speak **comfort** to His people.

i. In any group waiting to hear God's word, there are any number of hidden hurting hearts. It is important for those hurting hearts to hear a word of **comfort** from God's messenger. As one preacher put it, "Preach to broken hearts and you will never lack an audience."

c. **Speak comfort to Jerusalem**: This means that Jerusalem *needed* a word of comfort. This means that God *had* comfort to give them. God's comfort is not a hollow, positive-thinking, "There's-a-silver-lining-behind-every-cloud" kind of message. God always gives His people *reasons* for comfort.

i. The comfort comes with tender words, spoken to the heart. **Speak comfort** is literally, "'speak to the heart', like a young man wooing his girl (Genesis 34:3)." (Motyer) It is important for God's messengers today to *speak to the heart.*

d. **That her warfare is ended**: At the moment Isaiah spoke this, the battle may have still loomed. This may very well have been a prophetic word; even though there was still an army against them, as far as God was concerned, **her warfare is ended**. This was *reason* for comfort.

i. It is in this same sense that God speaks to us and tells us we can be *more than conquerors through Him who loved us* (Romans 8:37). The battle still looms, but as far as it concerns the believer in Jesus Christ, **her warfare is ended**, because *You are of God, little children, and have overcome them, because He who is in you is greater than he who is in the world* (1 John 4:4).

e. **That her iniquity is pardoned**: At the moment Isaiah spoke this, Jerusalem was well aware of her sin – Isaiah had made them aware of it! Yet, the prophet speaks of a day when comfort can be offered because **her iniquity is pardoned**. This is real comfort; to be recognized as a sinner – as one having **iniquity** – yet knowing just as much that our **iniquity is pardoned**. This was a *reason* for comfort.

f. **For she has received from the LORD's hand double for all her sins**: This declares the *basis* for the pardon of iniquity – the sin has been *completely paid for*. Isaiah, speaking in Old Covenant terminology, speaks of Jerusalem bearing the curse for disobedience described in passages like Leviticus 26 and Deuteronomy 28. But the same principle applies to the believer under the New Covenant; our **iniquity is pardoned** because our sin has been *paid for*. This is a *reason* for comfort.

i. Does it seem unfair that God would have a **double** payment for sin? "*Double* means 'to fold over, fold in half' (Exodus 26:9).... When something is folded over, each half corresponds exactly with the other half, and this would yield the thought of exact correspondence between sin and payment." (Motyer) A payment has been made, and it was *exactly* the payment that was needed.

ii. Our **iniquity** is never **pardoned** because God has simply decided to "let us off the hook." That would make God an unrighteous, wicked judge, something He could never be. But under the New Covenant, it is not *we* who have **received from the LORD's hand double for all her sins**; it is our sin-bearing Savior Jesus Christ, who **received** the cup of wrath **from the LORD's hand double for all** our **sins**.

2. (3-5) A voice in the wilderness prepares the way of the LORD.

The voice of one crying in the wilderness:
"Prepare the way of the LORD;
Make straight in the desert
A highway for our God.
Every valley shall be exalted
And every mountain and hill brought low;
The crooked places shall be made straight
And the rough places smooth;
The glory of the LORD shall be revealed,
And all flesh shall see *it* together;
For the mouth of the LORD has spoken."

a. **The voice of one crying in the wilderness**: Here, Isaiah speaks for the LORD's messenger, who cries out to the barren places.

b. **Prepare the way of the LORD**: The idea is that the LORD is coming to His people as a triumphant King, who has the road prepared before Him so He can travel in glory and ease. Every obstacle in the way must be removed: **every valley shall be exalted and every mountain and hill brought low; the crooked places shall be made straight and the rough places smooth**.

i. Whatever was wrong in the road must be corrected. The problems were not the same everywhere. Sometimes, the road in the valley needed to be lifted up; other times a road had to be cut through a passage in the mountains.

ii. The idea of preparing the way of the LORD is a word picture because the real preparation must take place in our hearts. Building a road is very much like the preparation God must do in our hearts. They are both expensive, they both must deal with many different problems and environments, and they both take an expert engineer.

c. **The glory of the LORD shall be revealed**: His glory is revealed to the prepared hearts described in the previous verses. And it is revealed without regard to nationality; **all flesh shall see it together**. This glory of the LORD is not revealed only to Jerusalem or Judah, but to every prepared heart. The certainty of this word is assured because *the mouth of the LORD has spoken.*

d. **Prepare the way of the LORD**: This passage of Isaiah 40:3-5 has a direct fulfillment in the New Testament, in the person and ministry of John the Baptist. Zacharias, the father of John the Baptist, knew this at the birth of his son (Luke 1:76). And three gospels directly relate this passage to the ministry of John (Matthew 3:3, Mark 1:3, and Luke 3:3-6).

i. Jesus was the coming Messiah and King, and John the Baptist's ministry was to be one **crying in the wilderness**, and through his message of repentance, to **prepare the way of the LORD**. We often fail to appreciate how important the *preparing* work of the LORD is. Any great work of God begins with great *preparation*. John wonderfully fulfilled this important ministry.

3. (6-8) The message of the voice in the wilderness.

The voice said, "Cry out!"
And he said, "What shall I cry?"
"All flesh *is* grass,
And all its loveliness *is* like the flower of the field.
The grass withers, the flower fades,
Because the breath of the LORD blows upon it;
Surely the people *are* grass.
The grass withers, the flower fades,
But the word of our God stands forever."

a. **What shall I cry?** The voice in the wilderness knew he had an important work, but wanted to know more exactly what his message should be.

b. **All flesh is grass**: The message is *the frailty of man*. Isaiah thinks of the beautiful green grass covering the hills of Judah after the winter rains, and how quickly the grass dies, and the hills are left brown and barren. This is how frail and weak man is. Even the beauty of man is fleeting and passes as quickly as spring wildflowers (**all its loveliness is like the flower of the field**).

i. **Because the breath of the LORD blows upon it**: Man is in this frail state at the pleasure of God. It is to God's glory and according to His plan that man is this frail, and the glory of man is so fleeting.

c. **The word of our God stands forever**: The message is *the permanence of God and His word.* In contrast to the frailty and fleeting glory of man (**The grass withers, the flower fades**), the **word of our God** endures.

i. **The word of our God** certainly *has* endured. It has survived centuries of manual transcription, of persecution, of ever-changing philosophies, of all kinds of critics, of neglect both in the pulpit and in the pew, of doubt and disbelief – and still, **the word of our God stands forever**.

ii. "Written on material that perishes, having to be copied and recopied for hundreds of years before the invention of the printing press, did not diminish its style, correctness, nor existence. The Bible, compared with other ancient writings, has more manuscript evidence than any ten pieces of classical literature combined." (Josh McDowell, *Evidence that Demands a Verdict*)

iii. In A.D. 303, the Roman Emperor Diocletian demanded that every copy of the Scriptures in the Roman Empire be burned. He failed, and 25 years later, the Roman Emperor Constantine commissioned a scholar named Eusebius to prepare 50 copies of the Bible at government expense.

iv. Voltaire, the French skeptic and infidel who died in 1778, said that 100 years from his time, Christianity would be swept from existence and passed into history, and that the Bible would be a forgotten book. Many years after Voltaire's death, the Geneva Bible Society used his press and his house to produce stacks of Bibles.

v. "Infidels for eighteen hundred years have been refuting and overthrowing this book, and yet it stands today solid as a rock. Its circulation increases, and it is more loved and cherished and read today than ever before. Infidels, with all their assaults, make about as much impression on this book as a man with a tack hammer would on the Pyramids of Egypt. When the French monarch proposed a persecution of the Christians in his dominion, an old statesman and warrior said to him, 'Sire, the Church of God is an anvil that has worn out many hammers.' So the hammers of the infidels have been pecking away at this book for ages, but the hammers are worn out, and the anvil still endures. If this book had not been the book of God, men would have destroyed it long ago. Emperors and popes, kings and priests, princes and rulers have all tried their hand at it; they die and the book still lives." (Hastings, cited in McDowell)

vi. "A thousand times over, the death knell of the Bible has been sounded, the funeral procession formed, the inscription cut on the tombstone, and committal read. But somehow the corpse never stays put." (Bernard Ramm, *Protestant Christian Evidences*)

d. **The word of our God**: This message, cried out by the voice in the wilderness, was meant to prepare hearts for the coming of the LORD by leading them into repentance. The understanding of our frailty and fleeting glory, contrasted with the eternal enduring of God and His word, should humble us in repentance before the LORD. It certainly worked in the ministry of John the Baptist (Luke 3:7-18).

e. **The word of our God stands forever**: Peter made a wonderful reference and application to this passage in 1 Peter 1:22-25.

i. There, he gives a stirring call for love among believers (*Since you have purified your souls in obeying the truth through the Spirit in sincere love of the brethren, love one another fervently with a pure heart*, 1 Peter 1:22).

ii. Then, using the passage from Isaiah 40:8, he says *why* we should love one another this way: *having been born again, not of corruptible seed but incorruptible, through the word of God which lives and abides forever, because "All flesh is as grass, and all the glory of man as the flower of the grass. The grass withers, and its flower falls away, but the word of the LORD endures forever." Now this is the word which by the gospel was preached to you.* (1 Peter 1:23-25)

iii. Peter makes a beautiful connection, showing that the enduring word Isaiah spoke of is the same word of the gospel that is preached and believed, bringing salvation.

iv. Peter also makes a beautiful application. Since this eternal, always potentially fruit-bearing seed is in us, we have both the *obligation* and the *ability* to have a *sincere love of the brethren.* Perhaps we could say that if we need more love for others, it begins with having more of the *incorruptible seed* set in our hearts and allowed to grow.

B. "Behold Your God!"

1. (9) An invitation to behold your God.

O Zion,
You who bring good tidings,
Get up into the high mountain;
O Jerusalem,
You who bring good tidings,
Lift up your voice with strength,
Lift *it* up, be not afraid;

Say to the cities of Judah,
"Behold your God!"

a. **You who bring good tidings, get up into the high mountain**: Isaiah speaks of a message so great – tidings so good – that they must be spread as widely as possible. From on top of **the high mountain**, the messenger can proclaim this great message to as many people as possible. It is a message that should be shouted out, so the messenger is told, **Lift up your voice with strength**.

b. **Say to the cities of Judah, "Behold your God"**: What is the great message, that should be shouted so loud? It is an invitation to **behold your God**. There is nothing greater for a believer to do than to study and to know their God.

i. The message isn't to give God a passing glance. No; we are invited to **behold your God**. It speaks of a study, of a long-term mission to know the greatness and the character of our God. It also shows how important it is for the message of God's preacher to focus on God. After every sermon, a preacher should ask, "Did I help the people to **behold your God**?"

ii. A great philosopher named Alexander Pope once wrote, "Know then thyself, presume not God to scan; the proper study of mankind is man." In one sermon, Spurgeon replied to that famous statement: "It has been said by someone that 'the proper study of mankind is man.' I will not oppose the idea, but I believe it is equally true that the proper study of God's elect is God; the proper study of a Christian is the Godhead. The highest science, the loftiest speculation, the mightiest philosophy which can ever engage the attention of a child of God, is the name, the nature, the person, the work, the doings, and the existence of the great God whom he calls his Father."

2. (10) Behold the returning LORD.

Behold, the Lord GOD shall come with a strong hand,
And His arm shall rule for Him;
Behold, His reward *is* with Him,
And His work before Him.

a. **Behold, the Lord GOD shall come with a strong hand**: One aspect of our God we should behold is *the fact of His return*. Our God will return to this earth, and He will come with power (**a strong hand...His arm shall rule**).

b. **The Lord GOD shall come**: When the LORD comes back, He comes to reward His people (**His reward is with Him**). He comes to inspect His work (**and His work before Him**). This is something important for us to know about our God.

3. (11) Behold the loving Shepherd.

He will feed His flock like a shepherd;
He will gather the lambs with His arm,
And carry *them* in His bosom,
***And* gently lead those who are with young.**

a. **He will feed His flock like a shepherd**: Another aspect of our God to behold is *His loving care as a shepherd.* The first thing a shepherd must do for his sheep is feed them, and the LORD feeds us like a shepherd feeds his flock.

i. Sheep must be directed to the good pasture and must be moved on to new pasture when they have stripped the grass bare. We need as much carefully directed feeding as sheep! "No creature has less power to take care of itself than the sheep; even the tiny ant with its foresight can provide for the evil day, but this poor creature must be tended by man or else perish." (Spurgeon)

ii. God loves to identify Himself with a shepherd. Many of the greatest men of the Bible were shepherds, and their character as shepherds points to Jesus Christ.

- *Abel* is a picture of Jesus, the sacrificed shepherd.
- *Jacob* is a picture of Jesus, the working shepherd.
- *Joseph* is a picture of Jesus, the persecuted and exalted shepherd.
- *Moses* is a picture of Jesus, the calling-out-from-Egypt shepherd.
- *David* is a picture of Jesus, the shepherd king.

b. **He will gather the lambs with His arm**: Our LORD shows special care for **the lambs**. The youngest, the weakest, are not despised – they are given special care by the LORD who first actively gathers them and will **carry them in His bosom**. He doesn't cast the weak **lambs** over His shoulder, as a shepherd might carry a sheep. Instead, He lovingly cradles **them in His bosom**, close to His heart. That is both a *safe* place and a *tender* place.

i. "To carry is kindness, but to carry in the bosom is loving-kindness. The shoulders are for power, and the back for force, but the bosom is the seat of love." (Spurgeon)

ii. "I see the Lord of angels condescending to personal labor. Jesus Christ himself gathers with his own arm and carries in his own bosom the lambs of his flock. He doth not commit this work to an angel, nor does he even leave it to his ministers; but he himself, by his Spirit, still undertakes it." (Spurgeon)

c. **And gently lead those who are with young**: The shepherd carries a rod and a staff and knows how to use them, but He also knows how to **gently lead those who are with young**. He knows exactly when to be gentle, and when more severe guidance should be used.

d. **Like a shepherd**: Jesus is given three great titles regarding His work as a shepherd.

i. *Jesus the Good Shepherd* (John 10:11-15). He is good in His care and sacrifice for the flock.

ii. *Jesus the Great Shepherd* (Hebrews 13:20). He is great in His glorious triumph over every enemy.

iii. *Jesus the Chief Shepherd* (1 Peter 5:4). He is the Chief over all His people in His return. At His return, Jesus also exercises another aspect of His role as Shepherd: He divides the sheep from the goats (Matthew 25:31-33). "Did you ever notice that the same Shepherd who saves the lost, will curse the finally impenitent? He shall separate them one from another as a shepherd divideth his sheep from the goats, and he shall set the sheep on his right hand, but the goats on the left. Then shall he say unto them on the left hand, 'Depart ye cursed.' What lips are those which pronounce those dreadful words? The Shepherd's lips." (Spurgeon)

4. (12) Behold the God over all creation.

Who has measured the waters in the hollow of His hand,
Measured heaven with a span
And calculated the dust of the earth in a measure?
Weighed the mountains in scales
And the hills in a balance?

a. **Who has measured the waters in the hollow of His hand**: Another aspect of our God to behold is *His authority over all creation*. Our God is so great, and so dominant over all creation, that He **has measured the waters in the hollow of His hand** and has **measured heaven with a span**.

i. This is another example of what we call *anthropomorphism* – speaking of God in human terms so we can partially understand who He is and what He does. God is not a being with the body of a giant, so large that all the waters of the earth could be cupped in His hand, or so large that the universe could be measured by the span of His hand. The Bible tells us that God the Father is spirit, so He does not have a body as we know it (John 4:24). But we understand exactly what the LORD tells us through the prophet Isaiah – God is so great, so dominant over all creation that we should stand in awe of His power and glory.

ii. Once my youngest son and I had a discussion about who in our family was bigger. We observed that his big brother was bigger than he was, and his big sister was bigger than the big brother, and mom was bigger than big sister, and I was bigger than mom was. Then my son looked at me and said, "But you're not bigger than God." That's something for everyone to remember.

b. **And calculated the dust of the earth in a measure**: It isn't just about size; it's also about smarts. God is so great in His wisdom and intelligence that He **calculated the dust of the earth in a measure**. God knows exactly how many grains of dust there are on the earth. Even if a person knew the number of hairs on their head (as God knows, according to Luke 12:7), they could never calculate the dust in their own house – much less **the dust of the earth**.

i. To take it further, God knows how heavy the mountains are (He **weighed the mountains in scales**), and the hills also for that matter! (**And the hills in a balance**)

5. (13-14) Behold the God of all wisdom.

Who has directed the Spirit of the Lord,
Or *as* His counselor has taught Him?
With whom did He take counsel, and *who* instructed Him,
And taught Him in the path of justice?
Who taught Him knowledge,
And showed Him the way of understanding?

a. **Who has directed the Spirit of the Lord, or as His counselor has taught Him?** Another aspect of God to behold is *His great wisdom*. He has the raw intelligence to know how much dust there is in the earth, and how heavy the mountains and the hills are. But more than that, God *has the wisdom to use that knowledge*. God is so wise, that no one **has directed the Spirit of the Lord**; no one **as His counselor has taught Him**.

i. **Who has directed the Spirit of the Lord**: In the Septuagint (the Greek translation of the Hebrew Old Testament used in the days of Jesus and the disciples), this is translated *Who has known the mind of the Lord?* The apostle Paul quoted this line in Romans 11:34.

b. **With whom did He take counsel**: God needs no **counsel**, no *instruction*, no *teacher*, and no one to show Him **the way of understanding**.

C. God's greatness is measured in comparison to others.

1. (15-17) God's greatness surpasses all nations.

Behold, the nations *are* as a drop in a bucket,
And are counted as the small dust on the scales;
Look, He lifts up the isles as a very little thing.
And Lebanon *is* not sufficient to burn,
Nor its beasts sufficient for a burnt offering.
All nations before Him *are* as nothing,
And they are counted by Him less than nothing and worthless.

a. **Behold, the nations are as a drop in a bucket**: The glory of a powerful nation is something to behold. We think of a huge military parade, with all the strength of the nation on display. But compared to God, it is *nothing*. The greatest glory of the greatest nation is **as a drop in a bucket** compared to the greatness and glory of the Lord God.

b. **Lebanon is not sufficient to burn, nor its beasts sufficient for a burnt offering**: If man were to take all the wood in the mighty forests of Lebanon and use it to make a burnt offering of all the animals of the land, it would not be enough to satisfy God. Man's best efforts cannot satisfy the honor and glory of God.

c. **They are counted by Him less than nothing and worthless**: In this chapter, God declares His greatness over all creation, but He never says of creation that it is **less than nothing and worthless**. But the nations have an arrogance, a pride against God that puts them lower than creation itself – He accounts them **less than nothing and worthless**.

2. (18-20) God's greatness surpasses all idols.

To whom then will you liken God?
Or what likeness will you compare to Him?
The workman molds an image,
The goldsmith overspreads it with gold,
And the silversmith casts silver chains.
Whoever is too impoverished for *such* a contribution
Chooses a tree *that* will not rot;
He seeks for himself a skillful workman
To prepare a carved image *that* will not totter.

a. **What likeness will you compare to Him?** There are many likenesses that represent the gods of the nations. How do they compare to God? They don't compare at all, because they are only the work of men's hands (**the workman molds an image**).

i. "Maybe we are not as crude as the ancient Israelites, though some nations are. However, some people worship a crucifix, others will worship the church, or idolize the preacher. Some people will bow before the gods of materialism, ambition, sex, even home and loved ones, and will substitute anything if only they can escape having to get down to the basic need of facing why it is that God does not guide or deliver." (Redpath)

b. **To prepare a carved image that will not totter**: The empty images that are the idols of the nations are so insignificant that they must be made so that they **will not totter**. They can't even stand up on their own! God has no rivals.

i. Look at the care you have to give to your idols. First, you have to choose good wood, because who wants to worship a rotting god? Then you must choose a skilled workman because who wants to worship a poorly made god? Then it has to be well designed because who wants to worship a god that keeps falling over? "Whenever Isaiah speaks about idolatry, he cannot keep from using the most cutting mockery." (Bultema)

3. (21-26) God's greatness is evident, as He is the Creator of all.

Have you not known?
Have you not heard?
Has it not been told you from the beginning?
Have you not understood from the foundations of the earth?
***It is* He who sits above the circle of the earth,**
And its inhabitants *are* like grasshoppers,
Who stretches out the heavens like a curtain,
And spreads them out like a tent to dwell in.
He brings the princes to nothing;
He makes the judges of the earth useless.
Scarcely shall they be planted,
Scarcely shall they be sown,
Scarcely shall their stock take root in the earth,
When He will also blow on them,
And they will wither,
And the whirlwind will take them away like stubble.
"To whom then will you liken Me,
Or *to whom* shall I be equal?" says the Holy One.
Lift up your eyes on high,
And see who has created these things,
Who brings out their host by number;

He calls them all by name,
By the greatness of His might
And the strength of *His* power;
Not one is missing.

a. **Have you not known? Have you not heard?** Isaiah can't believe that anyone could doubt the greatness of God when they see the glory of God's creation. First, He sits above all creation (**It is He who sits above the circle of the earth**). Second, He created it all (**Who stretches out the heavens like a curtain**).

i. Isaiah's amazement is well placed. How can anyone look at the glory and design evident in creation, and fail to understand that there must be a glorious designer behind such a glorious design?

ii. "This is one of the central Old Testament passages on the doctrine of creation. It teaches that the physical fabric of creation is a direct artifact of the Creator." (Motyer)

iii. Isaiah uses an interesting phrase when he describes God as the One **who sits above the circle of the earth**. How could Isaiah possibly know that the earth's shape was a circle? He probably didn't know, but the Lord who spoke through Isaiah did know.

iv. Every once in a while, unlearned critics talk as if Bible-believing people are members of the "Flat Earth Society" – people so out of touch with real science that they still insist the earth is flat. In response, we should be reminded that Augustine, perhaps the greatest of the church fathers, who lived about a thousand years before Columbus, professed that the earth was round, not flat. As well, in the thirteenth century, Thomas Aquinas, the most profound and prolific of medieval theologians, observed that the spherical shape of the earth could be empirically demonstrated. All they did was agree with Isaiah: **It is He who sits above the circle of the earth**.

b. **He brings the princes to nothing; He makes the judges of the earth useless**: God's power and glory are not only exalted above the inanimate creation, but also over men of power on the earth. When people have political power (**princes**) or legal power (**judges**) it is easy for them to think of themselves as gods! Through the message of Isaiah, the Lord sets this straight. All God needs to do is to **blow on them, and they will wither**.

c. **Who brings out their host by number; He calls them all by name**: God's mastery over all creation is shown by the fact that He can bring out all the stars **by number**, and then **He calls them all by name**. With the billions and billions of stars in the universe, it is staggering to know that God can number and name them all.

i. "The astronomers are still busily engaged in counting and classifying the stars, but Christ has described, counted and ordered them already." (Bultema)

D. Applying the knowledge of God's greatness.

1. (27-28) Having confidence in God's power and wisdom.

Why do you say, O Jacob,
And speak, O Israel:
"My way is hidden from the LORD,
And my just claim is passed over by my God"?
Have you not known?
Have you not heard?
The everlasting God, the LORD,
The Creator of the ends of the earth,
Neither faints nor is weary.
His understanding is unsearchable.

a. **Why do you say**: Having spent all of Isaiah 40 showing us the greatness and the glory of God, now Isaiah shows us how understanding this makes a difference in our lives – beyond the obvious compulsion we should feel to honor and worship this great God.

b. **Why do you say, O Jacob…"My way is hidden from the LORD, and my just claim is passed over by my God"?** Understanding the greatness and glory of God persuades us that there is nothing in our life hidden from God, and there is nothing neglected by God.

c. **Have you not known? Have you not heard?** The people asked this question in Isaiah 40:21 doubted there was a God who created all. The ones asked the same question in this verse seem to know there is a creator, but live as *practical* atheists. They don't seem to understand that the fact there is a God of all creation makes a difference in everyday life.

i. "How easy it is to believe in the infinite power of God and at the same time to feel that He is unable to meet our personal needs!" (Wolf)

d. **Have you not heard?** These practical atheists need to hear what they already know: that the Lord GOD is **the Creator of the ends of the earth**. Then they need to hear *about* the Creator: that He **neither faints nor is weary. His understanding is unsearchable**. Those who really believe these truths about God should live as if God is really there.

2. (29-31) Receiving the strength of the Lord.

He gives power to the weak,
And to *those who have* no might He increases strength.
Even the youths shall faint and be weary,
And the young men shall utterly fall,
But those who wait on the Lord
Shall renew *their* strength;
They shall mount up with wings like eagles,
They shall run and not be weary,
They shall walk and not faint.

a. **He gives power to the weak**: After explaining all the greatness and glory of God, now Isaiah explains another benefit we can receive from our God – He gives us His great power.

i. Notice who God gives power to: **the weak, and to those who have no might He increases strength**. Those who are proud and confident in their own wisdom and strength will receive no **strength** from God.

b. **Even the youths shall faint and be weary**: Those who thought themselves strong find themselves weak. God's strength is reserved for those who know they are **weak**, and know they **have no might**.

c. **But those who wait on the Lord shall renew their strength**: How do we receive this strength from the Lord? We receive it as we **wait on the Lord**. The idea behind **wait on the Lord** is not a passive sitting around until the Lord does something. Yes, God gives us strength; but we don't expect it to come as if He were pouring it into us as we sit passively. He brings it to us as we seek Him, and rely on Him, instead of our own strength. If we are weak, it is because we do not **wait on the Lord**.

i. We are also told that we **renew** our **strength**. It is strength that was once received when we first came to the Lord in **weakness** and **no might**. Then, that strength is renewed as we wait on the Lord. **Renew** is "from a basic meaning 'to change'...[it] comes to mean 'to put on afresh': here, 'keep putting on fresh strength.' (Motyer)

d. **They shall mount up with wings like eagles**: This is the *measure* of strength the Lord gives us – strength to soar above everything else.

e. **They shall run and not be weary, they shall walk and not faint**: This is the *purpose* of the strength the Lord gives us – strength to move forward and progress for Him. It isn't strength to show off, but strength to go forward in.

i. **Weak** in Isaiah 40:29 and **faint** in Isaiah 40:30 are the same Hebrew word, which means "failure through loss of inherent strength." **Weary** in Isaiah 40:30 is a different word, which means "exhaustion because of the hardness of life" (Motyer). If we are worn out for either reason, God is here to give us strength – if we will wait on Him.

f. Notice the order, because it seems strange. First, we **mount up with wings like eagles**. Then we **run**. Finally, we **walk**. Does it seem out of order? Not at all. First, we recognize that we soar up into heavenly places in Christ Jesus (Ephesians 2:6). Then we set ourselves on the course to run the race (Hebrews 12:1). Then we are in a good place to walk the walk (Colossians 2:6).

Isaiah 41 – Fear Not

A. The glory of God over the coastlands.

1. (1) A command and an invitation to the coastlands.

Keep silence before Me, O coastlands,
And let the people renew *their* strength!
Let them come near, then let them speak;
Let us come near together for judgment.

a. **Keep silence before Me, O coastlands**: The Hebrew word translated **coastlands** is also translated *islands* or *isles* in other passages, such as Isaiah 11:11 and 40:15. It is also translated with broader words like *territory* in passages like Isaiah 20:6. The idea is probably best expressed as "distant lands." Here, God is calling to *all nations* – even the "distant lands" – to **keep silence before** Him. Why? Because they are coming to God's courtroom: **Let us come near together for judgment**.

i. Bultema on **coastlands**: "a poetic name for the idolatrous distant nations." Motyer: "Isaiah uses the word [**coastlands**] as shorthand for the far reaches of the earth."

b. **And let the people renew their strength**: Isaiah 40:31 has just promised that *those who wait on the Lord shall renew their strength.* But here, God advises the **people** – those in the distant lands, who do not know Him – to **renew *their* strength** as they come into His courtroom. If you are going to contest with God, you had better be prepared.

i. The problem is that while those who wait upon the Lord have the Lord's limitless strength, those from distant lands have no god of strength to help them. "The repetition of the phrase 'renew their strength' (cf. 40:31) may well be ironic. Perhaps as the exiles renew their strength in the true God, so the nations are ironically exhorted to do the same – but in their man-made deities!" (Grogan)

c. **Let them come near, then let them speak**: God will allow the idol worshippers of all the world to come before Him and justify their idolatry. They will have the opportunity to speak, though they must enter His courtroom in silence, out of respect for His majesty.

i. There are many different reasons for silence. There is the silence of *shame*, the silence of *attention*, the silence of *submission*. Any one of these is a good reason to initially be silent in the LORD's presence.

2. (2-4) God reasons with the coastlands.

Who raised up one from the east?
Who in righteousness called him to His feet?
Who gave the nations before him,
And made *him* rule over kings?
Who gave *them* as the dust to his sword,
As driven stubble to his bow?
Who pursued them, *and* passed safely
By the way *that* he had not gone with his feet?
Who has performed and done *it*,
Calling the generations from the beginning?
I, the LORD, am the first;
and with the last I *am* He.

a. **Who raised up the one from the east?** God questions the idolaters from the distant lands, and asks them who authored this important event in human history – **who raised up the one from the east?**

i. Commentators warmly debate the identity of this **one from the east**. Most believe him to be either Abraham, the patriarch of the Jewish people and the father of the faithful, or Cyrus, the king who joined the Medes and the Persians into a fighting force which conquered Babylon – which, prophetically, is the broad time context Isaiah speaks to.

ii. Wolf speaks for those who believe Cyrus is spoken of: "Born east of Babylon in what is now Iran, Cyrus would move through country after country, conquering every king in his path. Shortly after 550 B.C., Cyrus was able to unify the Medes and the Persians and to defeat the powerful kingdom of Lydia in Asia Minor. Then he turned south to conquer Babylon (539 B.C.)." Bultema adds regarding Cyrus: "Both secular and sacred documents present him as righteous and good, and he can be called *righteous* or, as the text actually has it, *justice*, especially since he carried out the righteous acts of vengeance on Babylon and that of the deliverance of Israel."

iii. Clarke speaks for those who believe Abraham is the **one from the east**: "Some explain it of Abraham, others of Cyrus. I rather think that the former is meant; because of the character of the righteous man, or righteousness, agrees better with Abraham than with Cyrus."

iv. Who is it? It is a difficult decision, and either answer can be correct according to the context. On balance, it is best to see the **one from the east** as Abraham, because of the word of the LORD later in the chapter, in Isaiah 41:22: *Let them bring forth and show us what will happen; let them show the former things, what they were*. God appeals to idols and their worshippers and asks them to tell both the future and the past. Since Cyrus is mentioned in Isaiah 41:25 (*I have raised up one from the north... from the rising of the sun*), he is the figure that shows God's knowledge of the *future*. Abraham is the figure that shows God's knowledge of the *past*. Past and future – with the present sandwiched in-between – all belong to the LORD our God.

b. **Who.... Who.... Who**: As God invites those in distant lands to come and reason with Him, He shows them His greatness over all creation, and over all history. They must ask themselves, "Who is in control of the course of human events?" **Who has performed and done it, calling the generations from the beginning?**

i. This is always a relevant question. Is there a point, a direction to human history? Is it just a random, meaningless combination of undirected events? Is it a cycle, fated to repeat itself endlessly? Or, is there a God in heaven who directs human events, always moving to a final resolution and fulfillment? Our answer to this question influences almost everything in our lives.

c. **I, the LORD, am the first; and with the last I am He**: Here, the LORD God of Israel declares that *He* **has performed and done it, calling the generations from the beginning**. He lifts up and puts down kings and nations. He is **the first** and He is **the last**; He is the "bookend" both before and after the saga of human history, starting the story, ending the story, and keeping the whole story together.

i. If God is both the **first** and the **last**, then He also has authority over everything in-between. This means that there absolutely *is* a plan of God for human history, and He directs the path of human events toward His designed fulfillment. Our lives are not given over to blind fate, to random meaninglessness, or to endless cycles with no resolution. Instead, the LORD God who is **the first** and **the last** directs all of human history and even our individual lives.

ii. Jesus takes the same title of *the First and the Last* in Revelation 1:17 and 22:13. If the **Lord** is **the first** and **the last** according to Isaiah 41:4, and if Jesus is *the First and the Last* according to Revelation 1:17 and 22:13, since there cannot be *two firsts* or *two lasts,* Jesus must be the **Lord** God.

3. (5-7) The reaction of the coastlands.

The coastlands saw *it* and feared,
The ends of the earth were afraid;
They drew near and came.
Everyone helped his neighbor,
And said to his brother,
"Be of good courage!"
So the craftsman encouraged the goldsmith;
He who smooths with the hammer *inspired* him who strikes the anvil,
Saying, "It is ready for the soldering";
Then he fastened it with pegs,
***That* it might not totter.**

a. **The coastlands saw it and feared**: When they met this God of all authority and power, they **feared.** They were brought so low by this encounter with God that they had to encourage one another to go on! (**Everyone helped his neighbor, and said to his brother, "Be of good courage!"**)

i. This is a *logical* reaction. It is the same kind of reaction Peter had when he saw the great power of Jesus (Luke 5:8).

b. **So the craftsman encouraged the goldsmith**: What did they do with the fear they felt after their encounter with God? They *let the fear drive them away from the true God.* Instead of surrendering to this God of glory and majesty and power, they turned *from* God, and *made for themselves gods,* idols of gold.

i. Isaiah pours on the irony. It took a lot of work to make a good god. It took skilled workers (**the craftsman…the goldsmith…he who smooths with the hammer…him who strikes the anvil**). It took organization and teamwork (**"It is ready for the soldering"**). If you don't do it right, your god might not be able to stand up (**That it might not totter**).

ii. People still see something of God's power and glory, reject it, and then make their own god. This is Paul's whole message in Romans 1:18-25.

B. God encourages Israel.

1. (8-9) Israel is different from those in the distant lands.

But you, Israel, *are* My servant,
Jacob whom I have chosen,
The descendants of Abraham My friend.
You whom I have taken from the ends of the earth,
And called from its farthest regions,
And said to you,
"You *are* My servant,
I have chosen you and have not cast you away."

a. **But you, Israel, are My servant**: In contrast to the God-rejecting and idol-making people in distant lands, **Israel** – remember the name means, "Governed by God" – **Israel** is the **servant** of the LORD.

i. A **servant** of God would never make God into his own image, his own idea of what God should be. Servants don't tell their masters what to do, or what to be. Servants know who the master is and who the servant is.

ii. "Israel is twice addressed as *servant* (literally 'slave'), that is to say a person without position or rights – but this servant belongs to a great master." (Motyer)

b. **Jacob, whom I have chosen**: Lest Israel become proud, God pops their swelling quickly. If they are **Israel** – "Governed by God" – then they are also **Jacob** – "Conniving, untrustworthy con-man." They are only the **servant** of God because He has **chosen** them.

c. **The descendants of Abraham My friend**: Israel stood in this place because of their *family relationship* to Abraham. Since Abraham was the **friend** of God, so his **descendants** had a special place before God also.

i. Jehoshaphat knew that Abraham was the friend of God (2 Chronicles 20:7). James knew that Abraham was the friend of God (James 2:23). We are also the friends of God, not because of our relation to Abraham, but because of our relation to the Son of God, Jesus. *You are My friends if you do whatever I command you. No longer do I call you servants, for a servant does not know what his master is doing; but I have called you friends, for all things that I heard from My Father I have made known to you.* (John 15:14-15)

d. **You whom I have taken from the ends of the earth…And said to you, "You are my servant, I have chosen you and have not cast you away"**: Again, Israel's special place before God is because of *God's initiative*, not because of *Israel's achievement*. Israel is different from the idol-makers in distant lands because of God's work in them, not because of their own greatness.

2. (10-13) Fear not, for God's help is present.

Fear not, for I *am* with you;
Be not dismayed, for I *am* your God.
I will strengthen you,
Yes, I will help you,
I will uphold you with My righteous right hand.'
"Behold, all those who were incensed against you
Shall be ashamed and disgraced;
They shall be as nothing,
And those who strive with you shall perish.
You shall seek them and not find them—
Those who contended with you.
Those who war against you
Shall be as nothing,
As a nonexistent thing.
For I, the LORD your God, will hold your right hand,
Saying to you, 'Fear not, I will help you.'

a. **Fear not, for I am with you**: This is both a *command* and a *promise.* Israel is *commanded* to **fear not**. Fear, worry, and anxiety are often *sin.* When the God who rules over the nations as described in Isaiah 41:2-4, the God who chose us and loves us as described in Isaiah 41:8-9, when *that God* tells us **fear not**, we must take it seriously! But there is also a *promise.* We **fear not**, because the LORD has told us, **I am with you**. What more do we need? *If God is for us, who can be against us?* (Romans 8:31)

i. How much more prone to fear and discouragement we are when we are alone. But we are never alone because God has declared, **fear not, for I am with you**.

b. **Be not dismayed, for I am your God**: It was as if God said to His people, "Remember Me? The God of all power and glory? I'm that One. **I am your God**." Years ago, J.B. Phillips wrote a wonderful book titled, *Your God is Too Small.* In it, he showed how when people forget the greatness of God, they easily become **dismayed**. But God says, **be not dismayed, for I am your God**.

c. **I will strengthen you, Yes, I will help you, I will uphold you with My righteous right hand**: God's *strength* and *glory* make Him *able* to help us. But it is His *love* that makes Him say, "**I will** help you."

i. Idols must be *fastened...with pegs*, so they *might not totter* (Isaiah 41:7). You have to hold *them* up. But God holds *us* up; **I will uphold you with My righteous right hand**. You should never have a God that you have to hold up.

ii. Knowing this, do we see *the terrible nature of our fear and unbelief?* They say to God, "You are not with me. You are not the God of glory and might. You do not really love me."

iii. "Every truthful man feels that he has a right to be believed. He speaks upon the honour of an honest man, and if you say, 'I cannot believe you,' and even begin to lament that you have no faith in him, the reflection is not upon yourself, but on the person whom you cannot believe. And shall it ever come to this, that God's own children shall say that they cannot believe their God? Oh, sin of sins! It takes away the very Godhead from God, for if God be not true, he is not a God; and if he be not fit to be believed, neither is he fit to be adored, for a God whom you cannot trust you cannot worship." (Spurgeon)

d. **Behold, all those who were incensed against you shall be ashamed and disgraced**: God will deal with our enemies if we keep our trust in Him. He knows how to make our adversaries – whether they be men or devils – **ashamed and disgraced**.

i. **Behold, all those who were incensed against you shall be ashamed and disgraced** is, in part, an outworking of God's promise to Abraham in Genesis 12:3: *I will bless those who bless you, and I will curse him who curses you.* God has always crushed anti-Semitic nations and movements, and in the reign of the Messiah, He will crush them completely.

e. **For I, the LORD your God, will hold your right hand, saying to you, "Fear not, I will help you"**: In Isaiah 41:10, God promised to **uphold you with My righteous right hand**. That was God's hand holding us up. Now, we see God's hand holding our **right hand**, and giving us strength over fear, doubt, and our adversaries.

3. (14-16) Fear not, with God's help, no obstacle is too great.

"Fear not, you worm Jacob,
You men of Israel!
I will help you," says the LORD
And your Redeemer, the Holy One of Israel.
"Behold, I will make you into a new threshing sledge with sharp teeth;
You shall thresh the mountains and beat *them* small,
And make the hills like chaff.

You shall winnow them, the wind shall carry them away,
And the whirlwind shall scatter them;
You shall rejoice in the Lord,
***And* glory in the Holy One of Israel."**

a. **Fear not, you worm Jacob, you men of Israel**: The idea of a **worm** is connected to the name **Jacob**, but the idea of **men** is connected with the name **Israel**.

i. "In the rabbinical commentary on the five books of Moses, *Yelamedenu* is asked, Why are the Israelites called a *worm*? To signify, that as the worm does not smite, that is, *gnaw* the cedars, but with its mouth, which is very tender, yet it nevertheless destroys the hard wood; so all the strength of the Israelites is in prayer, by which they smite the wicked of this world, though strong like cedars, to which they are compared." (Clarke)

ii. "The name *Jacob*, as applied to Israel here, always points back to Israel's lowly and deceitful past, so that it is by no means an honor." (Bultema)

iii. **And your Redeemer**: "*Redeemer* is *goel*, see Isaiah 35:9, the Next-of-Kin who takes upon himself his people's needs as if they were his own." (Motyer)

b. **Behold, I will make you into a new threshing sledge with sharp teeth; you shall thresh the mountains and beat them small**: God will so help Israel and so empower them, that they will be able to cut down mountains as if they were a great **threshing** machine, removing mountains and seeing their dust blown away. The point is clear: *nothing*, not even a mountain, will stand in their way when God helps them.

i. "I don't know of any other than the Creator Himself who can take a weak worm and make it sharp with teeth! God can do that." (Redpath)

ii. Jesus expressed the same idea in Matthew 17:20: *If you have faith as a mustard seed, you will say to this mountain, "Move from here to there," and it will move; and nothing will be impossible for you.*

c. **You shall rejoice in the Lord, and glory in the Holy One of Israel**: When we overcome great obstacles with the help of the Lord, we know it is His work. We **rejoice in the Lord**, not in ourselves. We **glory in the Holy One of Israel**, not in ourselves.

4. (17-20) Fear not, God has abundant resources.

The poor and needy seek water, but *there* is none,
Their tongues fail for thirst.

I, the LORD, will hear them;
***I*, the God of Israel, will not forsake them.**
I will open rivers in desolate heights,
And fountains in the midst of the valleys;
I will make the wilderness a pool of water,
And the dry land springs of water.
I will plant in the wilderness the cedar and the acacia tree,
The myrtle and the oil tree;
I will set in the desert the cypress tree *and* the pine
And the box tree together,
That they may see and know,
And consider and understand together,
That the hand of the LORD has done this,
And the Holy One of Israel has created it.

a. **I will open rivers in desolate heights**: In response to the cry of the **poor and needy**, those whose **tongues fail for thirst**, God sends miraculous supplies of water to them. God has resources and supplies we know nothing about, and He loves to supply us from His hidden resources.

b. **I will plant in the wilderness the cedar and the acacia tree**: God will also make barren places fruitful, and full of beautiful forests. God can take the most barren **wilderness** and make it a forest.

i. "Water and shade are the two great needs of the desert traveller.... None of the trees mentioned are fruit trees: the point is shelter, not sustenance." (Motyer)

c. **That the hand of the LORD has done this, and the Holy One of Israel has created it**: When it all takes place, everyone will know this. Miraculous supplies of water and forests in the wilderness are impossible without God, so He gets the glory when the work is done.

C. Idolatry on trial.

1. (21) God calls idols and their worshippers to trial.

"Present your case," says the LORD.
"Bring forth your strong *reasons*," says the King of Jacob.

a. **Present your case**: God is fair. He will not condemn idols, the false gods of the nations, and those who worship them, without a fair trial. So He invited these idols and their worshippers to come and **present your case**. "Let's hear your side of the story." **Bring forth your strong reasons**. "Let's hear your best arguments."

b. **Says the King of Jacob**: This is the only place in the Bible where God uses this title. **King of Jacob** is used only here, but the title *king of Israel* is used 138 times in the Bible, mostly of men, but of the Lord God in Isaiah 44:6 and Zephaniah 3:15, and of Jesus in John 1:49 and 12:13.

2. (22-24) God examines the defendants – idols and their worshippers – at the trial.

Let them bring forth and show us what will happen;
Let them show the former things, what they *were*,
That we may consider them,
And know the latter end of them;
Or declare to us things to come.
Show the things that are to come hereafter,
That we may know that you *are* gods;
Yes, do good or do evil,
That we may be dismayed and see *it* together.
Indeed you *are* nothing,
And your work *is* nothing;
***He who* chooses you *is* an abomination.**

a. **Let them bring forth**: God invited idols to *present your case* in Isaiah 41:21. But none is presented; the next words are God's questioning of the idols. Why don't the idols present their case and defend themselves? Because they are dumb statues that can't speak! So, the questioning moves on, and God examines the defendants.

b. **Let them bring forth and show us what will happen**: If these idols really are gods, then they certainly know the future and the past. Then let them speak up. **Show us what will happen**. Then, **let them show the former things, what they were**. Gods know these things, don't they? Do it **that we may know that you are gods**.

c. **Yes, do good or do evil**: It is as if God stands in a courtroom, questioning a thousand idols of different sizes and designs, and finally cries out, "Do *something!* **Do good or do evil!** Can't you do *anything?*"

d. **Indeed you are nothing**: But they cannot do anything. So, the accusation is made based upon the evidence: **your work is nothing; he who chooses you is an abomination**.

i. Today, idolatry is still an abomination. Though few bow down to statues, many still fashion a god of their own opinion and decide that is the god they will respect. Even many churchgoers do this today. "The spiritual conflict experienced today is exactly of the same nature and of the same character as you find depicted here. The issue is still unsettled in the minds of men, though it is settled eternally in the mind of God. The world is still making every effort to put the best possible show upon its worship of the creature rather than the Creator. Its worship is more the patronizing of the shell of religion than bowing in submission before an empty cross, and occupied throne, and the King of kings in glory." (Redpath)

e. **Indeed, you are nothing, and your work is nothing**: Paul quoted this idea in 1 Corinthians 8:4, when he wrote, *Therefore concerning the eating of things offered to idols, we know that an idol is nothing in the world, and that there is no other God but one.*

3. (25-29) The LORD's summation: Idols are worthless, and man is so limited.

I have raised up one from the north,
And he shall come;
From the rising of the sun he shall call on My name;
And he shall come against princes as *though* mortar,
As the potter treads clay.
Who has declared from the beginning, that we may know?
And former times, that we may say, "*He is* righteous"?
Surely *there is* no one who shows,
Surely *there is* no one who declares,
Surely *there is* no one who hears your words.
The first time *I said* to Zion,
"Look, there they are!"
And I will give to Jerusalem one who brings good tidings.
For I looked, and *there was* no man;
I looked among them, but *there was* no counselor,
Who, when I asked of them, could answer a word.
Indeed they *are* all worthless;
Their works *are* nothing;
Their molded images *are* wind and confusion.

a. **I have raised up one from the north, and he shall come**: In contrast to the idols who can tell nothing of the future, the LORD knows. He knows that He will bring Cyrus from the north to conquer the Babylonians, who conquered Judah and Jerusalem and took them captive. God would use Cyrus to allow the Jews in exile to return (Ezra 1).

i. "Cyrus had the greatest respect for Jehovah, as we can read in his proclamation concerning the freeing of Israel in Ezra one. In it he states correctly that Jehovah had given him all the kingdoms of the earth." (Bultema)

ii. "The 'north' is included because the Persians conquered the lands north of Babylon before invading her borders." (Wolf)

b. **Who has declared from the beginning, that we may know?** Not the idols; they know nothing. Not man, for **I looked, and there was no man... Who, when I asked of them, could answer a word.**

c. **Indeed they are all worthless; their works are nothing**: Finally, the verdict is read at the trial. Apart from God, in the grand scheme of things, all of the greatness of man is **worthless**, and all the great **works are nothing**. And what of the idols? **Their molded images are wind and confusion**.

i. "This chapter is the great I WILL chapter of the Bible. No fewer than fourteen times in the scope of these verses does God reinforce His authority with the promise, 'I will.'" (Redpath) Look at them all:

- *I will strengthen you.* (Isaiah 41:10)
- *I will help you.* (Isaiah 41:10, 13, and 14)
- *I will uphold you with My righteous right hand.* (Isaiah 41:10)
- *I will make you into a new threshing sledge with sharp teeth.* (Isaiah 41:15)
- *I will open rivers in desolate heights.* (Isaiah 41:18)
- *I will make the wilderness a pool of water.* (Isaiah 41:18)
- *I will plant in the wilderness the cedar and the acacia tree.* (Isaiah 41:19)
- *I will set in the desert the cypress tree.* (Isaiah 41:19)
- *I will give to Jerusalem one who brings good tidings.* (Isaiah 41:27)

ii. This is a remarkable contrast with Isaiah 14 – the "I will" chapter of Satan. Here are the "I will" statements of Satan:

- *I will ascend into heaven.* (Isaiah 14:13)
- *I will exalt my throne above the stars of God.* (Isaiah 14:13)
- *I will also sit on the mount of the congregation.* (Isaiah 14:13)
- *I will ascend above the heights of the clouds.* (Isaiah 14:14)
- *I will be like the Most High.* (Isaiah 14:14)

iii. The "I will" statements of Satan were all proud and self-directed. Every "I will" of the LORD in Isaiah 41 is for the benefit and blessing of His people. Though Satan was lifted up in pride, and proclaimed "I will," none of them came to pass. But each and every one of God's "I will" statements will be fulfilled.

iv. "When God says, 'I will,' He says it with all the authority of omnipotence. He has foreseen every difficulty. He has studied every obstacle which may come in His way. He has anticipated every possible contingency. He knows the weakness of the one to whom He makes His promise, and yet He says, 'I will!'" (Redpath)

Isaiah 42 – The Servant's Song

A. The LORD speaks of His Servant.

1. (1-4) The character of the Servant.

"Behold! My Servant whom I uphold,
My Elect One *in whom* My soul delights!
I have put My Spirit upon Him;
He will bring forth justice to the Gentiles.
He will not cry out, nor raise *His voice*,
Nor cause His voice to be heard in the street.
A bruised reed He will not break,
And smoking flax He will not quench;
He will bring forth justice for truth.
He will not fail nor be discouraged,
Till He has established justice in the earth;
And the coastlands shall wait for His law."

a. **Behold! My Servant**: The LORD calls to all people – the people of Israel, and the coastlands – and tells them to **behold** (study, set focus upon) His **Servant**.

i. "The word *ebed* can refer to a slave (Exodus 21:20-21) or a vassal king (2 Samuel 10:19), an individual subject (Genesis 21:25) or a tributary nation (1 Chronicles 18:2, 6, 13). In all those cases the term refers to a person or group characterized by dependence and servitude." (Lindsey)

ii. The New King James Version rightly capitalizes **Servant** because the context demonstrates this is a clear reference to Jesus. Additionally, Matthew quotes Isaiah 42:1-5 and plainly says it is a prophecy fulfilled in Jesus (Matthew 12:16-21). So, in this, the LORD commands all peoples to put their focus on Jesus.

iii. Jesus described Himself as a servant in Matthew 20:25-28, Matthew 23:11, Mark 9:35, Mark 10:43-45. Peter, in his Acts 3 sermon, gives our Savior the title *His Servant Jesus* (Acts 3:13 and 3:26). In Acts 4, the praying people of God speak of *Your holy Servant Jesus* (Acts 4:27, 4:30). But Jesus isn't just *a* servant. He is *The Servant,* and everyone should **behold**, as the Lord says, **My Servant**.

iv. What do we see when we **behold** Jesus, the Lord's **Servant**? Among many things, we see Him as the **Servant**. As Jesus said in Matthew 20:26-28 (also recorded in Mark 10:43-45), *Whoever desires to become great among you, let him be your servant. And whoever desires to be first among you, let him be your slave; just as the Son of Man did not come to be served, but to serve, and to give His life a ransom for many.* When Jesus said *let him be your servant,* it means being a servant is a choice. When Jesus said *let him be your slave,* it showed how deep service should go. When He said that He *did not come to be served, but to serve,* it shows the essential heart of a servant. When Jesus said *and to give His life a ransom for many,* it showed how far servants go.

v. But Jesus, the **Servant**, is more than an *example* to us. He is our **Servant**. He serves us; not only in what He did in the past, but also, He serves us every day through His constant love, care, guidance, and intercession. Jesus did not stop serving when He went to heaven; He serves all His people *more effectively than ever* from heaven.

b. **My Servant whom I uphold**: This was certainly true for Jesus, but it is true also in the way the Lord deals with all His servants. He promises to **uphold** His servants. When someone is the servant of another, the servant is required to give full service and obedience to the master. But the master is also required to take care of the servant. The Lord always can say **My Servant whom I uphold**.

i. There may be another sense in this; Redpath believes it speaks of the Father's trust in and dependence on the Son. "The picture is taken from an Eastern court, where a monarch is in a procession, and as he walks he leans upon a favorite courtier. This verse, in fact, could well be translated, 'Behold, my servant, upon whom I lean.' It is an indication of a special favor and confidence. So we have the picture of God the Father leaning upon God the son, counting upon Him and trusting Him to fulfill all His purposes."

c. **My Elect One in whom My soul delights**: Jesus is the ultimate **Elect One**, our election is really a matter of being chosen in Jesus. As Paul wrote in Ephesians 1:4, *He chose us in Him before the foundation of the world.* **In whom My soul delights** shows that for the Lord, election is not a cold, calculating, technical thing. It is connected deeply with His love and approval. When God chooses someone, His **soul delights** in them. If you are chosen in Jesus before the foundation of the world, then God says, "My **soul delights** in you."

i. Understanding this helps us to receive God's favor, instead of trying to give Him a *reason* to delight His soul in us! Many of us are trying to *earn* the approval of God, instead of realizing it is His *free gift*, received by faith, because He has chosen – elected – to delight His soul in us.

d. **I have put My Spirit upon Him**: Jesus was filled with the Spirit and did ministry in the power and flow of the Holy Spirit (Matthew 3:16).

e. **He will bring forth justice to the Gentiles**: The ministry of the Servant, the Messiah, would not be restricted to the Jewish people. He would also have a ministry **to the Gentiles**, bringing justice and righteousness to them.

f. **He will not cry out, nor raise His voice**: This doesn't mean that Jesus never spoke loudly. It refers to His gentle, lowly heart and actions. Jesus didn't make His way by bluster and loud, overwhelming talk, but by the Spirit of God upon Him.

i. "He is not self-assertive: probably the three verbs here are cumulative, stressing his quiet, unaggressive demeanour, but *shout* ('shriek') could suggest that he is not out to startle, *cry out* ('raise his voice') not to dominate or shout others down, *raise his voice* ('make his voice heard') not out to advertise himself." (Motyer)

ii. "Think for a moment about the modesty of God. He is always at work: He guides the sun, the stars, and the universe. He controls every galaxy. He refreshes the earth constantly. But He works so quietly that many people now try to make out there is no God at all.... That is the hallmark of reality in service. God's artists do not put their signatures to the pictures they create. His ambassadors do not run after the photographer all the time to get their pictures taken. It is enough that they have borne witness to the Lord." (Redpath)

g. **A bruised reed He will not break, and smoking flax He will not quench**: This is another reference to the gentle character of Jesus. A reed is a fairly fragile plant, yet if a reed is **bruised**, the Servant will handle it so gently that **He will not break** it. And if flax, used for tinder to start a fire, does not flame but only smokes, He will not **quench** it into extinguishing. Instead, the Servant will gently blow on the **smoking flax**, fanning it into flame again.

i. Often we feel that God deals roughly with our weaknesses and failures. Just the opposite is true. He deals with them gently, tenderly, helping them along until the **bruised reed** is strong and the **smoking flax** is in full flame.

ii. "Think again of that reed: something that has been crushed, or hurt by unkindness, a life that is somehow bent and bruised and shattered, without strength or beauty. There is nothing attractive about a reed, and there is certainly nothing very pleasant about the circumstances in which it lives! Usually it grows in a smelly, unsavory swamp." (Redpath)

iii. "We call ourselves Christians, but if you are like me, sometimes you are desperately ashamed of how dimly your light burns. There is far more smoke than fire: so little prayer, so little real testimony, so much depression and discouragement. But the Lord says He will not extinguish the smoking flax." (Redpath)

iv. "He is not dismissive of others: however useless or beyond repair (*bruised reed*), however 'past it' and near extinction (*smouldering wick*) they may seem. The negative statements imply their positive equivalents: he can mend the broken reed, fan into flame the smouldering wick. The former has been internally damaged, the latter lacks the external nourishment of oil. The Servant is competent both to cure and to supply." (Motyer)

v. Jesus sees the value in a **bruised reed**, even when no one else can. He can make beautiful music come from a **bruised reed**, as He puts His strength in it! Though a **smoking flax** – used for a wick on an oil lamp – is good for nothing, Jesus knows it is valuable for what it can be when it is refreshed with oil. Many of us are like the **bruised reed**, and we need to *be strengthened with might through His Spirit in the inner man* (Ephesians 3:16). Others are like the **smoking flax** and can only burn brightly for the Lord again when we are drenched in oil, with a constant supply coming, as we are filled with the Holy Spirit.

vi. Jesus wants us to have His heart towards the lowly, broken, and hurting. It's easy to pass them by just as quickly as the priest and the Levite passed the man on the road to Jericho. "The superficial Christian worker ignores that kind of situation. He wants a sphere to serve where it will be worthy of his talent, if you please. A task where his abilities will be recognized and used, something that is big enough to justify all the training he has undergone. In the eyes of the Lord, the test of the real servant is, does he bend with the humility of Jesus Christ over a bruised reed and smoking flax?" (Redpath)

h. **He will bring forth justice for truth. He will not fail nor be discouraged**: The Servant is *gentle*, but not *weak*. **He will bring forth justice for truth**. There aren't two ways about it; it **will** happen, and failure or discouragement will not stop the Servant.

i. Isn't it wonderful that Jesus never gets **discouraged**? When we think of the job that He has to do, the obstacles He must overcome, and the tools He needs to work with, it is amazing that He never becomes **discouraged**. It is because He has all power and authority.

ii. **Fail** is the same word as **smoking** in **smoking flax He will not quench**. **Discouraged** is the same word as **bruised** in **a bruised reed He will not break**. "So here is the Servant of the Lord...there are no bruises about Him; He is no mere smoking flax. He is well able to do the task of redemption because He is free from all the weaknesses and failures of His people. He has no flaws or blemishes – He is perfection and majestic strength." (Redpath)

i. **Till He has established justice in the earth; and the coastlands shall wait for His law**: The work of the Servant will extend to the whole earth, and all the peoples – even those in the distant **coastlands** – shall serve Him.

2. (5-9) The LORD of glory and His promise to His Servant.

Thus says God the LORD,
Who created the heavens and stretched them out,
Who spread forth the earth and that which comes from it,
Who gives breath to the people on it,
And spirit to those who walk on it:
"I, the LORD, have called You in righteousness,
And will hold Your hand;
I will keep You and give You as a covenant to the people,
As a light to the Gentiles,
To open blind eyes,
To bring out prisoners from the prison,
Those who sit in darkness from the prison house.
I *am* the LORD, that *is* My name;
And My glory I will not give to another,
Nor My praise to carved images.
Behold, the former things have come to pass,
And new things I declare;
Before they spring forth I tell you of them."

a. **Thus says God the LORD**: The promise of the Servant and His ministry is so wonderful, that the One making the promise should state His credentials. Just as when we take out a loan, the bank asks for assurance we can fulfill our promise, so this verse is another "credit check" on God. **God the LORD** is more than happy to do so. First look *up*, because He **created the heavens and stretched them out**. Then look *down*, because He **spread**

forth the earth and that which comes from it. Then look *in a mirror*, because He **gives breath to the people on it**. The God who did such great things can fulfill His promises about the Servant.

b. **I, the Lord, have called You in righteousness, and will hold Your hand**: Specifically, this is a promise from the Lord to the Servant – Jesus Christ. Jesus must have received remarkable encouragement from passages like this when He faced difficult and trying times during His earthly ministry.

i. **Called You in righteousness**: "Because there was nothing unholy or unrighteous in My calling, You can be confident that the calling will be fulfilled."

ii. **Will hold Your hand**: "I am with You always, to love and guide You. I will never leave You. I am holding Your hand all the time!"

iii. **I will keep You**: "You will not get lost or left behind. I am always there to watch over You and **keep You**."

iv. **And give You as a covenant to the people, as a light to the Gentiles**: "You will fulfill the purpose I have called You to. You will bring salvation, not only to Your **people**, but also to those afar off, who seem beyond salvation."

v. **To open blind eyes, to bring out prisoners from the prison**: "I will use You to do miraculous works of restoration and healing, both physically and spiritually. You will be used to bring sight and freedom to many."

vi. What glorious promises, each fulfilled in the ministry of Jesus! By extension, these promises also belong to us. Jesus prayed, *As You sent Me into the world, I also have sent them into the world* (John 17:18). We are sent as Jesus was sent and can receive these same promises as belonging to us.

c. **I am the Lord, that is My name**: Such glorious promises need confirmation, and the assurance that the One making the promises is able to fulfill them.

i. **I am the Lord**: "This is the famous tetragrammaton, or name of *four letters*, which we write *Jehovah, Yehovah, Yehveh, Yeveh, Jhuh, Javah,* etc. The letters are Y H U H. The Jews never pronounce it, and the true pronunciation is utterly unknown." (Clarke)

d. **My glory I will not give to another**: First, *no one else* can fulfill these promises, because God will not *share* His glory with any other.

i. It is important to understand that Jesus shares in the glory of the Father. Jesus prayed, *And now, O Father, glorify Me together with Yourself, with the glory which I had with You before the world was.* (John 17:5) If God the Son and God the Father each share glory, and the LORD shares His glory with no one, it means that the Father and the Son are the LORD God. The LORD God – Yahweh – is one God in Three Persons.

e. **Behold, the former things have come to pass, and new things I declare**: God is master of both the past (**the former things**) and the future (**new things**). Being the master of both the future and the past, God has the present well in hand also.

i. We see this especially in the way that God can **declare...new things**, even **before they spring forth**. As Peter said, *so we have the prophetic word confirmed, which you do well to heed as a light that shines in a dark place* (2 Peter 1:19). God's prophetic word fulfilled shows us the confidence we can have in His word.

B. The work of the LORD's Servant.

1. (10-12) Praise for the victory of the Servant.

Sing to the LORD a new song,
***And* His praise from the ends of the earth,**
You who go down to the sea, and all that is in it,
You coastlands and you inhabitants of them!
Let the wilderness and its cities lift up *their voice*,
The villages *that* Kedar inhabits.
Let the inhabitants of Sela sing,
Let them shout from the top of the mountains.
Let them give glory to the LORD,
And declare His praise in the coastlands.

a. **Sing to the LORD a new song**: This sounds like a Psalm (Psalm 33:3, 40:3, 98:1, and others), because it is a song of praise. Who the Servant is and what He does is so glorious, it has to bring out a **new song** of praise.

b. **You coastlands and you inhabitants of them**: Who should sing this **new song**? Everyone who has been touched by the work of the Servant. Since even the **coastlands** were blessed by the Servant (Isaiah 42:4), they should praise Him also.

2. (13-17) The LORD brings judgment against all who serve false gods.

The LORD shall go forth like a mighty man;
He shall stir up *His* zeal like a man of war.

He shall cry out, yes, shout aloud;
He shall prevail against His enemies.
"I have held My peace a long time,
I have been still and restrained Myself.
***Now* I will cry like a woman in labor,**
I will pant and gasp at once.
I will lay waste the mountains and hills,
And dry up all their vegetation;
I will make the rivers coastlands,
And I will dry up the pools.
I will bring the blind by a way they did not know;
I will lead them in paths they have not known.
I will make darkness light before them,
And crooked places straight.
These things I will do for them,
And not forsake them.
They shall be turned back,
They shall be greatly ashamed,
Who trust in carved images,
Who say to the molded images,
'You *are* our gods.'

a. **The LORD shall go forth like a mighty man**: This day of praise is a day of victory for the LORD over all false gods. **He shall prevail against His enemies.**

b. **He shall stir up His zeal like a man of war…. He shall cry out, yes, shout aloud…. I will cry like a woman in labor**: The LORD does this work of judgment with *energy*. He isn't passive or dispassionate in His judgment. When the LORD sets things right on the earth, He does it with **zeal**.

i. The difference between **He shall cry out, yes shout aloud** and *He will not cry out, nor raise His voice* (Isaiah 42:2) shows the difference between the first and Second Coming of Jesus. The first coming was meek and lowly; the Second Coming will be loud and demonstrative.

c. **I will lay waste the mountains and hills**: No obstacle can get in the way of the LORD's work. **Mountains and hills** can't get in His way. **Rivers** and **pools** will not stop Him. Even the blindness of others will not prevent His plan. In the end, it is certain that **they shall be greatly ashamed, who trust in carved images**.

3. (18-20) The deaf and blind come to the Servant.

"Hear, you deaf;
And look, you blind, that you may see.
Who *is* blind but My servant,
Or deaf as My messenger *whom* I send?
Who *is* blind as *he who is* perfect,
And blind as the LORD's servant?
Seeing many things, but you do not
Observe; opening the ears, but he does not hear."

a. **Hear, you deaf; and look, you blind, that you may see**: Who are the **deaf** and the **blind** the LORD speaks to here? They are the **deaf** and **blind** among God's people. The LORD has already spoken to the blind among the Gentiles (Isaiah 42:16). Now, He speaks to the blind that He calls **My servant**, the deaf whom He calls **My messenger**.

i. Obviously, a **blind** man will have trouble being a good **servant**. A **deaf** man will have trouble being a good **messenger**.

b. **Seeing many things, but you do not observe**: This is a word to these blind ones who *think* they can see. They act as if they can see, but they really can't **observe** anything. They will stay blind and deaf as long as they can't admit their need.

c. **He does not hear**: What is the cure? It begins with knowing our condition. When the **deaf** know they are deaf, and the **blind** know they are blind, they know their need, and do not deceive themselves about their condition.

i. When Jesus healed a man born blind, He used the occasion to speak about spiritual blindness and its cure. In the diagnosis of Jesus, only those who *know* they are blind can be healed of their blindness. Jesus said, *"For judgment I have come into this world, that those who do not see may see, and that those who see may be made blind." Then some of the Pharisees who were with Him heard these words, and said to Him, "Are we blind also?" Jesus said to them, "If you were blind, you would have no sin; but now you say, 'We see.' Therefore your sin remains."* (John 9:39-41)

4. (21-25) The LORD defends His defrauded people.

The LORD is well pleased for His righteousness' sake;
He will exalt the law and make it honorable.
But this is a people robbed and plundered;
All of them are snared in holes,
And they are hidden in prison houses;
They are for prey, and no one delivers;

For plunder, and no one says, "Restore!"
Who among you will give ear to this?
***Who* will listen and hear for the time to come?**
Who gave Jacob for plunder, and Israel to the robbers?
Was it not the LORD,
He against whom we have sinned?
For they would not walk in His ways,
Nor were they obedient to His law.
Therefore He has poured on him the fury of His anger
And the strength of battle;
It has set him on fire all around,
Yet he did not know;
And it burned him,
Yet he did not take *it* to heart.

a. **The LORD is well pleased...He will exalt the law and make it honorable**: The LORD God is pleased to bring this justice on the earth, and to **exalt** and honor the law.

i. Though under the new covenant, we do not come to God on the basis of the law, it does not mean that the law of God is bad. As Paul wrote in Romans 7:12, *Therefore the law is holy, and the commandment holy and just and good.* The weakness of the law is not in the law, but in us. The law perfectly suits the purpose God intended for it: to display God's holy standard, to expose our sin, and to show us the need for salvation in Jesus.

b. **But this is a people robbed and plundered**: God looks upon His people and sees the pain and devastation the world, the flesh, and the devil has wrought upon them. They are **robbed and plundered**, they **are for prey, and no one delivers**. Worst of all, **no one says, "Restore!"**

c. **Who gave Jacob for plunder, and Israel to the robbers?** Who did this? Isaiah's answer is almost shocking: **Was it not the LORD, He against whom we have sinned?** In this circumstance, God allowed the low, defeated place of Israel as discipline for their sin, for their chosen blindness and deafness.

d. **For they would not walk in His ways, nor were they obedient to His law**: The painful and low place of Israel was meant to draw them back to the LORD. We can know that the LORD only used these measures after He had exhausted far gentler measures. Yet even these sharp measures did not work: **Yet he did not know...Yet he did not take it to heart**.

e. **It has set him on fire all around**: This correction from the LORD felt like fire to Israel, yet they did not respond to it. In 1 Peter 4:12-19, Peter also relates trials and correction from the Lord to fire: *Beloved, do not think* *it strange concerning the fiery trial which is to try you, as though some strange thing happened to you.... For the time has come for judgment to begin at the house of God; and if it begins with us first, what will be the end of those who do not obey the gospel of God?* God's purpose in the fiery trial is to bring us to repentance and softness of heart, and the more we resist that work, the more the fire will burn! We should respond as Peter said we should in 1 Peter 4:19: *Therefore let those who suffer according to the will of God commit their souls to Him in doing good, as to a faithful Creator.* Is the fire of God's correction burning away the sin and impurity in your life, or is it just making you blacker and harder?

Isaiah 43 – Fear Not

A. Reasons not to fear.

1. (1) Fear not, knowing you belong to the Lord.

But now, thus says the Lord, who created you, O Jacob,
And He who formed you, O Israel:
"Fear not, for I have redeemed you;
I have called *you* by your name;
You *are* Mine."

a. **Says the Lord, who created you…and He who formed you**: God speaks to His people as their *Creator*. God has a special and unique claim upon us because He is our Creator. When men forget or reject God as Creator, they fail in the most basic obligation they have to God.

b. **Fear not**: This is a *command*, accompanied by *promises*. By outward circumstances, the people of Judah had reason to be afraid of Babylon's army and exile. God points them past the present circumstances to both this command and promise.

c. **For I have redeemed you**: Not only did Israel have an obligation to God as their Creator but also as their *Redeemer*. He is the One who bought them out of literal exile and spiritual slavery.

i. The redeemer bought an unfortunate relative out of their slavery and debt. He rescued them and paid the slave price or debt they could not pay. When God calls Himself our *Redeemer*, it looks forward to the price that must be paid for our salvation.

d. **I have called you by your name; You are mine**: God *twice owns* His people. He has the right of ownership both as Creator and Redeemer. His ownership is *personal* because He says **I have called you by your name**. His ownership is *certain* because He seals it by saying **You are mine**.

i. Knowing that we belong to the LORD is a wonderful answer to fear. We can know that He holds us, protects us, guards us, and cares for us. We can know that He would not have created, redeemed, and called us unless He intended to finish His work in us. How can we be afraid when we know this God is for us, is looking out for our interests?

2. (2-7) Fear not, knowing the LORD is with you.

When you pass through the waters, I *will be* with you;
And through the rivers, they shall not overflow you.
When you walk through the fire, you shall not be burned,
Nor shall the flame scorch you.
For I *am* the LORD your God,
The Holy One of Israel, your Savior;
I gave Egypt for your ransom,
Ethiopia and Seba in your place.
Since you were precious in My sight,
You have been honored,
And I have loved you;
Therefore I will give men for you,
And people for your life.
Fear not, for I *am* with you;
I will bring your descendants from the east,
And gather you from the west;
I will say to the north, 'Give them up!'
And to the south, 'Do not keep them back!'
Bring My sons from afar,
And My daughters from the ends of the earth;
Everyone who is called by My name,
Whom I have created for My glory;
I have formed him, yes, I have made him.

a. **When you pass through the waters, I will be with you**: Through any potential obstacle, God will be with us. Deep waters? **I will be with you**. Must you **walk through the fire**? Then **you shall not be burned**. When God is with us, He is for us, and who can be against us?

i. Israel had and would have their trials, but we have ours also. Trials are inevitable; it doesn't say *if you pass through the waters*, it says **when you pass through the waters**. The text doesn't say, "When you walk on a luxurious padded carpet, I will be with you." It says God will be with us in the toughest of circumstances. Trials are varied; sometimes we face **waters**, sometimes **rivers**, and sometimes **fire**. Floods overwhelm, fires consume.

ii. The mention of the LORD's presence and protection in the **fire** reminds us of the story of the three sons of Judah cast into the Babylonian furnace because they would not bow or bend to worship an idol. They also were preserved in the fire by the presence of God (Daniel 3:19-25).

iii. This passage is also full of images from the Exodus from Egypt. "The statement, 'I am the Lord, your God' would remind every Jewish reader of Exodus 20, where the divine description is followed by the words 'who brought you out of Egypt, out of the land of slavery' (Exodus 20:2). So, learning from this past event, they could rest in his promise to bring them again into their own land." (Grogan)

iv. "Israel is just as indestructible as God's Word and Covenant are. Whoever can annihilate Israel can do more than Satan and all the powers of hell have been able to do in ages past. What is true of Israel, however, is equally true of the Church. Against it, too, the flames have raged and the waters have boiled but, according to His promise, the Lord Jesus has always been with her." (Bultema)

b. **Walk through the fire**: God helping us, we can do this. We don't have to panic, we don't have to fear, and we don't have to run as if we didn't trust God. He can so strengthen us in our trials that we can **walk through the fire**.

i. "Walking is the pace at which you go when you are not in a hurry, when you are not concerned or alarmed. When you are not burdened or anxious, then you walk. 'He that believeth shall not make haste' (Isaiah 28:16)." (Redpath)

c. **Since you were precious in My sight**: God here describes the *motivation* for His work of redemption. He loves us! We are **precious in** His **sight**! This is an Old Testament example of the truth in John 3:16: *For God so loved the world, that He gave His only begotten Son.*

i. "To prove His love for His people, God was willing to give Egypt, Cush, and Seba as a ransom for Israel. These three nations may symbolize Israel's great worth, or they may have been named in anticipation of the subsequent Persian conquests." (Wolf)

d. **Fear not, for I am with you; I will bring your descendants from the east**: God's presence and blessing with Israel would also be demonstrated by unleashing the shackles of their exile. They could have hope for the future because they knew they were **called** by the **name** of the LORD, and they were **created for** His **glory**.

i. **Whom I have created for My glory** means that God not only has created us but that He has created us *for a purpose*. If we have no Creator, then we are *purposeless*; but God has created us, and He did it for a purpose, creating us for His glory. This means that when we are glorifying God, we are fulfilling the purpose we were created for, and will therefore be the happiest and fulfilled.

B. Witnesses to the work of the Lord.

1. (8-9) The nations and the people of Israel are called to either prove their case or accept God's.

Bring out the blind people who have eyes,
And the deaf who have ears.
Let all the nations be gathered together,
And let the people be assembled.
Who among them can declare this,
And show us former things?
Let them bring out their witnesses, that they may be justified;
Or let them hear and say, "*It is* truth."

a. **Bring out the blind people who have eyes**: Previously, in Isaiah 42:19, the Lord spoke of His blind and deaf servants, who had willingly closed their eyes and ears to His truth and ways. Now, God tells these blind and deaf servants of His to come forth – with **all the nations** who will **be gathered together**.

b. **Who among them can declare this, and show us former things? Let them bring out their witnesses**: God invites His people (who are **blind** and **deaf**) and the nations to testify: to prove Him to be wrong or to prove that they are justified in their rejection of Him. It is as if God is saying, "You have chosen to worship and honor other gods. Come before Me now and justify yourself. Bring plenty of witnesses."

i. "We must not miss the pathos: imagine any litigant depending on the blind to testify to what they have seen and the deaf to what they have heard!" (Motyer)

2. (10-13) The Lord commissions His witnesses.

"You *are* My witnesses," says the Lord,
"And My servant whom I have chosen,
That you may know and believe Me,
And understand that I *am* He.
Before Me there was no God formed,
Nor shall there be after Me.

I, *even* I, *am* the LORD,
And besides Me *there is* no savior.
I have declared and saved,
I have proclaimed,
And *there was* no foreign *god* among you;
Therefore you *are* My witnesses,"
Says the LORD, "that I *am* God.
Indeed before the day *was*, I *am* He;
And *there is* no one who can deliver out of My hand;
I work, and who will reverse it?"

a. **You are My witnesses**: God's people had witnessed the greatness of God. If only Israel would remember the great things God had done among them, they would see each wonderful work of His as a *witness* to the truth that He is the only true God.

i. The idol worshippers have nothing to say as witnesses because their gods can do nothing. But the people of God are witnesses of His greatness and power. They have seen it and experienced it.

b. **And My servant whom I have chosen that you may know and believe Me**: A witness is a passive observer of what someone has done, and Israel had seen the great works of God. But they were more than passive observers; God called Israel to be His **servant**. That was why they were **chosen** – not to sit around and glory in their chosenness, but to *serve* the LORD, and to **know** the LORD and **believe** Him in every way.

c. **Before Me there was no God formed, nor shall there be after Me**: In clear, certain words, God says that not only is He the most high God, but that there are *no other gods* beside Him. There are no "junior gods." There are no "second class gods." **There was no God formed** before the LORD, and there will be no God formed after Him.

i. What about Biblical passages which some take to suggest there are other gods? For example, in John 10:34, Jesus quotes Psalm 82:6-7, saying *You are gods*. But the judges of Psalm 82 were called "gods" because in their office they determined the fate of other men. Also, in Exodus 21:6 and 22:8-9, God speaks to earthly judges under the Hebrew word *elohim* [gods]. In John 10, Jesus is saying "if God gives these unjust judges the title 'gods' because of their office, why do you consider it blasphemy that I call Myself the 'Son of God' in light of the testimony of Me and My works?" Jesus did not take the phrase *you are gods* of Psalm 82 and applying it to all humanity, or to all believers. The use of *gods* in Psalm 82 was a metaphor.

ii. In 2 Corinthians 4:4, Paul calls Satan *the god of this age*. Certainly, he does not mean Satan is a true god, a rival god to the Lord God. Satan can be called *the god of this age* because so many people regard him as god! But Paul made it clear in 1 Corinthians 8:4-5 that the idols the nations worship are merely *so-called gods*, and that *there is no other God but one.*

iii. This is an important point, because some – such as Jehovah's Witnesses – take the opinion that Jesus is indeed a god, but something of a "junior level god." They will allow that He is *mighty God* (Isaiah 9:6), but not that He is *Almighty God.* But when the LORD says through Isaiah, **before Me there was no God formed, nor shall there be after Me**, it proves there is only *one true God.* There are *figurative* or *metaphorical* gods, such as the judges of Psalm 82. There are *false gods* such as the devil or the idols of the nations. But there are no *true Gods* apart from the LORD, Yahweh, who is One God in Three Persons. Ironically, the Jehovah's Witnesses took their title from this very passage which proves their doctrine regarding Jesus is wrong.

d. **And besides Me there is no savior**: The LORD God is the only savior. Only He has **declared and saved** – there was no **foreign god among you** who did any good. He is our help and support. Sadly, we often turn to our only savior as a last resort, instead of as a first resource.

i. Since Jesus is clearly our savior (Philippians 3:20, 2 Timothy 1:10), and there is no other savior beside the LORD, then Jesus must be the LORD. The LORD, Yahweh, is One God in Three Persons.

e. **Therefore, you are My witnesses**: If Israel would remember that only the LORD has ever rescued them, they would not be so quick to turn to other gods and to turn away from the LORD. We should all be **witnesses** to the saving, rescuing, and healing work of the LORD.

f. **Indeed, before the day was, I am He**: God's credentials go beyond His saving work on behalf of His people. He comes before time itself. Before there was ever a day, God was. So, His strength is infinitely greater than anyone else's; He can rightly say **there is no one who can deliver out of My hand**. When God does something, no one **will reverse it**.

C. The LORD redeems a hard-hearted people.

1. (14-17) A promise to judge Babylon.

Thus says the LORD, your Redeemer,
The Holy One of Israel:
"For your sake I will send to Babylon,

And bring them all down as fugitives—
The Chaldeans, who rejoice in their ships.
I *am* the LORD, your Holy One,
The Creator of Israel, your King."
Thus says the LORD, who makes a way in the sea
And a path through the mighty waters,
Who brings forth the chariot and horse,
The army and the power
(They shall lie down together, they shall not rise;
They are extinguished, they are quenched like a wick):

a. **For your sake I will send to Babylon**: Isaiah prophesied before the Babylonians ever conquered Judah and sent the nation into a 70-year exile. Yet Isaiah prophesies, not only about the coming captivity but also beyond it to the eventual judgment upon Babylon for what they will do to Judah.

b. **Thus says the LORD, who makes a way in the sea**: At the time Isaiah prophesied, Babylon was an up-and-coming world power. Before they would be judged, they would be a world dominating super-power. How could Israel be confident that God was up to the job of delivering them and judging Babylon? All they had to do was look at God's great works in the past, such as when He made **a way in the sea** – when He parted the Red Sea so Israel could cross and escape the Egyptian armies (Exodus 14). Isaiah powerfully brings up these images when he writes of **the chariot and the horse, the army and the power** of these enemies of God's people, and how **they shall lie down together…they are extinguished**. Just as God overwhelmed the Egyptian armies that had enslaved Israel, so would He judge the Babylonians also.

i. This teaches us that we can always justify trusting God right now by remembering the great things He has done.

ii. This teaches us that we never want to oppose the LORD or His people.

c. **The LORD your Redeemer…the Holy One of Israel…your Holy One, the Creator of Israel, your King**: In just these few verses, look at the glorious titles of God. In this passage, prophetically intended to comfort Israel in the midst of their Babylonian captivity, God powerfully put forth images of His own strength and power.

2. (18-21) God promises His exiled people a new work.

Do not remember the former things,
Nor consider the things of old.
Behold, I will do a new thing,

Now it shall spring forth;
Shall you not know it?
I will even make a road in the wilderness
***And* rivers in the desert.**
The beast of the field will honor Me,
The jackals and the ostriches,
Because I give waters in the wilderness
***And* rivers in the desert, to give drink**
To My people, My chosen.
This people I have formed for Myself;
They shall declare My praise.

a. **Do not remember the former things**: As Isaiah wrote prophetically to Israel, they were mired in the desperate circumstances of captivity and exile. God wanted to put their eyes on the new work He would do, so He began with a reminder to **not remember the former things**. If they were stuck in the failure and sin and discouragement of the past, they would never go forward to the new thing God had for them.

i. It is a fascinating – and instructive – switch between Isaiah 43:16-17 and Isaiah 43:18. In Isaiah 43:16-17, Israel was told to look to the past by remembering the great things God did for them at the Red Sea. But in Isaiah 43:18, they were told, **do not remember the former things, nor consider the things of old**. This shows us that there is a sense in which we *must remember* the past, in terms of God's great work on our behalf. There is also a sense in which we *must forsake and forget* the past, with all its discouragement and defeat, and move on to what God has for us in the future.

b. **Behold, I will do a new thing**: Staying stuck in the past can keep us from the **new thing** God wants to do. If Israel stayed stuck in the discouragement and seduction of Babylon, they would never look for the **new thing** of release from exile.

i. We can make an idol out of the "new." We can err as the people of Athens did who *spent their time in nothing else but either to tell or to hear some new thing* (Acts 17:21). We can be tossed about by every wind of doctrine. But we can also err on the other side of the balance, and work against the **new thing** God wants to do.

ii. **Shall you not know it?** God asks the same question today. "Will you stay in step with My Spirit? When He leads into something new, **shall you not know it?**"

c. **I will even make a road in the wilderness**: Between the captivity in Babylon and the return to Israel lay hundreds of miles of **wilderness**. God's people didn't need to be afraid because God would **make a road in the wilderness**, provide **rivers in the desert**, and even protect His people from animals, because **the beast of the field will honor Me**, the LORD says.

i. Often, when God makes a promise, we worry about the details or the obstacles for the fulfillment of the promise. God replies to us, "Don't worry about it at all. **I will even make a road in the wilderness**. I have resources and plans you don't know about. Leave those problems to Me."

d. **They shall declare My praise**: This is part of fulfilling the purpose God created us for, as mentioned in Isaiah 43:7 (*Whom I created for My glory*). When we **declare** our **praise** for God, we are giving Him glory, and fulfilling one of the purposes we were created for.

i. This passage has in view Israel's prophesied deliverance from Babylon, but also more than that. It also has in mind the ultimate deliverance, brought by the Messiah.

ii. "From all which texts laid together, it appears that this latter deliverance, compared with that out of Egypt, is not to be confined to their freedom from the Babylonish captivity, but to be extended to the consequences of it, and especially to the redemption by Christ, because otherwise that Egyptian deliverance was more glorious and wonderful in many respects than the Babylonian." (Poole)

3. (22-24) The hard-heartedness of God's people.

But you have not called upon Me, O Jacob;
And you have been weary of Me, O Israel.
You have not brought Me the sheep for your burnt offerings,
Nor have you honored Me with your sacrifices.
I have not caused you to serve with grain offerings,
Nor wearied you with incense.
You have bought Me no sweet cane with money,
Nor have you satisfied Me with the fat of your sacrifices;
But you have burdened Me with your sins,
You have wearied Me with your iniquities.

a. **But you have not called upon Me, O Jacob**: Who is Isaiah speaking to? When is he speaking of? Isaiah may have come out of the prophetic future into the prophetic present and may be speaking to the people of Judah in his own day. He may still be speaking in the prophetic future and rebuking the hard-hearted complacency of many of the Babylonian exiles, most of whom had no interest in returning to the Promised Land.

b. **And you have been weary of Me**: In the flesh, sometimes we regard serving and obeying the LORD as a **weary** thing. We feel it is such a burden to serve the LORD. We think we are worse off for following His ways and we feel so oppressed and afflicted. Sometimes people say, "I just need to take a break," and essentially mean that they need to take a break from the LORD.

i. When we feel like this, it is *certain evidence* that we are not in step with Jesus, and the true nature of Jesus. He said, *Come to Me, all you who labor and are heavy laden, and I will give you rest. Take My yoke upon you and learn from Me, for I am gentle and lowly in heart, and you will find rest for your souls. For My yoke is easy and My burden is light.* (Matthew 11:28-30) If following God always seems like some great, weary burden – then you really aren't following Him.

c. **You have not brought Me the sheep for your burnt offerings**: When we are weary of the LORD like this, it often shows in our giving, and in immorality (**you have burdened Me with your sins**).

i. "Perhaps the Israelites were insincere in their worship. When they did bring offerings, they simply went through the motions of worship, and so God did not consider their empty sacrifices to be true sacrifices at all." (Wolf)

d. **You have burdened Me with your sins, you have wearied Me with your iniquities**: Isaiah spoke to God's people who felt "burnt out," burdened, and weary of the LORD. God replied to them, "You feel burdened? You feel weary? Try being Me! **You have burdened Me with your sins, you have wearied Me with your iniquities.**"

4. (25-28) The LORD's mercy to a hard-hearted people.

I, *even* I, *am* He who blots out your transgressions for My own sake;
And I will not remember your sins.
Put Me in remembrance;
Let us contend together;
State your case, that you may be acquitted.
Your first father sinned,
And your mediators have transgressed against Me.
Therefore I will profane the princes of the sanctuary;
I will give Jacob to the curse,
And Israel to reproaches.

a. **I, even I, am He who blots out your transgressions...I will not remember your sins**: What will God do with such a hard-hearted people? He will forgive them at the earliest opportunity. He will forget their sins.

Despite all their sin and disregard for God, He still loves His people and longs for their humble return.

i. Jesus' story of the Prodigal Son is a beautiful illustration of this principle. The Prodigal felt the father was a weary burden to be relieved, and he went his own way. But the father still loved him and was ready to forget all the sin as soon as the Prodigal humbly returned.

ii. **I will not remember your sins**: How can God forget? By simply choosing to not remember. God has forgotten our sin as being fully paid for by what Jesus endured on the cross. We can forget our sin also and put it far from us.

b. **Let us contend together; state your case**: God says to His people, "Do you want to justify yourself? Then do it. Present your best case." But no matter what they say on their behalf, God has a stronger argument against them: **Your first father sinned**. "You are a child of Adam, and his sin has infected the whole human race, including yourself. You are a sinner through and through from birth. Stop trying to justify yourself and humbly look to Me for salvation."

c. **And your mediators have transgressed against me**: Not only were they – and we – born in sin because of Adam, they also trusted in the wrong mediators. The ones they trusted to save them before God were sinners themselves. Looking to a perfect, sinless Mediator can only save us, *for there is one God and one Mediator between God and men, the Man Christ Jesus.* (1 Timothy 2:5)

d. **I will give Jacob to the curse**: Because of this deep sinfulness, and failure to look to God's solution for sin, there was only a **curse** for Jacob. Because we are born in sin, and when we reject God's Mediator, then all there is left for us is **the curse** and **reproaches**.

Isaiah 44 – The Lord, Your Redeemer

A. A promise to pour out the Spirit.

1. (1-4) Fear not, knowing the promise of the outpoured Spirit.

Yet hear now, O Jacob My servant,
And Israel whom I have chosen.
Thus says the Lord who made you
And formed you from the womb, *who* will help you:
"Fear not, O Jacob My servant;
And you, Jeshurun, whom I have chosen.
For I will pour water on him who is thirsty,
And floods on the dry ground;
I will pour My Spirit on your descendants,
And My blessing on your offspring;
They will spring up among the grass
Like willows by the watercourses."

a. **Yet hear now**: Though Isaiah 43 ended with a warning of judgment, it did not mean God would take back His promise of hope and restoration. Israel could still know the goodness of the Lord if they would only turn back to Him.

b. **Thus says the Lord who made you**: This reminds us that God is still active in and responsible for creation. He didn't just create Adam and Eve and then let the whole thing go. There is a sense in which God has **made** each one of us, so we each have a personal obligation to Him as our Creator.

c. **And you, Jeshurun, whom I have chosen**: The name **Jeshurun** means "the upright one." It is used here as a contrast to the name **Jacob**, even as *Israel* is sometimes used as a contrast to **Jacob**.

i. "The name *Jeshurun* appears only three more times in the Old Testament: Deuteronomy 32:15, 33:5, 26; and in all cases it is used of

Israel...this word bespeaks a wonder of grace, for He calls His deeply sinful people His beloved, His upright one." (Bultema)

d. **Fear not.... For I will pour water on him...I will pour My Spirit on your descendants**: This is a glorious promise to a humble, returning Israel. God will not simply give them His Spirit; He will **pour** out His Spirit on them as if **water** was poured over them.

i. This is a *freedom* in the giving of the Spirit. This is a *flow* in the giving of the Spirit. This is *abundance* in the giving of the Spirit. This is an *evident* giving of the Spirit. God wants to **pour** His Spirit upon His people! If you experience a few drops, God wants to **pour**. If you are bone dry, God wants to **pour**. If you know the pour, God wants to keep pouring! We must learn to stop saying "when" as God pours.

ii. "Without the Spirit of God we can do nothing; we are as ships without wind, or chariots without steeds, like branches without sap, we are withered; like coals without fire, we are useless; as an offering without the sacrificial flame, we are unaccepted. I desire both to feel and to confess this fact whenever I attempt to preach. I do not wish to get away from it, or to conceal it, nor can I, for I am often made to feel it to the deep humbling of my spirit." (Spurgeon)

iii. "I believe that, at this present moment, God's people ought to cry to him day and night that there may be a fresh baptism into the Holy Ghost. There are many things that are desirable for the Church of Christ, but one thing is absolutely needful; and this is the one thing, the power of the Holy Ghost in the midst of his people." (Spurgeon)

iv. Who receives this gift? **I will pour water on him who is thirsty**. When we are thirsty for the outpouring of the Spirit, ask for it and receive it in faith, we can expect to be poured on. God is looking for **dry ground** to pour out **floods** upon.

e. **And My blessing on your offspring**: God doesn't only want to pour His Spirit; He also wants to pour His blessing, on us and our **offspring**.

i. As the old hymn says:
Showers of blessing, showers of blessing we need.
Mercy-drops 'round us are falling,
But for the showers we plead.

f. **They will spring up among the grass like willows**: The effect of the poured-out Spirit is *life*. Life springs up and grows where the Spirit of God is poured out.

2. (5) The promise of belonging to the LORD.

One will say, "I *am* the LORD's";
Another will call *himself* by the name of Jacob;
Another will write *with* his hand, "The LORD's,"
And name *himself* by the name of Israel.

a. **One will say, "I am the LORD's"**: Another effect of the poured-out Spirit is that He identifies us as belonging to the Lord. When the Holy Spirit is poured out on us, we know we belong to the Lord, and we aren't afraid to say it. The Holy Spirit is an identifying *seal* upon the believer (Ephesians 1:13).

b. **Another will write with his hand, "The LORD's," and name himself by the name of Israel**: When the Holy Spirit is poured out on us, we *want* to take the name of the Lord. We want everyone to know we belong to Him, and He belongs to us.

i. Spurgeon on **Another will write with his hand, "The LORD's"**: "The text may have another rendering, for, if you notice, the word '*with*' in the text is in italics, to show that it was inserted by the translators. It might run thus: 'Another shall subscribe his hand unto the Lord.' This alludes to the custom which still exists, but which was more common in those days, of a servant being marked or tattooed in the hand with his master's name.... Paul alludes to this when he says, 'Henceforth let no man trouble me, for I bear in my body the marks of the Lord Jesus;' as much as to say, 'I am Christ's: I have had his name branded upon me.'"

B. The LORD alone is God.

1. (6-8) The LORD declares to witnesses that He alone is God.

Thus says the LORD, the King of Israel,
And his Redeemer, the LORD of hosts:
"I *am* the First and I *am* the Last;
Besides Me *there is* no God.
And who can proclaim as I do?
Then let him declare it and set it in order for Me,
Since I appointed the ancient people.
And the things that are coming and shall come,
Let them show these to them.
Do not fear, nor be afraid;
Have I not told you from that time, and declared it?
You *are* My witnesses.
Is there a God besides Me?

**Indeed *there is* no other Rock;
I know not *one*."**

a. **I am the First and I am the Last; besides Me there is no God**: The LORD has already taken this unique title in Isaiah 41:4, in the same context of proclaiming His glory against the feeble false gods. An idol can never be **the First**, because an idol needs someone to make him. An idol can never be **the Last** because they wear out and break. But the Lord GOD of Israel is both **the First** and **the Last**; He is completely unique, and **besides** Him **there is no God**.

i. "As *first* he does not derive his being from any other, but is self-existing; as *last* he remains supreme at the End." (Motyer)

ii. Jesus takes the same title of *the First and the Last* in Revelation 1:17 and 22:13. If the **LORD** is **the First** and **the Last** according to Isaiah 44:6, and if Jesus is *the First and the Last* according to Revelation 1:17 and 22:13, since there cannot be *two firsts* or *two lasts*, Jesus must be the **LORD** God.

b. **Who can proclaim as I do?** Because God is **the First** and **the Last**, He lives outside our time-domain and can **proclaim** things before they happen. He can proclaim **the things that are coming and shall come**. This shows God really is who He says He is, watching and directing the parade of human and cosmic history as it makes its course down His appointed path.

c. **Do not fear, nor be afraid**: Knowing these truths about God isn't only good for winning theological quiz games. When we really know who God is, and His great wisdom and authority over all things, it erases all **fear** in our lives.

d. **You are My witnesses. Is there a God besides Me?** As if God said to His people, "You are all witnesses of these truths. Tell Me yourself – is there any **God besides Me**?"

i. Because there is no other **God besides** the LORD, it means that God the Father is the LORD, God the Son is the LORD, and God the Holy Spirit is the LORD. *Yahweh* – the name translated by the small-caps LORD – is the Triune God, the One God in Three Persons. There are no "grades" or "degrees" to true deity. There are false gods, symbolic gods, and the true God – and the only true God is Yahweh, the LORD.

e. **Indeed there is no other Rock; I know not one**: Since God is the only God, He is the only *solid ground* to build our life upon.

2. (9-20) The folly of idol makers.

Adam Clarke writes of this passage: "The sacred writers are generally large and eloquent upon the subject of idolatry; they treat it with great severity, and set forth the absurdity of it in the strongest light. But this passage of Isaiah…far exceeds anything that ever was written upon the subject, in force of argument, energy of expression, and elegance of composition."

Those who make an image, all of them *are* useless,
And their precious things shall not profit;
They *are* their own witnesses;
They neither see nor know, that they may be ashamed.
Who would form a god or mold an image
***That* profits him nothing?**
Surely all his companions would be ashamed;
And the workmen, they *are* mere men.
Let them all be gathered together,
Let them stand up;
Yet they shall fear,
They shall be ashamed together.
The blacksmith with the tongs works one in the coals,
Fashions it with hammers,
And works it with the strength of his arms.
Even so, he is hungry, and his strength fails;
He drinks no water and is faint.
The craftsman stretches out *his* rule,
He marks one out with chalk;
He fashions it with a plane,
He marks it out with the compass,
And makes it like the figure of a man,
According to the beauty of a man, that it may remain in the house.
He cuts down cedars for himself,
And takes the cypress and the oak;
He secures *it* for himself among the trees of the forest.
He plants a pine, and the rain nourishes *it*.
Then it shall be for a man to burn,
For he will take some of it and warm himself;
Yes, he kindles *it* and bakes bread;
Indeed he makes a god and worships *it*;
He makes it a carved image, and falls down to it.
He burns half of it in the fire;
With this half he eats meat;
He roasts a roast, and is satisfied.

He even warms *himself* and says,
"Ah! I am warm,
I have seen the fire."
And the rest of it he makes into a god,
His carved image.
He falls down before it and worships *it*,
Prays to it and says,
"Deliver me, for you *are* my god!"
They do not know nor understand;
For He has shut their eyes, so that they cannot see,
***And* their hearts, so that they cannot understand.**
And no one considers in his heart,
Nor *is there* knowledge nor understanding to say,
"I have burned half of it in the fire,
Yes, I have also baked bread on its coals;
I have roasted meat and eaten *it*;
And shall I make the rest of it an abomination?
Shall I fall down before a block of wood?"
He feeds on ashes;
A deceived heart has turned him aside;
And he cannot deliver his soul,
Nor say, "*Is there* not a lie in my right hand?"

a. **Those who make an image, all of them are useless**: Isaiah will brilliantly show the foolishness of idol makers. A simple look at how idols are made shows how silly it is to regard them as gods, so the idol makers themselves **are their own witnesses** against themselves.

b. **The workmen, they are mere men**: Isaiah looked at the people who made idols and noticed that they themselves were only weak, frail men. The **blacksmith** becomes **hungry, and his strength fails**. The **craftsman** works hard with wood, but it is only wood. Half of the tree is made into an object of worship and trust, and the other half is burned for a warm fire and cooking.

c. **They do not know nor understand; for He has shut their eyes, so they cannot see**: How could the idol makers fail to see what is so obvious about the stupidity of idolatry? God has **shut their eyes** and shut their **hearts**.

i. Is this unjust of God? Is He condemning man for something that He is really responsible for? Not at all. They first loved the darkness and chose their blindness, then the Lord gave them what they wanted. Isaiah points to this when he writes, **no one considers in his heart,**

nor is there knowledge nor understanding to say…a deceived heart has turned him aside.

ii. It is the same way that God hardened the heart of Pharaoh (Exodus 4:21). Sometimes it says that Pharaoh hardened his own heart (Exodus 8:15), sometimes it says simply that Pharaoh's heart was hardened, without saying who did it (Exodus 7:13). Who really did it? When we consider the occasions where God hardened Pharaoh's heart, we must never think that God did it against Pharaoh's will. It was never a case of Pharaoh saying, "Oh, I want to do what is good and right and I want to bless these people of Israel" and God replying, "No, for I will harden your heart against them!" When God hardened Pharaoh's heart, He was allowing Pharaoh's heart to do what Pharaoh wanted to do – God was giving Pharaoh over to his sin (Romans 1:18-32).

iii. "The idolater chose a delusion and became deluded." (Motyer)

d. **He feeds on ashes**: The wooden idol from the craftsman's shop is just a warm fire away from being ashes. Worshipping and serving an idol – any false god – is as wise and as satisfying as eating ashes. We can only satisfy our soul in God.

e. **And he cannot deliver his soul, nor say, "Is there not a lie in my right hand"**: The one given over to a false god is so entranced in the lie that he is in bondage. He holds the idol in his **right hand** – the hand of power and authority – yet cannot see that it is a lie.

i. "The idolater picks up the figurine in his hand, holding it, but in reality it holds him. He is in bondage to *a lie*." (Motyer)

ii. "And such passages as these are added in such cases to give an account of the prodigious madness of sinners herein; because, as they wilfully shut their own eyes, and harden their own hearts, so God judicially blinds and hardens them, and gives them up to believe lies, and then it is no wonder if they fall into such dotages." (Poole)

3. (21-23) Remembering and praising the greatness and the glory of the true God.

"Remember these, O Jacob,
And Israel, for you *are* My servant;
I have formed you, you *are* My servant;
O Israel, you will not be forgotten by Me!
I have blotted out, like a thick cloud, your transgressions,
And like a cloud, your sins.
Return to Me, for I have redeemed you."
Sing, O heavens, for the LORD has done *it*!

Shout, you lower parts of the earth;
Break forth into singing, you mountains,
O forest, and every tree in it!
For the LORD has redeemed Jacob,
And glorified Himself in Israel.

a. **Remember these, O Jacob**: As Israel remembers the foolishness of making and worshipping idols, it should inspire greater trust and confidence in God. When we think about the alternatives to following the LORD, it should make us follow Him all the more closely.

i. As Peter said to Jesus, *Lord, to whom shall we go? You have the words of eternal life.* (John 6:68)

b. **Remember these, O Jacob**: If the foolishness of the alternative wasn't enough, God gives His people many more reasons to trust and love Him: **I have formed you, you are My servant…you will not be forgotten by Me…. I have blotted out, like a thick cloud, your transgressions…. I have redeemed you**. Any one of these would be reason enough, but combined, they are overwhelming.

c. **Sing, O heavens, for the LORD has done it**: This is the only logical reaction to seeing who God is. And if God's people won't do it, then creation itself will (**Shout, you lower parts of the earth; break into singing, you mountains**).

d. **For the LORD has redeemed Jacob, and glorified Himself in Israel**: Creation rejoices when God saves and glorifies Himself in His people. Paul developed this theme in Romans 8:19-22.

4. (24-28) The LORD demonstrates He is the true God by prophesying a future deliverer of Israel.

Thus says the LORD, your Redeemer,
And He who formed you from the womb:
"I *am* the LORD, who makes all *things*,
Who stretches out the heavens all alone,
Who spreads abroad the earth by Myself;
Who frustrates the signs of the babblers,
And drives diviners mad;
Who turns wise men backward,
And makes their knowledge foolishness;
Who confirms the word of His servant,
And performs the counsel of His messengers;
Who says to Jerusalem, 'You shall be inhabited,'
To the cities of Judah, 'You shall be built,'

And I will raise up her waste places;
Who says to the deep, 'Be dry!
And I will dry up your rivers';
Who says of Cyrus, '*He is* My shepherd,
And he shall perform all My pleasure,
Saying to Jerusalem, "You shall be built,"
And to the temple, "Your foundation shall be laid."'

a. **Thus says the LORD**: The LORD makes remarkable claims through this whole passage, and in these verses. He claims to be their **Redeemer**, the Creator of each person (**who formed you from the womb**), the Creator of all things (**who makes all things**), wiser and greater than anyone (**who frustrates the signs of the babblers**), who upholds His own (**who confirms the word of His Servant**), who resurrects dead cities (**who says to Jerusalem, "You shall be inhabited"**), and who has authority over all creation (**who says to the deep, "Be dry!"**). How can God back up such great claims?

b. **Who says of Cyrus**: God proves He is who He claims to be by announcing the name of a deliverer for Israel's Babylonian exiles – and Isaiah wrote this more than 200 years before Cyrus fulfilled this prophecy.

i. The prophet alluded to the king who would bring about Israel's release from captivity in Isaiah 41:2, but in this passage, amazingly, he mentions him by name. "*Cyrus*, whom God here designeth by his proper name *two hundred* years before he was born, that this might be an undeniable evidence of the certainty and exactness of God's foreknowledge, and a convincing argument, and so most fit to conclude this dispute between God and idols." (Poole)

ii. "This great passage, with its two explicit references to Cyrus, has attracted much scholarly discussion. For many modern scholars it represents the strongest argument for 'Deutero-Isaiah,' for they cannot conceive of supernatural predictive prophecy of such detail." (Grogan)

iii. Some believe that Isaiah wrote much of this, but someone after the events were fulfilled just wrote in the name **Cyrus**. This doesn't hold true, because the whole section is carefully written to dramatically reveal the name of **Cyrus**. Just the name couldn't have been written in later.

iv. "We can, of course, choose to disbelieve what it says, but we must not adjust its testimony to suit modern conventions, tastes or prejudices. The evidence of the Old Testament (as of the New) is that pre-knowledge of personal names is given when, for whatever reason, the situation warrants it (*cf.* 1 Kings 13:2 with 2 Kings 23:15-17; Acts

9:12). This special dimension of prediction is at home in Isaiah, who, more than any other prophet, makes prediction and fulfilment the keystone of his proof that the Lord is the only God." (Motyer)

v. "If the fact of predictive prophecy is accepted, we are in no position to set limits to its exercise, and, since the OT does not let us into the secrets of the mechanisms or 'psychology' of inspiration, we do not have the clues to decide what is possible and what is impossible. Within the total biblical context, the revelation of names is perfectly at home (see, *e.g.*, Genesis 16:11; Matthew 1:21; Luke 1:13)." (Motyer)

vi. "Josephus in his *Antiquities* relates that when Cyrus came across his name mentioned in this place in Isaiah 220 years before he lived, he was seized by a holy desire to fulfill what was written of him." (Bultema)

c. **He is My shepherd**: Cyrus was a **shepherd** in the sense that God used him to do something good and helpful for Israel.

i. "The lost sheep were to be rounded up and returned to their true fold in Judah by this foreigner...this oracle gives the first explicit reference in the Book of Isaiah to God's plans to rebuild the city." (Grogan)

ii. "Kings were called 'shepherds' as being guardians and carers of their people (56:11; 2 Samuel 24:17; 1 Kings 22:17; Jeremiah 2:8). The title here signifies that the coming conqueror is the Lord's appointed carer – even, as a shepherd would, to lead them into their proper pastures." (Motyer)

d. **He shall perform all My pleasure**: Cyrus was a special instrument in God's hand, for God's work. He would do the work of the Lord and open the door for the work of rebuilding **Jerusalem** and the **temple** after the Babylonians destroyed them.

i. The royal proclamations of Cyrus fulfilling this prophecy are found in Ezra 1:2 and 2 Chronicles 36:23.

e. **Who says to the deep, "Be dry"!** The specific work commissioned by Cyrus is described in detail, including drying up the waters and laying the foundation for the temple (**Your foundation shall be laid**).

i. Trapp on **Who says to the deep, "Be dry!"** "That will put it into the heart of Cyrus to dry up the Euphrates, and so to take Babylon."

ii. "*Foundations*: interestingly, as Ezra records (3:10-13; 5:16), in the days of Cyrus the rebuilding of the temple did not progress beyond the laying of the foundations." (Motyer)

iii. With such amazingly specific claims, it is no wonder that God proves who He is through predicted and fulfilled prophecy. *And so we have the prophetic word confirmed, which you do well to heed as a light that shines in a dark place, until the day dawns and the morning star rises in your hearts; knowing this first, that no prophecy of Scripture is of any private interpretation, for prophecy never came by the will of man, but holy men of God spoke as they were moved by the Holy Spirit.* (2 Peter 1:19-21)

Isaiah 45 – "Look to Me and Be Saved"

A. Looking to the God who chose Cyrus.

1. (1-3) God's calling and mission for Cyrus.

"Thus says the LORD to His anointed,
To Cyrus, whose right hand I have held—
To subdue nations before him
And loose the armor of kings,
To open before him the double doors,
So that the gates will not be shut:
'I will go before you
And make the crooked places straight;
I will break in pieces the gates of bronze
And cut the bars of iron.
I will give you the treasures of darkness
And hidden riches of secret places,
That you may know that I, the LORD,
Who call *you* by your name,
***Am* the God of Israel.**

a. **Thus says the LORD to His anointed, to Cyrus**: Isaiah carries on this remarkable prophecy from the previous chapter. In it, God announces – *by name* – the deliverer for His people from a coming captivity, and He does it 200 years before the man **Cyrus** is born.

i. **His anointed** means that Cyrus had a particular anointing from God for his work. God poured out His Spirit on a pagan king because God wanted to use that man to bless and deliver His people.

ii. "There is precedent for the divine anointing of a non-Israelite king, though in one passage only (1 Kings 19:15-16). Although the living God normally employed Israelites for such purposes, he is sovereign and may use whom he will." (Grogan)

iii. **Thus says the LORD to His anointed** means that this word was particularly directed to **Cyrus**. This was God's message to him, and Cyrus apparently listened. "These things Cyrus knew from reading the book of prophecy which Isaiah had left behind two hundred and ten years earlier." (Josephus, *Antiquities* XI, 5 [i.2], cited in Grogan)

b. **Whose right hand I have held**: Like many of us, Cyrus could look back on his life and career and see how the LORD held his hand the entire time. **To subdue nations before him and loose the armor of kings**: Cyrus had a remarkable military career.

i. "To his appointed and enabled one, to subdue many nations. Xenophon, in his first book...gives us a list of them. Cyrus subdued, saith he, the Syrians, Assyrians, Arabians, Cappodcians, Phrygians, the Lydians, Carians, Phoenicians, Babylonians, the Bactrians, Indians, Cilicians, Sacians, Paphloagonians, Maryandines, and many other nations. He also had a dominion over the Asiatics, Greeks, Cyprians, Egyptians.... He vanquished, saith Herodotus, whatever country soever he invaded." (Trapp)

c. **To open before him the double doors, so that the gates will not be shut... I will break in pieces the gates of bronze**: The armies of the Medes and Persians, under Cyrus, conquered the city of Babylon in a remarkable raid described in Daniel 5. According to the ancient historian Herodotus, while King Belshazzar of Babylon held a reckless party, Cyrus conquered the city by diverting the flow of the Euphrates into a nearby swamp; thus, lowering the level of the river so his troops could march through the water and under the river-gates. But they still would not have been able to enter, had not the bronze gates of the inner walls been left inexplicably unlocked. *God opened the gates of the city of Babylon for Cyrus* and put it in writing 200 years before it happened.

i. "In October 539 BC, Cyrus advanced into lower Mesopotamia and, leaving Babylon till last, conquered and occupied the surrounding territory. Seeing which way the wind was blowing, Nabonidus of Babylon deserted his city, leaving it in the charge of his son Belshazzar... the taking of Babylon was as bloodless and effortless as Daniel 6 implies." (Motyer)

d. **I will give you the treasures of darkness and hidden riches of secret places**: The night they conquered the city, Cyrus and his armies took all the staggering treasures of Babylon – and it was important that Cyrus know that *the LORD* had *given* it to him.

i. On the night Babylon fell, Cyrus probably had no great sense of the LORD's guidance or presence. He probably thought himself both brilliant and lucky. Often, we succeed in something only by the blessing and pleasure of God, and never see the miraculous hand of God behind it all.

ii. God certainly gave Cyrus **treasures**. Clarke cites Pliny: "When Cyrus conquered Asia, he found *thirty-four* thousand pounds weight of gold, besides golden vessels and articles in gold."

e. **That you may know that I, the Lord, who call you by your name, am the God of Israel**: God announced all of this 200 years before its fulfillment so that Cyrus would know and glorify the Lord. But the Lord also did it so Cyrus would show kindness to the people of God, granting them permission to return to the Promised Land from the captivity imposed on them by the Babylonians.

i. The royal proclamations of Cyrus fulfilling this prophecy are found in Ezra 1:2 and 2 Chronicles 36:23.

2. (4-7) The purpose behind God's calling and mission for Cyrus.

For Jacob My servant's sake,
And Israel My elect,
I have even called you by your name;
I have named you, though you have not known Me.
I *am* the Lord, and *there is* no other;
***There is* no God besides Me.**
I will gird you, though you have not known Me,
That they may know from the rising of the sun to its setting
That *there* is none besides Me.
I *am* the Lord, and *there is* no other;
I form the light and create darkness,
I make peace and create calamity;
I, the Lord, do all these *things*.'

a. **For Jacob My servant's sake**: Cyrus would like to think that God picked him because he was the smartest or most talented or strongest man available. Really, God's focus was on His people. It wasn't Cyrus that moved God to act, but the condition and cry of His people. It was for their **sake**.

i. "That all these victories were for the sake of little Israel is one of the ironies of God's control of history." (Grogan)

ii. "Cyrus is preferred in order that Israel might be released. Cyrus shall have a kingdom, but only in order that God's people may have their liberty. The Lord raises up one, and He puts down another. Behind all the drama of human events today there is a God who is planning for His church – through affliction and persecution, chastening and tribulation – to be perfected and prepared to inherit the Kingdom of God." (Redpath)

b. **I have named you, though you have not known Me…. I will gird you, though you have not known Me**: Cyrus didn't even know the LORD, yet God could anoint him, guide him, bless him, and use him. How much more should God be able to do through those who have at least a mustard seed's worth of faith in Him.

i. Proverbs 21:1 says, *The king's heart is in the hand of the LORD, like the rivers of water; He turns it wherever He wishes.* God can work in and through others in very unexpected ways.

c. **That they may know from the rising of the sun to its setting that there is none besides Me**: This was wonderfully fulfilled in Ezra 1:1-3. That passage shows how when Cyrus made his proclamation allowing the people of God to return to the Promised Land, that he acknowledged to the whole world the greatness and uniqueness of the LORD God of Israel.

i. *Now in the first year of Cyrus king of Persia, that the word of the LORD by the mouth of Jeremiah might be fulfilled, the LORD stirred up the spirit of Cyrus king of Persia, so that he made a proclamation throughout all his kingdom, and also put it in writing, saying, "Thus says Cyrus king of Persia: All the kingdoms of the earth the LORD God of heaven has given me. And He has commanded me to build Him a house at Jerusalem which is in Judah. Who is among you of all His people? May his God be with him, and let him go up to Jerusalem which is in Judah, and build the house of the LORD God of Israel (He is God), which is in Jerusalem."*

d. **I form the light and create darkness, I make peace and create calamity; I, the LORD, do all these things**: Simply put, Isaiah knows, Cyrus would know and declare to the whole world, and we should know today, that *God is in control.* Since this prophecy was given long before God's people went into the captivity Isaiah now announces deliverance from, they could be comforted through the captivity by knowing *God is in control.*

i. Isaiah's point is that there are not two gods or forces in heaven, one good and one bad, as in a dualistic "yin and yang" sense. "Cyrus was a Persian, and Persians had a dualistic concept of God and the world. Their good god they called Ahura-mazda and the evil god Angra-mainya. The former had created the light, the second the darkness." (Bultema)

ii. But God has no opposite. Satan is not and has never been God's opposite. There is one God. He is not the *author* of evil; evil is never "original," but always a perversion of an existing good. Yet God is the *allower* of evil, and He uses it to accomplish His eternal purpose of bringing together all things in Jesus (Ephesians 3:8-11 and 1:9-10). If God could further His eternal purpose by allowing His Son to die a wicked, unjust death on a cross, then He knows how to use what He allows for His eternal purpose.

iii. "Undoubtedly the Lord is no representative of evil as such, but He does make use of evil so that it may bring forth good." (Calvin, cited in Bultema)

iv. When God does great, miraculous things, it is easy to believe that He is in control. When times are hard and the trials heavy, we need to believe it all the more.

B. Looking to the God who created everything.

1. (8) God calls to the creation.

"Rain down, you heavens, from above,
And let the skies pour down righteousness;
Let the earth open, let them bring forth salvation,
And let righteousness spring up together.
I, the LORD, have created it.

a. **Rain down, you heavens**: The great God described in the previous passage can speak to the **heavens** and bring rain. It is true in the literal, natural sense; but it is also true in a literal *spiritual* sense. God can send a flood from heaven, and **let the skies pour down righteousness**.

b. **Let the earth open, let them bring forth salvation**: God can send His blessing from every direction. It comes **down** from the **heavens**, it comes up from the **earth**.

c. **Let them bring forth salvation, and let righteousness spring up together**: It is important to see that **salvation** and **righteousness** always **spring up together**. When God brings **salvation** to a life, He also brings **righteousness** to that life. They **spring up together**.

d. **I, the LORD, have created it**: What is God speaking of here? That He created the natural, physical world? Or that He created the invisible, spiritual world? Both are true, so both may be in mind here.

2. (9-10) The foolishness of resisting our Creator.

"Woe to him who strives with his Maker!
***Let* the potsherd *strive* with the potsherds of the earth!**
Shall the clay say to him who forms it, 'What are you making?'
Or shall your handiwork *say*, 'He has no hands'?

**Woe to him who says to *his* father, 'What are you begetting?'
Or to the woman, 'What have you brought forth?'"**

a. **Woe to him who strives with his Maker**: Knowing that God is the Creator of all things should make us hesitant to oppose Him in any way. It is as foolish as for **the clay to say to him who forms it, "What are you making?"**

i. It is foolish to oppose our Creator because since He made us, He can break us. If it is foolish to oppose our Creator because since He made us, He knows what is best for us. It is foolish to oppose our Creator because we owe the greatest obligation to Him.

ii. "The idea is quite commonly held that the Jews murmured about God's decree that a heathen would deliver them, and that these words are a rebuke." (Bultema)

b. **Or shall your handiwork say, "He has no hands"**: The only thing more foolish than the creature resisting and opposing the Creator is for the creature to believe there *is no Creator!* Isaiah pictures a clay pot, the **handiwork** of the potter saying, "My potter **has no hands**. I have no Creator!"

c. **Woe to him who says to his father, "What are you begetting"?** The begotten has no say in his coming to be. It is simply foolish and counter-productive for us to question and accuse God over how He made us. Each of us has our strengths and weaknesses, and we each have our triumphs and challenges. We simply need to accept what we are before God and look for His redeeming, transforming power to conform us into the image of His Son, Jesus Christ (Romans 8:29).

3. (11-13) The God of all creation will raise up Cyrus and deliver His people.

**Thus says the Lord,
The Holy One of Israel, and his Maker:
"Ask Me of things to come concerning My sons;
And concerning the work of My hands, you command Me.
I have made the earth,
And created man on it.
I—My hands—stretched out the heavens,
And all their host I have commanded.
I have raised him up in righteousness,
And I will direct all his ways;
He shall build My city
And let My exiles go free,**

Not for price nor reward,"
Says the LORD of hosts.

a. **I have made the earth, and created man on it**: Repeatedly through this extended section of Isaiah, God emphasizes His place as *Creator*. The importance put on this idea here shows us that knowing God as *Creator* isn't an option, or just a matter of text-book fights in the courts and public schools. When we reject God as *Creator*, we reject the God of the Bible, and serve a God of our own imagination. He really did make us, and it really does matter.

i. "In the Old Testament the Creator is not only the One who began everything, but also the One who maintains everything in existence, controls and guides everything." (Motyer)

b. **I will direct all his ways; he shall build My city and let My exiles go free**: The God of all power and creation uses that power on behalf of His people. He will direct the ways of the announced deliverer – Cyrus – and cause him to rebuild Jerusalem and release the people of God captive in a foreign land. And Cyrus would do it **not for price or reward**, but out of a conviction from God that he must do it (Ezra 1:1-3).

C. Looking to the LORD who is above all gods.

1. (14-17) When the LORD is revealed as the true God, idolaters submit, and God's people are saved.

Thus says the LORD:
"The labor of Egypt and merchandise of Cush
And of the Sabeans, men of stature,
Shall come over to you, and they shall be yours;
They shall walk behind you,
They shall come over in chains;
And they shall bow down to you.
They will make supplication to you, *saying*, 'Surely God *is* in you,
And *there is* no other;
***There is* no other God.'"**
Truly You *are* God, who hide Yourself,
O God of Israel, the Savior!
They shall be ashamed
And also disgraced, all of them;
They shall go in confusion together,
***Who are* makers of idols.**
***But* Israel shall be saved by the LORD**
With an everlasting salvation;

You shall not be ashamed or disgraced
Forever and ever.

a. **They shall walk behind you, they shall come over in chains**: Even as Israel was led away into captivity by means of a forced relocation, so one day Israel will be supreme among the nations and lead them as they and the LORD please.

b. **And they shall bow down to you.... saying, "Surely God is in you… there is no other God"**: The submission of the nations to Israel is not so much to Israel itself, as it is to the God of Israel.

c. **Truly You are God**: Isaiah here pours out an inspired flood of praise, describing God, exalting God, declaring confidence in God, receiving from God.

i. **Truly You are God, who hide Yourself**: It isn't that God hides Himself from the seeking sinner. Isaiah simply declares what Paul would later say in 1 Timothy 1:17: *Now to the King eternal, immortal, invisible, to God who alone is wise, be honor and glory forever and ever. Amen.*

ii. Bultema on **Truly You are God, who hide Yourself, O God of Israel, the Savior**: "When he sees how God for many centuries hides His face from Israel, he cries out these words, overcome by rapture and emotion. The LORD hides Himself from Israel during the *times of the Gentiles* (18:4; 40:27; 49:14; Hosea 3:3-5)…. So it is clear that we may not apply these words to a seeking sinner. From such God does not hide Himself. But when in the last days Israel will seek Him, she will find Him."

2. (18-21) The LORD declares His greatness and the foolishness of idolatry.

For thus says the LORD,
Who created the heavens,
Who is God,
Who formed the earth and made it,
Who has established it,
Who did not create it in vain,
Who formed it to be inhabited:
"I *am* the LORD, and *there is* no other.
I have not spoken in secret,
In a dark place of the earth;
I did not say to the seed of Jacob,
'Seek Me in vain';
I, the LORD, speak righteousness,

I declare things that are right.
Assemble yourselves and come;
Draw near together,
You *who have* escaped from the nations.
They have no knowledge,
Who carry the wood of their carved image,
And pray to a god *that* cannot save.
Tell and bring forth *your case*;
Yes, let them take counsel together.
Who has declared this from ancient time?
***Who* has told it from that time?**
***Have* not I, the LORD?**
And *there is* no other God besides Me,
A just God and a Savior;
***There is* none besides Me.**

a. **For thus says the LORD, who created the heavens**: By sheer repetition, Isaiah virtually *pounds* it into our awareness – that God is our Creator, and we have obligations to Him as our Creator.

b. **Who did not create it in vain, who formed it to be inhabited**: This brief statement – **who did not create it in vain** – is the Scriptural basis for a speculative doctrine known as the "Gap Theory."

i. The Gap Theory is based on a comparison between Isaiah 45:18 and Genesis 1:2, which they translate as *the earth became without form and void.* Here in Isaiah 45:18, God says that He did not **create it in vain**, and **vain** is the same Hebrew word for *void* found in Genesis 1:2. The idea is that God **did not create it in vain** (*void*), but that it *became without form and void* through Satanic attack and ages of desolation, which explains the vast geological ages and fossil remains which seem to date far beyond the history of the Bible. According to the Gap Theory, Genesis 1:3 and the following verses describe the *re-creation* of a world that was made *void* by Satan.

ii. The first thing to be said against the Gap Theory is that while to translate Genesis 1:2 (*The earth was without form, and void*) as *the earth became without form and void* doesn't follow the plainest understanding of the Hebrew grammar here. It is permissible, but a bit of a stretch. The most natural way to translate the passage is to say the *earth was without form and void* instead of the *earth became without form and void.*

iii. The other thing to be said against the Gap Theory is its use as an answer to interpretations of the fossil record. Those who believe in the

Gap Theory assign old and extinct fossils to this long and indefinite "gap" between Genesis 1:1 and 1:2. But whatever merit the Gap Theory may have, it cannot explain the extinction and fossilization of ancient animals. The Bible says plainly death came by Adam (Romans 5:12), and since fossils are the result of death, they could not have happened before Adam's time.

iv. Bultema on this verse and the Gap Theory: "We wish only to state that this text alone is not sufficient proof for it. In any case it is clear that the ultimate purpose of the earth is not to be void but to be inhabited by converted Israel and the converted nations."

c. **I did not say to the seed of Jacob, "Seek Me in vain"**: It is a wicked thing to think God ever says to His people, **"Seek Me in vain."** When we seek for God with all of our heart, we will find Him. Jeremiah 29:13 says, *and you will seek Me and find Me, when you search for Me with all your heart.* Hebrews 11:6 says, *he who comes to God must believe that He is, and that He is a rewarder of those who diligently seek Him.*

d. **They have no knowledge, who carry the wood of their carved image, and pray to a god that cannot save**: As the Lord declares His own greatness, faithfulness, and saving power, it naturally contrasts with the foolish idols of the nation – which must be carried, instead of being able to carry the one who worships them.

e. **Who has declared this from ancient time?** The amazing phenomenon of predictive prophecy shows that God is who He says He is, and that there is no other God besides Him.

f. **A just God and a Savior**: As much as anything else, this shows the amazing power, wisdom, and love of God. At first glance, it is impossible to see how **a just God** can be **a Savior** when justice demands that sinners be damned. But prompted by His great love, God fulfilled the righteous demands of His justice at the cross, so He could extend Himself to us as **Savior**, yet still remain **a just God**.

i. As Paul put it in Romans 3:26: *That He might be just and the justifier of the one who has faith in Jesus.*

3. (22-25) Looking to the Lord and finding salvation in surrender.

"Look to Me, and be saved,
All you ends of the earth!
For I *am* God, and *there is* no other.
I have sworn by Myself;
The word has gone out of My mouth *in* righteousness,
And shall not return,

That to Me every knee shall bow,
Every tongue shall take an oath.
He shall say,
'Surely in the LORD I have righteousness and strength.
To Him *men* shall come,
And all shall be ashamed
Who are incensed against Him.
In the LORD all the descendants of Israel
Shall be justified, and shall glory.'"

a. **Look to Me, and be saved, all you ends of the earth**: This simple but powerful statement shows the plan of salvation.

i. It shows the *simplicity* of salvation: all we must do is **look**. "One can read may books on theology which expound all kinds of things in an attempt to show how man can reach God, but these theories are far from the truth. The Holy Spirit needs exactly four letters, two of them the same, to tell us what to do: l-o-o-k. That is all. It is the simplest, basic thing any person can do, yet the most difficult to do in daily living." (Redpath)

ii. It shows the *focus* of salvation: we must look to **God**, and never to ourselves or to anything else of man. "Look unto ME, is His Word, which means looking away from the church because that will save nobody; away from the preacher because he can disappoint and disillusion you; away from all outward form and ceremony. You must look off from all this to the throne and there, in your heart, see the risen, reigning Lord Jesus Christ." (Redpath)

iii. It shows the *love* behind salvation: God pleads with man, "**Look to Me**."

iv. It shows the *assurance* of salvation: **and be saved**.

v. It shows the extent of God's saving love: **all you ends of the earth!**

b. **Look to Me**: In Numbers 21, the people of Israel were stricken by deadly snake bites, and Moses lifted up the image of a bronze serpent, raised on a pole, and the people who looked to it lived. The people were saved not by *doing* anything, but by simply *looking* to the bronze serpent. They had to trust that something as seemingly foolish as looking at such a thing would be sufficient to save them, and surely, some perished because they thought it too foolish to do such a thing.

i. So it says here in Isaiah: **Look to Me, and be saved, all you ends of the earth!** We might be willing to *do* a hundred things to earn our salvation, but God commands us to only trust in Him – to *look* to Him.

ii. "Wherever I am, however far off, it just says 'Look!' It does not say I am to see; it only says 'Look!' If we look on a thing in the dark we cannot see it, but we have done what we were told. So if a sinner only looks to Jesus, he will save him; for Jesus in the dark is as good as Jesus in the light, and Jesus when you cannot see him is as good as Jesus when you can. It is only 'look!' 'Ah!' says one, 'I have been trying to see Jesus this year, but I have not seen him.' It does not say see him, but 'look unto him!'" (Spurgeon)

c. **Look to Me, and be saved, all you ends of the earth**: On Sunday, January 6, 1850, a young man not quite sixteen years of age walked through a village street in a little town some fifty miles from London, England. On the bitterly cold day the snow fell heavily; but he was more concerned to find a church, because he was deeply conscious of his need of God, and of the breakdown, sin, and failure of his life even at that young age. As he made his way through the street with the snow falling, he felt it was too far to go to the church which he had intended to visit, so he walked down a back lane and entered a little Methodist chapel. He sat down on a seat near the back, and it was as cold inside as it was out! There were only about thirteen people there.

Five minutes after the service was due to begin at eleven o'clock, the regular preacher for the morning hadn't come. He had been delayed by the weather. So one of the deacons came to the rescue and began conducting the service, and after a little while announced his text: 'Look unto me, and be ye saved, all the ends of the earth: for I am God, and there is none else.' The deacon didn't know much, so he only spoke for about ten minutes.

Charles Spurgeon himself tells what happened: "I had been wandering about, seeking rest, and finding none, till a plain, unlettered, lay preacher among the Primitive Methodists stood up in the pulpit, and gave out this passage as his text: 'Look unto me, and be ye saved, all the ends of the earth.' He had not much to say, thank God, for that compelled him to keep on repeating his text, and there was nothing needed – by me, at any rate, – except his text. I remember how he said, 'It is Christ that speaks. "I am in the garden in an agony, pouring out my soul unto death; I am on the tree, dying for sinners; look unto me! Look unto me!" That is all you have to do. A child can look. One who is almost an idiot can look. However weak, or however poor, a man may be, he can look; and if he looks, the promise is that he shall live.' Then, stopping, he pointed to where I was sitting under the gallery, and he said, 'That young man there looks very miserable.' I expect I did, for that is how I felt. Then he said, 'There is no hope for you, young man, or any chance of getting rid of your sin, but by looking to Jesus;' and he shouted, as I think only a Primitive Methodist can, 'Look! Look, young man! Look now!' And I did look; and when they sang a hallelujah before they went home, in their own earnest way, I am sure I joined in it. It happened to be a day when the snow was lying deep and more was falling; so, as I went home, those words of David kept ringing through my heart, 'Wash me, and I shall be whiter than snow;' and it seemed as if all nature was in accord with that blessed deliverance from sin which I had found in a single moment by looking to Jesus Christ."

Somehow in a very strange and amazing way that young man looked from the depths of his soul into the very heart of God. He went out from the church, and he tells that as he walked through the streets, his burden had been lifted, never to return again. He walked with a new spring in his step, a new joy in his face, a new sense of peace in his heart. He had looked and lived.

d. **For I am God, and there is no other**: This is why we must look to the LORD, and to the LORD alone. Only He is God. Institutions are not God. The Church is not God. Pastors are not God. Brothers and sisters in Christ are not God. We don't look to them; we look to the LORD, for He alone is God.

e. **I have sworn by Myself**: When God confirms an oath, who does He swear by? He swears by Himself. There is no one greater, so He swears by His own holy name and character.

i. As Hebrews 6:13 says, *For when God made a promise to Abraham, because He could swear by no one greater, He swore by Himself.*

f. **That to Me every knee shall bow, every tongue shall take an oath**: The LORD here declares there will come a day when **every knee shall bow** to Him, and **every tongue** will swear by His greatness. Paul obviously quoted this passage in Philippians 2:10-11.

i. Paul's quotation of Isaiah 45:23 in Philippians 2:10-11 is overwhelming evidence of the deity of Jesus Christ. Clearly, in Isaiah 45:23 it is the LORD God speaking (*I, the LORD, speak*, Isaiah 45:19). Now, Paul clearly puts these high words and this high praise towards Jesus: *that at the name of Jesus every knee should bow, of those in heaven, and of those on earth, and of those under the earth, and that every tongue should confess that Jesus Christ is Lord, to the glory of God the Father.* Additionally, the confession is made that *Jesus Christ is Lord* – and the word *Lord* is the same word used in Paul's ancient Bible for "LORD" in the Old Testament.

g. **Surely in the LORD I have righteousness and strength**: This is the declaration of every believer. **Righteousness and strength** are found **in the LORD**, not in ourselves or anywhere else. Indeed, **in the LORD all the descendants of Israel shall be justified, and shall glory**.

Isaiah 46 – Dead Idols and the Living God

A. The idols of the nations are carried into captivity.

1. (1-2) The false gods are carried away on carriages.

Bel bows down, Nebo stoops;
Their idols were on the beasts and on the cattle.
Your carriages *were* heavily loaded,
A burden to the weary *beast.*
They stoop, they bow down together;
They could not deliver the burden,
But have themselves gone into captivity.

a. **Bel bows down, Nebo stoops**: **Bel** and **Nebo** were names of two false gods the idol-worshipping nations served. It is as if now God gets personal, "naming names" when it comes to idols; and now these false gods are brought low.

i. The names of the pagan gods **Bel** and **Nebo** are familiar to us in the names *Belshazzar* and *Nebuchadnezzar*.

ii. "In chapter 45 Isaiah declared that every knee will bow to the Lord, and here he pictures the gods of the great Babylon stooping low in humiliation." (Grogan)

b. **Their idols were on the beasts and on the cattle. Your carriages were heavily loaded**: Isaiah pictures God's people going into captivity, in a forced relocation. Loaded on to their **beasts** and **carriages** are their idols – even their idols are carried away into captivity, and loaded on the moving trucks! The bottom line is **they could not deliver the burden, but have themselves gone into captivity**.

2. (3-4) The Lord, the true God, will carry His people.

"Listen to Me, O house of Jacob,
And all the remnant of the house of Israel,

Who have been upheld *by Me* from birth,
Who have been carried from the womb:
Even to *your* old age, I *am* He,
And *even* to gray hairs I will carry *you*!
I have made, and I will bear;
Even I will carry, and will deliver *you*.

a. **Who have been upheld by Me from birth, who have been carried from the womb**: The false gods represented by silent and dead idols must be carried; but God carries His people. He carried them from before their birth, and He promises to continue to carry them (**even to gray hairs I will carry you!**).

b. **I have made, and I will bear; even I will carry**: This is the same Fatherly care Jesus spoke of in Luke 12:6-7: *Are not five sparrows sold for two copper coins? And not one of them is forgotten before God. But the very hairs of your head are all numbered. Do not fear therefore; you are of more value than many sparrows.* When we understand that has **made** us, and we are valuable to Him, then we can trust Him to **carry** us.

i. It's a worthy question: do you have to carry your gods, or does your God carry you?

3. (5-7) The Lord can save His people when the idols are helpless.

"To whom will you liken Me, and make *Me* equal
And compare Me, that we should be alike?
They lavish gold out of the bag,
And weigh silver on the scales;
They hire a goldsmith, and he makes it a god;
They prostrate themselves, yes, they worship.
They bear it on the shoulder, they carry it
And set it in its place, and it stands;
From its place it shall not move.
Though *one* cries out to it, yet it cannot answer
Nor save him out of his trouble.

a. **They lavish gold out of the bag**: Much money and attention are given to the production and care of our idols. Yet, **though one cries out to it, yet it cannot answer nor save him out of his trouble**. Isaiah again exposes the ironic folly of idolatry.

B. A call to remember.

1. (8-10) Remember that the Lord knows the beginning and the end.

"Remember this, and show yourselves men;
Recall to mind, O you transgressors.
Remember the former things of old,
For I *am* God, and *there is* no other;
***I am* God, and *there is* none like Me,**
Declaring the end from the beginning,
And from ancient times *things* that are not *yet* done,
Saying, 'My counsel shall stand,
And I will do all My pleasure.'

a. **Remember this, and show yourselves men**: We can gain the courage of **men** when we **remember** the things God tells us to remember. How much defeat we suffer in the Christian life through simply *forgetting*.

b. **Remember the former things of old…there is none like Me, declaring the end from the beginning**: God knows the **end** of every matter, of every course of circumstances, just as clearly as anyone else can see the **beginning** of it.

c. **Saying, "My counsel shall stand, and I will do all My pleasure"**: God knows the end from the beginning because He is much more than a passive observer of events. His **counsel shall stand**. His works and plans never fail, because He **will do all** His **pleasure**. God isn't just *watching* the entire parade of history, He is *directing* the parade.

i. The essential point is that God's people must *remember* this about the LORD – that He knows the end from the beginning and is in control over all things. When we **remember this**, we will **show yourselves men**. We can have tremendous courage in our God when we understand and remember who He is and what He does.

2. (11-13) Remember that the LORD will bring a deliverer to Zion.

Calling a bird of prey from the east,
The man who executes My counsel, from a far country.
Indeed I have spoken *it*;
I will also bring it to pass.
I have purposed *it*;
I will also do it.
Listen to Me, you stubborn-hearted,
Who *are* far from righteousness:
I bring My righteousness near, it shall not be far off;
My salvation shall not linger.
And I will place salvation in Zion,
For Israel My glory.

a. **Calling a bird of prey from the east, the man who executes My counsel**: This is another reference to Cyrus. God's people need to remember that God always has a deliverer for His people, even if He has to find one among pagan kings.

b. **My salvation shall not linger**: God's people need to remember that God's timing is always precise and wise. When we are **stubborn-hearted** we need to **listen** to the LORD and remember He never delays and is never late. God always has His deliverer, and always knows exactly when to bring His deliverance.

Isaiah 47 – Babylon Brought Low

A. The humiliation of Babylon.

1. (1-3) Babylon, represented as a woman, is humbled.

"Come down and sit in the dust,
O virgin daughter of Babylon;
Sit on the ground without a throne,
O daughter of the Chaldeans!
For you shall no more be called
Tender and delicate.
Take the millstones and grind meal.
Remove your veil,
Take off the skirt,
Uncover the thigh,
Pass through the rivers.
Your nakedness shall be uncovered,
Yes, your shame will be seen;
I will take vengeance,
And I will not arbitrate with a man."

a. **Come down and sit in the dust**: Isaiah pictures proud Babylon as a humiliated woman, who **shall no more be called tender and delicate**. She is stripped of her fine clothing and is forced to march in a forced relocation (**pass through the rivers**).

i. Bultema calls this "The bold image of a rich, frivolous and sensual young woman who, as a prisoner, is doomed to the despicable state of a slave and in every respect is treated like a Near-Eastern slave woman."

b. **I will take vengeance, and I will not arbitrate with a man**: The humiliation God will impose on Babylon is exactly the humiliation she put upon Judah and Jerusalem. When God humbles Babylon, He is taking **vengeance** and cannot be talked out of His judgment.

2. (4) The LORD of hosts is glorified.

As for **our Redeemer, the LORD of hosts** ***is*** **His name,**
The Holy One of Israel.

a. **As for our Redeemer**: Seemingly, Isaiah cannot help himself – when he sees how God will take vengeance on this enemy of God's people, he praises God and boasts in his **redeemer**.

b. **Our Redeemer**: This translates the great Hebrew word *gaal* or *goel*, the kinsman-redeemer.

i. Bultema on the Hebrew word for **Redeemer**: "A *gaal* had to be a close relative. Christ is this too, for according to His humanity He came forth from the Jews. A *gaal* had to be able to deliver. The Holy One of Israel does not lack this ability. Sometimes a *gaal* had to exercise bloody vengeance. Christ will work bloody vengeance upon Babylon for its oppression of His people. Frequently a *gaal* had to pay a ransom to free a prisoner. The Lord Jesus paid with His blood on Golgotha to ransom His people. On the basis of these considerations, to which could be added many more, it is evident that the name *Gaal* is very fitting for the Savior."

3. (5-7) Why God will humble Babylon.

"Sit in silence, and go into darkness,
O daughter of the Chaldeans;
For you shall no longer be called
The Lady of Kingdoms.
I was angry with My people;
I have profaned My inheritance,
And given them into your hand.
You showed them no mercy;
On the elderly you laid your yoke very heavily.
And you said, 'I shall be a lady forever,'
So **that you did not take these** ***things*** **to heart,**
Nor remember the latter end of them.

a. **I was angry with My people**: Babylon thought that she conquered Judah and Jerusalem through her own power. But Babylon didn't see that she really conquered them because God **was angry with** His **people**, and therefore used Babylon as an instrument of His work. God says, "You didn't know that I had **given them into your hand**."

b. **You showed them no mercy**: As an instrument in God's hand, Babylon was too enthusiastic in their attack on God's people. Even though God allowed it and used it, they still should have shown mercy to God's people. We are always safe when we take the path of mercy.

c. **And you said, "I shall be a lady forever"**: Babylon was *blind*, Babylon was *cruel*, and now Babylon is shown to be *proud and presumptuous*. For all these reasons, God promised to humble Babylon.

i. Bultema applies the sense of Isaiah 47:5-11 to the corrupt Church: "In her self-satisfaction and frivolous self-deception she says, *I shall be a lady*. She claims royal riches, power and honor for herself *for ever*. A queen feels she must reign, and that was also the Church's goal quite early. Soon it placed a cross on its steeple instead of on its shoulders. With all its veneration of the cross, it hated the cross in a spiritual sense and reached for the crown of the world." (Bultema)

B. The rebuke of Babylon.

1. (8-9) Why sudden humiliation comes to Babylon.

"Therefore hear this now, *you who are* given to pleasures,
Who dwell securely,
Who say in your heart, 'I *am*, and *there is* no one else besides me;
I shall not sit *as* a widow,
Nor shall I know the loss of children';
But these two *things* shall come to you
In a moment, in one day:
The loss of children, and widowhood.
They shall come upon you in their fullness
Because of the multitude of your sorceries,
For the great abundance of your enchantments.

a. **Hear this now, you who are given to pleasures, who dwell securely**: In the midst of her pride and arrogance (**I am, and there is no one else besides me; I shall not sit as a widow**), God brought another charge against Babylon. Judgment would also come **because of the multitude of your sorceries, for the great abundance of your enchantments**. Babylon was famous as a founding place and breeding ground for occult arts and practices.

2. (10-11) Babylon is rebuked for her pride and arrogance.

"For you have trusted in your wickedness;
You have said, 'No one sees me';
Your wisdom and your knowledge have warped you;
And you have said in your heart,
'I *am*, and *there is* no one else besides me.'

Therefore evil shall come upon you;
You shall not know from where it arises.
And trouble shall fall upon you;
You will not be able to put it off.
And desolation shall come upon you suddenly,
***Which* you shall not know.**

a. **You have trusted in your wickedness**: This is a searching insight into the heart of the proud sinner. They trust in their continuing wickedness to cover the tracks of their previous sin. They are clever, but their wisdom in wickedness has warped them (**Your wisdom and your knowledge have warped you**).

b. **Therefore evil shall come upon you**: And it did for Babylon, which was suddenly conquered in one night when they believed all was safe and secure (as recorded in Daniel 5).

i. The rebuke of Babylon's pride is a simple fulfillment of a principle repeated three times in the Scripture: *God resists the proud, but gives grace to the humble.* (Proverbs 3:34, James 4:6, 1 Peter 5:5).

3. (12-15) A challenge to the stargazers and sorcerers of Babylon.

Stand now with your enchantments
And the multitude of your sorceries,
In which you have labored from your youth—
Perhaps you will be able to profit,
Perhaps you will prevail.
You are wearied in the multitude of your counsels;
Let now the astrologers, the stargazers,
***And* the monthly prognosticators**
Stand up and save you
From what shall come upon you.
Behold, they shall be as stubble,
The fire shall burn them;
They shall not deliver themselves
From the power of the flame;
***It shall* not *be* a coal to be warmed by,**
***Nor* a fire to sit before!**
Thus shall they be to you
With whom you have labored,
Your merchants from your youth;
They shall wander each one to his quarter.
No one shall save you.

a. **Stand now with your enchantments and the multitude of your sorceries**: God challenged the sorcerers of Babylon to save the people from His judgment. After all, if they had real spiritual power, they should be able to. But their weakness in the face of the LORD's judgment would be exposed.

i. "For the Babylonians, sorcery also included a mood of complacency (v. 10), because the people relied on their magicians to predict the coming of the enemy and to defeat him. In Babylonia the intellectual and the magical were intertwined, the wise man being instructed in all the arts of the supernatural." (Grogan)

b. **Behold, they shall be as stubble, the fire shall burn them**: Not only could the sorcerers of Babylon not deliver others from God's judgment, but they also couldn't even deliver *themselves.* The fire of judgment that would come upon them would be severe; it would **not be a coal to be warmed by, nor a fire to sit before**.

i. "False religion may seem to offer the warmth of 'helpfulness', but it is not a *fire to sit by*, rather a *fire* which *will burn up*, a furnace of destruction." (Motyer)

ii. How many greatly underestimate the blazing strength of God's judgment! We see the same tragic thinking among those who say, "I won't mind going to hell. I'll party there with all my friends!" Some have even said that they will ski on the lake of fire! They think the fires of judgment will somehow be useful or comforting, but they are making a deadly mistake. Can there be a more dangerous sin?

c. **No one shall save you**: What a sobering final sentence. This is true for all who will not find their salvation in the LORD; if you will not look to Him and be saved, then certainly **no one shall save you**.

Isaiah 48 – Chastening and Mercy for Judah

A. The LORD clearly sees the hard hearts of His people.

1. (1-2) The LORD sees the hypocrisy of Judah.

"Hear this, O house of Jacob,
Who are called by the name of Israel,
And have come forth from the wellsprings of Judah;
Who swear by the name of the LORD,
And make mention of the God of Israel,
***But* not in truth or in righteousness;**
For they call themselves after the holy city,
And lean on the God of Israel;
The LORD of hosts *is* His name:

a. **House of Jacob, who are called by the name of Israel**: Judah should take notice of this opening statement. God identified His people as the **house of Jacob** – the name **Jacob** essentially meaning "deceiver, cheater" – and said they only have **the name of Israel**, not the character of **Israel**, which means "governed by God."

b. **And have come forth from the wellsprings of Judah**: The second statement of Isaiah 48 isn't any more complimentary to the southern kingdom of Judah. God reminded them of their tribal ancestor, **Judah**, who was noted for his cruelty (Genesis 37:26-27) and immorality (Genesis 38). The LORD spoke to His people and said, "You come from your father **Judah**." It was not a compliment.

c. **Who swear by the name of the LORD…but not in truth or in righteousness**: God exposed the sin of His people. They took His name, identified with **the holy city**, and gave the appearance that they did **lean on the God of Israel**. Yet it was only image, not reality, and God saw through the image to the reality.

i. Look at all Judah has: "An honoured name, an impeccable pedigree, a true religious allegiance, a privileged citizenship and a mighty God to rely on – but it is all unreal. There is no genuineness (*truth*) in it, nor does it satisfy the standards of God (*righteousness*)." (Motyer)

2. (3-5) The LORD sees that Judah has no excuse.

"I have declared the former things from the beginning;
They went forth from My mouth, and I caused them to hear it.
Suddenly I did *them*, and they came to pass.
Because I knew that you *were* obstinate,
And your neck *was* an iron sinew,
And your brow bronze,
Even from the beginning I have declared it to you;
Before it came to pass I proclaimed *it* to you,
Lest you should say, 'My idol has done them,
And my carved image and my molded image
Have commanded them.'

a. **I have declared the former things from the beginning…. Suddenly I did them, and they came to pass**: The LORD has shown Israel His power to declare the future in predictive prophecy. He did this **because I knew that you were obstinate**, knowing Israel's love of idolatry, He gave them irrefutable evidence.

b. **Lest you should say**: This means that Judah was without excuse. They knew the greatness and power of God, yet they still lived with only a religious image, without a spiritual reality.

3. (6-8) The LORD sees how deep the sinfulness of Judah is.

"You have heard;
See all this.
And will you not declare *it*?
I have made you hear new things from this time,
Even hidden things, and you did not know them.
They are created now and not from the beginning;
And before this day you have not heard them,
Lest you should say, 'Of course I knew them.'
Surely you did not hear,
Surely you did not know;
Surely from long ago your ear was not opened.
For I knew that you would deal very treacherously,
And were called a transgressor from the womb.

a. **You have heard; see all this. And will you not declare it?** It was as if the LORD was amazed that His people had seen all of His great power and glory, yet they still stood in stubborn rebellion against Him.

b. **For I knew that you would deal very treacherously, and were called a transgressor from the womb**: The LORD stated the reason why His people were so deeply sinful. They were sinners **from the womb**, so their sinfulness was deeply rooted.

i. It is a difficult concept for our individualistic ears, but the Bible teaches that we are sinners **from the womb**, and that we inherited a sin nature because we descend from Adam and sinned in Adam (Romans 5:12). It isn't our individual acts of sin that make us sinners; it is our descent from Adam. Our individual acts of sin merely prove that each of us is a **transgressor from the womb**.

B. The LORD's mercy to His undeserving people.

1. (9-13) The reason for the LORD's mercy to His people.

For My name's sake I will defer My anger,
And *for* My praise I will restrain it from you,
So that I do not cut you off.
Behold, I have refined you, but not as silver;
I have tested you in the furnace of affliction.
For My own sake, for My own sake, I will do *it*;
For how should *My name* be profaned?
And I will not give My glory to another.
Listen to Me, O Jacob,
And Israel, My called:
I *am* He, I *am* the First,
I *am* also the Last.
Indeed My hand has laid the foundation of the earth,
And My right hand has stretched out the heavens;
***When* I call to them,**
They stand up together.

a. **For My name's sake I will defer My anger**: Knowing how deeply sinful His people are, why would the LORD ever show mercy to His people? He does it for His **name's sake**. It isn't because Israel *deserves* mercy; indeed, mercy can never be deserved. God gives it to glorify Himself and to further His eternal purpose.

b. **I have refined you, but not as silver; I have tested you in the furnace of affliction. For My own sake, for My own sake, I will do it**: Why had a disobedient Israel felt refining fires from the LORD? Again, it was for the **sake** and honor and glory of the LORD.

i. Does it bother us to know that God allows trials and His refining fires in our lives for His **own sake**? We should remember that we are not at the center of the universe, but God is. Everything He does and allows furthers His eternal purpose.

c. **I am He, I am the First, I am also the Last…. My right hand has stretched out the heavens**: To answer any resentment among His people, God reminded them *why* He allowed things for His glory and to further His praise. He can do it because of who He is – the only True God, the God of all glory, the God of all eternity, the God of all Creation.

2. (14-19) The unfulfilled potential of God's disobedient people.

All of you, assemble yourselves, and hear!
Who among them has declared these things?
The LORD loves him;
He shall do His pleasure on Babylon,
And His arm *shall be against* the Chaldeans.
I, *even* I, have spoken; yes,
I have called him,
I have brought him, and his way will prosper.
Come near to Me, hear this:
I have not spoken in secret from the beginning;
From the time that it was, I *was* there.
And now the Lord GOD and His Spirit
Have sent Me.
Thus says the LORD, your Redeemer,
the Holy One of Israel:
"I *am* the LORD your God,
Who teaches you to profit,
Who leads you by the way you should go.
Oh, that you had heeded My commandments!
Then your peace would have been like a river,
And your righteousness like the waves of the sea.
Your descendants also would have been like the sand,
And the offspring of your body like the grains of sand;
His name would not have been cut off
Nor destroyed from before Me."

a. **The LORD loves him**: Though the LORD is the God of all glory and power, He is not some kind of narcissist. God is motivated by *love* for His people.

i. It is the LORD's *love* for us that makes Him want us to obey and praise Him. Love desires, quite properly, that things work according to their design and purpose. We were designed and purposed to obey and praise our Creator. God can call us to submit to Him, and honor Him, for *our good*, not to satisfy some need in God.

ii. So, just as much as it is the love of the LORD for His people that **shall do His pleasure on Babylon** – punishing this nation that set itself against His people – so it is the love of the LORD that allows the refining fires to touch His people.

b. **Come near to Me, hear this…. now the Lord GOD and His Spirit have sent Me**: This is the Servant of the LORD, the Messiah Himself speaking. Only He was **from the beginning**. The Messiah is pleading with His people.

i. "Finally (v. 16) another speaker mysteriously enters the prophecy. This verse has a number of features that have mystified commentators, who have been puzzled particularly by its final couplet. Young, Kidner, and other conservative commentators have argued that the new speaker introduced here (or in the whole verse) is in fact God's Servant, the Servant of the songs.... Perhaps he is introduced here because Cyrus' work is in fact simply a harbinger of the much greater deliverance he would bring to God's people." (Grogan)

c. **Oh, that you had heeded My commandments**: In light of His power and love for Israel, God laments their unfulfilled potential, unfulfilled because of their disobedience.

i. If they had only obeyed, **then your peace would have been like a river**. Peace as flowing, bountiful, and life-giving as **a river**.

ii. If they had only obeyed, then **your righteousness** would have been **like the waves of the sea**. Righteousness as certain, as unending, as reliable as **the sea**.

iii. If they had only obeyed, then **your descendants would have been like the sand**. Descendants as numerous and as dense in population as **the sand**.

iv. It is sobering to think what unfulfilled potential we have, and what disobedience or unbelief keeps us from everything God has for us. "Yes, I am deeply impressed with the simplicity of the road to revival. Just twenty-four hours' obedience in our lives, and we would be living in such a flood tide of Holy Spirit blessing that there would not be room enough to contain it!" (Redpath)

3. (20-22) Praise for the LORD's redemption – and a warning.

Go forth from Babylon!
Flee from the Chaldeans!
With a voice of singing,
Declare, proclaim this,
Utter it to the end of the earth;
Say, "The LORD has redeemed
His servant Jacob!"
And they did not thirst
When He led them through the deserts;
He caused the waters to flow from the rock for them;
He also split the rock, and the waters gushed out.
"*There is* no peace," says the LORD, "for the wicked."

a. **Go forth from Babylon! Flee from the Chaldeans! With a voice of singing**: Despite Israel's disobedience and unfulfilled potential, the LORD still loves them and will still free them from their captivity in Babylon. When they leave Babylon, they will go forth **with a voice of singing**.

b. **Declare, proclaim this, utter it to the end of the earth; say, "The LORD has redeemed His servant Jacob"**: God tells His people to declare His praises **to the end of the earth**. The whole world should know how great and merciful God is.

c. **"There is no peace," says the LORD, "for the wicked"**: Hand in hand with praise for the greatness of the LORD is a contrast – the destined misery **for the wicked**.

i. Often, it seems that the way of the **wicked** is peaceful. This was how it seemed to the Psalmist in Psalm 73; yet when he saw the end of the wicked, and gained perspective in the house of the LORD, he knew that ultimately, **there is no peace…for the wicked**.

ii. "Verse 22 is a refrain that occurs again in 57:21, and both times it comes at the end of a nine-chapter section." (Wolf)

iii. The broad section of Isaiah 40 through 48 focused on the promise of God's deliverance of His people from their captivity in Babylon, and the specific prediction of the Gentile king who would deliver them, Cyrus. Through the section, God shows that His desire to deliver His people proves His love, His ability to deliver His people proves His power, and His prophetic knowledge of the deliverer proves His uniqueness among all gods. Starting with Isaiah chapter 49, there is no longer a mention of Cyrus, now the focus is on the ultimate deliverer, the Messiah. Though there is still reference to the deliverance from Babylon's captivity, the real focus is on the ultimate deliverance the Messiah will bring.

Isaiah 49 – The Messiah's Mission

This chapter is full of our Lord Jesus Christ, and the words quoted could not possibly have their complete fulfillment in any other save in our Savior. (Alan Redpath)

A. The Messiah declares His mission.

1. (1-2) The call and the preparation of the Messiah.

"Listen, O coastlands, to Me,
And take heed, you peoples from afar!
The LORD has called Me from the womb;
From the matrix of My mother He has made mention of My name.
And He has made My mouth like a sharp sword;
In the shadow of His hand He has hidden Me,
And made Me a polished shaft;
In His quiver He has hidden Me."

a. **Listen, O coastlands, to Me**: As the context will show, these words come prophetically from the Messiah, the Servant of the LORD revealed in previous chapters. Here, He commands the **coastlands** – the distant lands of the Gentiles – to **listen** to Him.

b. **The LORD has called Me from the womb**: The Messiah, later revealed as Jesus Christ, was **called** from the **womb**. Actually, as shown in Micah 5:2, Jesus was called even *before* He was in Mary's womb, yet here He starts at the point which any man could most readily relate to.

c. **From the matrix of My mother He has made mention of My name**: This was fulfilled in Luke 1:31, where the LORD, through the angel Gabriel, declared the name of Jesus before the conception in Mary's womb.

d. **He has made My mouth like a sharp sword**: This means that the very words of the Messiah have power and authority. While some might need to brandish a weapon to show their authority, the Messiah needs only to speak.

e. **In the shadow of His hand He has hidden Me, and made Me a polished shaft; in His quiver He has hidden Me**: The Messiah prophetically proclaims that He is like a carefully made and polished arrow in the service of the LORD, ready to be used at the right time. This probably has reference to the "hidden" years of Jesus, when He lived in obscurity, as **a polished shaft** waiting in the **quiver** of the LORD.

2. (3-4) The Messiah's confidence in the LORD.

"And He said to me,
'You *are* My servant, O Israel,
In whom I will be glorified.'
Then I said, 'I have labored in vain,
I have spent my strength for nothing and in vain;
Yet surely my just reward *is* with the LORD,
And my work with my God.'"

a. **You are My servant, O Israel**: Since the rest of the context of this chapter indicates that this passage speaks of the Messiah, it is best to regard **Israel** as a reference to the Messiah. How can the LORD speak of the Messiah as **Israel**? First, because the Messiah *comes from* Israel, and is a representative of the nation. Second, because the Messiah *fulfills the name Israel*, which means, "governed by God."

i. "On the surface, the statement 'You are my servant, Israel,' explicitly identifies Yahweh's Servant as the nation Israel. But if that were the case, an apparent contradiction would arise in verses 5-6, in which the Servant's task is to bring Israel back to Yahweh and to the land... the view that 'Israel' is a title of the individual messianic Servant harmonizes most satisfactorily with the passage and context." (Lindsey)

b. **Then I said, "I have labored in vain, I have spent my strength for nothing and in vain; yet surely my just reward is with the LORD"**: The translators of the New King James do not believe these words belong in the mouth of the Messiah, because they do not capitalize the pronoun **my**, as they would if they believed it spoke of the Messiah. Yet these words can be set prophetically in the mouth of the Messiah, because surely Jesus was tempted by the discouraging thought that all His work was **in vain** and **for nothing**. Yet He triumphed over such temptation by declaring, **my just reward is with the LORD**.

i. When we consider what – and who – the Lord Jesus had to work with on this earth, we certainly must believe that one of the great temptations He faced was discouragement. This passage shows that even though He ministered in difficult and discouraging circumstances,

He never gave in to discouragement, but always put His trust in the LORD.

3. (5-7) The Messiah blesses Israel and the nations.

"And now the LORD says,
Who formed Me from the womb *to be* His Servant,
To bring Jacob back to Him,
So that Israel is gathered to Him
(For I shall be glorious in the eyes of the LORD,
And My God shall be My strength),
Indeed He says,
'It is too small a thing that You should be My Servant
To raise up the tribes of Jacob,
And to restore the preserved ones of Israel;
I will also give You as a light to the Gentiles,
That You should be My salvation to the ends of the earth.'"
Thus says the LORD,
The Redeemer of Israel, their Holy One,
To Him whom man despises,
To Him whom the nation abhors,
To the Servant of rulers:
"Kings shall see and arise,
Princes also shall worship,
Because of the LORD who is faithful,
The Holy One of Israel;
And He has chosen You."

a. **To bring Jacob back to Him**: This shows that an important aspect of the Messiah's mission was to bring Israel back to the LORD. This shows that ethnic Israel has an enduring place in God's plan, and that plan will be fulfilled when *all Israel will be saved* (Romans 11:26).

b. **It is too small a thing that You should be My Servant to raise up the tribes of Jacob...I will also give You as a light to the Gentiles**: Though part of the Messiah's mission is directed to Israel, He also has a mission **to the Gentiles**. What will the Messiah do for the Gentiles? **That You should be My salvation to the ends of the earth**. The Messiah would not simply *bring* salvation; He would **be...salvation to the ends of the earth**.

i. "Israel has light but needs restoration, while the Gentiles need both light and salvation." (Grogan)

c. **Thus says the LORD...to Him whom man despises, to Him whom the nation abhors**: The LORD speaks to His Messiah, and reveals that He will be One **whom man despises**, and **whom** His own **nation abhors**.

This is an important – yet lightly noted – prophecy of the rejection of the Messiah, by mankind in general and by Israel specifically.

d. **Kings shall see and arise, princes also shall worship**: Yet in the end, the Messiah will not be despised or abhorred. He will receive the worship and honor He deserves, because He is the **chosen** of the LORD.

4. (8-12) The glory of the Messiah's ministry.

Thus says the LORD:
"In an acceptable time I have heard You,
And in the day of salvation I have helped You;
I will preserve You and give You
As a covenant to the people,
To restore the earth,
To cause them to inherit the desolate heritages;
That You may say to the prisoners, 'Go forth,'
To those who *are* in darkness, 'Show yourselves.'
"They shall feed along the roads,
And their pastures *shall be* on all desolate heights.
They shall neither hunger nor thirst,
Neither heat nor sun shall strike them;
For He who has mercy on them will lead them,
Even by the springs of water He will guide them.
I will make each of My mountains a road,
And My highways shall be elevated.
Surely these shall come from afar;
Look! Those from the north and the west,
And these from the land of Sinim."

a. **In an acceptable time I have heard You, and in the day of salvation I have helped You; I will preserve You**: The LORD God extended His help and preservation to the Messiah all through His earthly ministry. Yet if there is any specific time that this promise was fulfilled, it was as Jesus died on the cross and trusted in the promise of resurrection.

i. It is beautiful to imagine Jesus comforting and strengthening His soul with these promises as He anticipated and endured the ordeal of the cross. He could *know*, based on this promise, that the LORD would hear, help, and preserve Him.

b. **And give You as a covenant to the people**: Jesus, the Messiah, doesn't merely *bring* a covenant; He *is* **a covenant to the people**.

c. **That You may say to the prisoners, "Go forth"**: Jesus' ministry set people free from bondage and imprisonment.

i. Jesus set the demon possessed free from the bondage of chains and demonic torture (Mark 5:1-15).

ii. Jesus set the sick and diseased free from the bondage of their infirmities (Luke 13:16).

iii. Jesus set the righteous dead captive in Hades free from their place (Ephesians 4:8).

iv. Jesus sets those in bondage to sin and the law free (John 8:33-36, Galatians 3:22-23).

d. **For He who has mercy on them will lead them, even by the springs of water He will guide them**: In an immediate sense, this refers to God's supply and sustaining of the exiles returning from Babylon to Judah, through the unseen hand of the Messiah. In the larger sense, it speaks of mercy and the provision of God for people as they return to Him in the last days, as they **shall come from afar**.

e. **I will make each of My mountains a road**: The mountains in the way of the returning exiles – both in near and far fulfillment – would seem to defeat the purpose of the LORD. But they will not.

i. Notice it says **each...mountain** (or, as in the King James Version, *all ... mountains*). "There is no exception in that great, but little word, *all.* There is nothing in life – no obstacle, no loneliness, no trial, no sorrow – which may not be a way into God's richest blessing. There is no situation of entanglement, nothing that you can possibly conceive, but this can be part of God's way to make His mountain a way of deliverance." (Redpath)

ii. Notice it says **My mountains**. The mountains in the way are still the LORD's mountains, allowed there for a purpose. And the purpose is not to torment you, or because He hates you. There is a loving, wise purpose for every mountain, and God wants to make **each of My mountains a road**.

iii. "[When you make] the commitment of your life to Jesus Christ without reservation, then you can go to meet your mountains and meet obstacles in Jesus – not to meet them outside Him, but in Christ. If you do that, then the mountain between you and God's land of blessing becomes the way into it." (Redpath)

f. **And these from the land of Sinim**: Some identify **Sinim** with a place in Egypt; others identify it with China. The idea is that God will bring back the captives (particularly in the far fulfillment) from every conceivable place.

i. "'Sinim' is probably Aswan, near the southern border of Egypt.... This assumes that 'Sinim' is derived from *sewenim*.... If the Masoretic Text is correct, a long standing interpretation connects Sinim with China." (Wolf)

ii. Grogan gives another perspective on **Sinim**: "It is most likely that Isaiah was being consciously obscure. Even unmapped places are known to God, and even from them he will gather his pilgrims."

B. The LORD's faithfulness to Zion.

1. (13-14) The LORD is praised for goodness to Zion – and an objection is raised.

Sing, O heavens!
Be joyful, O earth!
And break out in singing, O mountains!
For the LORD has comforted His people,
And will have mercy on His afflicted.
But Zion said, "The LORD has forsaken me,
And my Lord has forgotten me."

a. **Sing, O heavens! For the LORD has comforted His people**: It is simply assumed that the people the **LORD has comforted** will praise Him; here, the LORD calls for creation itself to add their voices in praise for all the Messiah has done.

b. **But Zion said, "The LORD has forsaken me"**: In the midst of this great praise for the Messiah and His saving work, **Zion** – speaking of the highest hill in Jerusalem, and the place of God's people by association – **Zion** objects. Zion believes, **"The LORD has forsaken me, and my Lord has forgotten me."**

i. The rest of Isaiah 49 and Isaiah 50 will answer this question. Because of their captivity in Babylon, Zion wonders "Does God really care about us?" God will answer, with strength and insight, this question that many have asked since.

2. (15-18) God does care, and the LORD proclaims His love and faithfulness to Zion.

"Can a woman forget her nursing child,
And not have compassion on the son of her womb?
Surely they may forget,
Yet I will not forget you.
See, I have inscribed you on the palms *of My hands*;
Your walls *are* continually before Me.

Your sons shall make haste;
Your destroyers and those who laid you waste
Shall go away from you.
Lift up your eyes, look around and see;
All these gather together *and* come to you.
***As* I live," says the LORD,**
"You shall surely clothe yourselves with them all as an ornament,
And bind them *on you* as a bride *does*.

a. **Can a woman forget her nursing child**: Though bizarre accounts of unspeakable cruelty surface from time to time, everyone knows that a **woman** will never **forget her nursing child**. Yet the LORD says, **Surely they may forget, yet I will not forget you**. The LORD's affection for His people is greater than the devotion a woman has for **her nursing child**.

b. **See, I have inscribed you on the palms of My hands**: This has an obvious and beautiful fulfillment in the nail-scarred hands of Jesus. As Jesus told Thomas in a post-resurrection appearance, *look at My hands* (John 20:27). When we see the nail-scarred hands of Jesus, we see how He has **inscribed** us on the **palms of** His **hands**. With such love, how could God ever forget His people?

c. **Your walls are continually before Me**: The **walls** refer to the walls of the city of Jerusalem, which figuratively speak of the health, the strength, the prosperity, and the security of God's people. God is always mindful of the condition of His people, despite the objections of a doubting Zion.

d. **Your sons shall make haste…. you shall surely clothe yourselves with them all as an ornament**: The LORD will bring back the exiled and captive sons of Zion to the Promised Land, and this will be **an ornament** for God's people. The LORD's love and faithfulness for Zion are also shown by His promise for their future. It isn't just demonstrated by the past and the present, but also by His future plans for them.

i. This promise was partially fulfilled in the return of the exiles from Babylon but will be ultimately fulfilled in the regathering of Israel in the last days.

3. (19-26) God does care, and He promises and affirms blessing for Zion.

"For your waste and desolate places,
And the land of your destruction,
Will even now be too small for the inhabitants;
And those who swallowed you up will be far away.
The children you will have,
After you have lost the others,

Will say again in your ears,
'The place is too small for me;
Give me a place where I may dwell.'
Then you will say in your heart,
'Who has begotten these for me,
Since I have lost my children and am desolate,
A captive, and wandering to and fro?
And who has brought these up?
There I was, left alone;
But these, where *were* they?'"
Thus says the Lord GOD:
"Behold, I will lift My hand in an oath to the nations,
And set up My standard for the peoples;
They shall bring your sons in *their* arms,
And your daughters shall be carried on *their* shoulders;
Kings shall be your foster fathers,
And their queens your nursing mothers;
They shall bow down to you with *their* faces to the earth,
And lick up the dust of your feet.
Then you will know that I *am* the LORD,
For they shall not be ashamed who wait for Me."
Shall the prey be taken from the mighty,
Or the captives of the righteous be delivered?
But thus says the LORD:
"Even the captives of the mighty shall be taken away,
And the prey of the terrible be delivered;
For I will contend with him who contends with you,
And I will save your children.
I will feed those who oppress you with their own flesh,
And they shall be drunk with their own blood as with sweet wine.
All flesh shall know
That I, the LORD, *am* your Savior,
And your Redeemer, the Mighty One of Jacob."

a. **For your waste and desolate places…will even now be too small for the inhabitants**: As the LORD brings the sons of Zion back to Israel, they will fill the land in a glorious way.

b. **There I was, left alone; but these, where were they?** The great blessing of the returning sons of Zion – in both near and far fulfillment – will come as an astounding surprise. God's blessing will seem to come from nowhere. Though the promise seems too good to be true, God confirms it with **an**

oath to the nations. God will rescue Israel from both their immediate and ultimate captivity.

i. **Kings shall be your foster fathers**: "Calvin and most expositors believe that the text teaches that one day the greatest in the nation will love and care for the children of the Church. This text has usually been made to serve as proof of the legitimacy of the church state (or state church); however, the prophet does not have the Church in mind here, but future Israel." (Bultema)

ii. Clarke on **They shall bow down to you with their faces to the earth, and lick up the dust of your feet**: "These expressions therefore of the prophet are only general poetical images, taken from the manners of the country, to denote great respect and reverence: and such splendid poetical images, which frequently occur in the prophetical writings, were intended only as general amplifications of the subject, not as predictions to be understood and fulfilled precisely according to the letter."

iii. "*Lick up the dust of thy feet* refers to the great honor which the great ones of the world will give Israel. It is mainly on the basis of this phrase that there is the practice of kissing the pope's feet." (Bultema)

c. **Even the captives of the mighty shall be taken away**: Babylon, the mighty empire, had taken Zion captive. But even they **shall be taken away**. God will show His strength and love for Zion by giving unto Babylon what Babylon gave unto Zion, even though they thought it unlikely, as shown by the question of Isaiah 49:24.

i. This was true for Zion when freed from the Babylonian captivity; it is even more true for those set free from captivity to Satan. Jesus spoke of spoiling Satan in Luke 11:21-22: *When a strong man, fully armed, guards his own palace, his goods are in peace. But when a stronger than he comes upon him and overcomes him, he takes from him all his armor in which he trusted, and divides his spoils.*

ii. "The pictures of eating *their own flesh* and drinking *their own blood* draw on the horrors of siege conditions. The reality is that those who oppose the Lord and his people experience the self destructiveness of sin – a recurring feature of the wars of the Lord." (Motyer)

Isaiah 50 – The Messiah's Steadfast Obedience

A. The Lord's question to Zion.

1. (1-2a) God does care and will lovingly confront those in Zion who doubted His care for them.

Thus says the Lord:
"Where *is* the certificate of your mother's divorce,
Whom I have put away?
Or which of My creditors *is it* to whom I have sold you?
For your iniquities you have sold yourselves,
And for your transgressions your mother has been put away.
Why, when I came, *was there* no man?
***Why*, when I called, *was there* none to answer?**

a. **Where is the certificate of your mother's divorce**: Essentially, God speaks to a doubting Zion, "You say I don't care about you anymore. You say I have divorced you. Very well then, produce the document. But there is none because I have not divorced you. You will see that **for your iniquities you have sold yourselves**. It is your own fault, and no one else's."

i. "The people of Israel in exile are likening themselves to a divorced wife, forgotten and forsaken of God. The Lord interrupts this kind of thinking, and breaks into it with a challenge to His people, saying: 'Where is the bill of divorcement? Produce it. Produce the bill and show me where I divorced you.' But Israel cannot do it. Of course she cannot find it, because He has never given it to her. God cannot divorce those whom He has taken into covenant relationship with Himself." (Redpath)

ii. "Divorce accuses unfailing love of failure; slavery accuses sovereign power of weakness and sovereign resources of inadequacy. The truth, however, is very different, for it was all a matter of due reward of *sins*." (Motyer)

b. **Why, when I came, was there no man?** Seeing that Zion's troubles come from their own disobedience, where is the **man** who will stand up for Israel? Who will contend their case before God?

i. Or, there may be another sense: "Here the Lord compares Himself to a man and father of a household who is treated shamefully by his own wife and children. When he came home, there was no one to welcome him and when he called, no one answered him. Hence, He who had the right to all their respect was treated as one without any rights." (Bultema)

2. (2b-3) God does care and reminds Zion of His power.

Is My hand shortened at all that it cannot redeem?
Or have I no power to deliver?
Indeed with My rebuke I dry up the sea,
I make the rivers a wilderness;
Their fish stink because *there is* no water,
And die of thirst.
I clothe the heavens with blackness,
And I make sackcloth their covering."

a. **Is My hand shortened at all that it cannot redeem?** The LORD now answers His own question. The answer to this rhetorical question is a definite, "No." Despite the doubts of Zion, the LORD's power and authority are beyond question.

b. **I clothe the heavens with blackness**: Heaven is in mourning, because of the sin and unbelief of God's people.

i. "Oh, the sorrow in the heart of God – the pang, the pain, the agony, the suffering – when His children sin!.... Sin in the lives of God's people clothes heaven with blackness and sackcloth." (Redpath)

ii. Spurgeon relates this to the crucifixion: "The last miracle recorded here, namely, that of covering the heavens with sackcloth, was performed by our Lord even when he was in his death agony. We read that, at high noon, the sun was veiled, and there was darkness over all the land for three black hours. Wonder of wonders, he who hung bleeding there had wrought that mighty marvel! The sun had looked upon him hanging on the cross, and, as if in horror, had covered its face, and travelled on in tenfold night. The tears of Jesus quenched the light of the sun. Had he been wrathful, he might have put out its light for ever; but his love not only restored that light, but it has given to us a light a thousand times more precious, even the light of everlasting life and joy."

B. The steadfast obedience of the Servant of the Lord, the Messiah.

1. (4-5) The care of God is dramatically shown in the Messiah's submission to the Lord.

"The Lord God has given Me
The tongue of the learned,
That I should know how to speak
A word in season to *him who is* weary.
He awakens Me morning by morning,
He awakens My ear to hear as the learned.
The Lord God has opened My ear;
And I was not rebellious,
Nor did I turn away.

a. **The Lord God has given Me the tongue of the learned**: The Messiah now prophetically speaks again, explaining that the Lord God has given Him the ability to speak wisely. But for what purpose? **To speak a word in season to him who is weary**. What a glorious use of **the tongue of the learned**.

b. **He awakens Me morning by morning**: The Messiah prophetically speaks of His daily, wonderful, deep fellowship with God the Father. It is in these times that Jesus heard from His Father, that He could say **He awakens My ear to hear as the learned**. The Messiah could speak with **the tongue of the learned** because in daily time with God He learned to **hear as the learned**.

c. **The Lord God has opened My ear, and I was not rebellious**: The Messiah, speaking prophetically, looks back to a custom described in Exodus 21:5-6, where a servant became a willing bondslave to his master. The sign of this willing servant was the ear opened by the piercing of an awl, done against the entry doorway of the master. This speaks of the total submission of the Messiah to the Lord God.

i. If, after the six years of servitude, a servant wished to make a life-long commitment to his master – in light of the master's goodness and his blessings for the servant – he could, through this ceremony, make a life-long commitment to his master. This was a commitment not motivated by debt or obligation, only love for the master.

ii. In the ceremony, the servant's ear would be pierced – opened – with an awl, in the presence of witnesses – then, *he shall serve him forever* (Exodus 21:5-6). Psalm 40:6 also speaks of this ceremony taking place between the Father and the Son, where the Psalmist speaks prophetically for the Messiah: *Sacrifice and offering You did not desire;*

my ears You have opened. Jesus was a perfect bond-slave to the Father (Philippians 2:7).

2. (6-9) The care of the LORD is shown in the courageous greatness of the Messiah's submission to the LORD.

I gave My back to those who struck *Me*,
And My cheeks to those who plucked out the beard;
I did not hide My face from shame and spitting.
"For the Lord GOD will help Me;
Therefore I will not be disgraced;
Therefore I have set My face like a flint,
And I know that I will not be ashamed.
***He is* near who justifies Me;**
Who will contend with Me?
Let us stand together.
Who *is* My adversary?
Let him come near Me.
Surely the Lord GOD will help Me;
Who *is* he *who* will condemn Me?
Indeed they will all grow old like a garment;
The moth will eat them up.

a. **I gave My back to those who struck Me, and My cheeks to those who plucked out the beard; I did not hide My face from shame and spitting**: This prophecy speaks in chilling detail of the sufferings of the Messiah. We know that Jesus was beaten on the back (Mark 15:15). We know Jesus was beaten on the face (Luke 22:63-65). We know that Jesus was mocked and spat upon (Mark 15:19-20).

i. There is no specific mention in the gospels of those **who plucked out the beard** of Jesus as part of His pre-crucifixion suffering, but from this passage in Isaiah we know it happened. What terrible agony Jesus endured! It is even more than what the gospel writers explain to us! "We have before us the language of prophecy, but it is as accurate as though it had been written at the moment of the event. Isaiah might have been one of the Evangelists, so exactly does he describe what our Saviour endured." (Spurgeon)

ii. "He suffered the deepest humiliation, for to pluck out the hair (of the beard) and to cover someone's face with spit was, according to Near-Eastern concepts, the most humiliating suffering that could be inflicted upon a man." (Bultema)

iii. "Many of us could give to Christ all our health and strength, and all the money we have, very heartily and cheerfully; but when it comes to a point of reputation we feel the pinch. To be slandered, to have some filthy thing said of you; this is too much for flesh and blood. You seem to say, 'I cannot be made a fool of, I cannot bear to be regarded as a mere impostor;' but a true servant of Christ must make himself of no reputation when he takes upon himself the work of his Lord. Our blessed Master was willing to be scoffed at by the lewdest and the lowest of men." (Spurgeon)

iv. Notice it carefully: **I gave My back** means that Jesus did it *voluntarily*. Can we still think that God does not care for us?

b. **For the Lord GOD will help Me**: In the midst of all this suffering, humiliation, and pain, the Messiah has an unshakable confidence in the help of the Lord GOD.

i. Can we have the same confidence in God? "It is pitiful for the Christian to refuse to suffer, and to become a fighting man, crying, 'We must stand up for our rights.' Did you ever see Jesus in that posture?" (Redpath) Instead, trust in the LORD and proclaim, **for the Lord GOD will help me**.

c. **Therefore, I have set My face like a flint**: Despite knowing the agony awaiting Him, the Messiah will have a steadfast determination to obey the Lord GOD and follow His way. His **face** will be set as hard as **a flint**, and nothing will turn Him aside.

i. This was exactly fulfilled in the life of Jesus, who was determined to go to Jerusalem, even knowing what waited for Him there. *Now it came to pass, when the time had come for Him to be received up, that He steadfastly set His face to go to Jerusalem.* (Luke 9:51)

ii. There are two kinds of courage – the courage of the moment, which requires no previous thought, and a "planned" courage, which sees the difficulty ahead and steadfastly marches towards it. Jesus had this kind of courage; He could see the cross on the horizon, but still set His **face like a flint**.

iii. Spurgeon has a wonderful sermon on this text titled, *The Redeemer's Face Set like a Flint*. These are his headings and points:

1. How the steadfast resolve of Jesus was tested.
    - By offers from the world.
    - By the persuasions of His friends.
    - By the unworthiness of His clients.
    - By the bitterness of the first few drops of suffering in Gethsemane.

- By the ease at which He could have backed out if He had wished to.
- By the taunts of those who mocked Him.
- By the full stress and agony of the cross.

2. How the steadfast resolve of Jesus was sustained.

- By His divine schooling.
- By His conscious innocence.
- By His unshakable confidence in the help of God.
- By the joy that was set before Him.

3. How to imitate the steadfast resolve of Jesus.

- When there is something right, stand for it.
- When you have a right purpose that glorifies God, carry it out.

d. **And I know that I will not be ashamed**: The courage of the Messiah isn't a passive resignation to fate. It is a confident assurance in the Lord God. He can set His **face like a flint** *because* He can say, **"I know that I will not be ashamed."**

e. **He is near who justifies Me; who will contend with Me?** This is the Messiah's way of anticipating the truth of Romans 8:31: *If God is for us, who can be against us?* If it isn't clear enough, He says it again: **Surely the Lord God will help Me; who is he who will condemn Me?**

i. In fact, the reason why Romans 8:31 applies to us is that it first applies to Jesus, and we are *in Christ.* If Jesus stands in this place of victory, then all those who are in Christ stand there also.

3. (10-11) The Servant of the Lord challenges all to submit to the Lord as He does.

**"Who among you fears the Lord?
Who obeys the voice of His Servant?
Who walks in darkness and has no light?
Let him trust in the name of the Lord
And rely upon his God.
Look, all you who kindle a fire,
Who encircle *yourselves* with sparks:
Walk in the light of your fire and in the sparks you have kindled—
This you shall have from My hand:
You shall lie down in torment.**

a. **Who among you fears the LORD? Who obeys the voice of His Servant?** Now the Messiah speaks to His people and challenges them to fear the **LORD** and obey **His Servant** – the Messiah Himself.

i. "Only he who knows how to obey can call others to obedience." (Motyer)

b. **Who walks in darkness and has no light? Let him trust in the name of the LORD and rely upon his God**: The Messiah guides His people into the path of light. Simply, **trust in the name of the LORD and rely upon** your **God**. It isn't necessarily easy, but it certainly is *simple.*

c. **Look, all you who kindle a fire**: We might think that this fire is a *positive* thing, but in light of the entire verse, it isn't positive. It is more like the *profane fire* of Nadab and Abihu described in Leviticus 10:1. If we **walk in the light of** that **fire and in the sparks you have kindled**, then we shall have **torment** from the hand of the LORD. This follows along the line of the Messiah's exhortation to **trust in the name of the LORD**, and not in our own efforts before God, which are like a *profane fire.*

i. "Those who 'light fires' refers to men who had their own schemes and their own gods. Because they had rejected the light of God's Word, they would face terrible punishment." (Wolf)

ii. "*Torment*...is only found here but its verb...guarantees its meaning of grief, pain and displeasure – even the 'place of pain' – specifically the pains of sin under the curse of God." (Motyer)

Isaiah 51 – Listen and Awake

A. "Listen to Me."

1. (1-3) Listen: The LORD's past faithfulness is a promise of future blessing.

"Listen to Me, you who follow after righteousness,
You who seek the LORD:
Look to the rock *from which* you were hewn,
And to the hole of the pit *from which* you were dug.
Look to Abraham your father,
And to Sarah *who* bore you;
For I called him alone,
And blessed him and increased him."
For the LORD will comfort Zion,
He will comfort all her waste places;
He will make her wilderness like Eden,
And her desert like the garden of the LORD;
Joy and gladness will be found in it,
Thanksgiving and the voice of melody.

a. **Listen to Me, you who follow after righteousness**: The LORD here speaks to His people, but His people have had trouble listening to Him. So, three times in this chapter, the exhortation is given: **Listen to Me**.

b. **Look to the rock from which you were hewn…. Look to Abraham your father, and to Sarah who bore you**: God counsels His people to look at His work in His people in days past. This is one of the great glories of God's word to us; it tells us how God has dealt with His people and gives us faith and guidance for His work in our lives – if we will **listen** to Him.

i. As Isaiah spoke to them here, God's people were in a discouraging place. They felt defeated, and the prophet told them to look at God's work in and through His people in days past.

ii. "Once a Christian gets eaten up with discouragement and unbelief it takes a great deal to shake him out of it. Those two emotions are the masterstrokes of Satan. So long as the child of God maintains an attitude of praise and trust in the Lord, then he is invincible. Once the devil gets him discouraged, that poor man is really going to take a knocking!" (Redpath)

c. **For I called him alone, and blessed him and increased him**: Abraham was one man, from one simple family. Yet God **called him alone** and **increased him**. This should remind His people today that God does not need many people to do a great work. He can bless and increase one man **alone**. Isaiah wanted God's people – in view here are the returning exiles from Babylon, and those of Israel's ultimate regathering – to not be discouraged of their small numbers but realize that just as He did great things with Abraham and Sarah, He can do great things through them.

d. **For the Lord will comfort Zion…He will make her wilderness like Eden…Joy and gladness will be found in it**: Remembering Abraham and Sarah should give them hope for this promise. The promise seems too good to be true, but by faithfully remembering God's work in people like Abraham and Sarah, they would have the faith to believe God's promise to them today.

i. This shows how *we* can benefit through God's work in the lives of *others*. When we hear of what God has done and is doing in the lives of others, it can build our faith for God's work in our own lives.

e. **He will make her wilderness like Eden, and her desert like the garden of the Lord**: This reminds us that though these promises had a near fulfillment in the return from Babylon's captivity, their ultimate fulfillment is in a regathered, blessed, and saved Israel in the millennium.

2. (4-6) Listen: The Lord's salvation and righteousness are forever.

"Listen to Me, My people;
And give ear to Me, O My nation:
For law will proceed from Me,
And I will make My justice rest
As a light of the peoples.
My righteousness *is* near,
My salvation has gone forth,
And My arms will judge the peoples;
The coastlands will wait upon Me,
And on My arm they will trust.
Lift up your eyes to the heavens,
And look on the earth beneath.

For the heavens will vanish away like smoke,
The earth will grow old like a garment,
And those who dwell in it will die in like manner;
But My salvation will be forever,
And My righteousness will not be abolished.

a. **I will make My justice rest as a light of the peoples**: When the Lord ultimately regathers, blesses, and saves Israel, He will also shine forth His **justice** to all the world – to Israel (**My nation**) and to all the nations (**the peoples**).

b. **For the heavens will vanish away like smoke, the earth will grow old like a garment**: These are references to phenomena surrounding the Second Coming of Jesus (Matthew 24:35, 2 Peter 3:7-10, Revelation 6:12-17). This is ultimately when the justice of the Lord will be displayed to Israel and all nations.

i. The judgment of the Lord isn't only evident in creation, but also upon humanity: **Those who dwell in it will die in like manner**.

c. **But My salvation will be forever, and My righteousness will not be abolished**: Those tied to the earth (not to heaven) will be cast away, and even the earth will **vanish away**. But never the **righteousness** or **salvation** of God. They remain and are more permanent than even the heavens and the earth. We don't have to be afraid that God will change His character (**My righteousness**) or His mind about us (**My salvation**). This is something to **listen** to.

3. (7-8) Listen: Fear God, not man.

"Listen to Me, you who know righteousness,
You people in whose heart *is* My law:
Do not fear the reproach of men,
Nor be afraid of their insults.
For the moth will eat them up like a garment,
And the worm will eat them like wool;
But My righteousness will be forever,
And My salvation from generation to generation."

a. **Listen to Me…Do not fear the reproach of men**: Knowing the permanence of the righteousness and salvation of the Lord, and the passing nature of the wicked (**For the moth will eat them up like a garment**), we should **listen** to God, and not be afraid of **men**.

i. I cannot imagine a true man saying, 'I love Christ, but I do not want others to know that I love him, lest they should laugh at me.' That is a reason to be laughed at, or rather, to be wept over. Afraid of being laughed at? Oh sir, this is indeed a cowardly fear!" (Charles Spurgeon, *The Secret of Love to God*)

ii. "Yet you are a coward. Yes, put it down in English: you are a coward. If anybody called you so you would turn red in the face; and perhaps you are not a coward in reference to any other subject. What a shameful thing it is that while you are bold about everything else you are cowardly about Jesus Christ. Brave for the world and cowardly towards Christ!" (Charles Spurgeon, *Cheer for the Worker, and Hope for London*)

b. **But My righteousness will be forever, and My salvation from generation to generation**: Knowing that the **righteousness** and **salvation** of the Lord are permanent and the opposition and mocking of the wicked are temporary, we should stand strong in faith. This is something to **listen** to.

B. "Awake, awake!"

1. (9-16) Wake up to the power and greatness of the Lord.

Awake, awake, put on strength,
O arm of the Lord!
Awake as in the ancient days,
In the generations of old.
***Are* You not *the arm* that cut Rahab apart,**
***And* wounded the serpent?**
***Are* You not *the One* who dried up the sea,**
The waters of the great deep;
That made the depths of the sea a road
For the redeemed to cross over?
So the ransomed of the Lord shall return,
And come to Zion with singing,
With everlasting joy on their heads.
They shall obtain joy and gladness;
Sorrow and sighing shall flee away.
"I, *even* I, *am* He who comforts you.
Who *are* you that you should be afraid
Of a man *who* will die,
And of the son of a man *who* will be made like grass?
And you forget the Lord your Maker,
Who stretched out the heavens
And laid the foundations of the earth;
You have feared continually every day

Because of the fury of the oppressor,
When *he has* prepared to destroy.
And where is the fury of the oppressor?
The captive exile hastens, that he may be loosed,
That he should not die in the pit,
And that his bread should not fail.
But I *am* the LORD your God,
Who divided the sea whose waves roared—
The LORD of hosts is His name.
And I have put My words in your mouth;
I have covered you with the shadow of My hand,
That I may plant the heavens,
Lay the foundations of the earth,
And say to Zion, 'You *are* My people.'"

a. **Awake, awake, put on strength, O arm of the LORD**: Here, the faithful believer calls out to the LORD, looking to Him for salvation. They know of God's great works in the past (**Awake as in ancient days**) but ask God to act on their behalf *now.*

i. Curiously, though it is phrased this way (and rightfully so), it is really more of a wakeup call to faith for the believer than an attempt to wake up God. Psalm 121:4 reminds us, *Behold, He who keeps Israel shall neither slumber nor sleep.* Yet it is still wonderful for the believer to call upon the LORD this way because it awakens *our* faith.

b. **Are You not the arm that cut Rahab apart, and wounded the serpent?** Among God's great works remembered is His defeat of **Rahab**. But when did God **cut Rahab apart**, and wound a **serpent**? The name **Rahab** means *pride*, and ever since the Garden of Eden, the **serpent** has been associated with Satan (Genesis 3:1-6). This speaks in poetic terms of God's victory over Satan, as it does also in Psalm 89:10.

c. **So the ransomed of the LORD shall return, and come to Zion with singing**: With every enemy defeated, and every obstacle taken care of, God's people are restored. This is another promise with both a near and an ultimate fulfillment.

d. **Who are you that you should be afraid of a man who will die**: With promises this glorious, and a God this mighty, we have no reason to fear man. Man can never undo God's plan for our lives. Compared to the great power of God, they are **like grass**.

e. **You forget the LORD your Maker...You have feared continually every day**: The two go together. We will only live in fear **continually every day** if we **forget the LORD**. When we **forget the LORD**, we forget His tender love and care for us: **I have covered you with the shadow of My hand… and say to Zion, "You are My people."** This is something to be *awake* to.

i. The phrase **I have covered you with the shadow of My hand** reminds us of how God covered Moses with His hand, as Moses hid in the rock and the LORD made His glory to pass before Moses (Exodus 33:17-23).

ii. The LORD would shelter and protect His people the same way. Nothing comes to us unless it has first passed through His counsel. "Ask the question again, 'Where is the fury of the oppressor?' And the answer comes, it is under the control of God. Even Satan, your fiercest foe, – God created him, God governs him, God can do with him just as he pleases. Then as to that poverty of which you are afraid, it will not come unless God permits it; and if it does come, the Lord can alleviate it." (Spurgeon)

2. (17-23) Wake up to the reality of God's wrath.

Awake, awake!
Stand up, O Jerusalem,
You who have drunk at the hand of the LORD
The cup of His fury;
You have drunk the dregs of the cup of trembling,
***And* drained it out.**
***There is* no one to guide her**
Among all the sons she has brought forth;
Nor *is there any* who takes her by the hand
Among all the sons she has brought up.
These two *things* have come to you;
Who will be sorry for you?—
Desolation and destruction, famine and sword—
By whom will I comfort you?
Your sons have fainted,
They lie at the head of all the streets,
Like an antelope in a net;
They are full of the fury of the LORD,
The rebuke of your God.
Therefore please hear this, you afflicted,

And drunk but not with wine.
Thus says your Lord,
The LORD and your God,
***Who* pleads the cause of His people:**
"See, I have taken out of your hand

The cup of trembling,
The dregs of the cup of My fury;
You shall no longer drink it.
But I will put it into the hand of those who afflict you,
Who have said to you,
'Lie down, that we may walk over you.'
And you have laid your body like the ground,
And as the street, for those who walk over."

a. **Awake, awake! Stand up, O Jerusalem**: This wakeup call is directed right at **Jerusalem**. God's people sometimes spiritually "fall asleep" and need to be awakened. Romans 13:11-12 says, *And do this, knowing the time, that now it is high time to awake out of sleep; for now our salvation is nearer than when we first believed. The night is far spent, the day is at hand. Therefore let us cast off the works of darkness, and let us put on the armor of light.*

b. **You who have drunk at the hand of the Lord, the cup of His fury**: A common picture of judgment in the Old Testament is the **cup** of God's wrath or **fury**. The idea is that God gives a cup "full" of His wrath to those who are under judgment, and they must drink it. Here, God calls Jerusalem to remember that they have **drunk at the hand of the Lord, the cup of His fury** when they experienced God's judgment through the Babylonians.

i. If possible, the image is even strengthened: **You have drunk the dregs of the cup of trembling, and drained it out**. Not only did Jerusalem drink the cup, but they also **drained it** – drinking down to the **dregs** at the bottom of the cup. They had experienced **desolation and destruction, famine and sword**, and this was God's cup for them.

ii. This powerful image was in the mind of Jesus when He prayed in the Garden of Gethsemane on the night before His crucifixion. When He prayed, *Father, if it is Your will, take this cup away from Me; nevertheless not My will, but Yours, be done* (Luke 22:42), He had in mind the cup of God's wrath He was about to drink – to the dregs – at the cross.

c. **See, I have taken out of your hand the cup of trembling, the dregs of the cup of My fury; you shall no longer drink it**: The Lord knows when to give the cup, and when to take it from His people. Now is time for their redemption and for the shame of their enemies, so the Lord promises, **I will put it into the hand of those who afflict you**. We should always be *awake* to God's timing and loving promises.

i. "When faith is weak men are in a dreadful hurry, but strong faith does not judge the Lord to be slack concerning his promise. As God achieves his purpose with infinite leisure, he loves a faith that is patient and looks not for its reward this day or the next. 'He that believeth shall not make haste': that is to say, he shall not be ashamed or confounded by present trials so as to rush upon unbelieving actions. Faith leaves times and seasons with God to whom they belong." (Spurgeon)

ii. **Who have said to you, "Lie down, that we may walk over you"**: This "barbaric practice...is well documented in the ancient Near East, featured especially, but not exclusively, in Assyrian inscriptions" (Grogan). But God will give this humiliation to those who humiliated His people.

Isaiah 52 – Joy When the LORD Reigns in Zion

A. When the LORD brings back Zion.

1. (1-3) Wake up to the LORD's redemption of Zion.

Awake, awake!
Put on your strength, O Zion;
Put on your beautiful garments,
O Jerusalem, the holy city!
For the uncircumcised and the unclean
Shall no longer come to you.
Shake yourself from the dust, arise;
Sit down, O Jerusalem!
Loose yourself from the bonds of your neck,
O captive daughter of Zion!
For thus says the LORD:
"You have sold yourselves for nothing,
And you shall be redeemed without money."

a. **Awake, awake! Put on your strength, O Zion**: The first **Awake, awake!** asked the LORD to *put on strength* (Isaiah 51:9). The second **Awake, awake!** asked Jerusalem to remember the LORD's judgments and promises. Now, the third **Awake, awake!** tells **Zion** to **put on strength** in light of the first two awakenings.

b. **Put on your beautiful garments…for the uncircumcised and the unclean shall no longer come to you**: Jerusalem could put on clothes of beauty and glory because the time of judgment was over. This shows that this passage has ultimate fulfillment in the very last days.

c. **You have sold yourselves for nothing, and you shall be redeemed without money**: Tragically, Jerusalem went after other gods like someone selling themselves **for nothing**. Yet, they would be blessed by being **redeemed without money**. God's mercy answered to their tragic sin.

i. **You shall be redeemed without money** – but it doesn't mean that it doesn't cost anything. The end of Isaiah 52 begins to describe the great cost of redemption, but it is a cost paid by another.

2. (4-6) The Lord vindicates His name before those who blaspheme His name.

For thus says the Lord God:
"My people went down at first
Into Egypt to dwell there;
Then the Assyrian oppressed them without cause.
Now therefore, what have I here," says the Lord,
"That My people are taken away for nothing?
Those who rule over them
Make them wail," says the Lord,
"And My name *is* blasphemed continually every day.
Therefore My people shall know My name;
Therefore *they shall know* in that day
That I *am* He who speaks:
'Behold, *it is* I.'"

a. **Those who rule over them make them wail…and My name is blasphemed continually every day**: God looks down and sees how the nations have oppressed His people. **Egypt** held them in captivity. The **Assyrian oppressed them**, and the Babylonians took them **away for nothing**, and ruled cruelly over them. Worse than how they treated God's people was their disrespect for the Lord Himself, whom they **blasphemed continually every day**.

b. **Therefore My people shall know My name**: Yet God will glorify Himself; first, He will do it among His own **people**. It is almost as if God said, "I can abide with My name being **blasphemed continually every day** among the nations. Just let it be known and praised among My people."

i. It is bad enough that the world does not know or honor God, but it is far more tragic when His own people do not know or honor Him.

c. **Therefore they shall know in that day that I am He who speaks**: In Isaiah's day, they *didn't* know that the Lord had spoken through His Word. This is to be expected among the nations but should never be so among God's people. But God promises there will come a day when **they shall know in that day that I am He who speaks**.

3. (7-10) The whole earth sees that the Lord redeems Zion.

How beautiful upon the mountains
Are the feet of him who brings good news,
Who proclaims peace,

Who brings glad tidings of good *things*,
Who proclaims salvation,
Who says to Zion,
"Your God reigns!"
Your watchmen shall lift up *their* voices,
With their voices they shall sing together;
For they shall see eye to eye
When the LORD brings back Zion.
Break forth into joy, sing together,
You waste places of Jerusalem!
For the LORD has comforted His people,
He has redeemed Jerusalem.
The LORD has made bare His holy arm
In the eyes of all the nations;
And all the ends of the earth shall see
The salvation of our God.

a. **How beautiful upon the mountains are the feet of him who brings good news**: Isaiah prophesies of the beautiful feet of those who bring the Gospel – the **good news**.

i. No wonder those who bring **good news** have beautiful feet; they are out partnering with God for the salvation of men. The **feet** speak of activity, motion, and progress, and those who are active and moving in the work of preaching the gospel have **beautiful…feet**.

b. **Who proclaims peace, who brings glad tidings of good things, who proclaims salvation, who says to Zion, "Your God reigns!"** The good news – news of peace, glad tidings, and salvation – can all be summed up in the glorious proclamation, **"Your God reigns!"** Where **God reigns**, **peace** reigns. Where **God reigns**, **glad tidings** reign. Where **God reigns**, **salvation** reigns. What a marvelous declaration – Our **God reigns.**

i. "The watchmen who see this happy return are probably those in Jerusalem who had long awaited the messengers. According to Ezekiel, the prophets were the leading 'watchmen' for the nation." (Wolf)

c. **The LORD has made bare His holy arm**: The thought beginning at Isaiah 51:9 (*Awake, awake, put on strength, O arm of the LORD!*) is completed. The LORD has shown His strength, the strength of **His holy arm**. No wonder it is a time for joy and singing.

i. "The expression *made bare his holy arm* is a Hebrew idiom derived from rolling up long, loose sleeves before starting to work. Then the arm was bared – the symbol of any mighty undertaking or initiative." (Bultema)

d. **In the eyes of all the nations; and all the ends of the earth shall see the salvation of our God**: God does not make His saving strength known just for those who are immediately rescued. He also does it as a witness and a testimony to others, so they can **see the salvation of our God**.

4. (11-12) A call to and confidence for those who will return.

Depart! Depart! Go out from there,
Touch no unclean *thing*;
Go out from the midst of her,
Be clean,
You who bear the vessels of the LORD.
For you shall not go out with haste,
Nor go by flight;
For the LORD will go before you,
And the God of Israel *will be* your rear guard.

a. **Depart! Depart! Go out from there**: Prophetically, this has both a near and a distant application. It was intended for the Babylonian captives Isaiah has prophesied to; but also, for those gathered to the LORD in the very end times. The call to separate from Babylon – both literal and spiritual – is a call to purity, for those **who bear the vessels of the LORD**.

i. 2 Timothy 2:21 has a wonderful promise for those **vessels of the LORD** who pursue purity: *Therefore if anyone cleanses himself from the latter, he will be a vessel for honor, sanctified and useful for the Master, prepared for every good work.*

b. **For you shall not go out with haste, nor go by flight; for the LORD will go before you**: When the salvation of the LORD comes – both in its near and its ultimate fulfillment – there is a sense of peace in the glorious work of the LORD, not a striving in **haste** or **by flight**.

B. The Servant of the LORD brings salvation to many nations.

1. (13-14) The exaltation and humiliation of the Servant of the LORD.

Behold, My Servant shall deal prudently;
He shall be exalted and extolled and be very high.
Just as many were astonished at you,
So His visage was marred more than any man,
And His form more than the sons of men.

a. **Behold, My Servant**: This passage, through the end of Isaiah 53, has in focus the **Servant** of the LORD. This is the Servant previously spoken of in Isaiah 42:1, and Isaiah 49:3 and 6.

i. The Ethiopian in Acts 8:34 asked a question about Isaiah 52:13 through 53:12: *Of whom does the prophet say this, of himself or of some other man?* This question is still asked today, and the answer is extremely important.

ii. Through the book of Isaiah, many have been called servants of the Lord in one way or another. This includes Isaiah himself (Isaiah 20:3), Eliakim (Isaiah 22:20), David (Isaiah 37:35), and Israel (Isaiah 41:8-9). But there is no doubt that the phrase is also used as a specific title for the Messiah, and this is what is in view here.

iii. The New King James Version rightly capitalizes **Servant**, because the context demonstrates this is a clear reference to Jesus. Additionally, Matthew quotes Isaiah 42:1-5 and plainly says it is a prophecy fulfilled in Jesus (Matthew 12:16-21). Additionally, in Matthew 8:16-17 the Bible takes this passage of Isaiah 52:13 through 53:12 and says it specifically applies to Jesus.

iv. Many are amazed that people – especially Jewish people – can read a chapter like this and miss Jesus. But really it isn't surprising. When we make up our minds about who Jesus is, it's easy to become blind and deaf to the plain, simple message of the word of God. Put away your pre-conceived notions and your cultural Jesus. Let the word of God tell you who He is.

b. **He shall be exalted and extolled and be very high**: The first words of the Lord in the mouth of the prophet regarding His Servant declare His victory. **He shall be exalted and extolled** means that the Messiah will triumph. There is no doubt about it. Before any of His suffering is announced, His glorious triumph is assured.

c. **His visage was marred more than any man**: This speaks of the cruel and vicious beating Jesus endured at the hands of His enemies. Jesus was beaten so badly on His face that He hardly looked like a man. The result was so shocking that **many were astonished** when they saw Jesus.

i. *Now the men who held Jesus mocked Him and beat Him. And having blindfolded Him, they struck Him on the face and asked Him, saying, "Prophesy! Who is the one who struck You?"* (Luke 22:63-64)

ii. The *astonishment* mentioned may be subtly referred to in the New Testament. On several occasions after His resurrection, the followers of Jesus were slow to recognize Him (Luke 24:16, John 20:14 and 21:4). On one occasion, they even seem awkward about His appearance: *Yet none of the disciples dared ask Him, "Who are You?" – knowing that it was the Lord.* (John 21:12) This may indicate that the *marred visage* of Jesus remained after His resurrection. We know that Jesus retained some of the scars of His crucifixion (Luke 24:40, John 20:25-28), perhaps this extends to His face as well. However, we should not be troubled by the thought of seeing an "ugly Jesus" in heaven. If those scars do remain, they will only *increase* His glory and beauty to our eyes, standing as badges of His matchless love.

iii. **More than any man** does not literally mean that by appearances, Jesus was beaten more severely than any man would ever be beaten. It is a poetic hyperbole used to express the terrible effect of the beating He endured.

2. (15) The cleansing of many nations.

So shall He sprinkle many nations.
Kings shall shut their mouths at Him;
For what had not been told them they shall see,
And what they had not heard they shall consider.

a. **So shall He sprinkle many nations**: Sprinkling is often associated with *cleansing from sin* in the Old Testament (Exodus 24:8, Leviticus 3:8, Numbers 19:21, Ezekiel 36:25). Here, the promise is that the work of the Messiah will bring cleansing to **many nations**.

i. The Messiah is certainly Israel's Messiah, yet He belongs to more than Israel. His saving, cleansing work will extend far beyond Israel to **many nations**.

b. **Kings shall shut their mouths at Him**: Though all will be astonished at His appearance, they will have nothing to say against Him. His glory and His great work will stop every word. When they spoke against Him before, it was in blindness, but now **what had not been told them they shall see**.

Isaiah 53 – The Atoning Suffering and Victory of the Messiah

"This chapter foretells the sufferings of the Messiah, the end for which he was to die, and the advantages resulting to mankind from that illustrious event.... This chapter contains a beautiful summary of the most peculiar and distinguishing doctrines of Christianity." (Adam Clarke)

A. The atoning suffering of the Servant of the LORD.

1. (1-3) How man saw the suffering Messiah.

Who has believed our report?
And to whom has the arm of the LORD been revealed?
For He shall grow up before Him as a tender plant,
And as a root out of dry ground.
He has no form or comeliness; and when we see Him,
***There is* no beauty that we should desire Him.**
He is despised and rejected by men,
A Man of sorrows and acquainted with grief.
And we hid, as it were, *our* faces from Him;
He was despised, and we did not esteem Him.

a. **Who has believed our report?** Prophetically, Isaiah anticipates at least two things here. First, he anticipates how strange and contradictory it seems that this suffering Messiah, whose *visage* is *marred more than any man*, is at the same time salvation and cleansing to the nations. Second, he anticipates the rejection of the Messiah, that many would not believe **our report**.

b. **To whom has the arm of the LORD been revealed?** In this context of the Messiah's suffering and agony, this line seems out of place. The **arm of the LORD** is a picture of His strength, power, and might. Yet we will see a Messiah weak and suffering. But the strength, power, and might of God will be expressed *in the midst* of this suffering, seemingly weak Messiah.

c. **He shall grow up before Him as a tender plant**: Jesus did **grow up**, as He *increased in wisdom and stature, and in favor with God and men* (Luke 2:52). But all the while, He was as **a tender plant** – of seeming weakness and insignificance, not like a mighty tree.

i. A **tender plant** is weak and vulnerable – unless it is **before Him**, that is, **before** the Lord God. In God's presence, that which seems to be weak is strong. If the plant is **before Him**, it doesn't even matter that the ground is dry. God will sustain it with His presence.

d. **As a root out of dry ground**: Jesus grew up in the Galilee region of Roman occupied Palestine. In respect to spiritual, political, and standard of living matters, it was indeed **dry ground**. God can bring the most wonderful things out of **dry ground**.

i. "Do not say, 'It is useless to preach down there, or to send missionaries to that uncivilised country.' How do you know? Is it very dry ground? Ah, well, that is hopeful soil; Christ is a 'root out of a dry ground,' and the more there is to discourage the more you should be encouraged. Read it the other way. Is it dark? Then all is fair for a grand show of light; the light will never seem so bright as when the night is very very dark." (Spurgeon)

e. **He has no form or comeliness…no beauty that we should desire Him**: Prophetically, Isaiah gives a more compelling description of Jesus than we find anywhere in the gospel accounts. Jesus was not a man of remarkable **beauty** or physical attractiveness (**comeliness**). This doesn't mean that Jesus was *ugly*, but it does mean that He did not have the "advantage" of good looks.

i. This means that when we try to attract people to Jesus through **form or comeliness**, or **beauty**, we are using methods that run counter to the nature of Jesus. "These days it appears that we must dress up the gospel to make it attractive. We have to use the methods of technique which must be smart, well-presented, streamlined. There must be something about the presentation of the gospel that will appeal to people...to what is called 'the modern mind.' I wonder if we stop to think that in our efforts to make the gospel message 'attractive' we are drawing a curtain across the face of Jesus in His humiliation? The only one who can make Him attractive is the Holy Spirit." (Redpath)

f. **He is despised and rejected by men, a Man of sorrows and acquainted with grief**: Jesus was not a "life of the party" man. It would be wrong to think of Him as perpetually sad and morose; indeed, He certainly showed great joy (such as in Luke 10:21). Yet He knew sorrow and **grief** so intimately that He could be called **a Man of sorrows**. This, among other reasons, made Him **despised and rejected by men**.

i. Most of our sorrow is really just self-pity. It is feeling sorry for ourselves. Jesus never once felt sorry for Himself. His sorrow was for others, and for the fallen, desperate condition of humanity.

ii. "He was also 'a man of sorrows,' for the variety of his woes; he was a man not of sorrow only, but of 'sorrows.' All the sufferings of the body and of the soul were known to him; the sorrows of the man who actively struggles to obey; the sorrows of the man who sits still, and passively endures. The sorrows of the lofty he knew, for he was the King of Israel; the sorrows of the poor he knew, for he 'had not where to lay his head.' Sorrows relative, and sorrows personal; sorrows mental, and sorrows spiritual; sorrows of all kinds and degrees assailed him. Affliction emptied his quiver upon him, making his heart the target for all conceivable woes." (Spurgeon)

iii. In 1 Timothy 3, one of the requirements for leaders in the church is that they be *soberminded*. This word describes the person who is able to think clearly and with clarity. They do not constantly joke but know how to deal with serious subjects in a serious way. It doesn't mean solemn and somber, but it does mean an appropriate seriousness.

g. **And we hid, as it were, our faces from Him; He was despised, and we did not esteem Him**: Because there was nothing outwardly beautiful or charismatic about the Messiah, mankind's reaction was to withdraw from Him, to despise Him, and hold Him in low esteem. This shows that men value physical beauty and charisma far more than God does, and when we don't see it, we can reject the ones God accepts.

2. (4-6) The Servant of the Lord bears our sin.

Surely He has borne our griefs
And carried our sorrows;
Yet we esteemed Him stricken,
Smitten by God, and afflicted.
But He *was* wounded for our transgressions,
***He was* bruised for our iniquities;**
The chastisement for our peace *was* upon Him,
And by His stripes we are healed.
All we like sheep have gone astray;
We have turned, every one, to his own way;
And the Lord has laid on Him the iniquity of us all.

a. **Surely He has borne our griefs and carried our sorrows**: At this point, the prophet does not have in mind the way the Messiah took our guilt and God's wrath upon Himself. Here, he has in view how the Messiah took our *pain* upon Himself. He made **our griefs** His own, and **our sorrows** as if they were His. The image is that He loaded them up and **carried** them on His back, so we wouldn't have to.

i. How many people carry around pain – **griefs** and **sorrows** – that Jesus really carried for them? He took them from us, but for it to do us any good, we must release them.

b. **Yet we esteemed Him stricken, smitten by God, and afflicted**: Curiously, this estimation was accurate. Certainly, the Messiah was **stricken**. He was **smitten by God**. He was **afflicted**. The problem was not in seeing these things, but in *only* seeing these things. Man saw the suffering Jesus but didn't understand the reasons *why*.

c. **But He was wounded for our transgressions, He was bruised for our iniquities; the chastisement for our peace was upon Him**: Yes, the Messiah was **stricken, smitten by God, and afflicted**. But now, the prophet explains *why*. It was *for us* – **for our transgressions...for our iniquities**. It was in our place that the Messiah suffered.

i. **Wounded** is literally "pierced through."

d. **And by His stripes we are healed**: Here, the prophet sees through the centuries to know that the Messiah would be beaten with many stripes (Mark 15:15). More so, the prophet announces that provision for *healing* is found in the suffering of Jesus, so **by His stripes we are healed**.

i. There has been much debate as to if Isaiah had in mind *spiritual* healing or *physical* healing. As this passage is quoted in the New Testament, we see some more of the thought. In Matthew 8:16-17, the view seems to be of *physical* healing. In 1 Peter 2:24-25, the view seems to be of *spiritual* healing. We can safely say that God has *both* aspects of healing in view, and both our physical and spiritual healing is provided for by the suffering of Jesus.

ii. However, some have taken this to mean that every believer has the right – the promise – to perfect health right now, and if there is any lack of health, it is simply because this promise has not been claimed in faith. In this thinking, great stress is laid upon the past tense of this phrase – **by His stripes we are healed**. The idea is that since it is in the past tense, perfect health is God's promise and provision for every Christian at this very moment, even as the believer has the promise to perfect forgiveness and salvation at this moment.

iii. The problem of this view – not even counting how it terribly contradicts the personal experience of saints in the Bible and through history – is that it misunderstands the "verb tense" of both salvation and healing. We can say without reservation that perfect, total, complete healing is God's promise to every believer in Jesus Christ, paid for by **His stripes** and the totality of His work for us. But we must also say that it is not promised to every believer *right now*, just as the totality of our salvation is not promised to us *right now*. The Bible says that we *have been saved* (Ephesians 2:8), that we *are being saved* (1 Corinthians 1:18), and that we *will be saved* (1 Corinthians 3:15). Even so, there is a sense in which we *have been healed*, are *being healed*, and one day *will be healed*. God's ultimate healing is called "resurrection," and it is a glorious promise to every believer. Every "patch-up" healing in this present age simply anticipates the ultimate healing that will come.

iv. What Christians *must not do* is foolishly "claim" to be healed, despite "mere symptoms" that say otherwise, and believe they are standing on the promise of Isaiah 53:5. What Christians *must do* is pray boldly and trust God's goodness and mercy in granting gifts of healing now, even before the ultimate healing of resurrection.

v. "'With his stripes we are healed.' Will you notice that fact? The healing of a sinner does not lie in himself, nor in what he is, nor in what he feels, nor in what he does, nor in what he vows, nor in what he promises. It is not in himself at all; but there, at Gabbatha, where the pavement is stained with the blood of the Son of God, and there, at Golgotha, where the place of a skull beholds the agonies of Christ. It is in his stripes that the healing lies. I beseech thee, do not scourge thyself: 'With his stripes we are healed.'" (Spurgeon)

e. **All we like sheep have gone astray; we have turned, every one, to his own way**: Here the prophet describes our *need* for the Messiah's atoning work. Sheep are stupid, headstrong animals, and we, like they, **have gone astray**. We have **turned** – against God's way, **every one, to his own way**.

i. We all have our own **way** of sin. The constant temptation is to condemn *your way* of sin, and to justify *my way* of sin. But each way that is our **own way** instead of the LORD's way is a sinful, destructive, damned way.

f. **And the LORD has laid on Him the iniquity of us all**: Here we see the partnership between the Father and the Son in the work on the cross. If the Messiah *was wounded for our transgressions*, then it was also **the LORD** who **laid on Him the iniquity of us all**. The Father judged our **iniquity** as it was **laid on** the Son.

3. (7-9) The suffering and death of the Servant of the LORD.

He was oppressed and He was afflicted,
Yet He opened not His mouth;
He was led as a lamb to the slaughter,
And as a sheep before its shearers is silent,
So He opened not His mouth.
He was taken from prison and from judgment,
And who will declare His generation?
For He was cut off from the land of the living;
For the transgressions of My people He was stricken.
And they made His grave with the wicked—
But with the rich at His death,
Because He had done no violence,
Nor *was any* deceit in His mouth.

a. **He was oppressed and He was afflicted, yet He opened not His mouth**: Despite the pain and the suffering of the Messiah, He never **opened...His mouth** to defend Himself. He was silent before His accusers (Mark 15:2-5), never speaking to defend Himself, only to glorify God.

b. **He was led as a lamb to the slaughter, and as a sheep before its shearers is silent, so He opened not His mouth**: The prophet repeats His previous point, that the Messiah will suffer without speaking to defend Himself. When Isaiah uses the phrase, **He was led as a lamb to the slaughter**, we should *not* take this as indicating that Jesus was a helpless victim of circumstances and was helpless as a lamb. Quite the contrary; even in His suffering and death, Jesus was in control (John 10:18, 19:11 and 19:30). Isaiah's point is that Jesus was **silent**, not helpless.

i. "If I were to die for any one of you, what would it amount to but that I paid the debt of nature a little sooner than I must ultimately have paid it? For we must all die, sooner or later. But the Christ needed not to die at all, so far as he himself was personally concerned. There was no cause within himself why he should go to the cross to lay down his life. He yielded himself up, a willing sacrifice for our sins." (Spurgeon)

c. **He was taken from prison and from judgment, and who will declare His generation?** This not only refers to the confinement of the Messiah before His crucifixion, but it also speaks of the fact that the Messiah died childless. There was no one to **declare His generation**.

d. **For He was cut off from the land of the living; for the transgressions of My people He was stricken**: This is the first indication in this passage that the suffering Servant of the LORD, the Messiah Himself, would *die*. Up to this point, we might have thought He would only have been severely beaten. But there is no mistaking the point: He is to be **cut off from the land of the living**.

i. "The phrase 'cut off' strongly suggests not only a violent, premature death but also the just judgment of God, not simply the oppressive judgment of men." (Grogan)

ii. This, among many aspects of this prophecy, demonstrates again that Isaiah cannot be speaking of Israel as the suffering Servant. As badly as Israel has suffered through the centuries, she has never been **cut off from the land of the living**. She has always endured, even as God promised Abraham.

iii. The prophet brings the point home again and again. The Servant of the LORD, the Messiah, suffers, but not for Himself, but for **the transgressions of My people**.

e. **And they made His grave with the wicked**: Jesus died in the company of **the wicked** (Luke 23:32-33), and it was the intention of those supervising His execution to cast Him into a common **grave with the wicked**.

f. **But with the rich at His death, because He had done no violence, nor was any deceit in His mouth**: Despite the intention of others to make *His grave with the wicked*, God allowed the Messiah to be **with the rich at His death**, buried in the tomb of the wealthy Joseph of Arimathea (Luke 23:50-56, Matthew 27:57-60).

i. The line **because He had done no violence, nor was any deceit in His mouth** is important. It shows that even in His death, even in His taking the transgressions of God's people, the Messiah never sinned. He remained the Holy One, despite all the pain and suffering. As a recognition of that, He was buried **with the rich at His death**, and would indeed be resurrected.

B. The victory of the Servant of the LORD.

1. (10-11) The Messiah's satisfaction.

Yet it pleased the LORD to bruise Him;
He has put *Him* to grief.
When You make His soul an offering for sin,
He shall see *His* seed, He shall prolong *His* days,
And the pleasure of the LORD shall prosper in His hand.
He shall see the labor of His soul, *and* be satisfied.
By His knowledge My righteous Servant shall justify many,
For He shall bear their iniquities.

a. **Yet it pleased the LORD to bruise Him; He has put Him to grief**: The prophet gloriously, and emphatically, states that the suffering of the Servant of the LORD was ordained by the LORD, even for His *pleasure!*

i. This was *God's doing!* **He has put Him to grief**! Jesus was no victim of circumstance or at the mercy of political or military power. It was the planned, ordained work of the LORD God, prophesied by Isaiah hundreds of years before it happened. This was *God's victory*, not Satan's or man's triumph.

ii. As Paul says in 2 Corinthians 5:19, *God was in Christ reconciling the world to Himself*. The Father and the Son worked together at the cross. Though Jesus was *treated* as if He were an enemy of God, He was not. Even as Jesus was punished as if He were a sinner, He was performing the most holy service to God the Father ever offered. This is why Isaiah can say, **yet it pleased the LORD to bruise Him** (Isaiah 53:10). In and of itself, the suffering of the Son did not please the Father. But as it accomplished the work of *reconciling the world to Himself*, it was completely pleasing to God the Father.

b. **When you make His soul an offering for sin**: The Hebrew speaks of a specific, sacrificial sin-offering as described in Leviticus chapter 5. The idea of a substitutionary atonement for sin cannot be more specifically stated.

i. And it was this – the becoming of the sin-sacrifice – more than the physical suffering that Jesus dreaded. "My Lord suffered as you suffer, only more keenly; for he had never injured his body or soul by any act of excess, so as to take off the edge from his sensitiveness. His was the pouring out of a whole soul in all the phases of suffering into which perfect souls can pass. He felt the horror of sin as we who have sinned could not feel it, and the sight of evil afflicted him much more than it does the purest among us." (Spurgeon)

c. **He shall see His seed, He shall prolong His days, and the pleasure of the LORD shall prosper in His hand**: The death, the burial, the offering of the Messiah does not end the story. He lives on! He lives to **see His seed**, His spiritual descendants. **He shall prolong His days**, and not be under the curse of death. And the life He lives after His death and burial is glorious; His life shall be lived prospering in **the pleasure of the LORD**.

d. **He shall see the labor of His soul, and be satisfied**: The Messiah will look upon His work – with full view of **the travail of His soul** – and in the end, He shall **be satisfied**. The Messiah will have no regrets. Every bit of the suffering and agony was worth it and brought about a satisfactory result.

i. As the last lines to the hymn by Maltbie Babcock put it:

This is my Father's world:
The battle is not done;
Jesus who died shall be satisfied,
And earth and heaven be one.

e. **By His knowledge My righteous Servant shall justify many, for He shall bear their iniquities**: It is in knowing the Messiah, in both who He is and what He has done, that makes us justified before God.

2. (12) The Messiah's work and reward.

Therefore I will divide Him a portion with the great,
And He shall divide the spoil with the strong,
Because He poured out His soul unto death,
And He was numbered with the transgressors,
And He bore the sin of many,
And made intercession for the transgressors.

a. **Therefore I will divide Him a portion with the great, and He shall divide the spoil with the strong**: The Messiah's glorious work will be rewarded. With the image of dividing the spoil after a victorious battle, we see that the Messiah ultimately triumphs.

i. Paul described this ultimate triumph in Philippians 2:10-11: *That at the name of Jesus every knee should bow, of those in heaven, and of those on earth, and of those under the earth, and that every tongue should confess that Jesus Christ is Lord, to the glory of God the Father.* That is a glorious reward.

ii. "It is a strange fact that I am going to declare, but it is not less true than strange: according to our text the extraordinary glories of Christ, as Saviour, have all been earned by his connection with human sin. He has gotten his most illustrious splendour, his brightest jewels, his divinest crowns, out of coming into contact with this poor fallen race." (Spurgeon)

iii. In the end, the sufferings and humiliation of Jesus only bring Him *more* glory and majesty! "I do see that out of this dunghill of sin Christ has brought this diamond of his glory by our salvation. If there had been no sinners, there could not have been a Saviour. If no sin, no pouring out of the soul unto death; and if no pouring out of the soul unto death, no dividing a portion with the great. If there had been no guilt, there had been no act of expiation. In the wondrous act of expiation by our great Substitute, the Godhead is more gloriously revealed than in all the creations and providences of the divine power and wisdom." (Spurgeon)

iv. Who does the Messiah **divide the spoil** with? **With the strong**; those strong in Him. We can share in the spoil of Jesus' victory! *If children, then heirs; heirs of God and joint heirs with Christ, if indeed we suffer with Him, that we may also be glorified together.* (Romans 8:17)

b. **Because He poured out His soul unto death**: This speaks of the *totality* of Jesus' sacrifice on the cross. **Poured out** means that it was all gone. There was nothing left, nothing more He could give.

i. "'He hath poured out his soul unto death.' I will say no more about it, except that you see how complete it was. Jesus gave poor sinners everything. His every faculty was laid out for them. To his last rag he was stripped upon the cross. No part of his body or of his soul was kept back from being made a sacrifice. The last drop, as I said before, was poured out till the cup was drained. He made no reserve: he kept not back even his innermost self: 'He hath poured out his soul unto death.'" (Spurgeon)

c. **He was numbered with the transgressors**: Jesus could never become a sinner; He could never be a transgressor Himself. Yet willingly, loving, **He was numbered with the transgressors**. Is there a rollcall taken for **transgressors**? Jesus says, "Put My name down with them." We would be shocked if a godly woman looked at a list of prostitutes and said, "Put my name down among them." Or what if a godly man looked at a list of murderers and said, "Number me among them." But that is what Jesus did for us, only to an even greater degree.

d. **He bore the sin of many**: Over and over again, the prophet emphasizes the point. The Servant of the Lord, the Messiah, suffers *on behalf of* and *in the place of* guilty sinners.

e. **And made intercession for the transgressors**: We know that presently, Jesus has a ministry of intercession (Hebrews 7:25). But Hebrews 7:25 speaks of intercession for the saints. This passage probably refers to Jesus' prayers on the cross itself.

i. This means the work of the Messiah is made available to **transgressors**. It is when we see ourselves as **transgressors** that we can reach out and receive His salvation.

Isaiah 54 – The Restoration of Israel, the Wife of the LORD

"Try and suck all the sweetness that you can out of this chapter while we read it. The personal application of a promise to the heart by the Holy Spirit is that which is wanted. The honey in Jonathan's wood never enlightened his eyes until he dipped the point of his rod into it and tasted it. Try and do the same. This chapter is the wood wherein every bough doth drip with virgin honey. Sip: taste, and be satisfied." (Charles Spurgeon)

A. The LORD speaks to Israel as His wife.

1. (1-3) Israel will be restored like a barren woman who bears many children.

"Sing, O barren,
You *who* have not borne!
Break forth into singing, and cry aloud,
You *who* have not labored with child!
For more *are* the children of the desolate
Than the children of the married woman," says the LORD.
"Enlarge the place of your tent,
And let them stretch out the curtains of your dwellings;
Do not spare;
Lengthen your cords,
And strengthen your stakes.
For you shall expand to the right and to the left,
And your descendants will inherit the nations,
And make the desolate cities inhabited.

a. **Sing, O barren, you who have not borne**: In ancient Israel, the **barren** woman carried an enormous load of shame and disgrace. Here, the LORD likens captive Israel to a **barren** woman who can now **sing** – because now **more are the children of the desolate than the children of the married woman**.

i. The Babylonian exile and captivity meant more than oppression for Israel; it meant shame, disgrace, and humiliation. God promises a glorious release from not only the exile and captivity, but also from the shame, disgrace, and humiliation.

ii. This passage is quoted by the Apostle Paul in Galatians 4:27, in reference to the miraculous "birth" of those under the New Covenant. Paul also probably intended the phrase **more are the children** to also indicate that the children of the New Covenant would outnumber the children of the Old Covenant.

b. **Enlarge the place of your tent**: The curse and shame of barrenness would be so completely broken, and Israel would be so fruitful, that they would have to expand their living space. This would be of particular comfort to the returning Babylonian exiles, who felt themselves small in number and weak. This promise would strengthen them.

2. (4-6) Israel will be restored like a widow who is rescued from her reproach.

"Do not fear, for you will not be ashamed;
Neither be disgraced, for you will not be put to shame;
For you will forget the shame of your youth,
And will not remember the reproach of your widowhood anymore.
For your Maker *is* your husband,
The Lord of hosts *is* His name;
And your Redeemer *is* the Holy One of Israel;
He is called the God of the whole earth.
For the Lord has called you
Like a woman forsaken and grieved in spirit,
Like a youthful wife when you were refused,"
Says your God.

a. **And will not remember the reproach of your widowhood anymore**: Just as God compared the disgrace of Israel to the shame of barrenness, now He compares their humiliation to the **reproach** of **widowhood**. Here, the Lord promises rescue from Israel's shame.

i. "*Shame…disgrace…humiliated* represent three synonymous Hebrew verbs sharing the fundamental idea of disappointed hopes, the embarrassment of expecting – even publicly announcing – one thing and then reaping another." (Motyer)

b. **For your Maker is your husband**: Though Israel might have been regarded as forsaken as a widow, the Lord promises to stand in the place of her **husband**.

i. Through the centuries, many a hurting woman has taken this promise for herself. Forsaken by a husband, or forsaken of a husband, they have found beautiful comfort in the promise that God would be a **husband** to them, when all others forsook them. The principle is true; God will supply and meet our emotional needs, and rescue us from our disgrace and shame, when others have forsaken us.

c. **The LORD of hosts is His name**: To comfort and strengthen His people, God reminds them of how glorious of a Savior He is. He is their **Maker**, He is the **LORD of hosts**, He is their **Redeemer**, He is the **Holy One of Israel**, and **He is called the God of the whole earth**. Not only does God supply a husband, but a great one – Himself.

i. The promise that the LORD will meet our needs when others forsake us does not leave us to a place of "second best." The LORD God can be a *greater* husband than any man can be. This is something for every *single* woman to remember and something no *married* woman should forget. An earthly husband can never fulfill every need that the great Heavenly Husband can.

3. (7-8) God explains His restoration of Israel.

"For a mere moment I have forsaken you,
But with great mercies I will gather you.
With a little wrath I hid My face from you for a moment;
But with everlasting kindness I will have mercy on you,"
Says the LORD, your Redeemer.

a. **For a mere moment I have forsaken you**: God never really forsook Israel, yet He recognized that they *felt* **forsaken**. God said, "**for a mere moment I** allowed you to feel that I **have forsaken you**."

b. **But with great mercies I will gather you**: The **forsaken** is in the *present* tense; the **great mercies** are in the *future* tense. But they are real, and give Israel cause to set their hope and trust in the LORD, though they feel forsaken at the moment.

c. **I hid My face from you for a moment; but with everlasting kindness I will have mercy on you**: The contrast is between the **moment** of feeling forsaken and the **everlasting** nature of the kindness that will come. When we feel tried and forsaken, we should recognize that it is just for a **moment**, and the **everlasting** blessing will certainly come.

B. Comfort and assurance to restored Israel.

1. (9-10) A promise to never forsake Israel.

"For this is like the waters of Noah to Me;
For as I have sworn
That the waters of Noah would no longer cover the earth,
So have I sworn
That I would not be angry with you, nor rebuke you.
For the mountains shall depart
And the hills be removed,
But My kindness shall not depart from you,
Nor shall My covenant of peace be removed,"
Says the LORD, who has mercy on you.

a. **For this is like the waters of Noah to Me**: Just as God promised that the flood waters of Noah's day would not cover the earth forever, so will His anger recede from Israel.

b. **For the mountains shall depart…but My kindness shall not depart from you**: Flood waters recede, and mountains do not. But even if **the mountains shall depart**, even if **the hills be removed**, the **kindness** of the LORD to His people will never **depart**. The **kindness** of the LORD is more certain than the **mountains** and the **hills**, and His **covenant of peace** is surer.

2. (11-17) Promises of prosperity, peace, and protection.

"O you afflicted one,
Tossed with tempest, *and* not comforted,
Behold, I will lay your stones with colorful gems,
And lay your foundations with sapphires.
I will make your pinnacles of rubies,
Your gates of crystal,
And all your walls of precious stones.
All your children *shall be* taught by the LORD,
And great *shall be* the peace of your children.
In righteousness you shall be established;
You shall be far from oppression, for you shall not fear;
And from terror, for it shall not come near you.
Indeed they shall surely assemble, *but* not because of Me.
Whoever assembles against you shall fall for your sake.
Behold, I have created the blacksmith
Who blows the coals in the fire,
Who brings forth an instrument for his work;
And I have created the spoiler to destroy.
No weapon formed against you shall prosper,
And every tongue *which* rises against you in judgment

You shall condemn.
This is the heritage of the servants of the Lord,
And their righteousness *is* from Me,"
Says the Lord.

a. **O you afflicted one, tossed with tempest and not comforted**: God cares about the **afflicted one**. He cares about the one **tossed with tempest**. He cares about the one who is **not comforted**. When someone is in this place – **afflicted**, **tossed**, and **not comforted** – it is easy for them to believe God doesn't care. But He does, and He gives precious promises to give strength.

b. **Behold, I will lay your stones with colorful gems…sapphires…. rubies…crystal**: God will lavish riches upon the hurting and afflicted. When someone feels afflicted, tossed, and not comforted, they feel *poor*, no matter how much money they have in the bank. God promises to make the afflicted truly *rich*.

c. **All your children shall be taught by the Lord, and great shall be the peace of your children**: When we are afflicted, tossed, and not comforted, we feel bad not just for ourselves, but also for our **children**. God gives precious assurance not only for us but also quiets our fears for our **children**.

d. **In righteousness you shall be established…you shall not fear…. whoever assembles against you shall fall for your sake**: God promises those who are afflicted, tossed, and not comforted will find protection and security in Him.

e. **No weapon formed against you shall prosper**: The sovereign God – who **created the blacksmith**, who **created the spoiler to destroy** – also has the power to protect. He can promise that **no weapon formed against you shall prosper**. Whatever weapon is raised against God's people is destined to be destroyed itself. God will ultimately even protect His people from criticism; indeed, **every tongue which rises against you in judgment you shall condemn**.

i. The Lord will not allow the **weapon formed against** His servants to **prosper**. Sometimes this means the Lord takes the **weapon** out of the hand of the enemy of His servants. Sometimes it means that God allows the **weapon** to strike but brings a greater good out of it than the pain of the immediate blow. In allowing this, God will not allow the **weapon** to **prosper** but transforms the violent sword into a trowel for building His kingdom.

ii. The **tongue which rises against you** can really hurt. "Satan leaves no stone unturned against the Church of God. He uses not simply the hand; but, what is oftener a sharper weapon, the tongue. We can bear a blow, sometimes, but we cannot endure an insult. There is a great power in the tongue. We can rise from a blow which smote us to the ground; but we cannot so easily recover from slander, that lays the character low." (Spurgeon) Yet, we can trust in the LORD's triumph. "The more accusers, the more acquittals; the more slander, the more honour; so the enemy may slander us as much as he pleases." (Spurgeon)

iii. This is not a blanket promise for any churchgoer. The LORD specifically says, **this is the heritage of the servants of the LORD**. Are you a **servant of the LORD**? Then you can rest easy in His promised protection. The LORD also says that this is a promise for those whose **righteousness is from Me** – from the LORD Himself – and not from themselves. When a person understands that their righteousness is really from the LORD, they are much more comfortable in letting the LORD protect their righteousness.

Isaiah 55 – An Invitation to Receive the Glory of the LORD's Restoration

A. An invitation to receive blessing.

1. (1-2) An invitation to be richly fed.

"Ho! Everyone who thirsts,
Come to the waters;
And you who have no money,
Come, buy and eat.
Yes, come, buy wine and milk
Without money and without price.
Why do you spend money for *what is* not bread,
And your wages for *what* does not satisfy?
Listen carefully to Me, and eat *what is* good,
And let your soul delight itself in abundance.

a. **Ho**: The prophet calls out, loud and clear, to all that can hear. This is an important announcement and is therefore prefaced with this unique call.

i. "Ho! – this is the gospel note; a short, significant appeal, urging you to be wise enough to attend to your own interests. Oh, the condescension of God! That he should, as it were, become a beggar to his own creature, and stoop from the magnificence of his glory to cry, 'Ho!' to foolish and ungrateful men!" (Spurgeon)

b. **Everyone who thirsts, come to the waters**: It is an invitation to **everyone** – specifically, to **everyone who thirsts**. Only those who thirst will **come to the waters**. If we aren't thirsty for what the LORD can give us, then we will never **come** to His **waters**.

i. Jesus may have had this passage from Isaiah in mind when He cried out, *If anyone thirsts, let him come to Me and drink.* (John 7:37)

c. **You who have no money, come, buy, and eat**: Those who do thirst, and answer the Lord's invitation, don't need to bring money. Their money won't really do them any good. They can simply bring their trust and faith and receive what God has to give them.

d. **Waters…. wine…milk**: It's all free. It isn't that the *entrance* into the Christian life is free, and then we must be charged to *advance* in the Christian life. It's all free; our growth is just as much a gift of grace as our salvation.

i. "You are not permitted to drink freely of water, and then to purchase wine. You are not invited to come and eat freely that which is good, and then to spend your labour for that which is fat. No, the richest dainties of God's house are as free as the bread he gives to hungry souls." (Spurgeon)

e. **Why do you spend money for what is not bread, and your wages for what does not satisfy?** In His invitation, God asked His people to ask themselves – "Why do I spend money for what can't **satisfy**?" This is a remarkably relevant question, in light of all the things we can pour our time and money and effort into – things which will never satisfy the way the Lord can satisfy.

f. **Listen carefully to Me, and eat what is good, and let your soul delight itself in abundance**: The invitation is clear. The offer is made, the provision is made, and everything is available – but we must still do some things.

i. First, we must **listen carefully**. The satisfaction God promises eludes those who will not both listen and listen **carefully**. It takes time, attention, and effort to **listen carefully**, and some aren't willing to do this.

ii. Second, we must **eat what is good**. This requires some discernment. We must choose **what is good**, and then **eat** that. Many just simply eat whatever spiritual meal is set before them, without taking care to see that it **is good**.

iii. Third, we must **let your soul delight itself in abundance**. Even when we **listen**, even when we **eat what is good**, we still must **let** our **soul delight itself in abundance**. You can sit down at a great spiritual meal, but by your stubborn or bad attitude, simply *not* **let your soul delight itself in abundance**.

2. (3-5) An invitation to be wonderfully led.

Incline your ear, and come to Me.
Hear, and your soul shall live;
And I will make an everlasting covenant with you—

The sure mercies of David.
Indeed I have given him *as* a witness to the people,
A leader and commander for the people.
Surely you shall call a nation you do not know,
And nations *who* do not know you shall run to you,
Because of the LORD your God,
And the Holy One of Israel;
For He has glorified you."

a. **Incline your ear**: The thought carries over from the idea of *let your soul delight itself in abundance*. Whoever will genuinely "feast" upon the word must consciously **incline** their **ear** towards what God will say. This explains why two people can listen to the same message, and one benefit and the other not. Often, the one who did not benefit simply did not **incline** their **ear** to the LORD.

b. **Hear, and your soul shall live**: The *benefit* from inclining your ear to God is impressive. When we do it, we have life for our **soul**.

c. **And I will make an everlasting covenant with you – the sure mercies of David**: For the one who will listen to the LORD, God promises a covenant. From Isaiah's perspective, this covenant is *still in the future* (**I will make**). The covenant is also characterized by **the sure mercies of David**.

i. God showed His great mercy to David; not only by sparing David's life when he was guilty of murder and adultery, but also in blessings and preserving and guiding David every day of his life. If God promises us the same mercy He showed to David, we are blessed indeed.

ii. As well, the **mercies of David** are **sure**. They are certain. God never gave up on David, never stopped showing him mercy. We can count on God when He promises to us the **sure mercies of David**.

d. **I have given him as a witness to the people, a leader and a commander for the people**: God promised the blessing of *good and wise leadership* as a part of His **sure mercies**. God gave David and his remarkable leadership as a gift to Israel; here God promised that He would keep giving this gift according to the pattern shown in David.

i. David was a **witness** in the sense that he had a real relationship, a real experience with God, and could speak to Israel as a **witness** of what he had seen and heard in that relationship with God. Notice that David was a **witness to the people**. A witness **to**, not *of* the people. David did not lead through popularity polls or just giving the people what they wanted. He witnessed something from God, and he gave testimony of it **to the people**.

ii. David was a **leader** for Israel, leading them spiritually, politically, and militarily. He led both by his godly example and his shepherd's heart. Notice that David was a **leader** and a **commander for the people**. Not a leader and a commander **of** the people, but **for the people**. He led with a shepherd's heart that genuinely desired God's best for the people.

iii. It's curious that David is used here as God's prototype for a leader. Curious in many ways, because David's reign can be seen as quite troubled. He came to the throne of Israel through much struggle and difficulty. He slipped into terrible scandal, marked by murder and adultery. There was incest, rape, and murder among his own children. His reign was marred by an ugly civil war, in which his own son almost deposed him. Yet David is here lifted up as a wonderful leader of God's people! This shows that David's heart after God meant more than outward success, comfort, and ease. It also shows that God's best and most effective leaders don't necessarily have it easy.

iv. David was a **commander** for Israel. Even with his tender shepherd's heart, his leadership was bold and out-front. Because he had a sense of the heart of God, being a man after God's own heart (1 Samuel 13:14), he could boldly lead God's people.

v. These prophecies are fulfilled *spiritually* when God gives wonderful, David-like leadership to His people. They will be fulfilled *ultimately* when David – literal King David in his resurrection body – reigns over Israel in the millennium, the 1,000-year reign of Jesus Christ over this earth.

- Of that time, Jeremiah 30:9 says, *But they shall serve the LORD their God, and David their king, whom I will raise up for them.*
- In Ezekiel 34:23-24 the LORD promises, *I will establish one shepherd over them, and he shall feed them; My servant David. He shall feed them and be their shepherd. And I, the LORD, will be their God, and My servant David a prince among them; I, the LORD, have spoken.*
- Ezekiel 37:25 continues, *Then they shall dwell in the land that I have given to Jacob My servant, where your fathers dwelt; and they shall dwell there, they, their children, and their children's children, forever; and My servant David shall be their prince forever.*

vi. We have indications that as God's people rule with Jesus over the millennial earth, people will be entrusted with geographical regions according to their faithfulness (Luke 19:12-19). It seems that David's glorious portion will be to rule over Israel.

e. **Surely you shall call a nation you do not know, and nations who do not know you shall run to you**: Was this addressed to Israel, or to David as the leader and commander of God's people? Possibly both. Certainly, its ultimate fulfillment is in the millennium, when the nations will flock to Israel (Isaiah 60:5, 60:9).

f. **Because of the LORD your God, and the Holy One of Israel; for He has glorified you**: Why do the nations flock to David and/or Israel? Because the LORD has lifted them up, in accordance with His blessings of restoration.

3. (6-7) An invitation to be forgiven.

Seek the LORD while He may be found,
Call upon Him while He is near.
Let the wicked forsake his way,
And the unrighteous man his thoughts;
Let him return to the LORD,
And He will have mercy on him;
And to our God,
For He will abundantly pardon.

a. **Seek the LORD while He may be found**: The prophet impresses a sense of *urgency* on God's people. "This is the time. God can be found *now*. Seek Him *now*." It isn't that God is hidden and can only be found now. It is that He can only be found when our hearts are inclined to look for Him, and that inclination itself is a gift from God! We must receive the gift and make the most of it while we have it. *Not seeking* and failing to **call upon Him while He is near**, means we will not receive the blessings He promises.

b. **Let the wicked forsake his way**: The prophet impresses the need for *repentance* among God's people. Repentance is simply turning around our **way** – turning from our own way, turning to God's **way**. Simply, this is what it means to **return to the LORD**, and we can never walk on God's way until we **forsake** our own **way**. The LORD's glorious restoration works in and through our repentance.

i. Isaiah made an important point when he wrote, **and the unrighteous man his thoughts**. Wickedness may be demonstrated by our actions (our **way**), but *unrighteousness* can be found in our very **thoughts**. The battleground for a righteous walk with the LORD is often found in our minds, in our **thoughts**.

ii. The Apostle Paul knew this also when he wrote of *bringing every thought into captivity to the obedience of Christ* (2 Corinthians 10:5), and how we must *not be conformed to this world, but be transformed by the renewing of your mind* (Romans 12:2).

c. **And He will have mercy on him**: What a glorious promise! When we turn to the LORD, **He will have mercy on** us! In fact, **He will abundantly pardon**! The problem is never that we turn to the LORD and find that He rejects us. The problem is that we fail to **return to the LORD**.

B. The glorious ways of the LORD.

1. (8-9) A reminder of the difference and distance between God and man.

"For My thoughts *are* not your thoughts,
Nor *are* your ways My ways," says the LORD.
"For *as* the heavens are higher than the earth,
So are My ways higher than your ways,
And My thoughts than your thoughts.

a. **For My thoughts are not your thoughts**: God doesn't *think* the way we do. We get into a lot of trouble when we expect that He should think as we do. Because we are made in the image of God, we can relate to God's **thoughts**, but we cannot master them.

b. **Nor are your ways My ways**: God doesn't *act* the way we do. He does things *His* way, and His **ways** are often not our **ways**. We get into a lot of trouble when we expect that God should act the way we do.

c. **For as the heavens are higher than the earth**: How far is the distance between God's thoughts and ours? How far is the distance between His ways and ours? The distance is as great **as the heavens are higher than the earth**.

i. Gloriously, in Jesus Christ, heaven has come down to earth, and we can have our thoughts and ways transformed to be *more like* God's thoughts and ways. This is what it means *to be conformed to the image of His Son* (Romans 8:29). The distance will never be closed; God will always be God, and we will always be human. But when our salvation is complete, and we are united with the LORD in glory, the distance will be as close as is possible.

ii. The difference and distance between God and man is revealed, *not* to discourage us from seeking Him, but to keep us humble as we seek. "You may conclude that it is not intended that you should understand the infinite, for you are told that his thoughts and ways are far above you; but you are required to seek him while he may be found, and call upon him while he is near." (Spurgeon)

2. (10-11) The glorious operation of the word of God.

"For as the rain comes down, and the snow from heaven,
And do not return there,
But water the earth,
And make it bring forth and bud,
That it may give seed to the sower
And bread to the eater,
So shall My word be that goes forth from My mouth;
It shall not return to Me void,
But it shall accomplish what I please,
And it shall prosper *in the thing* for which I sent it.

a. **For as the rain comes down**: Using the figure of the water cycle, the LORD illustrates the essential principle that His word **shall not return to Me void, but it shall accomplish what I please**. Rain and snow come down from heaven, and **do not return** before serving their purpose on earth (they **water the earth, and make it bring forth and bud**). The rain and snow eventually do return to heaven, but *not* before accomplishing their purpose on earth. Even so, God's word, when He sends it down from heaven, does not return to Him **void**. Instead, it always fulfills His purpose on earth.

i. This means that God is not just "talk." When He talks, His words *accomplish* His intended purpose. The word of the LORD has *power*, and it never *fails* in His intended purpose.

ii. "It is an irrevocable word. Man has to eat his words, sometimes, and unsay his say. He would perform his engagement, but he cannot. It is not that he is unfaithful, but that he is unable. Now this is never so with God. His word never returns to him void. Go, find ye the snowflakes winging their way like white doves back to heaven! Go, find the drops of rain rising upward like diamonds flung up from the hand of a mighty man to find a lodging-place in the cloud from which they fell! Until the snow and the rain return to heaven, and mock the ground which they promised to bless, the word of God shall never return to him void." (Spurgeon)

b. **Make it bring forth and bud, that it may give seed to the sower and bread to the eater**: The use of these pictures to illustrate the operation of God's word shows that God's word brings forth *fruit*. It also shows that the fruit has many different applications. The same grain that gives **seed to the sower** also gives **bread to the eater**.

c. **It shall accomplish what I please**: God's word has something to **accomplish**. God doesn't just speak to hear Himself talk. His word is not empty or lacking in power. This also means that God's word has a *purpose*. He didn't speak in unfathomable mysteries just to blow our minds, or confuse us, or leave things up to any possible interpretation. When God speaks, He speaks to **accomplish** a purpose.

d. **It shall prosper in the thing for which I sent it**: God's word doesn't barely get the job done. It **shall prosper** in the purpose God has for it. It is rich and full of life. *God's word always succeeds, and always fulfills God's purpose.*

i. This doesn't mean that it doesn't matter how God's word is presented. Sometimes a terrible sermon has been excused by saying, "God's word doesn't return void." The principle is clear and true from this passage of Isaiah, but because of the preacher's poor preparation or preaching, there has been little of God's word set before the people. The preacher can ignore, dilute, or obscure God's word so that little goes forth. When little goes forth, that little will succeed – but how much better if more of the whole counsel of God went forth to succeed.

3. (12-13) The joy and blessing of restoration.

"For you shall go out with joy,
And be led out with peace;
The mountains and the hills
Shall break forth into singing before you,
And all the trees of the field shall clap *their* hands.
Instead of the thorn shall come up the cypress tree,
And instead of the brier shall come up the myrtle tree;
And it shall be to the LORD for a name,
For an everlasting sign *that* shall not be cut off."

a. **For you shall go out with joy, and be led out with peace**: When God's people turn to Him, listen to Him, and His Word does His work in them, **joy** and **peace** are always the result. The joy is so great, that even the **mountains and the hills**, and the **trees of the field** join in.

b. **Instead of the thorn shall come up the cypress tree**: Where before there was barrenness and reminders of the curse (**the thorn**), now there will be beautiful and useful trees. The picture is clear; in His glorious work of restoration, God takes away the barren and the cursed, and brings forth beauty and fruit.

c. **It shall be to the LORD for a name, for an everlasting sign that shall not be cut off**: When the LORD restores, all the work is done for His **name**, and for His glory. When the LORD restores, the work is secure; it is **an everlasting sign that shall not be cut off.**

Isaiah 56 – A House of Prayer for All Nations

A. A promise for those outside the borders of Israel.

1. (1-2) A call to righteousness.

Thus says the LORD:
"Keep justice, and do righteousness,
For My salvation *is* about to come,
And My righteousness to be revealed.
Blessed *is* the man *who* does this,
And the son of man *who* lays hold on it;
Who keeps from defiling the Sabbath,
And keeps his hand from doing any evil."

a. **Keep justice, and do righteousness, for My salvation is about to come**: This prophetic Word is directed to God's discouraged people, who have slacked in obedience and righteousness. They see no reason to repent as long as things look down. God shakes them out of this by calling them to **keep justice, and do righteousness** in *anticipation* of what He will do.

i. It's like the person who says, "LORD, I'll start giving when You bless my finances." No; start giving now and do it in *anticipation* that God will bless obedience regarding your finances.

b. **Blessed is the man who does this**: There is both the *inherent* blessing of obedience and the *Old Covenant* blessing to the obedient.

2. (3-8) A promise for the foreigner and the outcast.

Do not let the son of the foreigner
Who has joined himself to the LORD
Speak, saying,
"The LORD has utterly separated me from His people";
Nor let the eunuch say,
"Here I am, a dry tree."
For thus says the LORD:

"To the eunuchs who keep My Sabbaths,
And choose what pleases Me,
And hold fast My covenant,
Even to them I will give in My house
And within My walls a place and a name
Better than that of sons and daughters;
I will give them an everlasting name
That shall not be cut off.
Also the sons of the foreigner
Who join themselves to the LORD, to serve Him,
And to love the name of the LORD, to be His servants—
Everyone who keeps from defiling the Sabbath,
And holds fast My covenant—
Even them I will bring to My holy mountain,
And make them joyful in My house of prayer.
Their burnt offerings and their sacrifices
***Will be* accepted on My altar;**
For My house shall be called a house of prayer for all nations."
The Lord GOD, who gathers the outcasts of Israel, says,
"Yet I will gather to him
***Others* besides those who are gathered to him."**

a. **Do not let the son of the foreigner who has joined himself to the LORD speak saying, "The LORD has utterly separated me from His people"**: Why shouldn't they say it? Because it isn't true. They may *feel* like they are **utterly separated…from His people**, but God promises they aren't. So, He says to them, "Don't say that!"

b. **Nor let the eunuch say, "Here I am, a dry tree"**: The **eunuch** is cited as an example of an *outcast*. Eunuchs were denied full participation in temple rituals (Leviticus 21:17-20). God didn't want them to accept their feelings of being cast out. Though they may *feel* that way, God's word is higher than their feelings.

i. Often when people feel like foreigners or outcasts, their feelings become a self-fulfilling prophecy. It is only in refusing to embrace such feelings, and choosing instead to trust in God's promise, that such feelings can be broken. If God says you belong, then you belong.

c. **To the eunuchs who keep My Sabbaths, and choose what pleases Me, and hold fast My covenant, even to them I will give in My house...a place and a name**: This is God's call to the one who feels like an outcast. Simply, He says, "Walk right. Live in obedience, and I will honor and bless you. I will give you **a place and a name** in My house."

i. For many, this isn't good enough. They demand the recognition and honor of men. It isn't enough for God to give them **a place and a name** in His house. They must have **a place and a name** among men. Life is easier and more pleasant when we have **a place and a name** among men, but we must be able to find contentment having our **place** and **name** only with God.

ii. The **place** and **name** we find with God is better than that among men. It is **better than that of sons and daughters**; it is **an everlasting name that shall not be cut off**.

iii. Wolf on **a place and a name**: "An interesting application of this verse is the 'Yad vaShem' (A Memorial and a Name), the building in Jerusalem to honor the Jews who died in the holocaust during World War II but whose names are recorded in perpetuity."

iv. This also prophesies the passing of the dominance of the Levitical order. Clearly, giving eunuchs **a place and a name** in God's house contradicted the command of Leviticus 21:17-20. But under a coming New Covenant, there is a higher principle at work than the shadows of the Levitical law.

d. **Even them I will bring to My holy mountain, and make them joyful in My house of prayer**: God's people had slipped into the idea that they were accepted by God no matter what, and that others were rejected by Him no matter what. Here, the Lord makes it clear that even when a foreigner or a eunuch follow hard after God and come to Him in obedience, He will receive them.

e. **For My house shall be called a house of prayer for all nations**: God wanted His temple – His **house** – to not only be a place where the Jewish people would worship Him but to be a **house of prayer for all nations**.

i. The violation of this principle made Jesus angry. When He came to the temple and found the outer courts – the only place where the Gentile **nations** could come to pray – more like an outdoor marketplace than a **house of prayer**, He drove out the moneychangers and the merchants (Matthew 21:13).

f. **The Lord God, who gathers the outcasts of Israel, says, "Yet I will gather to him others"**: Because of the pain of exile and captivity, Israel had become intensely self-focused. They believed God only really cared about them, and the rest of the nations (many of whom treated Israel cruelly) did not matter. But God wanted to expand the vision of Israel beyond her own borders, so they would know that God loved the perishing world and wanted them to love them also.

B. A promise to judge the blind leaders of God's people.

1. (9) A word to the beasts of the field.

All you beasts of the field, come to devour,
All you beasts in the forest.

a. **All you beasts of the field, come to devour**: The LORD God invites the **beasts of the field** to a great feast – to eat up the corpses of His enemies after they lay on the field of battle.

b. **Come to devour**: The same picture is used in Revelation 19:17: *Then I saw an angel standing in the sun; and he cried with a loud voice, saying to all the birds that fly in the midst of heaven, "Come and gather together for the supper of the great God, that you may eat the flesh of kings, the flesh of captains, the flesh of mighty men, the flesh of horses and of those who sit on them, and the flesh of all people, free and slave, both small and great."*

2. (10-11) A word about the unfaithful leaders of Judah.

His watchmen *are* blind,
They are all ignorant;
They *are* all dumb dogs,
They cannot bark;
Sleeping, lying down, loving to slumber.
Yes, *they are* greedy dogs
***Which* never have enough.**
And they *are* shepherds
Who cannot understand;
They all look to their own way,
Every one for his own gain,
From his *own* territory.

a. **His watchmen are blind**: The leaders of God's people are blind; judgment is on the way, but they don't see it and warn God's people. They don't fulfill their purpose as **watchmen**. They are **ignorant**, like **dumb dogs**, simply **sleeping**.

b. **They are shepherds who cannot understand**: These ungodly leaders are a sad contrast to the godly leadership personified by King David in Isaiah 55:3-5. These are unfaithful **shepherds**, who only look **everyone for his own gain**.

3. (12) A word from the unfaithful leaders of Judah.

"Come," *one says*, "I will bring wine,
And we will fill ourselves with intoxicating drink;

Tomorrow will be as today,
***And* much more abundant."**

a. **We will fill ourselves with intoxicating drink**: Worse than being passively ignorant and blind, they are actively wicked. As judgment approaches, they simply drink and get drunk.

b. **Tomorrow will be as today, and much more abundant**: Their blind faith in progress has replaced a reasoned faith in God. They are ripe for judgment and unprepared for judgment. Since the picture of Isaiah 56:9 relates to the pictures in the Book of Revelation regarding the return of Jesus, we can see this as a picture of the leaders of the unprepared world – perhaps even the unprepared church – at the return of Jesus.

Isaiah 57 – The Spiritual Adultery of God's People

A. Judah's idolatry is like spiritual adultery.

1. (1-2) The persecution of the righteous.

The righteous perishes,
And no man takes *it* to heart;
Merciful men *are* taken away,
While no one considers
That the righteous is taken away from evil.
He shall enter into peace;
They shall rest in their beds,
***Each one* walking *in* his uprightness.**

a. **The righteous perishes**: Carrying on the rebuke of Judah's leaders from the previous chapter, the LORD speaks to the persecution of the **righteous**. In this case, it is persecution through *neglect* (**the righteous perishes and no man takes it to heart**).

i. *When* Isaiah proclaimed this is important. Many critics of the Bible demand that Isaiah was written after the Babylonian exile because so many events after the exile are precisely prophesied. But the sins described in this chapter are strictly *before the exile*. This chapter is a marvelous proof that the book of Isaiah was written in the days of Isaiah, by one author, and before the exile.

ii. "There is no evidence of corresponding post-exilic practices. A prophet in the post-exile could not have written like this." (Motyer)

iii. "All in all we prefer to think of the reign of Manasseh, for the abominations of this king are all found in this chapter." (Bultema)

b. **The righteous is taken away from evil. He shall enter into peace**: Though the righteous were ignored and persecuted by the wicked leaders of Judah, God would not forsake them. When they perished, when **merciful**

men were **taken away**, God used it to bless the righteous, to take them **away from evil** and to allow them to **enter into peace**.

2. (3-10) The spiritual adultery of God's people.

"But come here,
You sons of the sorceress,
You offspring of the adulterer and the harlot!
Whom do you ridicule?
Against whom do you make a wide mouth
***And* stick out the tongue?**
***Are* you not children of transgression,**
Offspring of falsehood,
Inflaming yourselves with gods under every green tree,
Slaying the children in the valleys,
Under the clefts of the rocks?
Among the smooth *stones* of the stream
***Is* your portion;**
They, they, *are* your lot!
Even to them you have poured a drink offering,
You have offered a grain offering.
Should I receive comfort in these?
"On a lofty and high mountain
You have set your bed;
Even there you went up
To offer sacrifice.
Also behind the doors and their posts
You have set up your remembrance;
For you have uncovered yourself *to those other* than Me,
And have gone up to them;
You have enlarged your bed
And made *a covenant* with them;
You have loved their bed,
Where you saw *their* nudity.
You went to the king with ointment,
And increased your perfumes;
You sent your messengers far off,
And *even* descended to Sheol.
You are wearied in the length of your way;
***Yet* you did not say, 'There is no hope.'**
You have found the life of your hand;
Therefore you were not grieved.

a. **Whom do you ridicule?** The wicked among God's people made fun of the righteous. They mocked them, and God heard it. Here, the LORD challenges them, simply asking "Who do you think you are? Who are you mocking? **Are you not children of transgression, offspring of falsehood**?"

i. This speaks to a common sin of human nature – to see the sins or the problems of others while being blind to our own sins or problems.

b. **Inflaming yourselves with gods under every green tree**: Here, the LORD begins to expose the *spiritual adultery* of His people. They are "hot" with passion for other gods, worshipping them in the ritual worship places of Canaanite paganism (**every green tree…. among the smooth stones of the stream…. on a high and lofty mountain**).

i. In this picture, the LORD is the husband of Israel, and their passionate, chronic attraction for idols was like the lust of an adulterer. His people pursued the false gods like a lover runs after the focus of their love, and they yield themselves to the idols as a lover yields themselves to their beloved (**you have uncovered yourself to those other than Me**).

ii. "According to the presentation of verse seven, the whoredom of Judah is compared to that of an adulteress who has become so impudent that she no longer commits her sins in secret but publicly and shamelessly. She acts without any restraint and refuses to blush with shame." (Bultema)

c. **Under every green tree**: The picture of "spiritual adultery" is especially fitting, because many of the pagan gods the Israelites went after were "worshipped" with debased sex rituals. A **green tree** might be a place of such idolatry because the evergreen tree spoke of constant fertility.

d. **Slaying the children in the valleys**: One of the Canaanite gods the Israelites worshipped was named Molech, and he received children as sacrifices. Molech was "worshipped" by heating a metal statue representing the god until it was red hot, then by placing a living infant on the outstretched hands of the statue, while beating drums drowned out the screams of the child until it burned to death. Molech was one of the "lovers" God's people forsook the LORD for in their spiritual adultery.

i. People who would not make a small sacrifice for the LORD God would kill their own children for a pagan idol! "And as the love of harlots is oft hotter than that of husband and wife, so superstition many times outdoeth true religion." (Trapp)

e. **Even to them you have poured a drink offering, you have offered a grain offering**: These are the sacrifices that *should* have been given to the LORD. But His unfaithful people gave them to idols instead.

i. "For the devil is God's ape, and idolaters used the same rites and offerings in the worship of idols which God has prescribed in his own [worship]." (Poole)

f. **Also behind the doors and their posts you have set up your remembrance**: In Deuteronomy 6:4-9, God told Israel to inscribe His name and His word on every door post. Here, there was a perverse twisting of that – they remembered their pagan gods **behind the doors and their posts**.

i. "The sensitive Israelite reader would, of course, remember that it was the word of God – and, most aptly, the assertion that there is only one God – that was the be inscribed on the doors." (Grogan)

g. **You are wearied in the length of your way**: As time went on, the spiritual adultery of God's people wasn't rewarding. After the initial thrill of their spiritual adultery wore off, they were **wearied**. But even then, they would not repent (**Yet you did not say, "There is no hope"**).

B. God describes His dealing with His disobedient people.

1. (11-13) The end of God's patience with His people.

"And of whom have you been afraid, or feared,
That you have lied
And not remembered Me,
Nor taken *it* to your heart?
Is it not because I have held My peace from of old
That you do not fear Me?
I will declare your righteousness
And your works,
For they will not profit you.
When you cry out,
Let your collection *of idols* deliver you.
But the wind will carry them all away,
A breath will take *them*.
But he who puts his trust in Me shall possess the land,
And shall inherit My holy mountain.

a. **And of whom have you been afraid, or feared, that you have lied and not remembered Me**: Here, the LORD confronts the fact that His people *do not* fear Him, and that they *do fear* someone or something else. **Nor taken it to your heart**: Their superficial relationship was connected to a *low view of God*, and their *lack of respect* for Him.

b. **Is it not because I have held My peace from of old that you do not fear Me?** Why did God's people lack respect for Him? In part, because He showed mercy and did not punish their sin immediately. They made a crucial error, common to fallen humanity: they mistook God's mercy and forbearance for weakness or lack of resolve.

c. **I will declare your righteousness and your works, for they will not profit you**: God's people didn't trust in Him, and the things they did trust in – themselves, and their idols (**let your collection of idols deliver you**) could not help them. Their idols were so weak and helpless that **a breath will take them**.

d. **He who puts his trust in Me shall possess the land, and shall inherit My holy mountain**: This is the contrast to those who turned away from God. Trust in the LORD makes a person secure, while trust in one's self or in idols ends in ruin.

2. (14) A stumbling block removed.

And one shall say,
"Heap it up! Heap it up!
Prepare the way,
Take the stumbling block out of the way of My people."

a. **Heap it up! Heap it up**: This doesn't describe setting things in the way of those coming to God. Instead, using the same imagery as Isaiah 35:8, which describes a *highway* for God's people, meaning a raised road that is above all obstacles. **Heap it up** refers to the building of this road, so that God's people can return to Him without obstacle.

b. **Prepare the way, take the stumbling block out of the way of My people**: Whatever gets in the way of our getting right with God must be taken out of the way. In the following verses, the LORD deals with those obstacles.

3. (15-21) God describes the way of peace and restoration.

For thus says the High and Lofty One
Who inhabits eternity, whose name is Holy:
"I dwell in the high and holy *place*,
With him *who* has a contrite and humble spirit,
To revive the spirit of the humble,
And to revive the heart of the contrite ones.
For I will not contend forever,
Nor will I always be angry;
For the spirit would fail before Me,
And the souls *which* I have made.

For the iniquity of his covetousness
I was angry and struck him;
I hid and was angry,
And he went on backsliding in the way of his heart.
I have seen his ways, and will heal him;
I will also lead him,
And restore comforts to him
And to his mourners.
"I create the fruit of the lips:
Peace, peace to *him who is* far off and to *him who is* near,"
Says the LORD,
"And I will heal him."
But the wicked *are* like the troubled sea,
When it cannot rest, whose waters cast up mire and dirt.
"*There is* no peace,"
Says my God, "for the wicked."

a. **For thus says the High and Lofty One who inhabits eternity, whose name is Holy**: To be right with God, the first thing to do is to *understand His great majesty*. The LORD introduces Himself to His people with titles reflecting His great majesty and expects His people to *respond to Him* as such a glorious God.

b. **To revive the spirit of the humble**: Though God is **the High and Lofty One**, and lives **in the high and holy place**, at the same time He will live with men – with **him who has a contrite and humble spirit**. This is the second thing to being right before God: being **contrite and humble** before the God of great majesty.

c. **For I will not contend forever, nor will I always be angry**: The third thing to understand in getting right with God is *His great love*. Here, the LORD shows His mercy to His people but promises to relent and not be angry forever. Though God disciplined His people, He now says, **I have seen his ways, and will heal him; I will also lead him, and restore comforts to him.**

d. **Peace, peace, to him who is far off and to him who is near**: In His mercy, God invites all men to **peace** – both **him who is far off** and **him who is near**. Each one can receive God's *shalom*, which is more than the absence of hostility; it is the gift of precious well-being.

i. In Ephesians 2:17, Paul speaks of Jesus fulfilling this promise exactly: *And He came and preached peace to you who were afar off and to those who were near.* As revealed through Paul, God shows that **him who is**

far off refers to the Gentiles, while **him who is near** is the Jewish man. Both can come to **peace** through receiving God's gift through Jesus.

e. **But the wicked are like the troubled sea, when it cannot rest.... there is no peace...for the wicked**: In contrast to those who return to God, the **wicked** are still without **peace**. God's great mercy is held out to man – but it must be received.

i. "Their minds are restless, being perpetually hurried and tormented with their own lusts and passions, and with the horror of their guilt, and the dread of Divine vengeance due unto them, and ready to come upon them." (Poole)

ii. Isaiah 57:20-21 is a good example of how the sea was thought to be a dangerous, dark, restless place in the mind of the ancient Jews. No wonder that in the new heaven and the new earth, there is no more sea (Revelation 21:1).

Isaiah 58 – The Blessing of True Worship

A. The LORD exposes the shallow worship of His people.

1. (1-3a) God's people ask: "Why do our prayers go unanswered?"

"Cry aloud, spare not;
Lift up your voice like a trumpet;
Tell My people their transgression,
And the house of Jacob their sins.
Yet they seek Me daily,
And delight to know My ways,
As a nation that did righteousness,
And did not forsake the ordinance of their God.
They ask of Me the ordinances of justice;
They take delight in approaching God.
'Why have we fasted,' ***they say*****, 'and You have not seen?**
Why **have we afflicted our souls, and You take no notice?'**

a. **Cry aloud, spare not…tell My people their transgression**: God spoke loudly and directly. His people need to hear **their transgression** – but would they hear?

b. **They seek Me daily, and delight to know My ways**: God first described the *appearance* of their spiritual life. On the surface, it seemed that God's people loved Him and were devoted to Him. They had the reputation of **a nation that did righteousness**, and they looked like people who would **take delight in approaching God**.

c. **Why have we fasted…and You have not seen?** With this spiritual veneer, they felt God was unfair to them. It was as if they said, "LORD, we have **fasted**, but You still don't answer our prayer. Don't you know that we seek you **daily**, **delight to know** Your **ways**, do **righteousness**, and take **delight in approaching** You? Yet You do not answer our prayers!"

2. (3b-5) God exposes the shallow worship of His people.

**"In fact, in the day of your fast you find pleasure,
And exploit all your laborers.
Indeed you fast for strife and debate,
And to strike with the fist of wickedness.
You will not fast as *you do* this day,
To make your voice heard on high.
Is it a fast that I have chosen,
A day for a man to afflict his soul?
Is it to bow down his head like a bulrush,
And to spread out sackcloth and ashes?
Would you call this a fast,
And an acceptable day to the LORD?**

a. **In fact, in the day of your fast you find pleasure, and exploit all your laborers**: Enough with the image; now God exposes the reality. The reality was that His people didn't **fast** with the right heart and did it only as an empty ritual. The reality was that even on a day when they fasted, they still exploited their employees. God didn't accept their fasting when it wasn't connected with a sincere heart of obedience.

i. "How can any nation pretend to fast or worship God at all, or dare to profess that they believe in the existence of such a Being, while they carry on the *slave trade*, and traffic in the souls, blood, and bodies of men! O ye most [criminal] of knaves, and worst of hypocrites, cast off at once the mask of your religion; and deepen not your endless perdition by professing the *faith* of our *Lord Jesus Christ*, while ye continue in this traffic!" (Adam Clarke, writing in 1823)

b. **Indeed you fast for strife and debate, and to strike with the fist of wickedness**: They fasted for needs, certainly; but selfish needs like "LORD, help me win this argument." "LORD, help me defeat this person." Though their prayer was accompanied with fasting, it was still a selfish, even wicked prayer – so God did not answer.

c. **You will not fast as you do this day, to make your voice heard on high**: The purpose of their fasting was to glorify *themselves*, to make their **voice heard on high**. God says, "No more. **You will not fast as you do this day**."

d. **Is it a fast that I have chosen**: The kind of fasting God rebukes here is a hollow, empty, show, without the spiritual substance behind it. This isn't the kind of fast God has **chosen**. Even though they *do* all the right things in fasting (**bow down his head like a bulrush…spread out sackcloth and ashes**), God does not even **call this a fast**.

i. The people of Isaiah's day had the same problem as the Pharisees of Jesus' day. They trusted in empty ritual, apart from the spiritual reality. Real fasting – fasting that is partnered with real repentance, and isn't only about image – has great power before God (Matthew 17:21). But God sees through the hypocrisy of empty religious ritual, including fasting. In Jesus' parable of the Pharisee and the Publican, He told how the self-righteous Pharisee made a special point to say, "*I fast twice a week*" (Luke 18:9-14).

ii. It isn't that Isaiah or the Lord are down on fasting. They are down on *any* empty religious ritual. The answer isn't to stop fasting, but to get right with God and make your fasting more than superficial. As Jesus said to His people about the empty religious rituals of the Pharisees, *These you ought to have done, without leaving the others undone* (Matthew 23:23).

B. The character and blessings of true worship.

1. (6-7) The kind of worship and fasting most acceptable to God.

"*Is* this not the fast that I have chosen:
To loose the bonds of wickedness,
To undo the heavy burdens,
to let the oppressed go free,
And that you break every yoke?
***Is it* not to share your bread with the hungry,**
And that you bring to your house the poor who are cast out;
When you see the naked, that you cover him,
And not hide yourself from your own flesh?

a. **Is this not the fast that I have chosen: To loose the bonds of wickedness**: God tells His people, "If you want to fast the way that pleases Me, begin with getting right with your brothers and sisters. Stop oppressing others and reach out to help others."

b. **Loose the bonds of wickedness…undo the heavy burdens…let the oppressed go free…break every yoke**: First, they had to *stop* acting wickedly towards others. This means that getting right with God *begins* by stopping the evil we do towards others.

c. **Share your bread with the hungry…cover…not hide yourself from your own flesh**: Then, they had to *start* acting lovingly towards others. This means that getting right with God *continues* by *doing* loving things for other people.

2. (8-12) The blessings God promises for the true worshipper.

Then your light shall break forth like the morning,
Your healing shall spring forth speedily,
And your righteousness shall go before you;
The glory of the LORD shall be your rear guard.
Then you shall call, and the LORD will answer;
You shall cry, and He will say, 'Here I *am*.'
"If you take away the yoke from your midst,
The pointing of the finger, and speaking wickedness,
***If* you extend your soul to the hungry**
And satisfy the afflicted soul,
Then your light shall dawn in the darkness,
And your darkness shall *be* as the noonday.
The LORD will guide you continually,
And satisfy your soul in drought,
And strengthen your bones;
You shall be like a watered garden,
And like a spring of water, whose waters do not fail.
Those from among you
Shall build the old waste places;
You shall raise up the foundations of many generations;
And you shall be called the Repairer of the Breach,
The Restorer of Streets to Dwell In.

a. **Then your light shall break forth like the morning**: If God's people would couple their fasting with lives of righteousness and love, **then** they would see their prayers answered. They would have lives full of **light**, full of **healing**, full of **righteousness**, full of **the glory of the LORD**. When they call out to God, then **the LORD will answer**.

b. **If you take away the yoke from your midst, the pointing of the finger, and speaking wickedness**: Again, the LORD gives them three things to *stop* doing.

- They must stop oppressing others, treating them as animals bound with a **yoke**.
- They must *stop* **pointing…the finger** at others and see where they are to blame.
- They must *stop* **speaking wickedness**.

i. These are sins of *commission*. They are sins that we go out and *do* against the LORD and against others. If we will walk right with God, we must stop and guard against *sins of commission*.

c. **If you extend your soul to the hungry and satisfy the afflicted soul**: Again, the LORD gives them two things to *start* doing. They needed to minister to the hungry with more than food; they had to **extend** their **soul to the hungry**. They had to look for the **afflicted soul** and seek to **satisfy** it.

i. Failing to do these are sins of *omission*. They are things that we should have done, yet we have not. If we will walk right with God, we must open our eyes and do what is our loving duty before Him.

ii. This prayer, "A General Confession of Sin," from the *Book of Common Prayer* (1559 edition), expresses repentance for both sins of *commission* and *omission*:

Almighty and most merciful Father, we have erred and strayed from thy ways, like lost sheep. We have followed too much the devices and desires of our own hearts. We have offended against thy holy laws. We have left undone those things which we ought to have done, and we have done those things which we ought not to have done, and there is no health in us. But thou, O Lord, have mercy upon us miserable offenders. Spare thou them, O God, which confess their faults. Restore thou them that be penitent, according to thy promises declared unto mankind, in Christ Jesu our Lord. And grant, O most merciful Father, for his sake, that we may hereafter live a godly, righteous, and sober life, to the glory of thy holy name.

d. **Then your light shall dawn in the darkness, and your darkness shall be as the noonday**: To the repentant, God promises blessing. Not only will they have **light**, but even their **darkness shall be as the noonday**!

e. **The LORD will guide you continually**: This is a promise for those who do more than just empty religious rituals. To have the guidance of the LORD, empty religious ritual isn't enough. We need to seek God with both sincere hearts and sincere actions.

f. **And satisfy your soul in drought, and strengthen your bones**: Those who serve God with sincere hearts and actions enjoy a health and life of the soul that is impossible for the superficial follower of God to know.

g. **Those from among you shall build the old waste places**: Those who serve God with sincere hearts and actions also *accomplish* things for God's kingdom. They **build** and are **called the Repairer of the Breach, the Restorer of Streets to Dwell in**. You can't **build** anything for God's kingdom on the foundation of a superficial walk with God.

i. How there needs to be a rebuilding work today! "We live in a broken world. In every direction there are breaches which are wide and deep. There are broken hearts and broken homes, and that which once was sacred is but a waste place. Whereas once there was a carefully guarded fence around the sanctity of family life, sex life, and the right to personal privacy, now there is just a waste place. The wall of protection is in ruins, and life has lost all its meaning." (Redpath)

ii. All in all, this passage shows several characteristics of a life right with God.

- It is an enlightened life: **Your light shall dawn in the darkness**.
- It is a guided life: **The Lord will guide you continually**.
- It is a satisfied life: **And satisfy your soul in drought**.
- It is a fragrant life: **Like a watered garden**.
- It is a freshly sustained life: **Like a spring of water, whose waters do not fail**.
- It is a productive, healing life: **You shall build the old waste places**.

3. (13-14) True Sabbath keeping and the blessings of it.

"If you turn away your foot from the Sabbath,
***From* doing your pleasure on My holy day,**
And call the Sabbath a delight,
The holy *day* of the Lord honorable,
And shall honor Him, not doing your own ways,
Nor finding your own pleasure,
Nor speaking *your own* words,
Then you shall delight yourself in the Lord;
And I will cause you to ride on the high hills of the earth,
And feed you with the heritage of Jacob your father.
The mouth of the Lord has spoken."

a. **Call the Sabbath a delight…the holy day of the Lord honorable**: The **Sabbath** was another empty religious observance for the Jewish people of Isaiah's day. God calls them to take a delight in the *heart* and in the *purpose* of the Sabbath – to **honor Him, not doing your own ways**.

i. This fits in perfectly with the fulfillment of the Sabbath in light of the finished work of Jesus. We keep the Sabbath when we set aside every day to **honor Him**, and by **not doing your own ways** as a means of justifying ourselves.

ii. Are Christians required to keep the Sabbath today? The New Testament makes it clear that Christians are not under obligation to observe a Sabbath day (Colossians 2:16-17; Galatians 4:9-11), because

Jesus fulfills the purpose and plan of the Sabbath for us and in us (Hebrews 4:9-11).

iii. Galatians 4:10 tells us that Christians are not bound to observe *days and months and seasons and years*. The rest we enter into as Christians is something to experience every day, not just one day a week – the rest of knowing we don't have to work to save ourselves, but that our salvation was accomplished in Jesus (Hebrews 4:9-10).

iv. The Sabbath commanded here and observed by Israel was a *shadow of things to come, but the substance is of Christ* (Colossians 2:16-17). We have a rest in Jesus that is ours to live in every day. Therefore, since the shadow of the Sabbath is fulfilled in Jesus, we are free to keep any day – or no day – as a Sabbath after the custom of ancient Israel. However, though we are free from the legal obligation of the Sabbath, we dare not ignore the importance of a day of rest – God has built us so that we *need* one.

v. If anyone would insist on the Sabbath, they must also insist on the six-day work week. Exodus 20:9, in the command regarding the Sabbath, says *Six days you shall labor and do all your work*. Adam Clarke says on that passage, "He who idles his time away in the *six* days is equally culpable in the sight of God as he who works on the *seventh*." (Clarke)

b. **Then you shall delight yourself in the LORD**: When we keep the meaning of the Sabbath, not merely as an empty religious ritual, then **you shall delight yourself in the LORD**. God will bless us, and we **shall delight**, not only in the blessings, but **in the LORD** Himself. We know it is sure because **the mouth of the LORD has spoken**.

i. In this chapter, God exposed the emptiness of two religious rituals as practiced in Isaiah's day: fasting and Sabbath keeping. Both of these are expressions of *not doing* things. In fasting, you *don't eat*. In Sabbath keeping, you *don't work*. An important aspect of this chapter is showing us that what we *don't do* isn't enough to make us right before God. Our walk with God shouldn't only be defined by what we *don't do*. What do we *do for* the LORD?

Isaiah 59 – The Reality Check

A. The sin God sees.

1 (1) The problem of God's people: what the cause is *not*.

Behold, the Lord's hand is not shortened,
That it cannot save;
Nor His ear heavy,
That it cannot hear.

a. **Behold, the Lord's hand is not shortened, that it cannot save**: God's people wondered why God did not seem to rescue them from their trials. They wondered if perhaps God had diminished in strength – if His **hand** had become **shortened**. Isaiah the prophet assures them that this is not the case.

i. This touches on one of the greatest problems in practical theology: how can there be a God of love and all power when there is human suffering? If we loved someone and had the power to end their suffering, wouldn't we do it? Isaiah addresses those who wondered if God wasn't all-powerful, and that is why their suffering continues.

ii. Rabbi Harold Kushner wrote a remarkably wide-selling book titled *When Bad Things Happen to Good People* (1981). It sold more than four million copies and was on the *New York Times* best-seller list for a whole year. The whole point of his book is to say God is all-loving but not all-powerful, that God is good, but not sovereign. So, when bad things happen to good people, it is because events are out of God's control. Kushner advises his readers to "learn to love [God] and forgive him despite his limitations." This certainly is not the God of the Bible, because **the Lord's hand is not shortened, that it cannot save**. Isaiah simply says, "**Behold** this. See this."

b. **Nor His ear heavy, that it cannot hear**: Perhaps the problem isn't that God lacks power. Perhaps He lacks *knowledge* of our problem or *interest* in our problem. But this isn't the situation at all, as Isaiah reminds us. God's **ear** is not **heavy**. He can **hear** us just fine.

2. (2) The problem of God's people: what the cause *is*.

But your iniquities have separated you from your God;
And your sins have hidden *His* face from you,
So that He will not hear.

a. **But your iniquities have separated you from your God**: The problem isn't with God's power, His knowledge, or His interest. The problem is with our **iniquities**. Sin has **separated you from your God**.

i. In what way does sin separate us from God? Sin does not necessarily separate us from the *presence* of God, because God is present everywhere (Psalm 139:7) and even Satan can have an audience with God (Job 1:6). Sin does not separate us from the *love* of God, because God loves sinners (Romans 5:8). But sin still does separate.

- Sin separates us from *fellowship* with God, because at least at the point of our sin, we no longer think alike with God.
- Sin separates us from the *blessing* of God, because at least at the point of our sin, we are not trusting God and relying on Him.
- Sin separates us from some of the *benefits of God's love*, even as the Prodigal Son (Luke 15:11-32) was still loved by the father but didn't enjoy the benefits of his love when he was in sin.
- Sin separates us, in some way, from the *protection* of God, because He will allow trials to come our way to correct us.

ii. How easy it is for us to blame our problems on everything except our **iniquities**! We will even *blame God* before seeing that the problem is with us! We will deny *who God is* before seeing that the problem is with us.

b. **And your sins have hidden His face from you**: This explains why God's people no longer felt the face of the Lord shining on them (Numbers 6:25). It was their **sins**, not the inability of God to hear, or His lack of interest in hearing.

i. This helps us understand – at least in a small way – the cry of Jesus from the cross, *My God, My God, why have You forsaken Me?* (Matthew 27:46). As Jesus stood in the place of guilty sinners, there was some way in which the face of God the Father was **hidden** from Him. Not in an ultimate, absolute sense; but in some way. But that was for *our sins*, not His own.

3. (3-8) A detailed description of the sins of God's people.

For your hands are defiled with blood,
And your fingers with iniquity;
Your lips have spoken lies,
Your tongue has muttered perversity.
No one calls for justice,
Nor does *any* plead for truth.
They trust in empty words and speak lies;
They conceive evil and bring forth iniquity.
They hatch vipers' eggs and weave the spider's web;
He who eats of their eggs dies,
And *from* that which is crushed a viper breaks out.
Their webs will not become garments,
Nor will they cover themselves with their works;
Their works *are* works of iniquity,
And the act of violence *is* in their hands.
Their feet run to evil,
And they make haste to shed innocent blood;
Their thoughts *are* thoughts of iniquity;
Wasting and destruction *are* in their paths.
The way of peace they have not known,
And *there is* no justice in their ways;
They have made themselves crooked paths;
Whoever takes that way shall not know peace.

a. **Your hands are defiled with blood**: They practiced and approved of violence and murder.

b. **Your lips have spoken lies**: They lied with ease and regularity.

c. **No one calls for justice**: They did not share God's heart for what was fair and good; everyone simply thought in terms of their *own* good. Both **justice** and **truth** were distant concepts, and instead of **justice** there were **empty words**, instead of **truth** there were **lies**.

i. Motyer on **empty words**: "Isaiah is not describing but diagnosing. They may think they are acting sensibly but actually it is all nonsense."

d. **They conceive evil and bring forth iniquity**, as if they were snakes giving birth to more evil serpents, bringing nothing but death (**he who eats of their eggs dies**) and more evil (**from that which is crushed a viper breaks out**).

i. Clarke on **weave the spider's web**: "By their plots they weave nets, lay snares industriously, with great pains and artifice, whereby they may entangle and involve their poor neighbours in intricacies and perplexities, and so devour them, as the spider weaves her web to catch flies, and then to feed on them." But their webs will never cover them before God; **Their webs will not become garments, nor will they cover themselves with their works**.

e. **The act of violence is in their hands. Their feet run to evil**: Both hands and feet are given to sin. But it doesn't end there; even **their thoughts are thoughts of iniquity**.

f. **They have made themselves crooked paths; whoever takes that way shall not know peace**: Their choice and the consequences are plain. Their **crooked paths** will never lead them into the **way** of **peace**, meaning **peace** in the full sense of *shalom*.

i. Paul quoted Isaiah 59:7-8 in Romans 3:15-17. He used this passage, connected with other Old Testament passages, to demonstrate that man is a sinner from "head to toe."

ii. In light of all this sin, it is amazing – absolutely amazing – that God's people could still believe (as they did in Isaiah 59:1) that the problem was with God, and not them.

B. The effects of sin the people see.

1. (9-11) Because of their sin, darkness comes.

Therefore justice is far from us,
Nor does righteousness overtake us;
We look for light, but there is darkness!
For brightness, *but* we walk in blackness!
We grope for the wall like the blind,
And we grope as if *we had* no eyes;
We stumble at noonday as at twilight;
***We are* as dead *men* in desolate places.**
We all growl like bears,
And moan sadly like doves;
We look for justice, but *there is* none;
For salvation, *but* it is far from us.

a. **Therefore justice is far from us, nor does righteousness overtake us**: Because God's people had no interest in **justice**, God did not bless them with it. Because God's people did not care about **righteousness**, God did not bless them with it. This is the principle of Jesus stated in Matthew 13:12: *For whoever has, to him more will be given, and he will have* *abundance; but whoever does not have, even what he has will be taken away from him.*

b. **We look for light, but there is darkness**: Now, having given themselves over to darkness, when they wanted the light, it wasn't there. When you always have the light to go to, the darkness feels "fun." It seems mysterious and adventurous. But when the **light** is taken away, we despair in the darkness.

2. (12-15a) Confessing their sin and admitting their guilt.

For our transgressions are multiplied before You,
And our sins testify against us;
For our transgressions *are* with us,
And *as for* our iniquities, we know them:
In transgressing and lying against the LORD,
And departing from our God,
Speaking oppression and revolt,
Conceiving and uttering from the heart words of falsehood.
Justice is turned back,
And righteousness stands afar off;
For truth is fallen in the street,
And equity cannot enter.
So truth fails,
And he *who* departs from evil makes himself a prey.

a. **Our sins testify against us…. righteousness stands afar off**: Now God's people are in a better place. They have had their reality check and see things as they are. No longer do they blame the "shortened hand" of God, or His "heavy ear." They know it is because of their own **sins** that **righteousness stands afar off**.

C. The salvation and redemption the LORD sees.

1. (15b-16a) What the LORD saw.

Then the LORD saw it, and it displeased Him
That *there was* no justice.
He saw that *there was* no man,
And wondered that *there was* no intercessor.

a. **The LORD saw it, and it displeased Him, that there was no justice**: The state of God's people was no mystery to the LORD. They cried out in Isaiah 59:12-15a, stating how desperate their condition was – and the LORD knew it all along.

b. **He saw that there was no man, and wondered that there was no intercessor**: Not only was the state of God's people bad, but no one among them took the lead in getting it right. Where was the **man** who would lead the people in righteousness? He could not be found. Where was the **intercessor** who would plead God's case to the people, and the people's repentance to their God? **No intercessor** could be found.

2. (16b-19) What the Lord did.

Therefore His own arm brought salvation for Him;
And His own righteousness, it sustained Him.
For He put on righteousness as a breastplate,
And a helmet of salvation on His head;
He put on the garments of vengeance for clothing,
And was clad with zeal as a cloak.
According to *their* deeds, accordingly He will repay,
Fury to His adversaries,
Recompense to His enemies;
The coastlands He will fully repay.
So shall they fear
The name of the Lord from the west,
And His glory from the rising of the sun;
When the enemy comes in like a flood,
The Spirit of the Lord will lift up a standard against him.

a. **Therefore His own arm brought salvation for Him**: God waited and waited for a disobedient Israel to turn to Him. He waited and waited for a *man* to lead them back to Him, or an *intercessor* to plead before Him. None arose; so the Lord did it Himself. If a man or an intercessor would have stepped out, it would have saved Israel a lot of calamity. But the fact that no man or no intercessor stepped forward didn't ruin God's plan. He waited to work in partnership through a *man*. He waited to work through an *intercessor*. But God's work would still be accomplished if none arose.

b. **He put on righteousness as a breastplate, and a helmet of salvation on His head**: No man stepped forward to work with the Lord, so the Lord put on his armor and went to destroy His enemies, protect His people, and glorify His name.

i. Most people don't pick up the connection between Isaiah 59:17-18 and Paul's comments on our spiritual armor in Ephesians 6:10-17. In that passage, Paul calls that armor *the whole armor of God*, and it is God's armor in the sense that it belongs to Him – after all, He uses it here in Isaiah 59:17-18 – and He allows us to use it to fight for Him.

ii. We may see a connection. If we *don't* put on the armor of God and fight for Him, then eventually God will put it on Himself and fight for His glory. But God's preference is to work in and through us, with us using His armor.

c. **So shall they fear the name of the LORD from the west, and His glory from the rising of the sun**: This shows that the end result will be wonderful. In His ultimate victory – which He wants us to share in but will accomplish with or without us – the **glory** of the LORD will be known and respected from east to west.

d. **When the enemy comes in like a flood, the Spirit of the LORD will lift up a standard against him**. The enemies of the LORD will never triumph over Him. Even if they come in **like a flood**, and seem unstoppable, the LORD will **lift up a** battle-**standard against him**, and he will be stopped. God gives His people the glorious privilege of being *more than conquerors* (Romans 8:37) but will win the battle with or without us.

3. (20-21) What the LORD said.

"The Redeemer will come to Zion,
And to those who turn from transgression in Jacob,"
Says the LORD.

"As for Me," says the LORD, "this is My covenant with them: My Spirit who is upon you, and My words which I have put in your mouth, shall not depart from your mouth, nor from the mouth of your descendants, nor from the mouth of your descendants' descendants," says the LORD, "from this time and forevermore."

a. **The Redeemer will come to Zion**: After speaking in the third person through the prophet, now the LORD speaks in the first-person through the prophet. When He speaks, He declares: **The Redeemer** – the *goel* – **will come to Zion**.

i. The *goel* – sometimes translated *kinsman-redeemer*, here simply as **Redeemer** – had a specifically defined role in Israel's family life. The kinsman-redeemer was responsible to buy a fellow Israelite out of slavery (Leviticus 25:48). He was responsible to be the "avenger of blood" to make sure the murderer of a family member answered to the crime (Numbers 35:19). He was responsible to buy back family land that had been forfeited (Leviticus 25:25). And he was responsible to carry on the family name by marrying a childless widow (Deuteronomy 25:5-10). In these, we see that the *goel*, the kinsman-redeemer, was responsible to safeguard the *persons*, the *property*, and the *posterity* of the family.

ii. When the New King James Version capitalizes **Redeemer**, it does so rightly – because our *goel* is Jesus Christ. He is our near kinsman because He has added perfect humanity to His deity. He is the one who buys us out of slavery. He is the one who avenges wrongs done to us. He protects our inheritance and blesses and guards our posterity. This promise of the LORD in Isaiah 59:20 could be reworded, "I will send My Messiah, the **Redeemer** for all humanity, Jesus of Nazareth!"

b. **To those who turn from transgression**: Who does the **Redeemer** come to? **To those who turn from transgression**. The *goel* only worked for those who asked for His services and knew they needed Him.

c. **My Spirit who is upon you, and My words…shall not depart from your mouth…from this time and forevermore**: The **covenant** God makes with His people promises an *abiding Spirit* and an *enduring word.* God accomplishes His purpose in people and through all creation through both the **Spirit** and the **word**.

Isaiah 60 – The Glorious Light of God's Kingdom

A. The glory of Israel in the Kingdom of God.

1. (1-3) The glorious light of God's Kingdom.

Arise, shine;
For your light has come!
And the glory of the Lord is risen upon you.
For behold, the darkness shall cover the earth,
And deep darkness the people;
But the Lord will arise over you,
And His glory will be seen upon you.
The Gentiles shall come to your light,
And kings to the brightness of your rising.

a. **Arise, shine; for your light has come**: After the thick and desperate *darkness* described in Isaiah 59:9-10, this is the glorious rescue from the Redeemer. **Light has come** – so God tells His people to *respond* to it, and to **arise** and **shine**.

i. Darkness is for lying down; **light** is for rising up. Darkness is for gloom and sleep; **light** is for shining. When the **light has come**, we must respond, and **arise, shine**.

ii. First we receive God's light (**your light has come**), and then we have a service to perform (**arise, shine**). You can't shine until **your light has come**, but once it has come, there is something wrong if you don't **arise** and **shine**.

b. **And the glory of the Lord is risen upon you**: This is no earthly light; this is light that emanates from the **glory of the Lord**. This is like the light of Jesus in the Transfiguration, when *His face shone like the sun, and His clothes became as white as the light* (Matthew 17:2). Sometimes harsh, bright light can be disturbing or uncomfortable – but not this warm, wonderful light that pulsates from the **glory of the Lord**.

c. **Gentiles shall come to your light**: When the LORD lifts up His glorious light over Israel, the Gentile nations shall see it and be attracted to the light. Even **kings** will be attracted **to the brightness of** Israel's **rising**. This will be ultimately fulfilled in the Millennial Kingdom of Jesus when Israel is lifted up among all nations.

i. While in principle this chapter has application to all God's people, it is specifically directed to Israel, and will be fulfilled in the Millennial Kingdom. Not all have seen this. Adam Clarke writes, "The subject of this chapter is the great increase and flourishing state of the Church of God by the conversion and accession of the heathen nations to it." But the fact that the LORD speaks of the **Gentiles** here in opposition to the subjects of the prophecy shows He speaks to *Israel* as *Israel*. Replacement theology just doesn't work here, or anywhere.

2. (4-13) Great treasures come to Israel in the Kingdom.

"Lift up your eyes all around, and see:
They all gather together, they come to you;
Your sons shall come from afar,
And your daughters shall be nursed at *your* side.
Then you shall see and become radiant,
And your heart shall swell with joy;
Because the abundance of the sea shall be turned to you,
The wealth of the Gentiles shall come to you.
The multitude of camels shall cover your *land*,
The dromedaries of Midian and Ephah;
All those from Sheba shall come;
They shall bring gold and incense,
And they shall proclaim the praises of the LORD.
All the flocks of Kedar shall be gathered together to you,
The rams of Nebaioth shall minister to you;
They shall ascend with acceptance on My altar,
And I will glorify the house of My glory.
"Who are these *who* fly like a cloud,
And like doves to their roosts?
Surely the coastlands shall wait for Me;
And the ships of Tarshish *will come* first,
To bring your sons from afar,
Their silver and their gold with them,
To the name of the LORD your God,
And to the Holy One of Israel,
Because He has glorified you.

"The sons of foreigners shall build up your walls,
And their kings shall minister to you;
For in My wrath I struck you,
But in My favor I have had mercy on you.
Therefore your gates shall be open continually;
They shall not be shut day or night,
That *men* may bring to you the wealth of the Gentiles,
And their kings in procession.
For the nation and kingdom which will not serve you shall perish,
And *those* nations shall be utterly ruined.
"The glory of Lebanon shall come to you,
The cypress, the pine, and the box tree together,
To beautify the place of My sanctuary;
And I will make the place of My feet glorious.

a. **Your sons shall come from afar**: Through this passage, one of the great themes is *regathering*. We may suppose that in the Millennial Kingdom of Jesus, every Jewish person remaining on the earth will be gathered into the land of Israel from every nation on earth. The present-day regathering of Israel is a precious preview of this ultimate and complete regathering.

b. **The wealth of the Gentiles shall come to you**: Not only will they receive the treasure of their people, but also the literal treasure of **the Gentiles shall come to** Israel in the Millennial Kingdom. The nations will willingly give them their **wealth**, much as the Egyptians willingly gave the Israelites riches when they left Egypt (Exodus 12:35-36). So much will be given that they will need to keep the gates of the city **open continually**.

c. **They shall bring gold.... their silver and their gold with them**: Why do the nations bestow such riches on little Israel? First, they recognize that they thereby give it to God. They bring **their silver and their gold with them, to the name of the Lord your God, and to the Holy One of Israel**. Second, they do it because they see the work of God in Israel: **because He has glorified you**. So they willingly give to and serve Israel (**The sons of foreigners shall build up your walls, and their kings shall minister to you**).

d. **To beautify the place of My sanctuary; and I will make the place of My feet glorious**: Another reason the riches of the nations pour into Jerusalem in the Millennial Kingdom of Jesus will be to build and support the Millennial Temple. The Millennial Temple – described in great depth in Ezekiel 40-47 – stands as a place memorializing God's presence and work in history. There will apparently also be priests and sacrifices at the temple, but not for atonement – because atonement was finished at the cross. The sacrifices are for worship, consecration, and perhaps historical reenactment.

B. The glory of Israel in the Kingdom contrasted with their previous state.

1. (14-18) How the nations treated Israel, and how they will treat them in the Kingdom.

Also the sons of those who afflicted you
Shall come bowing to you,
And all those who despised you shall fall prostrate at the soles of your feet;
And they shall call you The City of the LORD,
Zion of the Holy One of Israel.
"Whereas you have been forsaken and hated,
So that no one went through *you*,
I will make you an eternal excellence,
A joy of many generations.
You shall drink the milk of the Gentiles,
And milk the breast of kings;
You shall know that I, the LORD, *am* your Savior
And your Redeemer, the Mighty One of Jacob.
"Instead of bronze I will bring gold,
Instead of iron I will bring silver,
Instead of wood, bronze,
And instead of stones, iron.
I will also make your officers peace,
And your magistrates righteousness.
Violence shall no longer be heard in your land,
Neither wasting nor destruction within your borders;
But you shall call your walls Salvation,
And your gates Praise.

a. **The sons of those who afflicted you shall come bowing to you**: Those who previously persecuted Israel, and specifically Jerusalem, will have a different heart and mind in the Millennial Kingdom. Then they will **come bowing** to Jerusalem; they will recognize it as **The City of the LORD**.

b. **Instead of bronze I will bring gold**: God will take what was old – and perhaps functional, but not full of glory – and replace it with far better things. More of a miracle than turning **bronze** to **gold** is turning **magistrates** to **righteousness**.

c. **Violence shall no longer be heard in your land, neither wasting nor destruction within your borders; but you shall call your walls Salvation,**

and your gates Praise: What a glorious transformation! From the violence and unrestrained bloodshed of Isaiah 59:6-8, to walls called **Salvation** and gates called **Praise**.

i. The ultimate fulfillment of these things waits because the Millennial Kingdom is not yet here. But the King of that Kingdom is here and wants to do some of that work on a different level. For example, a *home* can see a beautiful transformation right now. It can be said of a Christian home, *violence shall no longer be heard in your home, neither wasting nor destruction within your walls; but you shall call your walls Salvation and your doors Praise.*

d. **You shall know**: This explains *why* God does this. It is not because Israel is so great and has earned this as an achievement through hard work. He does it that **You shall know that I, the LORD, am your Savior and your Redeemer, the Mighty One of Jacob**. He does a work so great that all know it is His doing.

2. (19-22) How the LORD will treat Israel in the Kingdom.

"The sun shall no longer be your light by day,
Nor for brightness shall the moon give light to you;
But the LORD will be to you an everlasting light,
And your God your glory.
Your sun shall no longer go down,
Nor shall your moon withdraw itself;
For the LORD will be your everlasting light,
And the days of your mourning shall be ended.
Also your people *shall* all *be* righteous;
They shall inherit the land forever,
The branch of My planting,
The work of My hands,
That I may be glorified.
A little one shall become a thousand,
And a small one a strong nation.
I, the LORD, will hasten it in its time."

a. **The sun shall no longer be your light by day...but the LORD will be to you an everlasting light**: This is like the light of the New Jerusalem described in Revelation 21:23, where the LORD Himself is the light. But just as important as having the LORD as your **everlasting light** is having **your God your glory**, and to **glory** in no one or nothing else.

i. "In the old order of creation, life was governed rigidly by night and day and unpredictably by the fitfulness of sun and moon. But in the new order of salvation, the ruling principle is the changeless presence of the Lord." (Motyer)

b. **They shall inherit the land forever**: When we remember the context of Isaiah's prophecy, it makes it even more precious. Isaiah was mostly written under the shadow of coming defeat and exile. To those dispossessed people of God, Isaiah pointed them to a day when **they shall inherit the land forever**.

i. This promise would not be fulfilled because the people of God were so good. Rather, the LORD said that it would be seen as **the work of My hands, that I may be glorified**.

c. **I, the LORD, will hasten it in its time**: God didn't say it would happen soon, though in an eternal scale we might consider it soon. But God would **hasten it** – hurry it along, expedite it – **in its time**. When **its time** has come, the LORD will **hasten it**, but not before **its time**.

i. The promise seems too good to be true, and we are conditioned to think that if it seems too good to be true, it is. But God is too good *not* to be true.

Isaiah 61 – Out of the Mouth of the Messiah

A. What the Messiah will do.

1. (1a) The empowerment of the Messiah's ministry.

"The Spirit of the Lord GOD is upon Me,
Because the LORD has anointed Me.

a. **The Spirit of the Lord GOD is upon Me**: Here, Isaiah prophetically speaks for the Messiah, and the Messiah announces that He is blessed and empowered by **the Spirit of the Lord GOD.**

b. **The Spirit of the Lord GOD is upon Me**: In Luke 4:16-22, Jesus spoke in the synagogue of Nazareth, His hometown. He opened up the scroll to Isaiah 61 – perhaps an assigned reading, perhaps chosen by Him – and read from the beginning of the chapter through the first line of verse 2. When He sat down, He simply said *today this Scripture is fulfilled in your hearing.* Jesus is the person described in Isaiah 61:1-3 and He is the one **the Spirit of the Lord GOD is upon.**

i. If Jesus, the Son of God and God the Son, perfect in both His deity and humanity, needed the **Spirit of the Lord GOD**, how much more do we.

c. **Because the LORD has anointed Me**: This identifies the speaker as the Messiah because *Messiah* means "Anointed One." Passages such as 1 Samuel 2:10 refer to the Messiah as *His anointed.*

i. The word "anoint" means *to rub or sprinkle on; apply an unguent, ointment, or oily liquid to.* Persons in the Old Testament were often literally anointed with oil. For example, priests were anointed for their special service to the LORD (Exodus 28:41). Literal oil would be applied, but as a sign of the Holy Spirit upon their lives and service. The oil on the head was only the outward representation of the real, spiritual work going on inside them.

ii. As Christians under the New Covenant, we also have an anointing: *But you have an anointing from the Holy One* (1 John 2:20). In the New Testament sense, *anointing* has the idea of being filled with, and blessed by, the Holy Spirit. This is something that is the common property of *all* Christians, but something we can and should become more submitted and responsive to.

2. (1b-3) The ministry of the Messiah.

To preach good tidings to the poor;
He has sent Me to heal the brokenhearted,
To proclaim liberty to the captives,
And the opening of the prison to *those who are* bound;
To proclaim the acceptable year of the LORD,
And the day of vengeance of our God;
To comfort all who mourn,
To console those who mourn in Zion,
To give them beauty for ashes,
The oil of joy for mourning,
The garment of praise for the spirit of heaviness;
That they may be called trees of righteousness,
The planting of the LORD, that He may be glorified."

a. **To preach good tidings to the poor**: The Messiah announces that He is here to heal the damage that sin brings. Sin has done great damage, so there needs to be a great work of redemption.

b. **He has sent Me**: Because sin impoverishes, He will **preach good tidings to the poor**. Because sin breaks hearts, He will **heal the brokenhearted**. Because sin makes captives, He will **proclaim liberty to the captives, and the opening of the prison to those who are bound**. Because sin oppresses, He will **proclaim the acceptable year of the LORD**.

c. **He has sent Me**: Because sin is a crime that must be avenged, He will **proclaim…the day of vengeance of our God**.

i. Significantly, Jesus stopped reading before this sentence. He stopped in the middle of the prophecy, because to **proclaim…the day of vengeance of our God** is relevant to His *Second Coming*, not to His first coming. The comma in **year of the LORD, and the day of vengeance** has stood for almost 2,000 years. This shows us something of the nature of Biblical prophecy: it may "shift gears" and time frames quickly and without warning.

ii. We can compare a whole **year** of grace to a single **day** of vengeance.

d. **He has sent Me**: Because sin brings grief, He will **comfort all who mourn**.

i. The extent of the comfort and restoration is beautifully described. Instead of the **ashes** of mourning, He gives His people **beauty**. Instead of the **mourning** itself, He gives His people **the oil of joy**. Instead of **the spirit of heaviness**, He gives His people **the garment of praise**. Why do we sit in the ashes, why do we mourn, why do we indulge the **spirit of heaviness** when Jesus gave us something so much better?

ii. The word **beauty** has in mind a beautiful crown or head ornament. It is translated *exquisite hats* in Exodus 39:28 and *headdresses* in Isaiah 3:20. In mourning, ashes would be cast upon the head (2 Samuel 13:19). Here, the ashes are replaced with a beautiful crown.

e. **That they may be called trees of righteousness**: The restored place of God's people is glorious. They are as strong, beautiful, and useful as **trees** – and **trees of righteousness** at that. Most wonderfully, when people look at the trees, they see they are the **planting of the Lord**.

B. What God's people will do.

1. (4) God's people will rebuild what is ruined.

And they shall rebuild the old ruins,
They shall raise up the former desolations,
And they shall repair the ruined cities,
The desolations of many generations.

a. **They shall rebuild the old ruins**: God loves to restore **ruins**. He wants to use His people to restore and rebuild things that are broken down and **ruined**. Under the empowerment of the Spirit, and the ministry of the Messiah, God's people will be rebuilders.

b. **The desolations of many generations**: Even if the rubble has stood for **many generations**, God can still use His people to rebuild. A beautiful example – and partial fulfillment – of this is Nehemiah, who took the decades-old rubble of Jerusalem's walls and rebuilt the walls.

2. (5-6) God's people will be set apart to serve the Lord.

Strangers shall stand and feed your flocks,
And the sons of the foreigner
***Shall be* your plowmen and your vinedressers.**
But you shall be named the priests of the Lord,
They shall call you the servants of our God.
You shall eat the riches of the Gentiles,
And in their glory you shall boast.

a. **You shall be named the priests of the LORD, men shall call you the servants of our God**: God's people, under the anointing of the Spirit and the ministry of the Messiah, have a holy occupation. They are **priests of the LORD** and **servants of our God**. God provides others to take care of the **flocks** and to be **your plowmen and your vinedressers**.

3. (7) God's people will rejoice at God's great blessings.

Instead of your shame *you shall have* double *honor*,
And *instead of* confusion they shall rejoice in their portion.
Therefore in their land they shall possess double;
Everlasting joy shall be theirs.

a. **Instead of your shame**: What a change under the anointing of the Spirit and the ministry of the Messiah! No more **shame**. Now, **you shall have double honor**. No more **confusion**. Now, **they shall rejoice in their portion**. Indeed, **everlasting joy shall be theirs**, a joy that can never be taken away.

C. The everlasting covenant.

1. (8) The heart behind the covenant.

"For I, the LORD, love justice;
I hate robbery for burnt offering;
I will direct their work in truth,
And will make with them an everlasting covenant.

a. **For I, the LORD, love justice; I hate robbery for burnt offering**: The LORD explains how sacrifices such as a **burnt offering** can really just amount to **robbery** if the heart isn't right. Instead, **the LORD loves justice**. Sacrifices alone, and the sacrificial system in itself, are not enough.

b. **I will direct their work in truth, and will make with them an everlasting covenant**: God has an alternative to the sacrificial system. As God directs the work, and as He makes an **everlasting covenant**, then His heart will be fulfilled among the people.

2. (9) The covenant brings prominent blessings.

Their descendants shall be known among the Gentiles,
And their offspring among the people.
All who see them shall acknowledge them,
That they are the posterity *whom* the LORD has blessed."

a. **They are posterity whom the LORD has blessed**: This *everlasting covenant* brings blessing, and blessings so prominent that the blessed **shall be known among the Gentiles**. In fact, **all who see them shall acknowledge them**.

b. **Whom the Lord has blessed**: The writer to the Hebrews pronounces a blessing regarding this everlasting covenant: *Now may the God of peace who brought up our Lord Jesus from the dead, that great Shepherd of the sheep, through the blood of the everlasting covenant, make you complete in every good work to do His will, working in you what is well pleasing in His sight, through Jesus Christ, to whom be glory forever and ever. Amen.* (Hebrews 13:20-21)

3. (10-11) The covenant brings salvation and righteousness.

I will greatly rejoice in the Lord,
My soul shall be joyful in my God;
For He has clothed me with the garments of salvation,
He has covered me with the robe of righteousness,
As a bridegroom decks *himself* with ornaments,
And as a bride adorns *herself* with her jewels.
For as the earth brings forth its bud,
As the garden causes the things that are sown in it to spring forth,
So the Lord God will cause righteousness and praise to spring forth before all the nations.

a. **I will greatly rejoice in the Lord**: The blessed one's joy isn't in the blessing itself but **in the Lord**. This is the same thought later expressed in Philippians 4:4, where the Apostle Paul wrote, *Rejoice in the Lord always. Again I will say, rejoice!*

b. **For He has clothed me with the garments of salvation, He has covered me with the robe of righteousness**: The granting of salvation and righteousness to God's people is represented by the picture of clothing them.

i. These are *glorious* garments: **As a bridegroom decks himself with ornaments, and as a bride adorns herself with her jewels**.

ii. These are *given* garments: **For He has clothed me...He has covered me**.

c. **As the earth brings forth its bud**: The blessing of God *grows*. It isn't manufactured, but it *grows*. Even so, **the Lord God will cause righteousness and praise to spring forth before all the nations**.

i. There is a sense in which we can never *make* something grow. No one can get inside of a seed and "turn on" the genetic component that makes the seed **spring forth**, and **bud**. The blessing of life and growth is miraculously within the seed. But we can provide the right environment for the seed to bud, grow, and be fruitful. That's also how we receive and flourish in God's blessings. We can't "make" or "manufacture" them. But we can put our hearts and minds in the right environments of faith, fellowship, and obedience, to see blessing grow and flourish.

Isaiah 62 – A Glorious Future for Zion

A. Jerusalem is loved and protected.

1. (1-3) The coming righteousness and glory of Zion.

For Zion's sake I will not hold My peace,
And for Jerusalem's sake I will not rest,
Until her righteousness goes forth as brightness,
And her salvation as a lamp *that* burns.
The Gentiles shall see your righteousness,
And all kings your glory.
You shall be called by a new name,
Which the mouth of the LORD will name.
You shall also be a crown of glory
In the hand of the LORD,
And a royal diadem
In the hand of your God.

a. **I will not rest, until her righteousness goes forth as brightness**: Isaiah prophesied in a time when Jerusalem was still a functioning city but was spiritually corrupt. Here, he looks forward to the time when Jerusalem is desolate because she has been conquered by the Babylonians, and prophetically speaks comfort and assurance to her discouraged and downcast citizens. The LORD assures them that He **will not rest** until Jerusalem is restored by a shining **righteousness**.

i. This prophecy is directed towards **Zion** and **Jerusalem**. Although God is concerned with that area as an actual material place, it also stands as a representation of Israel, and in an even more general sense, as a representation of all God's people.

b. **The Gentiles shall see your righteousness**: When God lifts up Zion, then the nations see it and are brought to trust in the LORD themselves. The work God would do for Jerusalem was intended to have an effect on more than just Jerusalem but would extend to **the Gentiles** and to **all kings**.

c. **You shall be called by a new name**: Jerusalem will be so transformed that she will **be called by a new name**. Since the LORD is the author of the transformation, He is also the author of the new name (**which the mouth of the LORD will name**).

i. The thought is extended in Isaiah 62:4, where the LORD "exchanges" the old names of Jerusalem for her new names of glory and security.

ii. The idea of **a new name** also extends to Christians, in passages like Revelation 2:17 and 3:12. In heaven, when our transformation is complete, we will receive a new name that matches our completely transformed nature.

d. **You shall also be a crown of glory in the hand of the LORD**: Jerusalem will be so special to God that He will regard it as a **crown of glory**. We may be familiar with the idea that we will *receive* a crown; it is deeper and more wonderful to consider that we will **be a crown of glory in the hand of the LORD**.

i. Paul uses a similar twist on a familiar idea in Ephesians 1:18, where he says that the believer should understand *what are the riches of the glory of His inheritance in the saints*. The idea is not of our inheritance in the LORD, but of His inheritance in *us*. We often have only a superficial understanding of how precious we are to God.

2. (4-5) The LORD loves Zion as a bridegroom loves a bride.

You shall no longer be termed Forsaken,
Nor shall your land any more be termed Desolate;
But you shall be called Hephzibah, and your land Beulah;
For the LORD delights in you,
And your land shall be married.
***For as* a young man marries a virgin,**
***So* shall your sons marry you;**
And *as* the bridegroom rejoices over the bride,
***So* shall your God rejoice over you.**

a. **You shall no longer be termed Forsaken**: Jerusalem knew the experience of war and defeat and desolation. God's people knew what it was like to feel **Forsaken** and **Desolate**, so it is as if they could take those names.

b. **But you shall be called Hephzibah, and your land Beulah**: The days of **Forsaken** and **Desolate** will one day pass. There will come a day when Zion and God's people will know that God delights in them (**Hephzibah** means "My delight is in her"). There will come a day when Zion and God's people will know the unbroken presence and love of God, as a wife should know the presence and love of her husband (**Beulah** means "Married").

i. "With such economy of words and beauty of imagery Isaiah depicts the loving unanimity that characterise Zion and her intimate union with the Lord – which Revelation 19:7 foresees as the marriage of the Lamb." (Motyer)

c. **And as the bridegroom rejoices over the bride, so shall your God rejoice over you**: Zion and God's people will know how much the LORD loves them. His feeling towards them is more than an obligation-type love; instead, He will **rejoice over you**.

i. The same idea is beautifully communicated in Zephaniah 3:17: *The LORD your God in your midst, the Mighty One, will save; He will rejoice over you with gladness, He will quiet you with His love, He will rejoice over you with singing.* No wonder Paul made a special prayer that we could somehow begin to comprehend such love, that we *may be able to comprehend with all the saints what is the width and length and depth and height; to know the love of Christ which passes knowledge.* (Ephesians 3:18-19)

3. (6-9) The LORD promises to protect Zion.

I have set watchmen on your walls, O Jerusalem;
They shall never hold their peace day or night.
You who make mention of the LORD, do not keep silent,
And give Him no rest till He establishes
And till He makes Jerusalem a praise in the earth.
The LORD has sworn by His right hand
And by the arm of His strength:
"Surely I will no longer give your grain
As food for your enemies;
And the sons of the foreigner shall not drink your new wine,
For which you have labored.
But those who have gathered it shall eat it,
And praise the LORD;
Those who have brought it together shall drink it in My holy courts."

a. **I have set watchmen on your walls, O Jerusalem**: Because God loves and rejoices over Zion, He will protect them. Though they were conquered before by the Babylonians, the day will come when **He makes Jerusalem a praise in the earth.**

b. **Watchmen on your walls**: The **watchmen** have a constant duty. They **shall never hold their peace day or night. You who make mention**

of the Lord, do not keep silent, and give Him no rest till He makes Jerusalem a praise in the earth. The **watchmen** are not critics; they are prayer warriors, who constantly pray, giving God "**no rest**" until God's people and His city are restored.

i. Bultema on **I have set watchmen…they shall never hold their peace day or night**: "There is a threefold rich thought: (1) The Lord Himself does not rest with regard to Zion; (2) He does not want His petitioners to keep silence in their prayers for Israel; (3) and He does not want His people to leave Him alone concerning Israel's deliverance."

ii. "A restless Saviour calls upon his people to be restless, and to make the Lord himself restless – to give him no rest till his chosen city is in full splendour, his chosen church complete and glorious." (Spurgeon)

iii. "'Give him no rest' is our Lord's own command to us concerning the great God. I do not suppose any of you ever advised a beggar to be importunate with you. Did you ever say, 'Whenever you see me go over this crossing ask me for a penny. If I do not give you one, run after me, or call after me all the way down the street. If that does not succeed, lay hold upon me, and do not let me go until I help you. Beg without ceasing.' Did any one of you ever invite applicants to call often, and make large requests of you?…. He does in effect say, 'Press me! Urge me! Lay hold on my strength. Wrestle with me, as when a man seeks to give another a fall that he may prevail with him.' All this, and much more, is included in the expression, 'Give him no rest.'" (Spurgeon)

c. **The Lord has sworn by His right hand and by the arm of His strength**: No more will Jerusalem be plundered by those who would steal her **grain** or **new wine**. Instead, **those who have gathered it shall eat it, and praise the Lord**.

B. The Lord will visit Jerusalem.

1. (10) A way prepared for the coming of the Lord.

Go through,
Go through the gates!
Prepare the way for the people;
Build up,
Build up the highway!
Take out the stones,
Lift up a banner for the peoples!

a. **Prepare the way for the people**: Isaiah prophetically looks forward to the time for the LORD to fulfill these promises. Since His salvation is coming, they must **prepare the way for the people**. They need to **build up the highway**, so a smooth road without obstacles is ready to usher people to the LORD's salvation.

i. Previously through Isaiah great promises were made of a massive pilgrimage to Jerusalem, so roads must be built and the way must be prepared.

b. **Lift up a banner for the peoples**: Not only must the way be prepared, but it must also be *marked* by **a banner for the peoples**. Then not only will they be *able* to come, but they will also be *attracted* to come.

2. (11-12) The Messiah comes to Zion.

Indeed the LORD has proclaimed
To the end of the world:
"Say to the daughter of Zion,
'Surely your salvation is coming;
Behold, His reward *is* with Him,
And His work before Him.'"
And they shall call them The Holy People,
The Redeemed of the LORD;
And you shall be called Sought Out,
A City Not Forsaken.

a. **Say to the daughter of Zion, "Surely your salvation is coming"**: The way has been prepared and marked; now is the time for the LORD's salvation and Savior to emerge, and to come to Zion.

i. The Savior came to Zion, but not *only* to Zion. Isaiah makes it clear: **Indeed the LORD has proclaimed to the end of the world** this great news of the coming Savior.

b. **Behold, His reward is with Him**: When the Messiah comes to Zion, **His reward is with Him**. Revelation 22:12 is a quotation from this verse: *And behold, I am coming quickly, and My reward is with Me, to give to every one according to his work.*

i. Paul continues this idea in 1 Corinthians 3:8-14, saying how when we appear before the Lord, we will be judged according to our work for and with Him. On that day, *each one will receive his own reward according to his own labor.* (1 Corinthians 3:8)

c. **And you shall be called Sought Out, A City Not Forsaken**: Through her history, Jerusalem knew what it was like to be **Forsaken**. But in that day, she will be called **Sought Out**; everyone will know she was valued and chosen by God.

Isaiah 63 – Prayer from Captivity

A. The day of vengeance.

1. (1) A question and an answer: "**Who is this**?"

Who is this who comes from Edom,
With dyed garments from Bozrah,
This *One who is* glorious in His apparel,
Traveling in the greatness of His strength?—
"I who speak in righteousness, mighty to save."

a. **Who is this who comes from Edom**: This prophecy describes the day of the LORD's vengeance. He has come **from Edom** in the sense that He has judged there first, and now comes to the land of Israel. As the LORD arrives, He **is glorious in His apparel, traveling in the greatness of His strength**.

i. **With dyed garments from Bozrah** is also significant. **Bozrah** was the capital city of ancient Edom, and "The important city of Bozrah is singled out because its name means 'grape-gathering,' and Isaiah developed a detailed comparison between treading grapes and pouring out blood." (Wolf)

ii. "God's act of judgment against Edom is clearly conceived to be a putting right of the wrongs done to Zion, especially since the Edomites took advantage of Judah's weakness after the Fall of Jerusalem to the Babylonians." (Grogan)

b. **I who speak in righteousness, mighty to save**: This is the LORD's reply to the question in the prophecy. He identifies Himself by what He says (**I who speak in righteousness**) and what He does (**mighty to save**). Even in the midst of judgment, in His glory and strength, He wants men to know He is **mighty to save**, not only *mighty to judge*.

2. (2-6) A question and an answer: "Why are Your clothes red?"

Why is Your apparel red,
And Your garments like one who treads in the winepress?
"I have trodden the winepress alone,
And from the peoples no one *was* with Me.
For I have trodden them in My anger,
And trampled them in My fury;
Their blood is sprinkled upon My garments,
And I have stained all My robes.
For the day of vengeance *is* in My heart,
And the year of My redeemed has come.
I looked, but *there was* no one to help,
And I wondered
That *there was* no one to uphold;
Therefore My own arm brought salvation for Me;
And My own fury, it sustained Me.
I have trodden down the peoples in My anger,
Made them drunk in My fury,
And brought down their strength to the earth."

a. **Why is Your apparel red**: The prophet asks why the garment of the Lord is **red**, and the Lord answers, "**I have trodden the winepress alone.... their blood is sprinkled upon My garments**." This promise is fulfilled when Jesus returns to the earth, and this passage is clearly behind passages like Revelation 19:13 and 15: *He was clothed with a robe dipped in blood, and His name is called The Word of God.... Now out of His mouth goes a sharp sword, that with it He should strike the nations. And He Himself will rule them with a rod of iron. He Himself treads the winepress of the fierceness and wrath of Almighty God.*

b. **I have trodden the winepress alone**: This reminds us that this work of judgment belongs to Jesus Christ and He **alone**. Though we will be part of the heavenly armies that accompany Jesus (Revelation 19:14), the work of judgment belongs to Him **alone**. The point is even emphasized by Isaiah: **From the peoples no one was with Me.... My own arm brought salvation for Me; and My own fury, it sustained Me**.

i. In God's great plan of the Ages, Jesus accomplishes two things **alone**. First, He atones for our sin *alone*. He alone hung on the cross, bearing the weight of all our guilt. Second, He judges the world **alone**. God does not need us to execute His ultimate judgment; we leave that to Him.

ii. "You will hear one say, that such-and-such a good man was punished for his transgressions; and I have known believers think that their afflictions were punishments sent from God on account of their sins. The thing is impossible; God has punished us, who are his people, once for all in Christ, and he never will punish us again. He cannot do it, seeing he is a just God. Afflictions are chastisements from a Father's hand, but they are not judicial punishments. Jesus has tredden the wine-press, and he has trodden it alone: so we cannot tread it." (Spurgeon)

c. **The day of vengeance is in My heart**: These words, prophetically spoken by Jesus, sound almost foreign to us. We rarely think of **vengeance** being in the **heart** of Jesus, but He said *the Father judges no one, but has committed all judgment to the Son* (John 5:22).

d. **And the year of My redeemed has come**: In this, Isaiah prophetically explains *why* the Messiah can say, "**vengeance is in My heart**." It isn't because God loves punishing sinners, but He does love vindicating His **redeemed**.

i. Notice also the comparison: it is a mere **day of vengeance**, but an entire **year of My redeemed**. Each phrase is simply a poetic way of saying "time" but God fittingly uses the picture of a **day** in communicating His **vengeance**, and a **year** in expressing His grace.

B. The exile's prayer.

1. (7-14) Remembering the mercy and the might of the Lord.

I will mention the lovingkindnesses of the Lord
***And* the praises of the Lord,**
According to all that the Lord has bestowed on us,
And the great goodness toward the house of Israel,
Which He has bestowed on them according to His mercies,
According to the multitude of His lovingkindnesses.
For He said, "Surely they *are* My people,
Children *who* will not lie."
So He became their Savior.
In all their affliction He was afflicted,
And the Angel of His Presence saved them;
In His love and in His pity He redeemed them;
And He bore them and carried them
All the days of old.
But they rebelled and grieved His Holy Spirit;
So He turned Himself against them as an enemy,
***And* He fought against them.**
Then he remembered the days of old,

Moses *and* his people, *saying*:
"Where *is* He who brought them up out of the sea
With the shepherd of His flock?
Where *is* He who put His Holy Spirit within them,
Who led *them* by the right hand of Moses,
With His glorious arm,
Dividing the water before them
To make for Himself an everlasting name,
Who led them through the deep,
As a horse in the wilderness,
***That* they might not stumble?"**
As a beast goes down into the valley,
***And* the Spirit of the LORD causes him to rest,**
So You lead Your people,
To make Yourself a glorious name.

a. **I will mention the lovingkindnesses of the LORD…according to all that the LORD has bestowed on us**: This prayer is prophetically placed in the mouth of one of Judah's Babylonian exiles. Despite the agony expressed later in the prayer, the praying one first **will mention the lovingkindnesses of the LORD**. This is a glorious example of how, even in the lowest place, we can praise the LORD and remember His goodness.

i. Look at all that the troubled one has to thank God for: **great goodness…mercies…. He became their Savior…. His love…His pity…He bore them and carried them**. If this vocabulary of praise can come from an afflicted one, what excuse can we have for not praising God?

ii. **Lovingkindnesses** "is the Hebrew word *hesed*, the love that is faithful to the covenant." (Grogan) It can also be translated "steadfast love." It is one of the great words of the Old Testament, probably the closest Hebrew equivalent to the Greek word *agape*.

iii. **Surely they are My people, children who will not lie**: "The Hebrew word for *lie* contains even more than our word. It was applied to a fountain, pit or brook that contained no water any more and so disappointed the thirsty person, and to a fruit tree that no longer yielded any fruit (Habakkuk 3:17). With this one significant word, the Lord meant to say that His people will not deceive and disappoint Him." (Butlema)

b. **In all their affliction He was afflicted**: Isaiah knows the nature of God; that in the afflictions of His people, He is afflicted also. God is not a dispassionate, unfeeling observer when His people suffer. He suffers with them when they are afflicted.

i. **In all their affliction He was afflicted** is another reason why anti-Semitism is so wicked. When the Jewish people are persecuted and afflicted, the LORD is **afflicted** also. How tragic that institutional Christianity, pretending to act in the name of Jesus, **afflicted** the LORD Himself by persecuting the Jewish people.

c. **And the Angel of His Presence saved them**: This refers to the presence and work of Jesus among ancient Israel, especially among those delivered from Egypt.

i. "The *angel of His presence* is the Messiah.... Calvin sees in this angel merely a serving angel. But of this Angel it is said that He by His *love* and *pity* saved Israel; this can hardly be said of a created angel. It is the Christ who is meant here." (Bultema)

ii. "*Angel of his presence*: literally 'of his face'. We recognise people by face; 'face' is the Lord's very own presence (Psalm 139:7), among them in the person of his angel – that unique 'Angel of the Lord' (as in Genesis 16:7ff; 21:17; 22:11, 15; Exodus 3:2; 14:19; 23:20-23; Malachi 3:1) who speaks as the Lord and is yet distinct from him." (Motyer)

d. **But they rebelled and grieved His Holy Spirit**: Despite this outpouring of love and mercy from God, His people responded with cold, rebellious, unresponsive hearts. God had to deal with this in His people, so **He fought against them**.

i. In these few verses, we hear from God the Father (**My people, children who will not lie**), God the Son (**the Angel of His Presence**), and God the Holy Spirit (**His Holy Spirit**). Clearly, "There are Trinitarian overtones in the passage." (Grogan)

e. **Then he remembered the days of old**: In the midst of the LORD's discipline – in this case, prophetically speaking, the Babylonian exile – the praying one **remembered the days of old**. He **remembered** the mighty hand of God in **days of old** and knew that mighty hand could be raised again for His people.

i. Specifically, in this case, **he remembered** what the LORD did in the days of Moses and the Exodus. Since now they were in a place of exile (Babylon), the story of God's deliverance from Egypt had special relevance. The praying one wasn't there for the Exodus; he had to read about it in God's word. But he saw how God's great works in the past had meaning right now.

f. **As a horse in the wilderness…as a beast goes down into the valley**: Isaiah speaks of the *ease of progress* that Israel made during the Exodus, and how God will bless Israel again in their regathering and restoration. The result will be that **the Spirit of the LORD causes him to rest**.

i. **As a horse in the wilderness** should be understood in this sense: *as a horse in open country*. The idea is of unhindered, rapid progress.

ii. "In both these verses there is an allusion to the Israelites going through the Red Sea in the bottom of which they found no more inconvenience than a horse would in running in the desert." (Clarke)

2. (15-19) A plea for restoration.

Look down from heaven,
And see from Your habitation, holy and glorious.
Where *are* Your zeal and Your strength,
The yearning of Your heart and Your mercies toward me?
Are they restrained?
Doubtless You *are* our Father,
Though Abraham was ignorant of us,
And Israel does not acknowledge us.
You, O LORD, *are* our Father;
Our Redeemer from Everlasting *is* Your name.
O LORD, why have You made us stray from Your ways,
***And* hardened our heart from Your fear?**
Return for Your servants' sake,
The tribes of Your inheritance.
Your holy people have possessed *it* but a little while;
Our adversaries have trodden down Your sanctuary.
We have become *like* those of old, over whom You never ruled,
Those who were never called by Your name.

a. **Where are Your zeal and Your strength**: The prophet speaks honest words from the mouth of the praying one. Sometimes it feels that the **zeal** and the **strength** of the LORD are far away, and when we feel like that, we should do just what the praying one did: cry out to God.

i. **Return for Your servants' sake**: "The word 'return' may suggest the return of the shekinah glory to the temple as the symbol of God's dwelling among his people (as in Ezekiel 43:6-12)." (Grogan)

b. **We have become like those of old, over whom You never ruled**: The praying one looks at the condition of God's people and cries out in agony. Why has God allowed this? The praying one isn't accurate in all his theology, but he is an expert in expressing the pain of the human heart.

Isaiah 64 – The Remnant Prays

A. Requesting and remembering God's great works

1. (1-4) God's people plead for Him to come in power and glory.

Oh, that You would rend the heavens!
That You would come down!
That the mountains might shake at Your presence—
As fire burns brushwood,
As fire causes water to boil—
To make Your name known to Your adversaries,
***That* the nations may tremble at Your presence!**
Then You did awesome things *for which* we did not look,
You came down,
The mountains shook at Your presence.
For since the beginning of the world
***Men* have not heard nor perceived by the ear,**
Nor has the eye seen any God besides You,
Who acts for the one who waits for Him.

a. **Oh, that You would rend the heavens! That You would come down**: The prayer of the remnant continues from Isaiah chapter 63; here, the plea is for God to intervene from heaven.

b. **The mountains shook at Your presence**: Earlier in this prayer (Isaiah 63:11-13), the praying one remembered God's great work for Israel in the days of the Exodus. Here, the praying one also remembers how the LORD shook Mount Sinai when Israel camped there on their way from Egypt to the Promised Land (Exodus 19:17-18).

c. **Nor has the eye seen any God besides You, who acts for the one who waits for Him**: The praying one now trusts that since *he* is **one who waits for** the LORD, he also will see God act on his behalf.

i. **The one who waits for Him**: "There is, however, a special blessing connected with *waiting for the Lord.* Men, even church-going men, would rather *work* than *wait.* They also love the legalism more than the holiness of waiting. Church leaders of today think waiting for the Lord is foolish dreaming." (Bultema)

2. (5-7) The obstacle to God's great works: our great sinfulness.

You meet him who rejoices and does righteousness,
***Who* remembers You in Your ways.**
You are indeed angry, for we have sinned—
In these ways we continue;
And we need to be saved.
But we are all like an unclean *thing*,
And all our righteousnesses *are* like filthy rags;
We all fade as a leaf,
And our iniquities, like the wind,
Have taken us away.
And *there is* no one who calls on Your name,
Who stirs himself up to take hold of You;
For You have hidden Your face from us,
And have consumed us because of our iniquities.

a. **You meet him who rejoices and does righteousness**: The praying one asks the question, "What kind of man does the LORD answer in prayer?" In Isaiah 64:4, he noted that it was the *one who waits for* the LORD. Now the praying one expands the idea, and notes that the LORD will answer the prayer (**meet**) for the one **who rejoices and does righteousness**. The LORD will answer the prayer of the one **who remembers** the LORD **in** his **ways**.

b. **For we have sinned – in these ways we continue; and we need to be saved**: This explains the problem. The praying remnant knows that God only answers the prayers of the righteous man, yet it isn't the righteous man who needs **to be saved** from the disaster he has brought on himself. **And we need to be saved** is translated well by the NIV (New International Version) here as, *How then can we be saved?* The praying one then goes on to eloquently describe our state of sin.

i. First, our sin makes us **like an unclean thing**; it makes us unacceptable and unworthy before God. "Under the Jewish law you know that when a person was unclean he could not go up to the house of the Lord. He could offer no sacrifice. God could accept nothing at his hands; he was an outcast and an alien so long as he remained unclean." (Spurgeon)

ii. Even **all our righteousnesses are like filthy rags**. The good we may try to do is unacceptable and unclean before the LORD. Because we **are all like an unclean thing**, even the good we do is polluted. "Brethren, if our righteousnesses are so bad, what must our *un*righteousnesses be?" (Spurgeon)

iii. **We all fade as a leaf.** Our sinful condition has made us weak and unstable, with no lasting power before God.

iv. **Our iniquities, like the wind, have taken us away** means that we have no power to stand against temptation. Our sins carry us along like a hurricane wind.

v. **And there is no one who calls on Your name, who stirs himself up to take hold of You**: Even in our unclean, unstable condition, we didn't seek the LORD the way we should. We were lazy and complacent before the LORD.

vi. "The verbs *sin* and *angry* are perfect tenses – it was your fixed mind to be angry and ours to continue in sin." (Motyer)

vii. Taken together, this is a fearful description of our fallenness: "You must not merely know that you are lost, but you must feel it. Do not be content with simply feeling that it is so, but *mourn before God* that it is so, and *hate yourself* that it is so. Do not look upon it as being a misfortune, but as being your own wilful sin, and look upon yourselves, therefore, as being guilty sinners." (Spurgeon)

c. **Filthy rags**: "*Filthy rags* is 'a garment of menstruation'; bodily discharges were considered a defilement because they were the 'outflow' of a sinful, fallen human nature. So, even what we might consider to be in our favour, *righteous acts*, partake of the defilement of fallenness." (Motyer)

i. Preachers of previous generations thought this passage so extreme in its graphic description of sin's likeness that it should not be preached honestly. "If preachers knew properly the meaning of this word, would they make such a liberal use of it in their public ministry?" (Clarke) "The expression, 'filthy rags,' in the Hebrew, is one which we could not with propriety explain in the present assembly. As the confession must be made privately and alone before God, so the full meaning of the comparison is not meant for human ear." (Spurgeon)

ii. However extreme the phrasing, the point is important. Even the works that seem holiest from the outside can be corrupt and unrighteous. "Sirs, there is sin in our prayers; they need to be prayed over again. There is filth in the very tears that we shed in penitence; there is sin in our very holiness; there is unbelief in our faith; there is hatred in our very love; there is the slime of the serpent upon the fairest flower of our garden." (Spurgeon)

iii. "Those that seek to be saved by their works, Luther fitly calleth the devil's martyrs; they suffer much, and take great pains to go to hell.... We must do all righteousnesses, rest in none but Christ's, disclaiming our own best as spotted and imperfect." (Trapp)

d. **You have hidden Your face from us**: This is the first of two reactions God makes to the sinful condition of man. First, fellowship is broken, or at the very least, damaged. Second, the LORD has **consumed us because of our iniquities**. Our sinful condition has invited – even *demanded* – the righteous judgment of God.

B. A plea for the mercy of the LORD.

1. (8-9) Asking God to remember who His people are.

But now, O LORD,
You *are* our Father;
We *are* the clay, and You our potter;
And all we *are* the work of Your hand.
Do not be furious, O LORD,
Nor remember iniquity forever;
Indeed, please look—we all *are* Your people!

a. **But now, O LORD, You are our Father**: The praying one is in a desperate place; he needs the mercy of God because the justice of God condemns him. In his appeal for mercy, he first reminds God, "**You are our Father**. Please, LORD, have mercy on us as a loving **Father**."

b. **We are the clay, and You our potter**: Next, the praying one appeals for God's mercy because of God's sovereign power over each life. It is like saying, "LORD we are like clay in Your hands. Deal gently with us, and mold us according to Your mercy."

i. A father is always a father; he can never truly disown his children. A potter cannot disown the pot; it is only there because he made it. This is Isaiah's way of saying, "You're stuck with us LORD!"

c. **Do not be furious, O LORD, nor remember iniquity forever**: The praying one asks for mercy on account of "time served." It is as if he prays, "LORD, You had a right to **be furious** with us for a time. You had a right to **remember** our **iniquity** for a while. But please, LORD, do not **remember iniquity forever**."

d. **Indeed, please look–we all are Your people**: The praying one makes his final appeal for mercy on the simple grounds that "LORD, **we all are Your**

people. We are sinners, and deserve Your judgment, but we are still **Your people**. In a sense, LORD, You are stuck with us."

2. (10-11) Asking God to remember the condition of Zion.

Your holy cities are a wilderness,
Zion is a wilderness,
Jerusalem a desolation.
Our holy and beautiful temple,
Where our fathers praised You,
Is burned up with fire;
And all our pleasant things are laid waste.

a. **Zion is a wilderness, Jerusalem a desolation**: In his appeal for mercy, the praying one asks God to look closely at the terrible condition of His **holy cities**. As he draws attention to **our holy and beautiful temple**, he notes that it **is burned up with fire**. It is an eloquent and powerful way of pleading with God to act.

3. (12) Asking God to act.

Will You restrain Yourself because of these *things*, O LORD?
Will You hold Your peace, and afflict us very severely?

a. **Will You restrain Yourself because of these things, O LORD?** The praying one concludes up the prayer with a great question. The **these things** he refers to are not the desperate condition of Jerusalem and the temple (Isaiah 64:10-11). They are the descriptions of our sinful condition (Isaiah 64:5b-7). The praying one asks, "LORD, You know very well our sinful condition. But **will You restrain Yourself because of these things, O LORD?**"

b. **Will You hold Your peace, and afflict us very severely?** The sense is, "LORD, please show mercy! Will you always give us what we deserve?"

i. In this prayer, the praying one deals with what seems to be an impossible problem. Because of our sin (Isaiah 64:5b-7), we are in a desperate state and need the LORD's salvation. But the LORD only answers the prayers of a righteous man (Isaiah 64:4-5a) – and a righteous man wouldn't be in the place we are! Ultimately, the answer is found in the New Covenant, where *a righteous Man stands in our place and prays for us*. This is why Jesus invited us to pray in *His* name (John 14:13-14). When we pray in Jesus' name, *He is the righteous Man* who appeals to God for us.

Isaiah 65 – The LORD *Answers the Prayer of the Remnant*

A. The immediate answer: The LORD will indeed bless His genuine servants.

1. (1-7) The LORD sees the shallow repentance of the remnant.

"I was sought by *those who* did not ask *for Me*;
I was found by *those who* did not seek Me.
I said, 'Here I am, here I am,'
To a nation *that* was not called by My name.
I have stretched out My hands all day long to a rebellious people,
Who walk in a way *that is* not good,
According to their own thoughts;
A people who provoke Me to anger continually to My face;
Who sacrifice in gardens,
And burn incense on altars of brick;
Who sit among the graves,
And spend the night in the tombs;
Who eat swine's flesh,
And the broth of abominable things is *in* their vessels;
Who say, 'Keep to yourself,
Do not come near me,
For I am holier than you!'
These *are* smoke in My nostrils,
A fire that burns all the day.
"Behold, *it is* written before Me:
I will not keep silence, but will repay—
Even repay into their bosom—
Your iniquities and the iniquities of your fathers together,"
Says the LORD,
"Who have burned incense on the mountains

And blasphemed Me on the hills;
Therefore I will measure their former work into their bosom."

a. **I was sought by those who did not ask for Me**: The Jewish exiles in Babylon were examples of those who did **ask** for the LORD; but they would not find Him, because for the most part they sought Him insincerely. Yet, God would be **found by those who did not seek** Him – namely, the Gentiles.

i. Isaiah 63:7 through 64:12 is the prayer of the remnant, voiced through the prophet Isaiah. It is one of the most beautiful and moving prayers in the Bible. Yet it does not seem to be representative of the heart of the Jewish exiles in Babylon. Here, God speaks to that heart, a heart with a shallow repentance.

ii. Paul quotes this passage in Romans 10:20-21: *But Isaiah is very bold and says: "I was found by those who did not seek Me; I was made manifest to those who did not ask for Me." But to Israel he says: "All day long I have stretched out My hands to a disobedient and contrary people."* These were bold words indeed from Isaiah, "so bold, say Origen and others, that for this cause, among others, he was sawn asunder by his unworthy countrymen." (Trapp)

b. **I have stretched out My hands all day long to a rebellious people**: It wasn't that the LORD had ignored the Jewish exiles in Babylon, and others like them. He **stretched out** His **hands all day long** to them. Some responded (like Daniel, or like the one prophetically praying in Isaiah 63:7 through 64:12), but most were **a rebellious people**.

c. **Who walk in a way that is not good, according to their own thoughts**: This defines what it is to be **a rebellious people** – simply, to **walk in a way...according to their own thoughts**. To trust in our own wisdom, our own judgment, our own thinking, is to be among the **rebellious people**.

i. This idea is repeated in several different places in Scripture. The phrase in the book of Judges that characterized the wickedness of that age shows it: *everyone did what was right in his own eyes* (Judges 17:6, 21:25). Proverbs expresses the idea like this: *There is a way that seems right to a man, but its end is the way of death* (Proverbs 14:12, 16:25). To live **according to their own thoughts** may sound like freedom, but really it is bondage. God's solution to living **according to** our **own thoughts** is revealed in Romans 12:2, to *be transformed by the renewing of your mind.*

d. **A people who provoke Me to anger continually to My face**: The walk of these people, **according to their own thoughts**, expresses itself in the most offensive and unholy ways before the LORD. The people **sacrifice in gardens** to idols. They **sit among the graves**, breaking the commands against contact with the dead (Numbers 19:11). They **eat swine's flesh** and drink **the broth of abominable things**.

i. Each of these sins were grossly offensive to the LORD. It is tragic, but true, that walking **according to** our **own thoughts** will always lead us into direct, blatant, opposition to the LORD.

e. **Keep to yourself, do not come near me, for I am holier than you**: They could say this, even in the midst of such extreme offense before God. No wonder God considers such people as **smoke in My nostrils**. Therefore, judgment is promised to them: **I will not keep silence, but will repay… your iniquities and the iniquities of your fathers together**.

i. How could *anyone* think "**I am holier than you!**" when they were steeped in the sins described in this passage? This is a dramatic display of the *blindness* pride brings. They could say, "**I am holier than you!**" and really mean it, because of their complete blindness.

ii. Charles Spurgeon preached a sermon titled *Self Righteousness – A Smouldering Heap of Rubbish* on this text. In it, he describes how dangerous and insidious self-righteousness is. "Moreover, self-righteous men, like foxes, have many tricks and schemes. They condemn in other people what they consider to be very excusable in themselves. They would cry out against others for a tenth part of the sin which they allow in themselves: certain constitutional tendencies, and necessities of circumstances, and various surroundings, all serve as ample apologies. Besides this, if it be admitted that they are wrong upon some points, yet in other directions they are beyond rebuke. If they drink, they do not swear; and if they swear, they do not steal: they make a great deal out of negatives: if they steal, they are not greedy and miserly, but spend their gains freely. If they practice fornication, yet they do not commit adultery; if they talk filthily, yet they boast they do not lie. They would be counted well because they are not universally bad. They do not break every hedge, and therefore they plead that they are not trespassers. As if a debtor for a hundred pounds should claim to be excused because he does not owe two hundred: or, as if a highwayman should say, 'I did not stop all the travellers on the road; I only robbed one or two, and therefore I ought not to be punished.' If a man should willfully break the windows of your shop, I warrant you, you would not take it as an excuse if he pleaded, 'I did not break them all; I only smashed one sheet of plate glass.' Pleas which would not be mentioned in a human court are thought good enough to offer to God. O the folly of our race!" (Spurgeon)

iii. Spurgeon also focused his attention on the most religious of the self-righteous: "Those who come with the language of repentance but without the spirit of it, are sometimes the most self-righteous of all, for they say 'I am all right because I am not self-righteous.' They make a self-righteousness out of the supposed absence of self-righteousness. 'Thank God,' say they, 'we are not as other men are, nor even as these self-righteous people.' Hypocrites all the way through."

iv. Man is so corrupt that he can be self-righteous over almost *anything*. "This weed of self-righteousness will grow on any dunghill. No heap of rubbish is too rotten for the accursed toadstool of proud self to grow upon." (Spurgeon)

2. (8-16) A promise of blessing for the true servants of the Lord, and a promise of chastisement for the false or shallow servants of God.

Thus says the Lord:
"As the new wine is found in the cluster,
And *one* says, 'Do not destroy it,
For a blessing *is* in it,'
So will I do for My servants' sake,
That I may not destroy them all.
I will bring forth descendants from Jacob,
And from Judah an heir of My mountains;
My elect shall inherit it,
And My servants shall dwell there.
Sharon shall be a fold of flocks,
And the Valley of Achor a place for herds to lie down,
For My people who have sought Me.
"But you *are* those who forsake the Lord,
Who forget My holy mountain,
Who prepare a table for Gad,
And who furnish a drink offering for Meni.
Therefore I will number you for the sword,
And you shall all bow down to the slaughter;
Because, when I called, you did not answer;
When I spoke, you did not hear,
But did evil before My eyes,
And chose *that* in which I do not delight."
Therefore thus says the Lord God:
"Behold, My servants shall eat,

But you shall be hungry; behold,
My servants shall drink,
But you shall be thirsty;
Behold, My servants shall rejoice,
But you shall be ashamed;
Behold, My servants shall sing for joy of heart,
But you shall cry for sorrow of heart,
And wail for grief of spirit.
You shall leave your name as a curse to My chosen;
For the Lord GOD will slay you,
And call His servants by another name;
So that he who blesses himself in the earth
Shall bless himself in the God of truth;
And he who swears in the earth
Shall swear by the God of truth;
Because the former troubles are forgotten,
And because they are hidden from My eyes.

a. **"Do not destroy it, for a blessing is in it," so will I do for My servants' sake**: Despite the unholy rebellion and pride of some of the remnant, God still has His servants, and He will bless and restore them. They will be regathered into His land, for He says: "**My elect shall inherit it, and My servants shall dwell there**." He has a special place **for My people who have sought Me**.

i. The picture of Isaiah 65:8 is striking. The idea is that God finds a few "good grapes" among the corrupt **cluster** of His people. It is for the sake of these – **for My servants' sake** – that the LORD shows blessing and restores.

ii. "*Found* suggests that the grapes were oozing as they were picked and that this was specially prized. Hence *there is some good*.... Marvellously, then, the Lord finds his people a blessing, and he prizes and guards them." (Motyer)

iii. "If the Church had clearly understood this simple example, then, it would not have dared to teach Israel's total rejection. Even as He would have saved Sodom for the sake of five righteous people, so He will spare Israel, His vine, for the sake of His *servants*, the cluster of good grapes." (Bultema)

b. **But you are those who forsake the LORD**: Not all are numbered among the servants of the LORD. They are destined for judgment, **because, when I called, you did not answer; when I spoke, you did not hear, but did**

evil before My eyes, and chose that in which I do not delight. On top of all their other sins is the sin of simply refusing to *listen* to God's correction.

i. It is one thing for us to fall into sin through weakness or ignorance; such sin is indeed sin, and God must deal with it as such. But refusing to respond to the conviction of the Holy Spirit is far worse. It is bad enough to be speeding down the highway; it is worse to ignore the flashing red lights in your rearview mirror.

ii. Wolf on **Gad** and **Meni**: "They were presenting offerings to the gods 'Fortune' and 'Destiny,' so their destiny would be the sword."

c. **Behold, My servants shall eat, but you shall be hungry**: Because of this, the true servants of God among the remnant will be blessed, but the false servants will be cursed. Why? It is necessary, **so that he who blesses himself in the earth shall bless himself in the God of truth**. If God does not reward His true servants, and curse His false servants, then God is not shown to be **the God of truth**.

i. **The God of truth** is literally "the God of (the) Amen...the God who says 'amen' to all his promises, affirming their reality and his trustworthiness to keep them." (Motyer)

B. The ultimate answer: The LORD will redeem and remake all of creation.

1. (17-19) The promise of new heavens and a new earth.

For behold, I create new heavens and a new earth;
And the former shall not be remembered or come to mind.
But be glad and rejoice forever in what I create;
For behold, I create Jerusalem *as* a rejoicing,
And her people a joy.
I will rejoice in Jerusalem,
And joy in My people;
The voice of weeping shall no longer be heard in her,
Nor the voice of crying.

a. **Behold, I create new heavens and a new earth**: As the ultimate answer to the problem of man's sin, God will **create new heavens and a new earth**. This takes place after the millennium, the glorious thousand-year reign of Jesus Christ, when this very earth and sky is done away with and God makes **new heavens and a new earth**.

i. Peter used this promise to encourage believers to holy living: *Nevertheless we, according to His promise, look for new heavens and a new earth in which righteousness dwells* (2 Peter 3:13). In the book of Revelation, John also sees this: *Now I saw a new heaven and a new earth, for the first heaven and the first earth had passed away. Also there was no more sea* (Revelation 21:1).

ii. From John's context we see that this **new heavens and a new earth** comes *after* the Great White Throne judgment (Revelation 20:11-15) and is connected not with the millennial earth, but with the eternal state. If all we had to go by was Isaiah's statement, we would automatically connect this **new heavens and a new earth** with the millennial earth, because immediately after Isaiah 65:17-19, we clearly find the millennial earth described. But based on what we find in 2 Peter and Revelation, we must see that Isaiah is in the prophetic habit of switching quickly from one time frame to another, speaking of the eternal state in Isaiah 65:17, and of the millennial earth in Isaiah 65:20-25.

b. **And the former shall not be remembered or come to mind**: This is another indication that Isaiah 65:17 does not speak of the millennial earth. Other passages of Scripture referring to the millennium show that there will be definite remembrance of **former** times on the earth. The whole temple ritual existing in the millennial earth (Ezekiel 40-46) will be a remembrance of the **former** days of Levitical sacrifice. The **former** nations of the world will remain (after judgment) and will serve the LORD and Israel (Psalm 72).

c. **I create Jerusalem as a rejoicing**: There will be a **Jerusalem** in the eternal state, in the **new heavens and a new earth**. Revelation describes – in stunning imagery – the descent of the *New Jerusalem* from heaven to the new earth (Revelation 21:2-27). It is in this Jerusalem, the eternal New Jerusalem, that the **voice of weeping shall no longer be heard in her, nor the voice of crying.**

i. John clearly connects this promise to the New Jerusalem: *And God will wipe away every tear from their eyes; there shall be no more death, nor sorrow, nor crying. There shall be no more pain, for the former things have passed away* (Revelation 21:4).

2. (20-25) The blessed state of the millennial earth.

"No more shall an infant from there *live but a few* days,
Nor an old man who has not fulfilled his days;
For the child shall die one hundred years old,
But the sinner *being* one hundred years old shall be accursed.
They shall build houses and inhabit *them*;
They shall plant vineyards and eat their fruit.
They shall not build and another inhabit;
They shall not plant and another eat;

For as the days of a tree, *so shall be* the days of My people,
And My elect shall long enjoy the work of their hands.
They shall not labor in vain,
Nor bring forth children for trouble;
For they *shall be* the descendants of the blessed of the LORD,
And their offspring with them.
"It shall come to pass
That before they call, I will answer;
And while they are still speaking, I will hear.
The wolf and the lamb shall feed together,
The lion shall eat straw like the ox,
And dust *shall be* the serpent's food.
They shall not hurt nor destroy in all My holy mountain,"
Says the LORD.

a. **No more shall an infant from there live but a few days…for the child shall die one hundred years old**: Quickly – as is the prophetic habit – Isaiah shifts gears, and now speaks not of the eternal state, but of the millennial earth. There will be death in the millennial earth, but in the transformed biology and ecology of the world under the reign of Jesus Christ, people will live incredibly longer, as they did in the days before the flood.

i. In the millennial earth, people will live so long that if someone dies **being one hundred years old**, people will consider that one **accursed**.

b. **They shall build houses and inhabit them; they shall plant vineyards and eat their fruit**: The millennial reign of Jesus Christ will not only be a time of biological transformation; it will also be a time of *social* transformation when perfect justice reigns over the earth. Never again will someone be robbed of the fruits of their labor. If you **build** a house, no one will steal it from you. You will **inhabit** that house. If you **plant vineyards**, no one will steal the fruit of it. You will **eat their fruit**. God gloriously promises, **My elect shall long enjoy the work of their hands**.

i. This may not sound like much, but for those who live in profoundly *unjust* times, this simple justice sounds like a miracle.

ii. One significant reason there will be such justice on the millennial earth is because Satan will be bound for these 1,000 years, unable to work his destructive mischief on the earth (Revelation 20:1-3).

c. **They shall not labor in vain, nor bring forth children for trouble; for they shall be the descendants of the blessed of the LORD, and their offspring with them**: There will be babies born and children raised in the millennial earth, and this is another indication that we are not in the eternal state. In the eternal state, we *neither marry nor are given in marriage, but are like angels of God in heaven* (Matthew 22:30). In the millennial earth, those allowed to enter are blessed of the LORD, and they and their **descendants** will populate the earth.

d. **It shall come to pass that before they call, I will answer; and while they are still speaking, I will hear**: The millennial reign of Jesus Christ will not only be a time of biological and social transformation. It will also be a time of profound spiritual transformation and intimacy. There will be an immediate and constant sense of the presence of God, and His knowledge will cover the earth (Isaiah 11:9).

i. This does not mean that everyone on the millennial earth will be saved; only that the *opportunity* for such close relationship will be widely enjoyed. We know that not all will be saved during the millennial earth because:

- At the conclusion of the time of the millennial earth, Satan is released from his confinement and finds many willing servants on the earth (Revelation 20:7-9), whom he gathers for one last – and strikingly futile – rebellion against God.
- Zechariah 14:16-19 and Psalm 2 describe the firm rule of the Messiah during the millennial earth, dealing decisively with those who do not surrender to His reign, enforcing righteousness all over the earth.

ii. Though not all will be saved on the millennial earth, we may suppose that the proportions will be reversed. Today, it is but a remnant that is saved because *many are called but few are chosen* (Matthew 22:14) and *broad is the way that leads to destruction, and there are many who go in by it. Because narrow is the gate and difficult is the way which leads to life, and there are few who find it* (Matthew 7:13-14). In the millennial earth, the *few* will be those who *don't* know the LORD and are not saved.

iii. One of the reasons why most are saved and know the LORD on the millennial earth is because not all survivors of the Great Tribulation are allowed to populate the millennial earth. After the Great Tribulation – which in judgment reduces the population of the earth by at least a third (Revelation 9:15, 18) – Jesus Christ will return to the earth, and in the judgment of the nations, determine who will be allowed to populate the millennial earth (Matthew 25:32-34). The millennial earth will have a "screened" population, that in terms of righteousness, will not be *perfect*, but better than the present earth.

e. **The wolf and the lamb shall feed together**: The millennial earth will also see a remarkable *ecological* transformation. No longer will predators stalk their victims. Instead, even **the wolf and the lamb** will get along, and **the lion shall eat straw like the ox**.

f. **"They shall not hurt nor destroy in all My holy mountain," says the Lord**: This is the glorious result of the transformation that happens during the millennial earth. The world will be different biologically, spiritually, socially, and ecologically.

i. The Bible speaks powerfully to other aspects of the millennial earth. Tragically, the Church through history has often ignored or denied the promise of the millennial reign of Jesus Christ. The early church until Augustine almost universally believed in an earthly, historical reign of Jesus, initiated by His return. Tyconius (in the late 300's) was the first to influentially champion a spiritualized interpretation, saying that this Millennium is *now* (*amillennialism*). His view was adopted by Augustine, the Roman Catholic Church and most Reformation theologians. Growing out of *amillennialism* is the doctrine of *postmillennialism* is an outgrowth of amillennialism, saying the millennium will happen in *this* age before Jesus' return – but that the church will bring it to pass. But the clear teaching of the Bible isn't *amillennialism* or *postmillennialism*, but what is called *premillennialism* – the teaching that Jesus Christ will return to this earth *before* the millennial earth, and *He* will establish and govern it directly. There are more than 400 verses in more than 20 different passages in the Old Testament which deal with this time when Jesus Christ rules and reigns personally over planet earth.

- King David will have a prominent place in the millennial earth (Isaiah 55:3-5, Jeremiah 30:4-11, Ezekiel 34:23-31, Ezekiel 37:21-28, and Hosea 3:5).
- There will be blessing and security for national Israel in the millennial earth (Amos 9:11-15).
- The Millennium a time of purity and devotion to God (Zechariah 13:1-9).
- Israel will be a nation of prominence in the millennial earth (Ezekiel 17:22-24).
- There will be a rebuilt temple and restored temple service on the millennial earth (Ezekiel 40-48, Ezekiel 37:26-28, Amos 9:11, and Ezekiel 20:39-44).

- The New Testament specifically promises a literal reign of Jesus Christ (Luke 1:32-33).
- In their resurrected state, the saints will be given responsibility in the Millennial Earth according to their faithful service (Luke 19:11-27, Revelation 20:4-6, Revelation 2:26-28; Revelation 3:12, Revelation 3:21, and 1 Corinthians 6:2-3).

Isaiah 66 – Rejoicing in God's Ultimate Victory

A. The Lord will repay His enemies.

1. (1-2) The greatness of God, and proper response of man.

Thus says the Lord:
"Heaven *is* My throne,
And earth *is* My footstool.
Where *is* the house that you will build Me?
And where is the place of My rest?
For all those *things* My hand has made,
And all those *things* exist,"
Says the Lord.
"But on this *one* will I look:
On *him who is* poor and of a contrite spirit,
And who trembles at My word.

a. **Heaven is My throne, and earth is My footstool**: Here, the Lord puts things back into proper perspective. We can never understand much of anything until we understand that the Lord God is enthroned in heaven, and that the earth is under His command – indeed, the **earth is** His **footstool**.

i. Stephen quoted Isaiah 66:1-2 in Acts 7:49-50, agreeing with Solomon and Isaiah about the greatness of God the Creator.

b. **Where is the house that you will build Me?.... But on this one I will look: on him who is poor and of a contrite spirit, and who trembles at My word**: We may want to serve God – but serve Him *our* way. We may want to **build** God something, but what can we **build** that is worthy of God? Instead, what God really wants from us is a **poor** and **a contrite spirit**, and to tremble at His **word**.

i. **Contrite** is literally "'lamed' or disabled, here used with spiritual significance: one who is aware of the damage wrought by sin, of personal inability to stand upright before God." (Motyer)

ii. Are you one of those who **trembles at** God's **word**? "They tremble at the searching power of God's Word. Do you never come into this place and sit down in the pew, and say, 'Lord, grant that thy Word may search me and try me, that I may not be deceived'? Certain people must always have sweets and comforts; but God's wise children do not wish for these in undue measure. Daily bread we ask for, not daily sugar." (Spurgeon)

2. (3-4) God's answer to empty religious ritual.

"He who kills a bull is *as if* he slays a man;
He who sacrifices a lamb, *as if* he breaks a dog's neck;
He who offers a grain offering, *as if he offers* swine's blood;
He who burns incense, *as if* he blesses an idol.
Just as they have chosen their own ways,
And their soul delights in their abominations,
So will I choose their delusions,
And bring their fears on them;
Because, when I called, no one answered,
When I spoke they did not hear;
But they did evil before My eyes,
And chose *that* in which I do not delight."

a. **He who kills a bull as if he slays a man**: In the empty religious ritualism, God's people thought they were pleasing God. But the LORD says that when a man **kills a bull** in sacrifice, it is **as if he slays a man**. Their religious ritualism *added* to their sin, it didn't take it away.

b. **Just as they have chosen their own ways…so will I choose their delusions**: God's people chose their rebellion against Him, and they persisted in it despite His continual warnings. As an extreme display of judgment, God will **choose their delusions** and send a delusion among them.

i. This is a sobering reminder of what God will do on the earth during the Great Tribulation, as described by Paul in 2 Thessalonians 2:11: *God will send them strong delusion, that they should believe the lie*. But what will happen during the Great Tribulation is just the ultimate fruit of what God does all the time among men. When we reject God and seek our own delusion, He may send one to us.

ii. An example of this kind of delusion are those who believe that the world was created out of *nothing* or by *chance*. What could be more delusional than to believe that something can come from nothing? To believe that *chance* actually has some kind of "power"? Yet for those who insist on believing it, God will give them over to this delusion.

c. **Because, when I called, no one answered, when I spoke they did not hear**: How can we keep from being given over to a delusion? By answering the LORD when He calls, by hearing Him when He speaks. It's really that simple.

3. (5-6) The LORD repays His enemies.

Hear the word of the LORD,
You who tremble at His word:
"Your brethren who hated you,
Who cast you out for My name's sake, said,
'Let the LORD be glorified,
That we may see your joy.'
But they shall be ashamed."
The sound of noise from the city!
A voice from the temple!
The voice of the LORD,
Who fully repays His enemies!

a. **Your brethren who hated you, who cast you out for My name's sake, said, "Let the LORD be glorified, that we may see your joy."** Here, Isaiah shows how those with a shallow, empty religion mock those of genuine faith. First, empty religion *hates* genuine faith (**hated you**). Second, empty religion *rejects* true faith (**cast you out**). Third, empty religion *acts in the name of the LORD* (**for My name's sake**). Fourth, empty religion mocks with spiritual sounding words (**"Let the LORD be glorified, that we may see your joy"**).

b. **But they shall be ashamed**: Most importantly, empty religion will never ultimately triumph. At the end of days, if not before, **they shall be ashamed**, when they hear **the voice of the LORD, who fully repays His enemies!**

B. The LORD comes with fire.

1. (7-11) Rejoicing in the deliverance of Jerusalem.

"Before she was in labor, she gave birth;
Before her pain came,
She delivered a male child.

Who has heard such a thing?
Who has seen such things?
Shall the earth be made to give birth in one day?
Or shall a nation be born at once?
For as soon as Zion was in labor,
She gave birth to her children.
Shall I bring to the time of birth, and not cause delivery?" says the Lord.
"Shall I who cause delivery shut up *the womb*?" says your God.
"Rejoice with Jerusalem,
And be glad with her, all you who love her;
Rejoice for joy with her, all you who mourn for her;
That you may feed and be satisfied
With the consolation of her bosom,
That you may drink deeply and be delighted
With the abundance of her glory."

a. **Before she was in labor, she gave birth**: Isaiah prophesies a day when the victory will come easily to Jerusalem, when she will be as the promise of Romans 8:37, *more than conquerors through Him who loved us*. Here, she gives birth – but without pain! Truly, **who has heard such a thing?**

b. **Rejoice with Jerusalem**: All God's people are called to share in Jerusalem's joy. The time of deliverance, victory, and vindication have come! **Be glad with her, all you who love her**! If God's people will do this, it will be a blessing for them also: **that you may feed and be satisfied with the consolation of her bosom**.

i. This intense, great, rejoicing may sometimes make the world uncomfortable and make us the target of mocking. "Very seldom are believers nowadays charged with being fanatical, nor even with being too enthusiastic; and this is a sign that we are below the right heat. When the world calls us fanatics we are nearing that point of ardour which is our Lord's due." (Spurgeon)

2. (12-17) The Lord comes in judgment.

For thus says the Lord:
"Behold, I will extend peace to her like a river,
And the glory of the Gentiles like a flowing stream.
Then you shall feed;
On *her* sides shall you be carried,
And be dandled on *her* knees.
As one whom his mother comforts,
So I will comfort you;

And you shall be comforted in Jerusalem."
When you see *this*, your heart shall rejoice,
And your bones shall flourish like grass;
The hand of the LORD shall be known to His servants,
And *His* indignation to His enemies.
For behold, the LORD will come with fire
And with His chariots, like a whirlwind,
To render His anger with fury,
And His rebuke with flames of fire.
For by fire and by His sword
The LORD will judge all flesh;
And the slain of the LORD shall be many.
"Those who sanctify themselves and purify themselves,
***To go* to the gardens**
After an *idol* in the midst,
Eating swine's flesh and the abomination and the mouse,
Shall be consumed together," says the LORD.

a. **Behold, I will extend peace to her like a river**: When the Messiah returns in glory and triumph, the **peace** of Jerusalem will be like a gentle, powerful river that is never disturbed. But not Jerusalem alone: **And the glory of the Gentiles like a flowing stream**.

b. **As one whom his mother comforts, so I will comfort you**: God speaks with supreme tenderness to His faithful servants. No one can comfort like a mother, and God will bring that kind of comfort to His people.

i. "This is a peculiarly delightful metaphor. A father can comfort, but I think he is not much at home in the work. When God speaks about his pity, he compares himself to their father: 'Like as a father pitieth his children, so the Lord pitieth, them that fear him.' But when he speaks about comfort, he selects the mother. When I have seen the little ones sick, I have felt all the pity in the world for them, but I did not know how to set to work to comfort them; but a mother knows by instinct how to do it." (Spurgeon)

c. **The hand of the LORD shall be known to His servants, and His indignation to His enemies**: When the Messiah returns in glory and triumph, for some it will be a great blessing – and for others it is be nothing but judgment. Indeed, **the LORD will judge all flesh; and the slain of the LORD shall be many**.

d. **Those who sanctify themselves and purify themselves, to go to the gardens, after an idol in the midst**: When the Messiah returns in glory and triumph, He will see through those who practice empty religion. They **"shall be consumed together," says the Lord.**

3. (18-21) The Lord gathers and restores His people.

"For I *know* their works and their thoughts. It shall be that I will gather all nations and tongues; and they shall come and see My glory. I will set a sign among them; and those among them who escape I will send to the nations: *to* Tarshish and Pul and Lud, who draw the bow, and Tubal and Javan, *to* the coastlands afar off who have not heard My fame nor seen My glory. And they shall declare My glory among the Gentiles. Then they shall bring all your brethren for an offering to the Lord out of all nations, on horses and in chariots and in litters, on mules and on camels, to My holy mountain Jerusalem," says the Lord, "as the children of Israel bring an offering in a clean vessel into the house of the Lord. And I will also take some of them for priests *and* Levites," says the Lord.

a. **I will gather all nations and tongues; and they shall come and see My glory**: God has promised a great regathering work among Israel; but He will also do a regathering work among the whole world, some from **all nations and tongues** to see His **glory**.

i. One place this finds ultimate fulfillment is around the throne of God (Revelation 5:9-10).

ii. "God says that He will set a *sign* among the nations. This sign is the same as the *sign of the Son of man* (Matthew 24:30)." (Bultema)

b. **Those among them who escape I will send to the nations...to the coastlands afar off who have not heard My fame nor seen My glory**: Isaiah makes prophetic reference to the missionary calling and work of God's people. Of course, God had a missionary intent for Israel, that they would be a priesthood among the nations (Exodus 19:6) and a light to the Gentiles. But even more pointedly, God has commanded the church **to the nations**, to **declare My glory among the Gentiles**.

i. "They are sent to *Tarshish* (Spain, France and Italy) to *Pul* (a region in Africa) and to *Lud*, which according to some is the same as Lydia, though it seems preferable to take *Pul* and *Lud* together for all of Africa. Tubal was a son of Japheth, whose descendants settled in north-eastern Europe or Russia and *Javan* is the biblical name for Greece." (Bultema)

ii. In a limited sense, this is fulfilled by the missionary outreach of the church through centuries. But this is only a partial fulfillment. Ultimately, these may be the 144,000 witnesses during the Great

Tribulation; they may be Jewish evangelists in the days of the millennial earth.

c. **Then they shall bring all your brethren for an offering to the Lord out of all nations**: As part of God's ultimate work, as the missionaries go out, the people of Israel ultimately come back, in a magnificent regathering. This is partially fulfilled now in Israel's regathered state; but will be ultimately fulfilled in the millennial earth of the Messiah.

i. Many years ago there was a remarkable example of modern-day regathering from the Arutz 7 news agency in Israel:

"Thirty-seven members of the Bnei Menashe tribe in India – believed to be descendants of the Ten Lost Tribes – arrived in Israel on Friday. The new arrivals, many of whom have relatives in Israel among the 450 Bnei Menashe who have arrived within the last five years, were brought to Israel under the auspices of the Jerusalem-based Amishav organization. Amishav is dedicated to locating descendants of the Lost Tribes and returning them to the Jewish people. 'This is a historic moment for the Jewish people,' said Amishav founder and chairman Rabbi Eliyahu Avichail, who has devoted his life to finding and assisting the descendants of the Lost Tribes of Israel. 'After a lengthy and difficult separation, the Bnei Menashe are being reunited with the Jewish people in the Land of Israel. This is a triumph of faith. Their return to Zion marks the closing of a historical circle.'"

The Bnei Menashe, with a rich oral tradition tracing themselves back to the Israelite tribe of Menashe, continue to practice many uniquely Jewish customs. About 3,500 Bnei Menashe decided to formally return to the Jewish people about 30 years ago, and began living a fully Jewish life to the best of their ability in accordance with Jewish law. Rabbi Avichail learned of their existence about 20 years ago, and began to investigate their claims to Jewish ancestry. After making several visits there and carefully studying their claims and the relevant history, Rabbi Avichail consulted with leading rabbinical authorities and concluded that there is convincing evidence linking the Bnei Menashe with the Jewish people. Among the evidence, Rabbi Avichail notes their ancient tradition speaking of the Patriarchs Abraham, Isaac, and Jacob; their custom of circumcising male children on the 8th day after birth; and their sacrificial ceremony on an altar reminiscent of the Jewish Temple in which the Hebrew Biblical name of G-d, Mount Sinai, Mount Moriah and Mount Zion are mentioned.

d. **And I will take some of them for priests and Levites**: The idea is that in that day, God will extend the priesthood beyond its previous boundaries.

This is ultimately fulfilled in the church because saints are called *priests* (1 Peter 2:5-9, Revelation 1:6, 5:10, 20:6).

i. "Just as in Isaiah's day only some were priests and Levites, but through them Israel was constituted as the Lord's priestly people, so now he foresees Gentiles incorporated on equal terms, into equal privileges." (Motyer)

4. (22-24) The certainty of both the LORD's judgment and His restoration.

"For as the new heavens and the new earth
Which I will make shall remain before Me," says the LORD,
"So shall your descendants and your name remain.
And it shall come to pass
***That* from one New Moon to another,**
And from one Sabbath to another,
All flesh shall come to worship before Me," says the LORD.
"And they shall go forth and look
Upon the corpses of the men
Who have transgressed against Me.
For their worm does not die,
And their fire is not quenched.
They shall be an abhorrence to all flesh."

a. **And it shall come to pass...all flesh shall come to worship before Me**: Here, God describes His ultimate triumph. Through the majestic book of Isaiah, the nations have been judged and often condemned. But God has an ultimate plan to reach the nations, seen in its ultimate fulfillment in Revelation 5:9-10. God will take people from every tribe and tongue, and **"all flesh shall come to worship before Me," says the LORD.**

i. Isaiah puts it into the context of **from one New Moon to another, and from one Sabbath to another, all flesh shall come to worship before Me**. Significantly, Isaiah began the book with a condemnation of the shallow worship of God's people at the time of the New Moons and Sabbaths (Isaiah 1:12-15). Now, after the greatness of the LORD's work, all that is different.

b. **And they shall go forth and look upon the corpses of the men who have transgressed against Me**: Some from every tribe and tongue will have a destiny of ultimate triumph; some also will have the destiny – freely chosen – of ultimate tragedy. Using the images of eternal damnation (**their worm does not die, and their fire is not quenched**), Isaiah describes the fate of those who reject God – even if they had the veneer of empty religion.

i. "After this life, and at the day of judgment, they shall go into eternal torments; where they will feel a work of conscience that shall never die, and a fiery wrath of God upon their souls and bodies that shall never go out." (Poole)

ii. The book of Isaiah closes with a sobering contrast, revealing the ultimate, eternal *importance* of this present life. Each life can choose its destiny: **worship** or the **worm**. Which is it for you?

Bibliography

Bultema, Harry *Commentary on Isaiah* (Grand Rapids, Michigan: Kregel Publications, 1981)

Calvin, John *Commentaries on the Book of the Prophet Isaiah 1-32* and *Commentaries on the Book of the Prophet Isaiah 33-66* (Grand Rapids, Michigan: Baker, 1979)

Clarke, Adam *The Holy Bible, Containing the Old and New Testaments, with A Commentary and Critical Notes, Volume IV – Isaiah to Malachi* (New York: Eaton and Mains, 1827?)

Erwin, Gayle "The Government," *Servant Quarters*, January-February 1999 Newsletter, from www.servant.org

Grogan, G.W, "Isaiah" *The Expositor's Bible Commentary, Volume 6* (Grand Rapids, Michigan: Zondervan, 1985)

Jennings, F.C. *Studies in Isaiah* (New York: Loizeaux Brothers, 1950)

Lindsey, Duane *The Servant Songs: A Study in Isaiah* (Chicago: Moody Press, 1985)

Maclaren, Alexander *Expostions of Holy Scripture, Volume Six* (Grand Rapids, Michigan: Baker, 1984)

Martin, Alfred *Isaiah – The Salvation of Jehovah* (Chicago: Moody Press, 1956)

McDowell, Josh *Evidence that Demands a Verdict* (Campus Crusade, 1972)

Morgan, G. Campbell *An Exposition of the Whole Bible* (Old Tappan, New Jersey: Revell, 1959)

Motyer, J. Alec *Isaiah: An Introduction and Commentary* (Downers Grove, Illinois: Inter-Varsity Press, 1999)

Poole, Matthew *A Commentary on the Holy Bible, Volume 2 – Psalms through Malachi* (London, Banner of Truth Trust, 1968)

Ramm, Bernard *Protestant Christian Evidences* (Chicago, Moody Press: 1959)

Redpath, Alan *Faith for the Times: Studies in the Book of Isaiah* (Grand Rapids, Michigan: Fleming H. Revell, 1976)

Spurgeon, Charles Haddon *The New Park Street Pulpit, Volumes 1-6* and *The Metropolitan Tabernacle Pulpit, Volumes 7-63* (Pasadena, Texas: Pilgrim Publications, 1990)

Strong, James *Strong's Exhaustive Concordance – Deluxe Edition* (Nashville, Tennessee: Thomas Nelson, 1980)

Tenney, Merrill C. *Interpreting Revelation* (Grand Rapids, Michigan: Eerdmans, 1970)

Trapp, John *A Commentary on the Old and New Testaments, Volume 3 – Proverbs to Daniel* (Eureka, California: Tanski Publications, 1997)

Wolf, Herbert M. *Interpreting Isaiah: The Suffering and Glory of the Messiah* (Grand Rapids, Michigan: Zondervan, 1985)

As the years pass I love the work of studying, learning, and teaching the Bible more than ever. I'm so grateful that God is faithful to meet me in His Word.

For the second time I am tremendously grateful to Alison Turner for her proofreading and editorial suggestions, especially with a challenging manuscript. Alison, thank you so much!

Thanks to Brian Procedo for the cover design and the graphics work.

Most especially, thanks to my wife Inga-Lill. She is my loved and valued partner in life and in service to God and His people.

David Guzik

David Guzik's Bible commentary is regularly used and trusted by many thousands who want to know the Bible better. Pastors, teachers, class leaders, and everyday Christians find his commentary helpful for their own understanding and explanation of the Bible. David and his wife Inga-Lill live in Santa Barbara, California.

You can email David at
david@enduringword.com

For more resources by David Guzik,
go to www.enduringword.com

CPSIA information can be obtained
at www.ICGtesting.com
Printed in the USA
BVHW030623080123
655820BV00020B/32